Robert

'Traditional religions' have not always yielded to Christianity and Islam, nor become devalued by modern secular ideas and commoditisation. In describing the shifting boundaries between these phenomena, David Parkin shows how indigenous African rites and beliefs may be reworked to accommodate a variety of economic systems, new spatial and ecological relations between communities, and the locally variable influences of Islam and Christianity.

Among the Giriama people of Kenya, there are pastoralists living in the hinterland; farmers, who work land closer to the coast; and migrants, who earn money as labourers or fishermen on the coast itself. Wherever they live, they revere an ancient and formerly fortified capital, located in the pastoralist hinterland, which few of them ever see or visit. Those who live closest to the sacred place – the pastoralists – are commonly believed to share in its purity, while those engaged in wage labour are often thought to be furthest removed spiritually from the cultural essence of the Giriama. The idea of the sacred is here made up of these different spatial perspectives, which sometimes conflict. As the site of occasional large-scale ceremonies, however, the settlement becomes specially important at times of national crisis. It then acts as a moral core of Giriama society, and a defence against total domination and assimilation.

Cambridge Studies in Social and Cultural Anthropology

Editors: Ernest Gellner, Jack Goody, Stephen Gudeman, Michael Herzfeld, Jonathan Parry

80

Sacred void

Kigango: a hardwood ancestral memorial standing in a maize field and dating back to about 1880.

SACRED VOID

Spatial images of work and ritual among the Giriama of Kenya

DAVID PARKIN

The right of the
University of Cambridge
to print and sell
all manner of books
was granted by
Henry VIII in 1534.
The University has printed
and published continuously
since 1584.

CAMBRIDGE UNIVERSITY PRESS

Cambridge

New York   Port Chester

Melbourne   Sydney

Published by the Press Syndicate of the University of Cambridge
The Pitt Building, Trumpington Street, Cambridge CB2 1RP
40 West 20th Street, New York, NY 10011, USA
10 Stamford Road, Oakleigh, Melbourne 3166, Australia

First published 1991

Printed in Great Britain at the University Press, Cambridge

British Library cataloguing in publication data

Parkin, David. *1940–*
Sacred void: spatial images of work and ritual among the Giriama of
Kenya. – (Cambridge Studies in Social and cultural
anthropology)
1. Kenya. Giriama. Social Life
I. Title
967.6204

Library of Congress cataloguing in publication data

Parkin, David J.
Sacred void: spatial images of work and ritual among the Giriama of Kenya /
David Parkin.
    p.   cm. – (Cambridge studies in social and cultural
anthropology: 80)
ISBN 0 521 40466 5
1. Giryama (African people) – Religion. 2. Giryama (African
people) – Social life and customs. I. Title. II. Series.
BL2480.G57P37 1991
299'.68395 – dc20 90–24158 CIP

A list of books in the series will be found at the end of the volume

ISBN 0 521 40466 5 hardback

For Nathan, Sasha and Andrew

Contents

Illustrations

Kigango: a hardwood ancestral memorial standing in a maize field
and dating back to about 1880. Photograph by David Parkin. *frontispiece*

Preface

This book, like one of its subjects, has accidental as well as intended beginnings, the tension between which constitutes its theme. It is relevant, therefore, to say how it came about.

I have spent some thirty-four months among the Giriama over the period from 1966 until 1985 (with a further three weeks in 1988). The first thirteen months were spent in Kaloleni location, well within the Giriama agricultural and coconut palm-growing area, from August 1966 until September 1967 inclusive. Some of the findings of that study were published in Parkin (1972), in which I tried to show how peoples' adherence to what they believed to be customary beliefs and practices masked their increasing dependency on a cash-crop market determined by an international supply and demand for their produce. Despite the emergence of cash-crop farmers and entrepreneurs, the colonial and, later, the new independent central government administration had consistently called the Giriama, and other coastal peoples, economically unmotivated and backward, often addressing the people as such at rallies and meetings, many of which I attended. The point of my 1972 monograph was to indicate that this construction of the Giriama by outsiders did not in the least match their own perception of themselves as being already involved in modern economic changes and as including among them successful entrepreneurs, nor did it reflect any objective measures that could be taken: for generations, in fact, the Giriama had produced traders of great skill and wealth who mediated between Swahili and Arabs on the Kenya coast and the bulk of the Giriama and related peoples.

It became obvious to me that these external colonial and post-independence judgements of the Giriama people and their values were part of a more general negative evaluation of them as secondary in all respects to the Muslim coastal Arabs and Swahili, both of whom had received privileged status, some autonomy, and even admiration for their culture and literature, during the colonial and protectorate period of British government. To this was added the often unfavourable view of the Giriama held by missionaries of all denominations, who despaired of the slow, almost non-existent conversion to Christianity among the Giriama, compared with such up-country peoples as the Kikuyu, Luo and Luhya, all of whom had converted in large number to Christianity, and to a wage-based work ethic, despite a later exposure to these phenomena. The Giriama became famous for their rebellion against British rule in 1914, and colonial and missionary records constantly refer to Giriama 'resistance', not only to wage labour, but also to Islam and Christianity, the latter of these two being regarded with regret but the former being seen as, at least, compensation.

Christianity has only in very recent years begun to make an impact on the Giriama. Islam has, however, been practised along the East African coast for almost as long as the religion itself. By trading produce from the interior, principally grain and ivory, and by fleeing into the vast hinterland whenever threatened, the Giriama hardly needed to labour for cash nor to embrace coastal Islam, except, indirectly, during occasional inland famines, when they might marry daughters to Muslims in exchange for scarce food grown at the more fertile and rain-fed coast. By itself, though, this did not result in large-scale conversion of Giriama to Islam. Later, Swahili-Arab wealth declined as the ban on slavery reduced the labour available for their coastal plantations.

This symbiotic relationship appears to have become especially precarious in recent decades, possibly as a result of population growth, and of the increasing dependency on the use of cash and on the means to acquire it, including cash-crop farming and wage-labour nearer the coast itself. As a result, more and more Giriama moved towards the eastern coastal area. During a thirteen-month period from August 1977 to September 1978, therefore, I carried out fieldwork with a view to understanding how coastal Muslims and inland Giriama interacted with and viewed each other, economically, politically and culturally. This time, however, I lived in a Muslim Swahili-speaking village, around whom were dotted migrant non-Muslim Giriama small homesteads. The experience was startling, for it seemed that, in many respects, each group viewed the other in mirror-image terms: what the one did and approved of, the other abhorred. Yet, there were common cultural elements which were also sometimes recognised as such by the two peoples, who would often stress their common coastal identity in opposition to up-country Kenyans and outsiders.

Whereas, during the first period of fieldwork, I used mainly the Giriama language, on this latter occasion I used Swahili (which I had learned years earlier) as well as the closely related Giriama. Much of the material collected on the coast during this latter period of fieldwork remains unpublished, and constitutes the basis of a projected third volume on the disparate origins and complex interplay of elements of local Islam. Between the two long periods of fieldwork (during 1968–69, while at Nairobi University, and for a few weeks in each of 1971 and 1972), I spent time in yet another area of Giriama country, the western bushland and near-savanna where cattle are herded, returning there for two periods of three and two months in 1984 and 1985.

This latter fieldwork provided a third ecological and cultural perspective, alongside that of the coast, dominated by Islam, small urban centres, and maritime activities, principally fishing, and that of the immediate hinterland of Giriama, characterised by cash-crop farming.

My intention all along was to write a book about the interrelationship between these three ecological and cultural areas, and, indeed, this book partially fulfils that aim. Increasingly, however, another theme persistently presented itself. In the hinterland of Giriama country, there is a traditional capital, located away from large population clusters. For generations it has been almost uninhabited. Outside observers had tended to regard it as little more than an anachronism, and Giriama themselves were divided between the majority who revered it but had little to do with it and who insisted that only a few special elders could talk about it, and these latter who stressed its importance but kept their visits to, and links with it, rather quiet. Over the years, I saw the relationship between peoples living in the three ecological zones as a kind of statement: the transition from the interior cattle zone, through the farming area, to the coast itself, was the direction many Giriama saw themselves taking as a people, namely, from an ideal of rural, pastoral independence uninfluenced by Islam and Christianity, to coastal economic dependency framed by adherence both to the two world religions and to a newly burgeoning consumerist culture drawn indirectly from tourism. During Giriama national crises, the silent majority would join the elders and point to their traditional capital as the source of their cultural essence and the moral safeguard against complete politico-economic encapsulation. Through the accident of crisis, then, they, like myself, would find it hard to ignore the ontological power of this largely unvisited and distant place. The choices and intentions induced by ecological constraints were, then, periodically rephrased in the idiom of this almost empty national site, whose significance simply would not go away.

One way of discussing the recent concern in anthropology with ethnographic writing, is to admit not necessarily to 'distortion' in our representations of other societies but to the implicit theory contained in our ethnographies. We can never, of course, ever faithfully represent how other peoples act and think, and it is true that our accounts may sometimes consolidate the authority of the writers to the possible detriment of those written about. Such ethical considerations are not to be dismissed lightly and deserve continuing debate. In general, however, we are impressionists whose depictions strike chords in each others' works, and who periodically stand back and compare. The work of explicit comparison usually amounts to a theoretical stock-taking and clarification of the subject, as we seek to account for our respective stances, and it is to such conclusions that we turn when we seek a state-of-the-art statement. Yet such statements are always prefigured in the ethnographies which inform them, and which I regard, therefore, as implicitly and not simply *pre*-theoretical. It seems necessary to make this claim at a time when the writing of intensively acquired ethnographic data has been severely questioned and when major fund-awarding bodies need constant reassurance that what anthropologists do in the field cannot possibly be shortened or standardised. The theory implicit in the present book turns on the idea that, in trying to resolve the existential dilemmas that make up their personal and social worlds, people constantly re-order their justifications, a common enough activity among us all, whether writing or speaking.

This book does not reproduce previously published material, except for a few passages from Parkin 1982b, and either introduces Giriama beliefs and practices for the first time, or elaborates on those mentioned briefly elsewhere. It is definitely not, then, the book of the articles. I have placed vernacular noun terms in the singular, denoted therefore by such familiar Bantu prefixes as *mu-*, *ki-*, *ka-*, *dzi-*, *lu-*, and (*n*), except where a plural was the appropriate form.

Formal thanks must first go to the President's Office, Republic of Kenya, for permission to carry out the fieldwork for this study, and to the Institute of African Studies, University of Nairobi, for affiliation. I am grateful, also, to the School of Oriental and African Studies, the Social Science Research Council (as it was), the British Academy, and the Nuffield Foundation, who have each made generous contributions to the research on which the study is based. Of those in whose homes I have lived, I would especially like again to acknowledge my debt to the late Johnstone Muramba, and to thank Charo Mboro, Charo Mugandi, Raphael Menza Charo, Joseph Karisa, Anthony Kazungu, Juma Athmani, and his mother, Fatuma. I also acknowledge my debt to his now deceased father, Athmani Juma. It has been a long time, and I hope that they, or theirs, will regard this work as worth their many efforts and encouragement. I thank Monica Parkin, both for having shared most of the fieldwork with me, and for having read this book meticulously from cover to cover and for commenting most valuably on it. One or two people have commented on a chapter, but I have mostly benefited from conversations in which I have sounded out colleagues and friends on ideas. Thus recalled are, at least, Bill Arens, Pierre Bonte, Michael Bourdillon, Cynthia Brantley, Abner Cohen, Elisabeth Copet-Rougier, Lisa Croll, Richard Fardon, Mark Hobart, Ivan Karp, Katama Mkangi, Brian Morris, Fred Morton, John Peel, Aidan Southall, Tom Spear, Paul Spencer, and Martha Wenger. I have especially benefited from the publications of Brantley and Spear, while Mkangi has not only shared his sociological knowledge of coastal peoples during our long association, but has made me painfully aware of the extraordinary price of political courage that people like him are prepared to pay. Two unknown readers for the Press also deserve thanks for their insightful suggestions, as does Jessica Kuper, the publishing editor, for her courteous advice and help. John Middleton also generously made available to me the papers and notes on which he based his edited version of the district officer, Champion's interpretation of Giriama society (Champion 1967). Finally, I single out those of my students who, over the years, have worked in the Kenya coastal area, and whose unflagging enthusiasm was an inspiration. It is not always recognised how much so-called supervisers are, in fact, indebted in their own research to their research students. Let me, therefore, return thanks to Robert Peake, Susan Beckerleg and Gaye Thompson, who, with Monica Udvardy of Uppsala University, have significantly advanced our understanding of Kenya coastal society. As well as commenting on some of the draft chapters, the latter two have produced studies concentrating on the study of Giriama women, which I regard as complementing this book in many respects.

Introduction

Space and religion

Quietly and undeclared as such, a loose assemblage of thinking has entered social science and the humanities. Perhaps it is pre-paradigmatic, to use Kuhn's now time-honoured expression (1956). It is the language and study of positions, stances, moves, panoptic views and close or distant gazes, in short, of spatial orientation and separation, and their effect and control in human society, and on theories about society.[1]

At the same time, religion, ritual, sacrifice and the sacred have again become objects of focused anthropological study, after a period, roughly from 1960 to 1980, when they were superseded either by semiological and structuralist studies of myth and of rites treated as myth, or by interpretative studies of symbolism. Numerous studies of ritual and religion as isolable, self-determining phenomena have appeared since about 1980.[2] Such studies appear to have freed

---

[1] It derives largely from Foucault (for example 1972a, 1972b, 1973, 1978; and see Hirst 1985), either directly, as in Rabinow's recent study of French colonial urban planning and architecture (1989), or indirectly as in such critiques and counter-critiques of anthropological method as Clifford and Marcus (1986) and Fardon (1990). A parallel view of how spatial metaphors and positions characterise anthropological language as well as being part of what anthropologists study, is found in such different studies as Salmond (1982, 1985), Ardener (1987, 1989: 142–54), and Needham (1987), and, for East African societies, Thornton (1980), Moore (1986), and Brandstrom (1990).

[2] This is evident from a count of 102 monographs listed and briefly summarised by Morris in his recent introductory text on the anthropology of religion (Morris 1987: 329–40). Since about 1980 there has been an extraordinary proliferation of ethnographic monographs focused on religion, ideas of the sacred, ritual, sacrifice and prayer, few of which claim theoretical adherence to either structuralism or methodologically self-conscious kinds of hermeneutic interpretivism. From about 1960 until 1980 such books are surprisingly few, with more on semiological and structuralist approaches to symbolism rather than specifically on religion and on such concepts as ritual and the sacred, which, as obvious 'odd-job words', are during this time used hesitantly, if at all, in such studies. Apart from that of Lévi-Strauss, it is possible that the influence of Edmund Leach may have been critical here, especially but not exclusively in Britain. His own work on Kachin ritual in 1954 re-defined this concept and also Durkheim's opposition between sacred and profane and, in effect, ushered in his own commitment to structuralist analyses of symbolism, myth and Biblical texts, which perhaps began in 1958 and 1961 with his essays on magical hair and on time, respectively, and continued at least until 1983, with a paper on Moses (Leach 1958, 1961 and 1983).

The period since 1980 appears to be one in which, following Needham (1975), the polythetic

themselves, so to speak, from Lévi-Strauss's stricture that religion is no more than one of a number of systems of classification (1963) and of ritual as cognitively subsumed within and even inferior to myth (1966: 232–244).

Both developments, a discourse on and through spatial concepts, and the re-entry of sacred ritual and religion as phenomena for-themselves, are linked reactions. The treatment of constructed spaces as 'statements' is part of the post-modernist attempt to dissolve the kind of dichotomy that would separate the human observer as all-knowing and autonomous from spaces, landscapes and buildings, upon which he or she acts. Paralleling this, the renewed interest in ritual and religion is, as indicated, a post-structuralist dissatisfaction with the structuralist reduction of these phenomena to little more than systems of logical classification and transformation.

There are also two significant influences of a topical and pragmatic nature. The interest in space is an aspect of the wider interest in the global environment as polluted and polluting, while that in religion and ritual is part of the general attempt in Western society to understand how, in the face of allegedly the greatest ever secularising forces, ideologically supported until recently by Marxism, religious fundamentalism and its insistence on sacred and proper ritual have emerged as the most powerful method of popular persuasion in much of the world.

This book seeks to explore this relationship between space as statement and construction, and the sacred as defined and defining. It argues that to talk about the sacred is to think and talk about space, and to some extent vice versa: that when people speak and write about the sacred, they tend to essentialise it in terms of places occupied by it; and that discussion of human spaces is likely, eventually, to refer to a central point imbued with extra-human, or spiritual, significance.

The usage of the two terms space and sacred in anthropology denotes fluid genealogies, but it is necessary to retrace some early assumptions in order to reach present understandings of them. In this introduction I deal mainly with space. In the conclusion I turn more fully to the sacred. The reason for this separation will, I hope, become clear at that point, which will have been arrived at ethnographically.

Anthropological studies of space, often linked to the study of time, have reflected a constant interest. They are by no means recent. They have included analyses of bodily position, posture and the distinction between right and left,

nature of such terms is broadly accepted, but in which the perceptual phenomena to which they allude persistently recur as themes attracting analysis. For me, the study which classically sets this agenda is Lewis's analysis of initiation rites in Papua New Guinea which consistently asks what ritual is at the same time as it is constructed through description. Such concepts thus return in a sometimes curious amalgam of contestable and essentialist assumptions. Morris's survey, though extensive, cannot be complete and, in addition to works cited elsewhere in this and other chapters, we may add others not included, such as Bourdillon and Fortes (1980), Davis (1982), Heusch (1985), Sanday (1986), Bloch (1986), Caplan (1987) and Metcalf (1989).

though more common concerns have been the symbolism of house architecture, homestead patterns and burial positions.

This eclectic view is in fact ethnographically fair, for it would be surprising if Western and non-Western models of spatial boundaries, position, and directionality were isomorphic. 'Space' is a broad enough category in Western scientific and lay thinking, despite having been the object of special study in physics and philosophy. Many non-Western languages have no specific term for an abstract concept of space, which is therefore treated by them as a more culturally embedded and so less isolable feature of thought and action. Traditionally in anthropology, however, the analytical drive has been to distinguish spatial categories as sometimes independent and sometimes dependent elements of social organisation.

Three responses to Durkheim
In the early pages of *The Elementary Forms of the Religious Life*, Durkheim sets forward his view that peoples' ideas of time and space are socially derived (1915: 10–12). He draws here on his and Mauss's findings with regard to Zuni, Sioux and Chinese spatial and temporal concepts (1963 (1903): 43ff., 68–75), and on his analysis of Australian societies. With regard to space, Durkheim and Mauss in fact start out by showing that it is the geographical areas occupied by clans, families and moieties which are at the basis of all other systems of classification such as those of colour, totemic animals and divinatory powers. It was self-evident for Durkheim and Mauss that such social groups as clans were necessarily also territorially defined. While briefly acknowledged as in some way basic, this territorial aspect then becomes subordinated to the social, especially in Durkheim's opus. It is, for instance, the collective religious enthusiasm of a group occupying a particular area of land, in relation to other groups, which provides the model for other forms of classification, not the identification with the land itself.

At first, this seems unexceptionable. After all, it might be argued, territory can have no significance for humans unless it is in some way differentiated from other territories, whether or not through human settlement: people only identify areas in relation to other areas. The same kind of argument is earlier advanced by Durkheim with regard to the more abstract notion of space. He says that Kant was wrong to see it as a 'vague and indetermined medium . . . purely and absolutely homogeneous'. Durkheim argues that such an idea 'could not be grasped by the mind' and that we can only understand space by differentiating objects and areas as being either north, south, east or west, as right or left, or up or down, and so on. These distinctions, moreover, are seen as necessarily social in origin, being common to the people of a single civilisation. He provides what he sees as 'cases where this social character is made manifest' (implying that the earlier examples of orientation are therefore cognitively latent?) as in some Australian and North

American societies 'where space is conceived in the form of an immense circle, because the camp has a circular form; and this spatial circle is divided up exactly like the tribal circle, and is in its image' (Durkheim 1915: 11).

Subsequently, anthropologists have talked in terms of a correspondence between spatial and social organisation, which may be regarded as a key feature of a so-called Durkheimian approach.[3] None, to my knowledge, has wished to challenge Durkheim on the extent to which an idea of space as indeterminate and homogeneous can in fact be grasped by the human mind and can, moreover, become a key element in social and religious organisation, as will be argued in this book.

What, then, have been the anthropological responses to the Durkheimian claim that spatial derives from social differentiation? First, Lévi-Strauss turns Durkheim on his head and argues that the human differentiation of such elements of the landscape as rocks and mountains, as well as specific flora and fauna, can in fact be used to classify social groups, which, in turn, can return to the environment, so to speak, and differentiate it and themselves still further, and so on. In this two-way process of mutual classification, the 'mythogeographical' and the social become part of each other, with neither thereafter cognitively prior to the other (Lévi-Strauss 1966: 162–168). But even in this formulation, no consideration is given to the possibility that a people's idea of space as an undifferentiated void might be socially significant.[4]

Second, Eliade makes a distinction between sacred space which is recognised as such by 'religious man', having been consecrated as a human settlement, and profane space which is homogeneous and undifferentiated and, in this state of void, mirrors the emptiness of men without religion. Sacred space is heterogeneous in that it constitutes a break from the bleak outside, is a centre giving

---

[3] Mary Douglas's distinction between 'grid' and 'group' societies, or aspects of society, is the most celebrated modern example of such correspondence, in this case of bodily posture, cosmology and degree of social boundedness (Douglas 1970). Other studies, such as those of Cunningham (1973 (1964)), Hobart (1978) and Turton (1978) analyse indigenously recognised spatial directions, axes, concentricities and internal and external boundaries in, for example, the building, structure and organisation of houses, and show how spatial exclusions and positions legitimate social hierarchies by making them locally acceptable parts of the natural environment.

[4] A notable structuralist account is that of Christine Hugh-Jones, who outlines what she acknowledges is her own model of underlying socio-spatial correspondences among the Northwest Amazonian Pira-parana Indians of Colombia. But she notes also that, while the people themselves distinguish the fanned river system of western radial headwaters which feed the 'Milk River' as where evil spirits live, and the eastern mouth of the river as where human culture originates, there is an area on each side of the mouth which is geographically unmarked in their eyes. It is 'empty of significance' and is correspondingly absent in their ideology (Hugh-Jones 1979: 237–241). It is, in other words, clearly a notion of undifferentiated space, yet, in constituting a socio-geographic 'absence', may, I suggest, give 'presence' or essence to the other spaces. Littlejohn's study of the Temne house may also be regarded as structuralist. He shows how the directions taken by different parts of a house both disclose and resolve the 'light' and 'dark' sides of humanity (1967). More recently, as an exercise in regional comparison, Kuper outlines some transformations in the structure of South African Bantu homesteads (Kuper 1975, 1980), which result from the remarkable affinities underlying Bantu cultural ideas and assumptions.

mankind orientation or direction in the world, and consists of internal divisions which are examples of human creativity: the living spaces of the homes or village, and the arrangement of a church, temple or traditional city. Modern cities are characterised as unconsecrated, inhabited for the most part by desacralised man, and as therefore amorphous and lacking the centrality that gives moral and religious direction (Eliade 1959: 20–65, 1954: 6–21). Eliade, unlike Durkheim and Lévi-Strauss, does then take into account the role played in human under- standing by an idea of space as homogeneous and undifferentiated, which is indeed at the basis of his definition of the profane. But its social significance is only ever negative, a state to be transcended and forsaken, and the broadness of Eliade's generalisations and his use of examples compare uncomfortably with the analytical finesse of Durkheim and Lévi-Strauss. That said, those broad ideas have in fact, directly and indirectly, helped spawn a distinctive and scholarly approach to the study of space in modern social anthropology.

This has principally taken the form of studies of religious pilgrimage to a sacred centre, which is held by the pilgrims to contrast with the ordinariness, profanity or wilderness of all other places. Since the work of the Turners (Turner 1974a, 1974b, and Turner and Turner 1978; see also Eickelman 1976), there has been an outpouring of analyses of journeys to shrines, holy cities and other sacred places (for example Sallnow 1987, Werbner 1977 and 1989, Gold 1988, Rasnake 1988 and Schlee (forthcoming), to take the most recent examples). Such sacred centres become focal points not only for a religion but often also for trade routes and political authority and boundaries. They provide the mobile popu- lations that sustain such trade and polities and the spirituality enabling individ- ual pilgrims to transcend them. Their key feature is that they are geographically fixed centres, constituting, in Eliade's terms, an absolute reality and touchstone to which pilgrims can refer to answers concerning their own origins and destinies.[5]

These movements of people to fixed centres thus presuppose a degree of pre- dictability regarding the nature of place, journey and benefits. People set out to arrive and return within a reasonably specific period of time. Occasionally, in Yamba's study of Hausa pilgrims in the Sudan who have been claiming for a long time that they are bound for Mecca but who have in fact settled in mid-journey, this certainty is tempered by constraints (Yamba 1990). The sacred destination then has to be worked at as an ideal to be achieved against all odds.

This possibility of unpredictability in peoples' movements, whether or not as pilgrims, introduces the third and remaining response to Durkheim that I identify. It is already evident in the Chinese geomancers' view of their environ-

---

[5] Although concerned more with territorial cults than with sacred centres visited by pilgrims, the studies edited by Werbner (1977) and Schoffeleers (1979) show the extent to which features of the landscape become not only ecological but also spiritual markers in the boundaries and relationships between peoples.

ments, including compass directions and features of landscape, as being either benign or malignant depending on a range of factors which have to be diagnosed, and which will determine where and how a building should be erected or a grave placed and positioned (Freedman 1969). It is given a theoretical guise in the approach, for instance, of the archaeologist, Ian Hodder (1986), and in the anthropological work of Bourdieu (1973, 1977, 1981) and of Moore (1986). Here, spatial categories do not, or do not necessarily, correspond with social distinctions nor encode themes, but are actually worked at and constantly reinterpreted by the people of a culture, sometimes being changed in the process. Their constant reinterpretation is part of the work of everyday practice.

Moore provides a full ethnographic exemplar of the approach. She studies spatial notions and directionality among the Marakwet of Kenya through the metaphor of a cultural text which can be read and 'worked at' by members of the society who move through and act in spaces. She argues that such spatial texts represent ideology, such as men's superiority over women, but that this ideology is itself produced within the material conditions of history. She also says that people can in practice choose how to respond to that ideology. Moore's ambitious attempt to bring together history and human agency, and people's interpretative use of ideology as represented in spatial texts, is to be applauded. Another use for the metaphor of text which can also be explored is the idea of space as a clean or blank sheet, of indeterminate size, and ready to be written on. Over-reliance on such metaphors in analysis is notoriously dangerous. I introduce this one simply to make the point that, among the people who are the subject of this book, the Giriama of Kenya, there are times when they appear to regard their own sacred centre in this way, as a place periodically to be cleaned, made blank and re-written without respect to previously existing boundaries of space and time. These are moments when such space is indeed rendered amorphous, homogeneous and indeterminate, a deliberate void. They are times, too, when the space stands liminally, betwixt and between what we may for the moment translate as sacred and profane states.

This liminal state is not that between two phases of a rite of passage. It is rather an intermediary perception of space, set between two others. On the one hand there is the centre, a former fortified settlement, in its sacred state. On the other hand, there is the area outside it, which is made up of the contrasting ecological zones of cattle-herders, farmers and fishermen, and of labour migratory routes and longer term population shifts. For reasons which I shall explain, this spatial complexity is often seen by Giriama as contaminating the purity of the sacred centre, pushing it in the direction of desacralisation. The Giriama response to this threat is, so to speak, to hold the centre, and to re-imagine it anew, cleansing it and re-working it back into its sacredness.

Three understandings of space

I do not wish to use the terms sacred and profane in a mutually exclusive sense, nor do I start from this opposition. As a starting point, I incline more to Van Gennep's view of the sacred as only ever relational and 'pivotal' as he calls it (1960: 12–13). In fact, beyond this introduction I do not use the term profane again in this book, except briefly in the final chapter. Nor is the idea of the sacred held to have fixed boundaries. What is contrasted by the Giriama with the sacred centre is not profanity, but greater or lesser amounts of sacredness depending on circumstances, relationships, and stances. There is constant semantic spillage. Thus, the western ecological zone of cattle-keepers around the sacred centre is itself often contrasted with the eastern areas of farmers and fishermen as being closer to tradition and a sense of 'pure' Giriama identity. Sometimes, though less often, it is a northern area which is regarded in this way, much less so than in the past. At the same time, practical considerations and competition characterise relations between people of the west and east, and other regions. My use of the term sacred, as is evident from its own history, therefore ranges over ideas of the pure, the autochthonous and the customary as well as the absolute and holy. This is, as best as one can, to translate Giriama usage, in which terms like 'clean/pure' (*-eri*), 'wholesome/adult' (*-zima*) and 'earth/origin' (*tsi*) commonly presuppose each other.

Focusing in this way on what I translate as Giriama ideas of the sacred is not a narrow exercise in cultural relativism. On the contrary, the intention is to question English usage of the concept through Giriama ideas, and so to broaden comparative understanding. This seems to me to be the original sense in which a reflexive anthropology was proposed: constantly to recast cultural ideas and analytical concepts in terms of the light they may throw on each other, rather than to document the personal self-understanding that may be gained from fieldwork, as seems to have become the general sense of the term in anthropology.

It follows from this that my view of Giriama society must overlap to some extent with those commonly expressed by Giriama themselves. Thus, in this study I see space as understood in three ways: as a fixed centre amenable to being regarded as absolutely sacred; as a relational pattern of ecological zones and human movements; and as an indeterminately regarded amorphism, without centre, boundary or even content. I could dub these centrist, relational and amorphist respectively, and see them as arising from the above interrogation of Eliade, Durkheim, Lévi-Strauss, Moore and others. No doubt they have been honed by such interrogation and by other influences both before and after fieldwork. At the same time it has to be emphasised that it was Giriama themselves who also contributed to making such distinctions, as far as I can judge, whilst I did fieldwork. This perennial question of relative influence is insoluble but not pointless, for it obliges us at least to record what we think were the original inspirations for an analysis drawn from the fieldwork itself. Whether what we record did so inspire is yet another question.

In the case of the Giriama, at least, I constantly met the following views. On the one hand, they say, their traditional capital or centre, called the Kaya, is a fixed, central place with inviolable boundaries and unquestionable sacredness. Rather like Newton's void having existence without objects in it, it does not need persons in it for it to remain sacred and central, and indeed it is often empty or almost empty for long periods. On the other hand, Giriama speak of the western part of Giriama country in which the Kaya stands in terms of its contrast with the eastern part. The west is 'traditional' and the east 'modern'. The west comprises the Giriama sacred centre while the east merges and mixes boundaries and peoples and lacks a definitive centre. The Kaya is a centre while the east and west are defined relationally, just as, internally, the east comprises different peoples and places standing in cross-cutting relationships to each other. As with Leibniz's view, such spaces only have existence and meaning through the relationships of people and objects within them, relations which are always liable to change. The Giriama thus juxtapose an absolutist or centrist with a relational view of the spaces they occupy.

How, then, do I add to this binary distinction commonly made by Giriama the third idea of a spatial category as amorphous and indeterminate? No such category is explicit in Giriama conversation, and I justify it as a part of Giriama thinking on the following grounds. In referring to the Kaya as not needing people to live in it, Giriama sometimes speak of it as their 'earth' (*tsi*) and as consubstantive with their whole country (using the term -*zima*). Giriamaland itself is still regarded by Giriama as having clear administrative boundaries, being made up of specific locations and sub-locations in Kenya's coast province, despite the fact that increasing numbers of the 350,000 Giriama spend much or all of their time outside and that more and more non-Giriama now live among them within their boundaries. The Kaya is physically demarcated by a large ring of forest, but in its consubstantive sense of 'being' all of Giriama country, and therefore as partaking in its welfare, the Kaya has unbounded significance. It is believed to affect and be affected by what goes on in Giriama country and among all Giriama, whether or not they are currently living in Giriamaland. Evils afflicting or incurred by Giriama contaminate the Kaya, while abuse of the Kaya damages the fertility of Giriama farms, cattle and married couples. The Giriama, their country and their Kaya undergo unpremeditated cleansing from time to time. This may take the form of a large-scale witch-hunt, the sacking and replacement of Kaya elders, or the ritual and physical clearing and cleansing of the Kaya, as well as through homestead rites involving washing and sweeping carried out under the auspices, or with the authority, of the Kaya.

Many of these activities, which are organised or led by Kaya elders and others associated with them, in fact often occur outside the Kaya and take the form of journeys undertaken by individuals or, as in the case of a witch-hunter, he and his team, who pass through one locality after another, beyond Giriamaland itself. The journeys and activities draw their legitimacy from the Kaya but at the same time rewrite its significance, just as they in effect redefine the boundaries of Giriama society by drawing attention to the continuing dispersal and mixture of its population. At such times, which are never predictable, it is difficult for me to call the Kaya an absolute and set sacred centre, since so many other forces are currently at work challenging its status. Its fate seems to hang in the balance, and it seems about to become just another important but desacralised item of the western landscape and so to derive its distinctiveness from its contrast with the east rather than from any intrinsic sacredness. But such times of doubt may be superseded, and seem historically to have been superseded, by a reassertion of its centrality and sacredness. It then partly continues as before, but it also partly assumes a new identity: its last triumph or miracle is the one most easily remembered and differs from preceding ones. Let me return for the last time to the metaphor. The sacred Kaya as spatial text, having been wiped clean, is rewritten to include earlier lines but also at least a few innovative ones. It is a liminal idea of homogeneous space positioned between a centre and an uncentred complexity, whose interrelationship is always in the making.

Contrary to Durkheim's assertion cited above, it is only by mentally grasping such an idea of undifferentiated spatial amorphousness that the Giriama could redefine the relationship between their sacred centre and the shifting movements and relationships occurring within and beyond their country. The centre and the country have, so to speak, to be brought into line with each other, that is to say, made mutually consistent and not absurd. There is, after all, considerable potential absurdity in the claim that a virtually uninhabited central place in a remote area surrounded by primeval forest can govern the lives of 350,000 people variously engaged in different rural and urban livelihoods. It is through the idea of the centre as having become undifferentiated and without shape that it can be refashioned to meet current Giriama needs, just as social and ecological complexities in other areas have to be reconciled with their view of a common origin, and hence shared identity, in the unfathomable knowledge and secrets of the Kaya.

There are many ethnic groups throughout the world who define themselves by reference to a fixed centre which only a minority of them live in or have ever visited. If such centres do not exist, it becomes imperative that at some stage they have to be invented. This cultivation or invention of a central place is likely to contrast with the fact that the group's members are in reality widely dispersed. The result is that there will be two understandings of space, as I have suggested is explicitly the case among the Giriama: of a fixity giving essence to the central place; and of cross-cutting and merging boundaries that never settle. The idea of spatial fixity lends itself to neat correlations and correspondence which nevertheless come under threat, such as the idea that the Kaya stands for purity and tradition. Spatial restlessness defies tautologous parallels and demands constant re-interpretation. As with the idea of spatial fixity, it must always be worked at. It is during this process of working-at that a once internally ordered but now cluttered space becomes cleared and then redifferentiated.

Pilgrims and their absence

It is of course commonly the case that the shrines and sacred places that are the objects of pilgrimage occasionally undergo clearing and cleansing and, although I know of no such reports, may need to be redefined periodically in conformity with peoples' changing expectations. But the Giriama sacred Kaya stands in a different relationship to population movement from that of pilgrims and their centres. While pilgrims move towards a shrine, the Giriama have over the years moved away from the Kaya. As I explain in chapter two, it was once highly populated, but now it and the surrounding area are seen over the years as having lost their population to other, more distant areas. Nor do Giriama in the least subscribe to a hope or myth of return. It is enough that the place itself, its forest, and its medicines and knowledge, remain in an uncontaminated state. There is yet another difference. The presuppositions of pilgrims are that they follow and seek relatively predictable voyages, marked routes, manageable time-scales and spiritual benefits. However, the character and destiny of the Kaya is always regarded as hedged around with uncertainty, so mirroring the doubts expressed by Giriama themselves concerning their own future both as individuals trying to wrest a livelihood from diminishing land and resources and as a group confronted by a burgeoning of alien culture, religions and ideology near and among them. When people visit the Kaya, perhaps to take an oath or participate in a trial by ordeal, to acquire medical knowledge, to be blessed, or as one of a number summoned to cleanse it, it is always in a crisis occurring without warning.

None of this is to deny the possibility of the Kaya becoming at some future stage a shrine for Giriama pilgrims to visit. The leader of a new indigenous Christian sect tried in fact to capture the Kaya for his church in the late 1980s (Thompson 1990: 117–144). Had he been successful, and had his sect in time become sufficiently widespread among the Giriama that they identified it as exclusively their own, treating it as their most salient expression of ethnic identity, we could certainly speculate that the Kaya might have become a sacred centre attracting pilgrims drawn from a by now vastly dispersed Giriama population, forced to live far afield as a result of extensive labour migration. While this is pure speculation, it is a reasonable inference to be drawn from the current status of the Kaya and of the political economy of Kenya. The uninhabited and even abandoned sacred centre is, then, the flip-side of the pilgrims' shrine or holy city. Historically the two may be transformations of each under, say, some alternating conditions of economic expansion, contraction, and population movements. This can be left as speculation bordering on hypothesis for further study.

It is strange that this contrastive type has gone amiss in anthropology, for there are a number of reports of important and sometimes central places which are remote, with none or very few people living in them, but which possess key ritual, medical and other knowledge, and are only irregularly and rarely visited by outsiders claiming to be culturally and ethnically connected to the centre. The most celebrated are perhaps the sacred places of various Australian Aborigine peoples, which are left behind and revisited in criss-crossing migrations and are permanently inscribed in landscapes. They commonly make up the distinctive Aboriginal cultural construction called in English and identified in the literature as The Dreaming. Part of The Dreaming is the continuous identification of remote and sacred places which are always being temporarily abandoned but which remain owned by and therefore central to an individual and his descendants. There is a vast and fascinating panoply of works on this phenomenon, much of it mentioned by Myers in the latest, intriguing study to focus on Aboriginal spatial concepts and organisation (Myers 1986: 152–155 and elsewhere). In Africa itself, Fardon (1991) presents a study of the Chamba people of Cameroon and Nigeria which turns on a distinction between two areas: one well populated and unsure of its ritual knowledge, and the other a much less peopled autochthonous area from which Chamba originated and where truly authentic knowledge is believed to reside. Finally, there are echoes of the idea of an empty or nearly empty sacred place in the example of the Merina ancestral villages of Madagascar described by Bloch, which contain the often large and ornate tombs of kinship groups, most members of whom expect to be buried in them despite having lived at a distance from their village for some generations. While maintaining links with the ancestral lands does furnish practical advantages, there is nevertheless a moral attachment to people's 'home' areas and what Bloch calls 'a continuing sacred existence' in them (Bloch 1971: 105–137). Comparing Bloch's, Fardon's and Myers' analyses with that of Sallnow concerning Andean pilgrimage (Sallnow 1987), there is a striking cosmological contrast attending the difference between shrines which attract population flows and sacred sites which are remembered more than visited. While the pilgrim shrines stand out as definitive statements of regional and personal order, the distant and nearly empty sacred places more hesitatingly evoke questions about a knowledge that is assumed to exist in them but is not always accessible.

The Giriama Kaya is of the latter kind, and is set, as I have mentioned, in an area characterised as remote from more populous and economically active and socially diverse areas. In calling it sacred and yet differentiating it from the more historically assertive shrines normally visited by pilgrims, we raise questions about the nature of the sacred as a concept, a task attempted in the concluding chapter.

Outline of the argument

As regards the layout of this book, the first chapter begins in the west of southern
Kilifi district, and describes the powerfully expressed images held by Giriama of
this cattle-keeping zone and of the Kaya within it. We see how fantasies of the
west as ecologically self-sufficient both draw on and nurture the sense of timeless Giriama independence vested in the Kaya. A condensed twenty-year history
of the relationship between a young witch-finder and some Kaya elders throws
into relief the doubts that at least some people have of these elders' use of their
powers. But the elders regain control, supported by and encouraging popular
belief in the greater powers of the Kaya as a place. The second chapter describes
some of the qualities which make this almost empty Kaya sacred in the eyes of
all some of the time, and of most all the time. It is sacred, yet it is also a fount of
power which is used politically to defend the Kaya and the Giriama people but
also to control them internally. The Kaya may be sacred but it is clear to people
that the Kaya elders are not, and that they pursue their ambitions as did former
big men and as do modern politicians.

Chapter three asks, then, how do western cattle-herders living near the Kaya
manage to sustain the image held of them as proudly closer to the heart of Giriama
tradition. After all, if Kaya elders are regarded frankly as motivated by personal
ambitions as well as by concern for the Kaya and the Giriama people, why should
the people of the cattle zone not also be so regarded? In fact, the westerners do
subscribe to the image of themselves as closer to custom and as less dependent
on external economic forces, and it is easy to see why. For instance, despite the
harshness of their livelihood, they sell few of their cattle on the open market,
perhaps one or two at a time, keeping most for milk production, funeral sacrifices
and, above all, bridewealth transactions. They operate a remarkable system of
dividing and 'hiding' their herds with relatives and affines in different areas, so
spreading the risks of disease, drought, and poor pasture, and lessening the likelihood of dependent sons and brothers pressing their claims. Cattle owners may
have either successfully opposed the introduction of government ranch schemes
for over twenty years, or at least have continued to herd and hide their cattle in
the time-honoured way. They are probably poorer overall than many of the
Giriama who live in the more fertile eastern and coastal areas of Kenya, and they
suffer droughts, the decimation of herds and famine more often. Yet they continue to be regarded by easterners, and to regard themselves, as independent of
the 'contaminations' of the largely Muslim coast. Elements of truth, ideal and
inaccuracy slide into each other.

The cattle-keepers' sense of autonomy is preserved in their marriage choices
and practices, which are discussed in chapter four. They rarely marry women
from the east, whom they regard as unable to remain long in the arid west, an
observation which is in fact borne out by figures on marriage. Yet women from
the west are able to enter petty trade and are far from repressed in this respect:

they take milk to the agricultural east and return with palm wine to sell in the cattle zone. This evokes contrasting but false or exaggerated stereotypes. Men in both east and west fear that eastern women, exposed to capricious and demanding Islamic spirits and influences, are less likely to make stable marriage partners and are more likely to seek personal independence in coastal small towns or the city of Mombasa, though very few do so. Western women, favoured for their stable marriages and alleged acceptance of male control, in fact convert their stable base into a dependable trading clientele in both west and east, so securing some financial autonomy. Male fears and exaggeration point up the idealisation of the west and its Kaya as an area of pure, unchanging Giriama identity in which women are indisputably dominated by men, and of the east as losing this identity.

These and other more general fears are heightened at funerals, described in chapter five, which are the most elaborate of all Giriama homestead rituals. They are attended by hundreds of people from both west and east: it is true that distantly resident easterners and westerners do not often inter-marry, but they come to each others' funerals by being invited as affines of affines and so on, in a chain-like sequence of overlapping locally endogamous areas which stretches from west to east. Funerals are both emotionally heavy and excitable occasions. There is the fear of death before the body is buried. Women's and men's song and dance groups hurl sexual and other forms of abuse at each other, and at the deceased, his or her relatives, and the local chief and sub-chiefs. The funerals seem at times to go beyond the rules supposed to govern them and threaten to get out of control, like the fear, grief, anger and insults that are expressed at them. Dramatically, men assume control, taking heirs aside, urging them and others to get the money to spend on livestock and palm wine for sacrifice and consumption, and explaining to the congregation how the funeral should henceforth proceed. Funerals, in short, throw open questions of Giriama authority, including that of the Kaya elders, and of the Kaya itself as a sacred centre.

Quietly punctuating the course of funerals, however, are various purificatory words and gestures aimed at washing and clearing away deathliness and putting it outside the homestead. They seem to be a hinted counterpoint to more explicit cleansing rites carried out in homesteads, at which the hierarchy of Kaya command comes to its fore, as discussed in chapter six. The most significant rite is that held to purify a homestead of the effects of a form of adultery which is tantamount to incest and which is especially feared for the infertility caused to members of the homestead. It is believed to be able to wipe out whole agnatic lines. It is strongly held by Giriama, both from east and west, that it is in fact in the large homesteads of the western cattle area where this kind of incest mostly occurs, for it is in these that brothers and their wives live together in large number and so where temptation is greatest. A paradox is that while the Kaya ensures the fertility of the Giriama people and their land, the greatest single cause of homestead infertility is believed to occur among the people of the cattle zone around the Kaya. The power of the Kaya elders is, so to speak, tested and perhaps even challenged by this fact, for it is diviners and herbalists who are needed to purify the homesteads. Yet, the main work of these diviners and herbalists is to diagnose and reverse the effects of witchcraft. Witchcraft, however, is said to be prevalent in the smaller, more closely congregated homesteads of the over-crowded east. Incest and witchcraft are, then, each associated with west and east, but it is eastern practitioners who come to the aid of the west, a curious reversal of the supreme power that is otherwise attributed to the Kaya and its elders. This theme of the subversion of the west by the east is continued in chapter seven, where the hierarchy of diviners and herbalists is based on the role played by eastern Islamic spirits from the coast, who are often the means by which many women and some men enter divination or gain extra spiritual power, with men doctors also able to buy additional Islamic medical knowledge.

Chapter eight shows how the sources of this subversion do indeed stem from the once predominantly Muslim narrow coastal strip, but that there are other new and powerful influences. These include up-country migrants who have settled there, European package tourism, the proliferation of mass-produced consumer articles and, to a lesser extent, Pentecostal Christianity. Islamic influence seems likely in fact to become secondary in due course. A new possessory spirit, or more properly a re-defined one, has arisen in this coastal area which kills whomever it desires. Inland spirits rarely kill. According to many Giriama the new spirit epitomises the ruthlessness and ancestral rootlessness of the recent coastal culture of consumerism, where even love leads to destruction. Yet some Giriama, though still a minority, continue to migrate to the area, as land or opportunities diminish, especially in the east. It is a dilemma of identity of which they are aware and which they will discuss with each other, provisionally resolving the issue by pointing to the sacred Kaya in the west as the repository of Giriama autonomy and as that which finally defines them, but which hardly any of them have ever visited. Though relatively few, such Giriama, particularly those who may never return to Giriama country, stand at the edge of an ancestral world.

In the concluding chapter I ask in what sense we can continue to call the Kaya sacred, for its pragmatic appeal as an identity tag seems paramount rather than its magnetism as, say, a place of worship or pilgrimage. Can it truly be said to instill a sense of awe and obligation among people who live at such a distance? I answer by suggesting a view of the sacred as made up of many perspectives which shift constantly in relation to each other and are contestable, but which play on the idea of the empty, the clean, the re-imaginable and the infinitely deferrable. For example, the Kaya has taken on an aura of restorative power the more it has become removed in space and time from the everyday activities of the people. On the other hand, though remote, it is sufficiently a part of the Giriama people and their land that it can become contaminated by their 'dirt' and so require purification. It is also a supreme place of violent sacrifice, where, as in rain-making and cleansing ceremonies, a ram, the animal of peace and purity, is slaughtered in an exaggerated manner recognised as jarring to the senses and sentiment. The same method of killing the ram is employed in ordinary homestead purificatory ceremonies, so that it is a form that every Giriama is familiar with. Writ large in its effects when carried out in the Kaya, it is as if the ram takes on contradictory forces which pull Giriama to the fold of the Kaya and push them away: promising them the alleged independence of the Kaya and its western surroundings, but recognizing their need to work and labour in areas not always of their choosing.

1

Fantasies of the west

Contrasting spaces

Westwards into the hinterland of southern Kilifi district, beyond the last of the palm trees in a place called Miyani, you can hear voices carrying along shallow ridges in the terrain. Linking the speakers are small paths between homesteads set perhaps a kilometre apart, some closer, some further. It is rare to hear the sound of a motor vehicle. But this is the 1980s. Surely in an area in which cattle are raised and milk produced, only 50 or so kilometres from the Port of Mombasa, there ought to be the noise of buses and trucks fetching and carrying people and goods. In fact it used to be like this. In the years after independence in 1962 and until the mid and even late seventies, the milk was regularly collected by entrepreneurs, while for those women who wished to sell milk directly to consumers and return with palm wine, there was always some morning and after-noon transportation to market centres. But the entrepreneurs and transporters withdrew their services for lack of profit. Now the women normally have to walk the fifteen or so kilometres to the small township of Kaloleni or the similar distance to the trading centre of Mariakani (see Map 1).

Some 45 kilometres to the north of Miyani at a one-shop settlement called Dulukiza, a bus stands idle. It is in full working order but its Kenyan Asian owners see no point in running it and would be happy to sell it. Business has been bad, they say, and their trade has withered like the bush around them in an area now commonly short of rain. One has to travel another fifteen kilometres, to Vitengeni, to find a bus regularly running to the coastal town of Kilifi. From about 1968 until 1978 this hinterland area suffered frequent droughts, since when the situation has only improved intermittently.

Softening the difficulties a little, a water pipeline has been extended to Gotani. Gotani consists of a road junction, two shops and the office and compound of the chief of Kayafungo location, of which nearby Miyani is a sub-location. A communal tap has been installed at Gotani, around which women from some-times great distances assemble, some setting out by foot before sunrise, in order

Map 1. Giriamaland and the Kenya coast

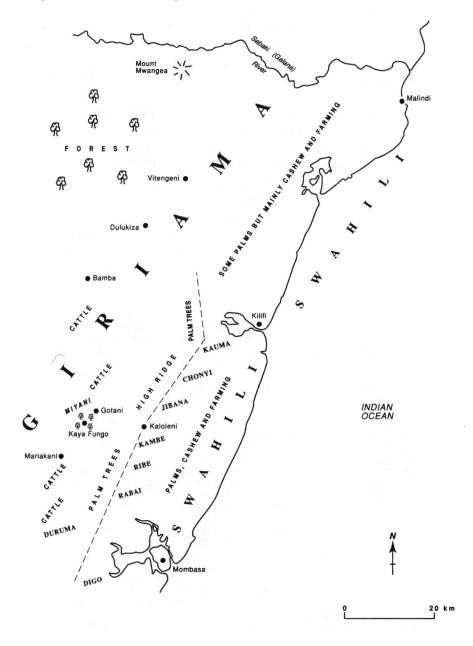

to return home by midday. More pipelines are promised and there is growing confidence that this will be done and that more people will benefit. Perhaps, indeed, there may even be a reversal of the alleged out-migration of people from the dry, inland pastures to the wetter, fertile region closer to the coast where the coconut palms grow. Perhaps land-starved farmers from the densely settled coastal zone will repopulate the more arid areas and keep livestock as well as growing maize and other crops.

But these are hopes for the future. The story here is of what has happened until now. It is of a people who have constantly moved over the generations within their own lands. In recent years many have poured eastwards towards the fertile coast. This movement was accelerated after the First World War, or rather after the unsuccessful rebellion by the Giriama in 1914 against British rule, further increasing after the Second World War and again in the years after independence when, in the late sixties and seventies, package tourism provided short-term cash employment and long-term illusions. A smaller number went to or remained in the western cattle area, sometimes joined by those who found little for themselves nearer the coast.[1] Yet others compromised, so to speak, by building a

---

[1] From 1962 to 1979 the population of the agricultural eastern coastal half of Kilifi district grew from 96,007 to 203,864, an increase of 112% over seventeen years. The population density increased from 72 persons per square kilometre to 153. I include within this mainly farming area the locations of Kauma, Kaloleni, Duruma, Chonyi, Jibana, Kambe-Ribe, Rabai, Mtwapa, Mavueni-Takaungu, Junju, Tezo-Toka, Ganda and Magarini, and the towns of Kilifi and Malindi (the latter, now a tourist centre, increasing 300% in population from 5,818 to 17,457). I exclude Mombasa district, which comprises the town and its environs, which grew from 179,500 to 341,148, an increase of 90%.

By contrast, the western cattle area grew less quickly over the same period, from 53,305 to 90,467, an increase of 70%. The population density grew from 17 to 29 persons per square kilometre. Included in this area are the locations of Bamba, Kayafungo, Mariakani, Ganze and Vitengeni, which, since administrative location and ecological boundaries do not coincide, inevitably also contain some heavily populated predominantly farming rather than cattle-keeping areas. These will have weighted the population and density increases more than would be the case had exclusively cattle-keeping areas been singled out.

We get some broad idea of longer-term changes by looking at census figures of (southern) Kilifi district taken in 1929 (reported in Kelly 1960). For instance, Ganze location actually had fewer people in 1962 (7,480) than in 1929 (7,649), and by 1979 had only reached 10,850. Similarly, in 1929 the locations of Kayafungo and Mariakani numbered 8,330 and 7,333 respectively, only reaching 13,981 and 10,536 by 1962. In other words, it is only since 1962 that Mariakani, Kayafungo and Bamba (not identified as such in the 1929 census) have expanded significantly. Contrasting with that early very low growth rate, Kaloleni location had only 4,352 people in 1929 but had tripled to 12,785 by 1962. Since 1962, of course, the western locations of Kayafungo and Bamba, but not Ganze, have grown much more than they did in the preceding period.

Taken as a whole, the western area, contrary to local statement, is clearly not losing its population in an absolute sense, though it often appears visibly to be so, since its slower rate of growth is partly attributable in particular areas to the departure of mainly young men, and sometimes their families, for the east, either to work for cash or to farm, though the latter option is nowadays rare, given the growing land pressure in the east. The vastly discrepant population densities also give visible expression to the claim that the west is losing its population to the east. (Sources: The Government of Kenya Census Reports for 1962, 1969 and 1979.)

house in the cattle zone, visiting it occasionally, and working for cash in or around Mombasa and Malindi.[2]

Of those who remained in the cattle zone a few were primary schoolteachers, for there are four such schools in the Miyani and nearby area catering for a population of about 1250 children. Others were men who preferred simply to raise livestock. Later, as jobs in the coastal area, as in Kenya generally, declined, some young men stayed because there was now nowhere for them to go. Women rarely moved except to accompany husbands, or, in a few cases, to be married to men nearer the coast.

The Giriama often characterise the two populations in the following way: people at the densely populated coast are ambitious, seek land, know the value of such cash crops as the coconut palm, its tapped wine and cashew nuts, and send their children to schools, dress their women in European or Swahili manner, may be Christian or Muslim, and are swiftly forgetting their cultural heritage; those living in the less crowded cattle area know Giriama customs and traditions better than the others, are not greedy but share and are more hospitable, live in large homesteads surrounded by relatives, prefer their women to wear the traditional cotton *hando* dress, and continue to venerate their *koma* ancestors. Crude impressions or not, the more you travel westwards away from the coast and into the dry arid bushland, the more you do seem enveloped by a sense of Giriama antiquity and authenticity, and the more eastwards to the coast, the more

[2] Given the problem of growing land pressure in the eastern farming area, fewer families are now able to migrate there from the west, should they need to do so. An increasing tendency is for westerners instead to seek wage employment in either Mombasa or the line of small towns and centres along the coastal strip.

A smaller proportion of almost landless people in the east actually move into the west, usually to try to farm rather than to herd cattle, but attempting to do so in areas unfavourable to farming. It appears to be an act of desperation. Typical of a harrowing report is that for 1975, for instance, when population pressure along the coastal belt prompted migration to the hinterland, where people ploughed large areas of land, 'which might never produce a crop but may succeed to trigger the start of a desert in the range areas. Most of the peasants are now on famine relief and unless alternative settlement or drought-proven [*sic*] crops are found, . . . they will continue to be a liability to the state . . . ' (Coast Province Annual Report, Range Management Division for 1975). That and the previous year, 1974, had been ones of persistent drought in the rangeland areas, with most springs and dams drying up, and with large losses of livestock. The combination of population pressure in the agricultural areas and drought in marginal areas, then becomes especially calamitous. Until a generation or two ago, there was more two-way migration between the cattle and farming areas. Stereotypes distinguishing cattlemen from farmers are of longstanding but are perhaps now even more accentuated as movement between the two modes of livelihood becomes restricted, or as, within the range areas, migrant farmers attempt to work land that cattlemen and government live-stock officers regard as suitable only or mainly for pasture.

It was at this time, too, that there were reports within the range lands of 'land-grabbing', pre-sumably as a result, in certain areas, of competition for land between incoming farmers and pre-existing cattlemen. Should a man wish to leave an eastern farming area to raise cattle in the west then he would do so through, usually, matrilateral ties while he is young, but I have few such cases.

Thus, although the population of the east has indeed grown more quickly overall than that of the cattle-keeping west, there is by no means an absence of migration, or attempted migration, in the opposite direction.

apparent is the overlay of Islam and, to a much lesser extent, of Christianity, with its individualistic trappings of third world capitalism, and with the fast coastal road humming to jetline coaches bound for Malindi and Lamu and rattling to *matatu* taxis and minibuses.

Poverty is nevertheless the shadow that lies across the arid and fertile zones alike. While some families have too few livestock to compensate for the limited maize harvests of the west, others nearer the coast may live as no more than squatters on land from which they always face the threat of eviction, despite the government priority that such people be offered plots on settlement schemes when they become available. In the face of such poverty stand the few large homesteads in the west whose heads own hundreds of cattle, and whose counterparts are the rare coastal farmers who have built up their land holdings and expanded into shop ownership and the transport business.

It is not however the gradations and extremes of wealth that people constantly talk about. It is, after all, well observed that family fortunes can crumble long before they result in family dynasties, and that memories of the rich reach back to their earlier, more ordinary circumstances. The line of road from Mombasa to Malindi was paved in 1969 and as a result is now studded with trading centres and emerging towns which advertise the possibility of concrete success which may be lost as quickly as it was won. It is rather the amazing regional contrast that is a common topic of Giriama conversation.

Taking the fertile farming area first, there is the ethnic jumble of the coastal strip, consisting roughly of three categories: such other fellow Mijikenda of the Giriama as the Jibana, Chonyi, Ribe, Kambe, Kauma, Rabai, Digo and Duruma, many of whom are recent immigrants while others may have been settled there for generations; the Swahili, Arabs and Asians of various strata and historical origins; and more recently the immigrants from up-country, including the Bantu-speaking Kikuyu, Kamba and Luhya, and the Nilotic-speaking Luo.

Second, further inland within this farming zone, there are the customary lands of the Giriama, where coconut palms, cashew nut and other trees and crops are grown and which includes the important trading centre and township of Kaloleni.

Third, built on a hill which was chosen as its site by the CMS mission at the end of the nineteenth century, the western side of Kaloleni faces out over the most inland area: the dry hinterland of the Giriama cattle zone which lacks the ethnic and economic diversity of the coast and the cash cropping of the middle palm-belt area.

While Giriama distinguish these three areas and also divide themselves in this way between farmers and keepers of livestock, they embrace both activities to some degree and see the cattle zone as the repository par excellence of Giriama lore, and the palm belt (itself once a cattle area, at least in Kaloleni, in the nineteen twenties) as having lost much that is traditional, the more so as it approaches the predominantly Muslim shoreland. There is indeed a consensus among

Giriama as far as I can judge: that the shoreline is one of ethnic admixture, which is not without its excitement, fancies, and promises, while, passing through the intermediary and fertile coconut and agricultural areas to the dry zone eventually bordering the Tsavo plains, there is the suggestion of Giriama purity, symbolised by the presence of the traditional Giriama capital, the Kaya.

It is tempting to regard this as a gross fiction. After all, the clan sections found in the cattle area in which I have worked, Miyani and nearby, contain branches deriving from other Mijikenda groups and are sometimes themselves of such non-Giriama origins. So much for ethnic purity. Similarly, people who raise cattle, goats, and sheep for meat, milk or sale, are as much at the mercy of fluctuating economic demands as are farmers and wage-earners. What people seem to be saying when they point to well-known areas like Gotani, Bamba, Mwangea or Viragoni, as repositories of pure Giriama custom, is that they are visible and tangible instances of a continuity with the past. They are seen as spatially somewhat remote sources of customary knowledge accessible in its details to only a few, but regarded generally as historically important.

This westwards gaze is, then, an expression of cultural identity. Paradoxically, the more the Giriama become involved in the ethnic and economic diversification and dependency of the coast, the more the western hinterland takes on the character of an autochthonous region considered essential for the preservation of Giriama identity. Like the European tourists on the coast who merge holiday brochure with personal contact, younger Giriama who mix with them have begun to romanticise about their own past and to bring it forward to the geographical present of the western zone, away from the sea and crowded populations.

For the easterner, the polarisation of the west as remote cultural ideal and of their own area as more concerned with immediate reality, is often elaborated in different ways. I have, for instance, heard Giriama so-called land squatters near the coast talk of the independence of the west and the subordination of the coastal area. In the intermediary zone further inland, Giriama farmers competitively seek profits as well as subsistence from their coconuts, palm wine and cashew nuts, but then compare their lack of land with what they see as an abundance in the west, glossing optimistically over the fact, of which they are normally aware, that cattle and goats require a much lower man–land ratio and that the land is much less suitable for farming.[3]

---

[3] I give the examples of the two locations in which I have worked (see Parkin 1972 for Kaloleni). Kaloleni borders Kayafungo location, which includes Miyani, and is a farming area heavily dependent on coconut palms, which grow in great profusion. It has a land density of 178 persons per square kilometre. It simply cannot accommodate many more farmers without radically altering the ecology, for instance by uprooting the palm trees. Would-be farming migrants are obliged to seek settlement in other eastern, less densely populated locations, or in the coastal strip. Therefore, Kaloleni's population increase over the period 1962–1979 was only 56%. Probably for the same reason, neighbouring Jibana, with the same palm-dependent ecology and with a huge rural population density of 262 persons per square kilometre, increased by only 26%.

The population of Kayafungo, by contrast, increased by 61%, despite its inhabitants' claim that

Western Giriama themselves subscribe to the view that they are closer to 'true' Giriama custom than people in the east, despite the fact that the west has its share of mundane problems like anywhere else. The west is, after all, subject to less rainfall than the east, and is more distant from clinics, hospitals, secondary schools and large shops, and has for years seen young men migrate to the fertile east and to large towns.

The view of the western bush and grassland area as one embracing authentic custom is partly based on its remoteness from modern developments in the cash-cropping agricultural east and the increasingly tourist-influenced coast. However, it is also in the west that the Giriama traditional capital is located. This remarkable fortified settlement, called the Kaya, is set within a small area of primeval forest surrounded by bushland. All known Giriama medicines are said to be found in the Kaya forest, which, according to a recent ethno-botanical expedition, does indeed contain enormous herbal riches (Hawthorne *et al.* 1981). The forest has been fiercely defended by most Giriama against attempts at its appropriation or destruction, not always successfully. Up to the middle of the nineteenth century it and its immediate environs accommodated many, some would say all, of the then 10–20,000 Giriama people, who were grouped there for mutual protection against successive invasions of Maasai, Oromo, and possibly Arabs and Swahili. Mutoro has suggested that it was also once part of a network

many of its people are leaving for the east and the coast. Kayafungo land density is, however, only 81 persons per square kilometre and includes on its eastern and south-eastern borders some relatively well-watered farming land. In its drier areas, also, some try to farm but, on the whole, the population increase there is indeed slowed by the less favourable farming terrain and the need to depend primarily on livestock. Miyani sub-location, for instance, has a lower density of 59 persons per square kilometre.

For Kayafungo location as a whole (total population in 1979 of 22,562 men, women and children), which is often characterised by government livestock officers as 'overgrazed', I estimate that its cattle population varies between 12,500 (after the 1974 drought) and 21,500 (for instance, during the better weather of the earlier seventies) herded on about 40,000 acres of cleared grazing land, distributed among some four hundred men who are both homestead heads and herd owners, and who hold the cattle in trust for male dependents. But since herd owners never disclose how many cattle they have, these being hidden in a variety of other herds in the manner described in chapter three, neither my own nor the local tax assessment of the number of cattle in the area should be taken as more than a rough guide. In addition to the cattle there are many more goats, perhaps four times as many, and a few thousand sheep which are kept mainly for sacrificial purposes.

The hides of cattle which have been sacrificed at funerals are collected, dried and sold. The sale of hides at Mariakani cattle auctions is much greater than that of live cattle. As regards live cattle, over a four-year period no more than one or two per cent of cattle were reported as sold at the auction, though an indeterminately greater number are sold to fellow Giriama, mostly for funeral sacrifices, especially to people in the eastern farming areas. The proportion of cattle reported as sold as hides, most of them at the Mariakani auction (and very few among fellow Giriama), ranges from 12% to 39% (median 22%). Such hides include those of young male animals, for it is these which are commonly sacrificed at funerals. Their sale indicates the scale of funerals as well as their nutritional and symbolic importance, as discussed in chapter five. The hides of cattle which have been sold to eastern farming areas and sacrificed there are more likely to be sold in Mombasa or to a coastal dealer and so would need to be added to the above number in order to know what proportion of cattle are sacrificed. Cows are, of course, allowed to live longer than young bulls, with most heifers being used in bridewealth transactions and then bred and milked, as the Giriama themselves emphasise (see chapter four).

of Kayas among the different Mijikenda peoples (for whom no common self-appellation then existed), who would trade with each other and with coastal Swahili and Arabs for goods that each could not itself produce (Mutoro 1987: 90–92, 264–266).

For most Giriama most of the time, the Kaya stands supreme as the unquestioned and absolute centre of Giriama knowledge and tradition, with the western area in which it stands often associated with it. It is a living example of Giriama authenticity. Distinguished from preceding settlements,[4] and from the Kayas of other Mijikenda groups by the name Kaya Fungo, after its most prominent leader, it now supersedes in importance the area north of the Tana river, in Somalia, called Singwaya. This is otherwise regarded as the place from which the Giriama and certain other Mijikenda peoples came (Spear 1978) and remains a significant reference point of origin in traditions told by older men and for burial positions (where, when a body is lain on its right side and with its feet pointing towards the west, the eyes of a deceased man or woman face in a northerly direction towards this origin in Singwaya).

However, while the Kaya stands on its own as the Giriama centre of knowledge and ritual, the comparison of east and west more ambiguously rests on an idealised polarisation of economic as well as cultural factors. In fact, the comparison of places is one of the ways in which polarisation is expressed. If we have to give an essence to such polarisation, we might say that it is of remoteness and continuity on the one hand and of immediacy and the contingent on the other. The Singwaya origin myth has the north as the remote and continuous and the south as the contingent, while the current beliefs about the Kaya emphasise west and east as having these attributes.

West and east, north and south, dry cattle zone and coastal strip, tradition and modernity, the remote and the immediate, and other contrasts that are made by the Giriama, have no ontological priority one over the other. All are aspects of one or other of the 'spaces' in which Giriama individuals place themselves and their activities. Nor, I imagine, can this be an experience of the Giriama alone. Is it not also that of any people who engage in the paradox of cultivating a geographical idealisation of their past while at the same time regarding other areas as currently providing a better livelihood?

We see the same mix of idealised time and space and of contingent and

---

[4] Adopting a geographical model of central-place distribution in his archaeological survey, Mutoro distinguishes between the main Kayas of each of the nine Mijikenda peoples and smaller 'daughter' Kayas. He identifies the expansion after 1750 from nine to twenty-four Kayas among all Mijikenda (1987: 83, 98). thus, among the Giriama, Kisini was the nearby 'daughter' of Kaya Fungo, with Singwaya, in the far north, also 'daughter' (though whether Kaya Fungo is the 'parent' is not clear). This is not, apparently, the Singwaya figuring in the Mijikenda origin myth, but is possibly named after it, though further archaeological research will surely help clarify the situation. The main point for this analysis is that, though largely uninhabited, the main Kaya Fungo (or Kaya Giriama as it is also known), has retained its primary status, with the sites of the 'daughter' Kayas of little or no significance for most Giriama today.

immediate activities in the work and images of the dozen or so Giriama elders who nominally operate from the Kaya. Alongside the Kaya's sacred status, its elders are and always have been periodically involved in political events. Their legitimacy derives from the Giriama belief in the sacredness of the Kaya, for they themselves are certainly regarded as ordinary mortals who have reached their powerful positions through their age and political skills. They are in no way regarded as divine or as temporarily occupying sacred bodies. The place, the Kaya, has the power, and the elders, and by extension all Giriama through them, draw on this power.

Yet, because the Kaya elders are not regarded as themselves sacred or divine but as subject like any other persons to greed, unjustifiable anger, and feelings of revenge, they are by no means beyond criticism and may even be removed from the Kaya, though only by other Kaya elders listening to popular discontent and prepared to compete with each other. Though themselves entitled to their position through seniority, the Kaya elders' internal rivalry reflects much of the competition that occurs between Giriama authorities and leaders elsewhere in the country.

Generally, the authorities to whom a Giriama traditionally appeals are commonly at a distance, socially, geographically and metaphysically. To be legitimate they must be moving in the direction of inaccessibility, but must never reach it. It is not that they should behave in an aloof manner. It is rather that they should be known to be among a few who are able to draw on recognised knowledge and forces which are specific to Giriama cosmology or which have, like certain elements of Islam, been incorporated in Giriama thinking. Those who are most recognised in this way are indeed the Kaya elders, but it is a presentation of themselves which lesser figures aspire to. Their success or failure in this respect is a factor of personal achievement which sometimes rests uneasily with the customary explanation that age is the most important attribute conferring authority.

Just as people fear different elements of the cosmology and feel more or less vulnerable to it, so they may differ in their judgement of particular figures of authority. Is this leader too young to be remote and therefore an authority, or is it precisely his ability to detect witches so effectively and to work miracles despite being young that places him apart? Is this elder too obviously concerned with his own immediate, material profit or is his skill in accumulating wealth the evidence of his exceptional power that places him at a distance from other men? As I show below, such questions did in fact confront the Giriama during the period from 1966 to 1988 (and no doubt at other times) as they encountered new definitions of themselves in the rapidly expanding politico-economic world of post-colonial Kenya.

Alongside the idea of unquestionable Kaya sacredness, then, positions of leadership and authority are subject to contestation. Pragmatic contestation and sacred unquestionability, while at times in conflict, both contribute to Giriama ideas of themselves as a people. Before describing in the next chapter their centring of the Kaya as an autochthonous source of ritual power and knowledge, I show how its elders are obliged to defend and advance their position against opposition, and how this reflects wider socio-cultural pressures and possibilities.

In the following micro-history we see how Giriama identity depends not on observed similarities among them but on a range of complementary character- istics which are articulated by leaders struggling to exert control over definitions of what it is to be a Giriama. The different aspects of Giriama identity are held together, made complementary, by the relationship of the eastern to western Giriamaland, with the believed inviolability of the Kaya articulating this relationship.

Witch-hunter from nearby, elders from afar (Case history 1)
Phase one: 1966–1970. Breaking with the elders
Let me start in 1966, the first year in which I lived among the Giriama, for an event which threw into relief the spatial opposition of much Giriama thought and explanation, and suggested the view of political power as drawing upon a play of remote possibilities and urgent needs.

It is no exaggeration to say that during the year of 1966 and for at least five years thereafter, the attention of the Kenya nation as a whole, and not just the coastal province, was captured by the achievements of a coastal witch-finder nicknamed Kajiwe, The Uncrushable (literally 'little rock'). A young man in his early twenties, Kajiwe was not in fact a Giriama but was of the Mijikenda sub- group, the Rabai, a matter of some importance as I shall show.

His activities have been described in some detail elsewhere (Parkin 1968, 1970; Brantley 1979) and for my present purposes I need not repeat them. Here I wish to show how he stood in relation to a number of other authority figures. In particular, I want to show that he personified the conflicts found among the more densely populated and ethnically mixed peoples of the coast and its immediate hinterland. By contrast, the group known as the Kaya elders (*azhere a Kaya*) evoked and appealed to a notion of customary harmony believed by many Giriama to obtain only in the remote hinterland of their country.

Adopting what was regarded by ordinary people as his own special technique for discovering witches, Kajiwe swept through much of Mijikenda country, promising to eradicate the practice of witchcraft. At least one Kenya government minister made the parallel between his popularity and that of the Alice Lenshina prophetic movement of Zambia a couple of years previously, a movement to be sadly echoed years later in 1987 through Alice Lakwena and her followers in Uganda, many of whom lost their lives confronting government guns. While the Kenya government wished therefore to treat the witch-hunt with caution, it also saw in it the possibility of ending the undeniably pervasive belief in witchcraft among the Mijikenda. The alleged economic backwardness of the Mijikenda was put down to fear on the part of individual Mijikenda that they dare not progress in farming, trade, school or any enterprise lest they be struck down by the jealousy of neighbours or relatives. Kajiwe was in fact given written permission for his witch-hunt by government representatives, with the knowledge and consent of the Kenyan president himself, Jomo Kenyatta, a frequent visitor to the coast. Eradicating witchcraft beliefs was seen as a possible spur to economic development.

However, while consenting to it, the government did wish the witch-finding movement to be systematically regulated. It appointed as custodians members of a registered ethnic welfare organisation called the Mijikenda Union, which had been set up in 1945. The Mijikenda Union, as it was organised in 1966 and at periods before and shortly after, is a key to understanding Giriama ideas of power and political process.[5] It is made up of elders, a number of whom appear in other contexts: some are resident elders of the Kaya or periodically live there; some of these, and others, are members of the secret oathing society called the Vaya; one is, or was, a government-appointed ex-chief; and another is himself a traditional doctor renowned throughout the Coast Province. Before unpacking the significance of these different organisations and links, let me continue with the story of Kajiwe.

Having given the movement its blessing, the government expected Mijikenda administrative locations to be 'cleansed' of their witches one by one. Kajiwe was to follow a strict programme of visits by spending a limited time in each. The Mijikenda Union elders were to ensure that he did this and that the Vaya elders administered their oaths to suspected witches discovered by Kajiwe, with no violence being committed against proven witches. The elders were expected to accompany the young man on his journeys.

A number of the elders of the Mijikenda Union and the Vaya society are entitled to live in the Kaya. Most do not, though may stay for short periods, with at least the head or leader of the Kaya, variously called *mtawali wehu* (our ruler), *baba wehu* (our father), or *muhongoni*, literally 'the main pole supporting the cross-beams of a traditional house', living at the traditional capital more or less permanently. This right to reside in the Kaya is an aspect of the dignity and respect accorded to any elder who is expected to command from a position of settled authority.

---

[5] I have discussed some of the Mijikenda Union's activities in Parkin 1972: 24–25, 90–97. The Union was set up in 1945, at about the same time as the term, Mijikenda, was coined for political and welfare purposes to express what were perceived to be the common interests of the separately named nine peoples. The following are some early administrative references: *Digo District Annual Report*, 1945, 1946, 1948–52, and 1954; *Kilifi District annual Report*, 1953; *Malindi Sub-District Annual Report*, 1948 and 1949; *Coast Province Annual Report*, 1945, 1947–49, and 1952; *Kilifi District Handing Over Reports*, 19/3/46, 4/3/49, and 14/4/49. I thank Dr F. Morton for drawing most of these to my attention.

Within weeks of the government permit having been granted, however, the elders, collectively called the Kaya elders, lost control of the movement. Kajiwe moved swiftly and indiscriminately from one location to another, ignoring the official timetable. The elders could not keep up with him. He demanded money ('fees') from witches he had exposed while at the same time taking it upon himself to remove their instruments of sorcery, disregarding the expectation that the Kaya elders were to be responsible for extracting confessions through their use of oaths. One old man accused by Kajiwe died of a heart attack. Muslims and their sacred literature became increasingly the butt of Kajiwe's and his supporters' attacks, and Kajiwe contemptuously dismissed even the Kaya elders.

The young witch-hunter was regarded by the Kaya elders and government as having gone beyond his official remit and, after a court trial in Mombasa which drew hundreds of supporters pleading on his behalf, Kajiwe was sentenced to eighteen months' imprisonment.

Phase two: 1971–1988. With the elders again

After serving a year Kajiwe was released and for a while became a more settled practitioner of traditional medicine. However, more quietly, he continued to respond to requests coming from different areas of Mijikenda country to deal with witchcraft problems, and he became quite wealthy.

Public support for him still grew and, once again, he became a major public figure, this time by administering oaths as protection against witchcraft rather than to suspected witches as in a trial by ordeal. Kajiwe worked with a well-organised cadre of young men. The government appears to have been alarmed by the Mijikenda-wide unifying aspects of the movement, possibly seeing in it the potential for political subversion. Kajiwe was therefore placed in detention as a security risk by the coast provincial commissioner under the Public Security Preservation Act.

From October 1970 to January 1971 there were some extraordinary exchanges both in the press and in the Kenyan parliament concerning his detention, with many opposition MPs interpreting the action as an attempt to crush the emerging communal and political solidarity of the Mijikenda people. The Mijikenda Union had already been curbed in 1969 for, among other reasons, holding customary moots to settle litigation deemed by government as the work of its own courts, and so not even these elders were available to act as custodians of or spokesmen for Kajiwe's activities. Without the formal umbrella of the Mijikenda Union, the Kaya elders generally, including those of the Vaya secret society, were unable effectively to articulate their protest at what became seen among the Mijikenda People as government 'interference' in their own local-level affairs.

During the early period of Kajiwe's activities in 1966–67, the Kaya elders (here including those of both the Mijikenda Union and the Vaya society) had been marginalised by Kajiwe, with not even the Vaya elders able to administer their oaths beyond an initial few weeks. By 1970–71 these same Kaya elders were once more on Kajiwe's side, expressing a widely held resentment that his work should have been hindered by government action. They argued that he no longer accused (sometimes violently) individual witches, but now peacefully exhorted whole communities to give up the practice and the thinking behind witchcraft.

The mood of Kajiwe's early period, then, was interpreted as one of aggressive confrontation with witches, which the elders and the government both rejected. His later one, however, was of highly organised, community-based appeal, with which the elders concurred, but which the government saw as an undue degree of local autonomy or 'lawlessness' in the words of the country's Vice-President (later President) during a parliamentary debate of 9 December 1970.

Kajiwe remained in detention for nearly two years. Thereafter he resumed his activities but at a much less public level and, operating from his own home, continued to enhance both his reputation as a successful doctor, and his wealth and property.

Once Kajiwe had been tamed, so to speak, it was possible for the Kaya elders and others to emphasise his harmlessness and indeed his benefit to the Mijikenda in offering a way to eliminate witchcraft. But, as I indicated above, the Kaya elders and Kajiwe had during his earlier period been much opposed to each other. This opposition is part of that between remote continuity, as expressed through the Kaya elders operating from their traditional Giriama capital, and the immediate and contingent, seen in the accelerating fear and panic with which Kajiwe was associated and which periodically denote a new wave of witchcraft attacks and accusations which are often blamed on coastal habits and ritual powers, including those of Muslims.

By the mid nineteen eighties Kajiwe continued to operate from his home, now even more wealthy but no longer responsible for extensive witch-hunts or communal oath-giving. He thus fits into the career pattern of other major witch-finders in the region, who move from a kind of itinerant adventurism to the settled state of successful local herbalist businessman.

As Kajiwe's public image lost its dramatic quality, that of the Kaya elders was suddenly enhanced, in 1988, as a result of their successful efforts at rain-making. The whole coastal region, including much of the normally well-watered fertile coastal strip, had suffered full or partial drought over the preceding two years. By May 1988 the rains were again overdue.

At this time, the current senior elder of the Kaya (called Mungwari) learned that his son, a diviner, had been told by one of his possessory spirits that the Kaya was being spoiled by evil. The son urged his father to get the local chief's permission to purify the Kaya. The several reasons given by the spirit as having caused the Kaya's contamination were that: people had been entering the sacred place wearing shoes; Europeans (tourists) had been coming to the Kaya; goats and cattle had been slaughtered there (with normally only the pure and peaceful ram allowed to be sacrificed in cleansing and fertility ceremonies); radios had been played in it; people had worn shirts while visiting (only seamless clothes should be worn, such as a traditional cotton wrap); and that women other than the wives of Kaya elders (who are permitted) had also entered.

The chief gave his immediate permission. The MP for the area contributed 600 shillings for the slaughter of a black ram in the Kaya (a ram being traditionally used for purificatory ritual, as discussed in chapter three). The elders then called reportedly 'all' (and certainly numerous) homestead heads in Giriama country to a meeting outside the chief's office in Gotani, seeking more money for the ram(s) and for a white cloth (called *msimbiji*) on which the ram is slaughtered. At the ceremony the elders reinstated the rules of Kaya entry and conduct, and prayed for rain, the fertility of the soil and the Giriama people, and for their protection from evil.

Within days rain did indeed fall throughout Mijikenda country. This dramatic success prompted the Kaya elders of the other Mijikenda groups to hold purificatory rain-making ceremonies before the second rains, during September of 1988, again with considerable evident success. Among the Rabai, for instance, comprising a much smaller area and population than the Giriama, adults were fined by the chief and Kaya elders if they did not help clear the Kaya for the ceremony, for it too had become neglected and overgrown. The ritual was on 9 September and heavy rain fell on the 11th. Throughout Mijikenda country these fruitful rain-making ceremonies, phrased in the idiom of cleansing the Kayas, were discussed excitedly, whether or not they concerned one's own group.

As one Giriama man put it, 'These Kaya events always happen in a crisis', whether to do with drought, famine, epidemics (of people, plants and cattle), political protest, or alongside such witch-finding movements as that led by Kajiwe. The crises prompt rituals of purification taking place in the Kaya, which is seen to undergo a complete and utter cleansing, both for itself and on behalf of all Giriama country. It is an act which aims to clear out all the accumulated evil and contamination incurred by neglect of the Kaya and its rules. Ordinarily it is homesteads and individuals who are purified or cleansed of the evil that is associated with 'dirt' or contamination affecting a place and a person. This is evident in a number of cases in this book, especially in chapter six, where the distinctively violent sacrifice of the ram is discussed. But the occasional cleansing of the Kaya refers not just to its own destiny but to that of the people outside as a whole. Cleansing is thus a common Giriama theme, elevated to special significance with respect to the Kaya, and is part of its definition as a sacred centre.

In this brief history of events affecting the Kaya elders of the west and the witch-finder from the east, there is an alternation of power and interest. In 1966, and for some time thereafter, Kajiwe politically overshadowed the Kaya elders. By 1988, the roles had been reversed. Indeed, Kajiwe played no part at all in the rain-making ceremonies.

Yet, we have to look at the Kaya elders and the witch-finder as each complementing the other. They have, as institutional figures, continued over the generations, for Kajiwe was preceded by other famous witch-finders, just as the elders are continually replaced. They do not, however, merely repeat a historical pattern. They are alternating markers of the old and new, acting like templates which are at each crisis redrawn, if only slightly. They preserve something of the old shape, yet also modify it, so that it is recognisable as both old and new at the same time.

Witch-finder and elders compared

We see something of this simultaneity in the contrasting characterisations held by the Giriama of the Kaya elders and of Kajiwe. We can see them as dramatic personae who are handed lines but who improvise as they go along. What is however constant is that while the elders enter, so to speak, from the west, Kajiwe comes from the east. Space defines them as they define it. I begin with the images held of Kajiwe.

Representing Kajiwe

Kajiwe's very origins and life career before becoming a witch-finder are at variance with Giriama ideas of their own traditional continuity. He is from the Rabai group, who in fact adopted Mijikenda language and some customs and so historically were only grafted on to the six northern Mijikenda groups hailing from Singwaya (including Giriama, Chonyi, Jibana, Kauma, Kambe, and Ribe) (Spear 1981: 12). His early life also associates him more with the non-Giriama coast than with the hinterland. He had for some years worked at sea as a fisherman.

Kajiwe's companions talked of his miraculous powers even then. They claimed, for instance, that he could induce edible crabs and lobsters to come to him by whistling at them. More dramatic is the story of his apparent drowning when, out at sea in a dug-out vessel which capsized, his friends searched for him in vain, gave up hope of finding him and swam to the shore to carry the sad news to his parents and family in Rabai location. They looked for him for seven days and, assuming the worst, prepared a funeral (*hanga*) which lasted seven days. Thirty days later, as they were about to slaughter cattle and goats at the second funeral or wake (*nyere za mwezi*), Kajiwe (Tsuma Washe as he was known) appeared. Puzzled at their amazement, he merely remarked that the day before he had been in a boat which had capsized and had had to swim back. He had also, he pointed out, found a star (*nyota*) in the sea while swimming back and proceeded to display it, as he did in his later activities as witch-finder. The star, which he carried in his hand and showed me, was in fact a large Whitefriars glass paper-weight. But, in 1966, the version of it as a star was commonly accepted as further evidence of his prowess.

Further claims made on his behalf were that, after his father refused Kajiwe's unspecified request for 1000 shillings, the young man set up a successful produce business in Tanga, another coastal town, and thereafter went to Mecca on his savings, there learning a great deal from important Muslim men. He returned, now recognised as a doctor (*muganga*) by non-Muslims. One doubter, a Muslim Koran teacher (*mwalimu*), insisted that he lacked curative powers. Using his star, a mirror and a wristwatch, Kajiwe then described in detail what the doubting Muslim had done at various times during the day. He also threatened the man that he would spit twice outside his mosque and deter worshippers from ever again attending it. The Muslim's doubts were swiftly settled.

Kajiwe was the latest in a long line of witch-finders, many of whom shared similar methods, and all of whom represented an alternative source of ritual power to that of the Kaya elders and the Vaya society's famous oath of the hyena (*kiraho cha fisi*). In other words, rather like prophets, the witch-finders address themselves to contingencies, in this case rampant witchcraft. Even when they promise a utopia or better order of things, they are concerned with immediate measures to eliminate the witchcraft as a route to the improved life. Kajiwe him-self urged people to abandon the use of traditional medicines which he identified as the source of witchcraft (some might say sorcery) and poisoning. He stressed instead the value of modern hospitals, schools and Christianity, regarding Islam as ritually powerful but as also producing many harmful medicines and beliefs (views which he may well have partly reversed if a recent report is correct: *Sunday Nation*, 7 January 1990).

The Kaya elders, on the other hand, stress a putative continuity of Giriama tradition in almost all they say and do. They are also, as I have indicated, located in the Kaya, or are at least symbolically resident there, and so at some distance from other Giriama. They comprise some of the oldest men in the society, certain Vaya members among them included, the Mijikenda Union by contrast com-prising men who are middle-aged.

While Kajiwe, a Rabai working on behalf of all Mijikenda, encapsulates ethnic admixture and innovative ideals, the Kaya elders personify the Giriama insistence on ethnic purity and exclusiveness over a range of contexts. Thus, a young man wishing to present himself to the Kaya elders for instruction in Giriama folklore must demonstrate that he is a 'pure' Giriama in the male line, for only such a person is supposed to receive the most detailed secrets. I myself of course encountered this attitude during my fieldwork despite earnest attempts and gradual success in learning the Giriama language.

The notion of secrecy, of meeting and taking decisions secretly (*njama*), is a dynamic one, in that it gives life, as well as value, to activities and knowledge. It seems to be linked and sometimes almost synonymous with the term for pledge (*njagama*), giving the idea that secret knowledge is held in trust for the whole Giriama community. If that secrecy is compromised, for example through its release to such ineligible persons as youngsters or non-Giriama, the view of many Giriama is that their customs and distinctiveness become contaminated. Secrecy and purity are then aspects of the same idea and are part of the political legitimacy based on trust at a distance, to which I have already referred. The socially distant Kaya elders have to be seen in this light, and in contrast to the young witch-finder Kajiwe whose whole attempt was to unmask, as he saw it, this secrecy, so menacing the elders' position.

Representing elders

The Mijikenda Union, in which the Kaya elders played a central role, had become effectively defunct by 1988. The rain-making ceremonies of that year rekindled the image of the power of the Kaya and seemed to show how transitory the Mijikenda Union and its call for secular political unity were. The Union was in fact only one of a number of possible institutional outlets for the expression of this power and unity, which were manifested in different ways.

Some of the Mijikenda Union elders entered county council politics and found themselves more in the townships of Kilifi and Malindi than in the rural areas where they and Kajiwe sought to confront witchcraft. The Mijikenda Union was no overnight phenomenon, however. It had (and has) its roots in customary ideas of authority which extend to the Kaya. The Mijikenda Union was established in 1945, with its headquarters in Mombasa. This was when the term, Mijikenda, was first used. The Union's main objective in those days was to ensure that individual Mijikenda who had died in Mombasa should be transported to their home area for burial. Money had to be collected for this purpose, which was called Mijikenda.

The term Mijikenda (or Midzichenda in the vernacular) replaced the pejorative Wa-Nyika by which the people were known by Swahili, Arabs and Europeans and which means, dismissively, 'people of the bush'. Mijikenda can also be rendered as 'the nine Kaya' (Makayachenda) and points to the idea both of the unity of the Mijikenda people and of the fact that each has or had a major capital or Kaya at its heart.

Early on I was given a highly idealised picture of Mijikenda segmentary unity, which the Mijikenda Union sought to encapsulate, and which presupposes Kaya sacredness. The nine peoples known as the Giriama, Chonyi, Jibana (Dzihana), Kambe, Kauma, Ribe (Rihe), Digo, Rabai (Rahai) and Duruma make up the

Mijikenda. Each of the nine peoples has its main Kaya or capital. In the case of the Giriama, the people are divided into six sections (called *mbari*) which may once have been exogamous clans. Each section is divided into clans which are for the most part exogamous today and also called *mbari*. Further division results in sub-clans, within but not beyond which widows may be inherited, and also called *mbari*, but sometimes also *lukolo*, which may also be the term used for even smaller segments. Finally, a homestead is known as *mudzi*, for which the term in the Digo dialect is in fact *kaya*. In other words *mudzi* and *kaya* both mean homestead-village, but in the case of all the Mijikenda groups except the Digo, kaya refers specifically to the main capital in each, where, until the late nineteenth century, the bulk of the people lived for mutual protection against either Oromo or, later, Maasai invaders.

Brantley has suggested that until the late nineteenth century, the Kaya of the Giriama provided an authoritarian focus for judicial and political control (1979: 114–115). Each of the six sections or major clans had its own residential area within the Kaya. Cutting across such clan differences were those of generation and age sets, from which were derived a supreme council of elders called *kambi*, who were supported by the Vaya secret society's use of its hyena oath (Brantley 1978). During the latter half of the nineteenth century, possibly as a partial result of Pax Britannica limiting Oromo and Maasai raids and possibly due also to increased population, the Giriama moved out of and away from their Kaya and spread eastwards, northwards, and even westwards and inland towards the Taru desert.[6] Now that they were dispersed, the Giriama developed many local versions of the institutions formerly located exclusively in the Kaya: each neighbourhood (*lalo*) would have its council of elders, with some members of the Vaya society able to administer oaths, and would be made up residentially of a number of small clan settlements interspersed one with the other. Yet, despite this dispersal, which continues today with Giriama migrating as individuals rather than as clan segments to areas outside as well as within Giriama country, the idea persists of the Kaya and its elders as final arbiters of Giriama autochthony. In other words, just as the opposition of Kajiwe to the Kaya elders was that of the contingent to the remote, so, among the Giriama themselves, the Kaya elders are the solidary and settled counterpart to population movement and spread.

Giriama politicians such as the famous Kenyan nationalist, the late Ronald Ngala, his son Katana Ngala, and others since, go to the Kaya and are blessed (*ku-haswa*) by the elders before a major political campaign or election. It is Kaya elders who are invoked as customary authorities. The colonial government, for instance, in 1914, forced the elders to conduct a peace-making ceremony after

[6] The district officer, Kelly, had earlier suggested 1860 as about the date of dispersal (*Kilifi Political Records*), which roughly accords with Brantley.

the Giriama rebellion against the British (see chapter seven), and throughout the later colonial period regarded them as the only consistently strong representative power. The Kaya elders' use of this power in 1966 over Kajiwe and in 1988 over rain and evil has already been described.

While no more than a few old men and their wives might actually be found at the Kaya at any one time, and sometimes no more than the senior elder, their guardianship of Giriama knowledge has been undisputed since the Kaya dispersal. Nor, despite their absence from the Kaya, have they been totally hidden from public view, despite their shadowy existence. They have remained significant, partly because the Kaya itself, as a physical place, is a constant point of reference, and partly because elders, while sometimes living in it, have also moved around in Giriama country as members of the once important Mijikenda Union, of the Vaya secret society, and, later, as county councillors. Some of the elders, for instance those in the Mijikenda Union, have not even reached the age at which they could even become residents of the Kaya, despite being eligible for membership of the Vaya society. But they are still subsumed within the general appellation of 'Kaya elders', for it is assumed that they too may eventually be entitled to full Kaya as well as Vaya membership, in addition to which they are frequently called to the Kaya for meetings and blessings before undertaking major political, judicial and representative tasks.

The age-grading of elders and Kaya elders is paralleled by the age-based succession of Kaya 'kings' (as *muhongoni* or *mtawali wehu* have been translated to me by some Giriama). Thus, during the period I have outlined, Pembe Bembere was the senior from 1966 to 1974 but was succeeded in turn by Machuko, for a short while, by Karisa Kabani (allegedly responsible for having allowed tourists into the Kaya and even for having sold a sacred *mwandza* drum to one of them), by Daniel Chai for only a few weeks before his death, and by Mungwari, the cleanser of the Kaya in 1988.

In this way, extreme age bordering on death goes together with purificatory powers emanating from the Kaya, which include those that ensure the fertility of the land and its people, and those that censure their abuse.

Case summary

The term, Kaya elders (*azhere a Kaya*), clearly refers, then, to a socially ageing process of political responsibility, rather than to a clearly bounded group of people. It refers, once again, to the principle of continuity by which the aged are eventually replaced by those immediately below them. In neither of these respects do witch-finders like Kajiwe fit into the process, for they have inserted themselves into history as events which are jarringly contingent on a believed massive build-up of witchcraft. But, by the very fact that witch-finders do succeed each other in some kind of cyclical manner (Willis 1968) we can see them as continuous. But it is not a continuity that Giriama recognise as being of their own making, nor is it an on-going testimony to Giriama customary purity and distinctiveness.

Within its overall aim of unity, the Mijikenda Union carefully preserved the distinctiveness of the nine groups by allocating a branch of the union to each. At the same time each branch had a representative from each of its sub-groups. This at least was the ideal, which therefore carried a version of the segmentary principle from the Giriama Kaya, with its representative system of six sections or clans, into modern political organisation. The similarity of aims, activities, and organisational pattern, and the overlap in membership between the Mijikenda Union, and the Kaya and the Vaya society, were recognised by the incumbents themselves. Indeed, as I have mentioned, the Mijikenda Union was curbed in 1969 precisely because it organised local-level moots to resolve disputes concerning land, marital, bridewealth, and witchcraft accusations, making use of Vaya and other oaths, but in effect usurping the right of the local government court to judge such matters. As was the case with Kajiwe, even the Mijikenda Union, and by implication the Kaya and Vaya elders, came afoul of the government when its activities were seen to have shaded into the judicial and the political.

We see that the political potential of both Kajiwe and the Kaya elders (including the Mijikenda Union), so different in their internal aspects, evoked common government protest when this potential was seen to increase local and ethnic autonomy. This is of course a common theme in both colonial and independent African states. It is moreover the background against which is set the Giriama movement of power as I have begun to describe it.

The Kaya, as a sacred place, strikingly accommodates such shifts of power. In its periodic acts of purification, the Kaya processes events, so to speak, and registers them as part of a changing Giriama identity, and as matters both requiring and providing sanctification. Take, for instance, the incorporation of modern politicians in the Kaya cleansing, as described in the above case history. It is really only since a few years before Kenya's independence in 1963 that, first, nationalist leaders like Ronald Ngala, and, later, as in 1988, local Members of Parliament, sought blessings in the Kaya and actively tried to contribute to its well-being, up-keep and sacred standing. During the colonial era, the Kaya had ambivalent status in the eyes of European government officials. Sometimes they encouraged it as an indigenous sacred instrument of rule, which could be used in turn to control insurgent Giriama. At other times, they saw it and its elders as the very threat they sought to contain.

In embodying knowledge the Kaya is held to define and explain the new powers, influences and boundaries to which the Giriama people are variously subject. For much of the time the Kaya enjoys a spatial ambiguity: its sacredness transcends physical boundaries yet at the same time is rooted in its territorial fixity and location. It can, therefore, accommodate within its purview new understandings of its relevance to the Giriama people. At one time, it provided a focus for rebellion against (and afterwards surrender to) the British. It later provided the sanctity that modern Kenya politicians claimed. It has also in recent generations, as the present case history shows, legitimised the need for witchcraft eradication and acknowledged the expertise of those gifted to do so, like Kajiwe, yet has retained its power as the source of final wisdom on such matters. It is the Giriama imaginative space in which events and knowledge are re-ordered.

Conclusion

The image I have is of two forms of power operating among the Giriama: concentrated and dispersed. Each is manifested in a number of different ways. The Giriama view of the Kaya as a fixed sacred place is an example of concentrated power, while a sense of dispersed power, occasionally spilling over from the Kaya, is evident in their spatial contrast between the west and east, and, within the eastern area, between various places and different peoples' cross-cutting movements, migrations and affiliations. The complementary histories of the Kaya elders and of the witch-finder can also be read as statements about the west and east respectively. The very idea of Giriama ethnic identity, of their definition of themselves as a relatively bounded cultural and linguistic group, is hinged on the contrast they make between their western and eastern areas. While the east is made up of social movement and migration, the west comprises the timeless purity of the Kaya, which must periodically be cleansed of accumulated contamination and the effects of neglect. If the Giriama were to abandon this view of the Kaya and its allegedly traditional western setting, they would be immersed in the ethnic jumble and socio-economic complexity of the eastern coastal area, which, as the failed attempts of witch-finders show, is never regarded as even temporarily cleansed of evils. Given their linguistic and cultural proximity to other Mijikenda groups, and the ease with which some Mijikenda peoples have adopted Islam and, more recently, Christianity, it is doubtful if a sense of Giriama distinctiveness would survive without the Kaya as an ultimate point of customary reference.

Yet the Kaya remains largely uninhabited and is located in an area whose population has grown more slowly than that of the eastern agricultural area and the coastal region, so fostering the belief that the west is actually in some parts losing its people. In the following chapter I describe the continuing centrality of the Kaya under such unlikely conditions and suggest that, both at the present time and historically, the Kaya has managed to disperse its powers while retaining them, as if drawing on an infinite fount.

2

Western Kaya, sacred centre

The Kaya as sacred centre

In being regarded by Giriama as absolute centre, dependent on no other places nor even requiring that elders live and work within it, the Kaya is clearly seen as an intrinsic source of ritual power as well as providing its elders with legitimacy in their handling of crises affecting the Giriama people as a whole. The Kaya is also regarded as the ultimate reference of their customs and identity. Yet, at the same time, the Giriama have a legend (shared by other Mijikenda peoples) of having migrated to the Kenya coastal hinterland from an original area, Singwaya, in Somalia, and of having had previous Kayas (see Spear 1981: 37 and *passim*, and Morton 1977 and Walsh 1987 for a critique and summary of the debate on Mijikenda origins). These two claims to autochthony need not be contradictory, for, in their migration southwards from Singwaya in the sixteenth century, the Giriama, and other Mijikenda groups said to come from there, apparently carried with them protective magic called *fingo*. These objects, which for each Mijikenda group may have been either a large stone, as among the Giriama, or a large pot of medicines, were buried right at the centre of each Kaya as it was settled by the new arrivals. When, therefore, the Giriama speak of their Kaya as being at the origin of their cultural identity, they may be referring metonymically to the buried sacred object as a refraction of Singwaya and so as continually still a part of that geographically distant, former centre. The *fingo* thus carried within it the power and 'life' of Singwaya, and then transplanted it on the Kaya sites. This refractory image of the *fingo* is further borne out by the suggestion of lesser kinds being placed at the right of each entrance to the Kaya, thus protecting it at its perimeter, with the main *fingo* providing protection, and itself being protected, at the centre (Mutoro 1987: 47).

However plausibly this may explain the sense of continuity between Singwaya and the Kaya, it is a fact that it is the Kaya and not Singwaya which people talk about in ordinary conversation. I myself, even as early as 1966, only ever encountered unprompted reference to Singwaya during burials, when the deceased is laid on his or her right side with the eyes looking north (or rather, slightly north-west) to Singwaya. The historian, Spear, was able to amass a vast number of traditions relating to Singwaya (1981), but these were elicited according to the normal method of oral history, and were neither part of everyday discourse nor known in detail by any other than elders of sometimes great age. Going further, I later witnessed some funerals carried out in the eastern area approaching the coast, where it was not the northerly direction of Singwaya that was held to justify the position of the corpse but where, instead, the claim was that the body was so positioned as to enable the head to face the coast or even, in some cases, so that the eyes might look to Mecca. This uncertainty concerning spatial orientation is discussed further in chapter five. By contrast, the sense of autochthony associated with the Kaya is shared by everyone, male and female, young and old, westerner and easterner. We have, then, to ask whether the more outspoken focus on the Kaya is of recent origin, and whether there is in effect a shift taking place in ideas of indigenous origin and centrality of existence. For the moment, at least, the story of the transplanted *fingo* bridges the somewhat tacit view of Singwaya origins and the explicit notion of Kaya sacredness.

Among the Giriama the *fingo* object is in fact called *ngiriama*, related to the word for witness (*mugiriama*) and clearly, then, extending to indicate the people, their sacred object, and the distinctive value they place on witnessing all transactions among them (hence the title of Parkin 1972). Such witnesses are principally elders, each identified by their exogamous clan (*mbari*) and, traditionally, generation-set (*rika*). Spear has drawn on documentary and oral sources to describe the make-up of the Kaya as it was before the dispersion from it of Giriama from the mid nineteenth century onwards (1978: xxi, 1–7, 46–50, 58–60, 127–128). He tells how the Giriama grouped themselves in the Kaya into six sections (or clans, as he calls them, also called *mbari*), each of which had its own large meeting house (*lwanda*) surrounded by the individual homesteads of fellow clan members. Eventually the sections sub-divided into the present-day exogamous clans, in addition to which other clans developed as a result of the assimilation of other Mijikenda and outsiders.

Cleared from dense, primeval forest, the Kaya was several hundred yards across, with a wooden fence all round it and two paths cut into it, each with three, or four (Mutoro 1987: 47), manned, heavy wooden gates protected by medicines. One path was located in an east-west direction and the other north-south. Today the forest is still dense and primeval, with thickets of aloes, sansevieria, acacia, commiphora, and prickly pear and comprising some 1000 hectares, according to the 1976 annual report of Kilifi district. (My impression was of a much smaller area, and Mutoro, who has mainly worked on some non-Giriama Kayas, puts the area at from ten hectares upwards (1987: 280).) The burial site of the *ngiriama* protective magic is in a small uncleared circle at the centre of the Kaya, near to which was a large, general meeting house called *moro*, where discussions would take place among men representing all sections and clans. At each end of the meeting place were a fig and a baobab tree, both important in many contexts of ritual and belief. Here, also, was and still is the special *mwandza* friction drum, which, even today, is kept, partly covered by banana leaves, in a little hut which is open at the sides. A non-member of the Kaya who happens to catch sight of the drum must pay a fine, lest he die, a fear and obligation taken most seriously as I observed on one occasion. Stones marking graves and also memorial posts for dead members of the Gohu society who had also become Kaya elders (see chapter eight) testify to the claim that resident Kaya elders were and are buried there rather than in their own homesteads outside the Kaya. The further claim that Kaya elders living outside are brought to the Kaya for burial there at the approach of death is less easy to substantiate but is an interesting indication of the focal attachment to the Kaya that is said to transcend the external, dispersed ties of homestead and clan (Mutoro 1987: 50).

No more than twelve or so of the most ancient elders are entitled to stay overnight in the Kaya. Each of the six Giriama major sections (or exogamous 'clans' as they may once have been) is represented by one or two such elders, with the two large sections of Kiza and Kidzini sometimes receiving more.[1] But, while this appears to be the limit on those allowed to reside there, the term 'Kaya elders' has come to refer to many influential elders who are not exceptionally senior, but who participate in the judicial and ritual activities organised from and in the name of the Kaya. They visit the Kaya during the daytime for meetings. They number another twelve, most of whom are also members of the Mijikenda Union referred to in the last chapter, which in its early days in the nineteen forties was set up expressly with the purpose both of repatriating the corpses of Mijikenda people who had died away from home and of contributing towards the upkeep of the Kaya. Overlapping with these elders are the members of the Vaya society, whose numbers are indeterminate since they are now spread throughout Giriama society. Out of a population of about 15,000 in the general area in which I worked, I knew of five elders identified as Vaya members, and there were reputedly others further afield.[2] Only two were of the same exogamous patri-

[1] The six sections are associated with certain characteristics and even rights. For example, it is the Kiza who are supposed to have carried the *ngiriama* stone all the way from Singwaya and to have ritual priority in the Kaya, while the six clans of the Kidzini are entitled to know and remedy the effects of the oath of a secret society called the Habasi, which is less restrictive in its membership than the Vaya. A typical Habasi oath is planted in a person's field of growing crops as a deterrent against thieves and will cause incessant bleeding to any thief. A responsibility of the Habasi and of the Kidzini Kaya elders is to uproot such an oath once the crops have been harvested lest an innocent child be affected by harmlessly helping him- or herself to some remaining produce.

[2] These identified themselves in 1966 as Kalume Muramba (MwaMweni clan), Baya wa Maunda (MwaMweni), Kazungu wa Deni (MwaBayaMwaro), Katsole wa Murimba (MwaKiza *sic*), and Kaldio wa ? (Milulu *sic*). (The last two bracketed names are in fact those of two of the six Giriama sections comprising several exogamous clans.) These men insisted that the use of the hyena or Vaya oath (presumably by non-Vaya and non-Kaya elders) had to be preceded by going to the Kaya and getting written permission there. I do not know of cases where the oath was given without such

clan. Dispersion of clan membership is expected, since oathing ceremonies and the cure of those who have broken or been captured by oaths requires that at least two elders be present and that they be of a different clan from the victim and from each other. As was evident in 1966 in the case of Kajiwe the witch-hunter, in 1988 during the rain-making ceremonies, and on other occasions in between, the number of prominent elders exercising influence on the 350,000 or so Giriama at any one time is surprisingly few, perhaps no more than 30 (including the twelve entitled to stay at the Kaya). In providing a rallying-point, however, the Kaya effectively magnifies their significance, and draws into its orbit the co-operation of many chiefs and sub-chiefs in locations throughout Giriama country.[3]

Recruitment to the Kaya is a long-term process. A middle-aged man, or even a younger one, may help the existing Kaya elders in their work for many years. He may eventually be invited to join the Vaya society, or, failing this, gradually become more and more central to the activities of the Kaya and its elders. The case of Daniel Chai illustrates this latter, more gradual, process of incorporation.

Daniel Chai was born in about 1900. By 1926, having been to Divinity School, he was in fact a Christian preacher, an activity he was still pursuing in 1936 (CMS Log Book, Kaloleni). By 1959 he had clearly long since become a lapsed Christian, and the Kilifi district annual report for that year refers to him as a (literate) 'secretary' to the then senior Kaya elder, Zia Gunga. Younger than the elders, but with a missionary education and experience, he handled their correspondence, the circulation of notices to fellow Giriama, and the frequent petitions and demands to government. He and the elders are accused in the district report of trying to set up a rival government to the colonial adminis-tration. By 1966, at the time of the Kajiwe movement, when I first met him, he was secretary of the Malindi branch of the Mijikenda Union, headed by the great herbalist, Vaya member and former Kaya elder, Kabwere Wanje (himself the son of a Kaya and Vaya elder). In this role Chai also acted as spokesman for the then head of the Kaya, Pembe Bembere, and as moderator between the Kaya elders, Kajiwe and Kabwere. By the mid nineteen eighties, now very old, he was elected

permission, sanctions against which are, allegedly, that the Vaya would plant corrective members against the culprit or that the effects of the oath would rebound on him.

[3] It may be, however, that, with the great increase in population over the years, other venues and organisations are emerging which provide alternative opportunities for leadership, both for elders and younger persons, and for women as well as men. My impression is that in 1966 the Giriama still looked to the Kaya elders, including the Mijikenda Union and the Vaya, as their sole supreme authorities. By the late 1980s an indigenous church movement, dubbed Umwenga by Thompson (1990: 117–144), emerged as the example of a possible basis of a new rallying-point. Even so, it is remarkable that the leader of the Umwenga movement, which started in the early 1970s, still desperately sought the legitimation of the Kaya by asking to be incorporated in it. The Kaya elders refused his advances and offers of spiritual assistance, as did the orthodox churches he approached, and the Kaya's perceived centrality was left unaffected. As regards women, the movement linked itself to the legendary prophetess, Mipoho, merging her identity and achievements with Mikatalili, the woman leader of the Giriama rebellion against the British in 1914. As with the rise of Pentecostal churches along the coast strip, the movement's adherents included a majority of women (Parkin 1979b: 282 n. 3; Thompson 1990: 119).

by the Kaya elders as 'father' of the Kaya, but died within a very short time. He was apparently never a member of the Vaya society, though I do not know whether this was out of preference or because he was not encouraged by other Vaya to join them in their meetings.

Since the Second World War, other elders have linked their work with the Mijikenda Union and/or with local government to that of the Kaya elders, and, as they grew older and retired, became more fully involved in the Kaya. Kaya elders are invariably men of many roles, which they perform and crystallise on behalf of the Kaya. Recruitment to the Kaya is, then, through a kind of long-term apprenticeship, sometimes through the Vaya society but sometimes through service to Kaya elders generally, not all of whom are Vaya members. In the past, at least, the women's Kifudu society appears to have enabled women similar access to the Kaya, and there seems little doubt as to the significance of women's roles there (Thompson 1990: 90–98, Udvardy 1990: 209–223).

The inner circle of the twelve or so Kaya elders entitled to reside in the Kaya are regarded as having supreme knowledge of the oaths and other medicines. The Vaya elders, not all of whom are yet old enough to join the inner circle, also administer them. Oathing is the activity perhaps most regarded with respect among the Giriama. There are numerous types of oaths, many of them now simply purchased without reference to the Kaya. One or two elders even claim that the famous hyena oath can also be purchased, though most say that only the Kaya elders really know how to prepare and give it. Certainly, definitions of its composition vary and it is still very much the case that the administration of oaths, of whatever kind, by senior Kaya elders is considered the most efficacious, and it is they who are regarded as most likely to be able to reverse the incessant bleeding that follows the breach of the hyena and some other male elders' oaths. These are, according to Udvardy (1990: 116), quite unlike the female oaths placed by the women's Kifudu society, which cause blemishes and abrasions to the skin, that is to say, cause harm to the exterior of the body.

There can be no doubt that such experiences of the Kaya reverberate among Giriama generally and, in conjunction with its benefits, show why so many out-side observers call it a sacred place. The number of attributes can be listed almost indefinitely and yet find general agreement. For instance, the forest is the source of all known medicines; others, like the *ngiriama*, are kept within the Kaya itself; the very soil (*tsi*) of the Kaya, like the forest itself, is associated with the fertility and well-being of all Giriama country; diviners and herbalists may seek ultimate validation of their powers by reference to the Kaya; the most powerful oaths are available there; should a witch enter the Kaya, he or she will die from the effects of their own witchcraft; a number of rules of dress and behaviour must be observed on pain of harm not just to the individuals involved but to the country generally; politicians are blessed there; and, as was shown in the last chapter, it is still the venue for effective rain-making ceremonies, and was apparently so in the past for other ceremonies of purification which banished plagues, epidemics and famines, and sought success in war.

An elder showed an uncanny sense of the power to be derived from mixing and transcending categories by explaining how, in their construction and choice of site of the Kaya, the Giriama had overcome the normal distinction between forest and homestead by making the forest their home (Thompson: personal communication). As in the cosmology of many societies, fertility is ensured through the engagement of difference, as in prescriptive marriage between different clans. In 'marrying' forest with home the Kaya is thus the procreative powerhouse of all Giriama, and is sometimes called the umbilicus (*kitovu*) to which the rest of the country is attached. Most significantly, it is also referred to as 'the clean/pure village' (*mudzi mueri*), which, I suggest, can be extended to an idea of it as sacred or holy, depending on our use of these terms: purification occurs everywhere among the Giriama, in their homesteads as well as in the Kaya, repulsing contamination incurred through transgressions and restoring fertility through transcendental power.

A sacred place is of course only so to those who believe in its powers, and the Giriama Kaya has had many invaders over the two hundred and fifty years during which, according to Spear, the Giriama have resided in it. Earlier were the Oromo and Kwavi Maasai, and most recently the British in 1914, who actually dynamited the main trees and gates of Kaya Fungo and burned all the trees and houses inside. This British reprisal against the Giriama elders who had encouraged the rebellion against the colonial government, revealed a split among the Giriama between the anti-colonial majority and the few headmen loyal to the government. Brantley gives a vivid reconstruction of the scene as the loyalist Giriama silently and unprotestingly watched the destruction of the Kaya, to be followed by angry younger men and other elders who accused the loyalists of having 'sold the land' and of having colluded with the government in destroying Giriama traditions (1981: 111).

The significance of this event is twofold. First, it is reminiscent of the way in which, in 1988, certain Kaya elders were held to have allowed strangers easy access to the Kaya and to have 'sold out' to the interests of tourists who, allegedly, used to visit it. As in 1914, young and middle-aged as well as elderly Giriama joined forces in condemning this action and in repairing the Kaya (in a moral sense rather than physically, in 1988). Only by 'purifying' the Giriama and other Kayas of the contaminating effects of transgressions and visits by strangers, could they restore the rain and fertility to the country (as described in the preceding chapter).

Second, both incidents indicate that not all Giriama have undivided respect for the sacredness of the Kaya, and that a small minority is prepared either to collude with its enemies or to exploit it commercially. As I discuss in chapter eight, this resembles the way in which a small number of Giriama and other Mijikenda who are influenced by the newly emerging consumerism of the modern coastal culture, are judged by other Giriama as flouting custom and threatening the group's long-term socio-cultural distinctiveness. Respect and disrespect for the Kaya is thus replicated in broader judgements of ethnic and cultural commitment. This is an element that recurs throughout the practice and discussions of rites and beliefs, becoming in effect an arena of contestation between competing interpretations of Giriama customary rules or even of what is required to be a 'proper' Giriama.

It seems likely that the idea of the Kaya as sacred centre has been intensified, and even exaggerated if not invented, only since the Giriama ceased to live in and around it in the second half of the nineteenth century. A former district officer by the name of Kelly (1960: 4), drawing from Kilifi district political records and from the work of Krapf (1860), Cashmore (1961) and Prins (1952), and from indigenous accounts, makes the interesting observation that the Kayas among the Mijikenda people as a whole were not previously treated as sacred places but simply as fortified towns protecting their inhabitants from enemy raids. Under such conditions, the pragmatic, trading and defensive uses of the Kaya might well have been foremost in people's minds, while at the same time the *fingo* protective magic would have been regarded as part of these defences, which were periodically strengthened by the ceremonial installation of generation sets (Brantley 1978), called *mung'aro*. In other words, the definition of the Kaya as a timeless distillation of customary essence and identity may well have been subordinated, if it was even that, to the mechanics, rituals and medicines of survival, trade and warfare.

Since then, the evacuation of the Kaya from the mid nineteenth century onwards perhaps parallels its growing mythicisation as a source of sacredness, the more so as practical problems and questions of ethnic identity confronting the Giriama are increasingly located in the east and along the coast, away from the Kaya, as indeed they are now. Ideas of the sacred cannot be expected to persist without some occasional demonstration of their practical efficacy, as in the Kaya elders' rain-making successes or in the recourse that may be had from time to time to the power and knowledge of oaths and women's fertility rituals (see Thompson 1990: 92–3). Reinforced by such occasional empirical proofs, however, beliefs in the sacred may flourish when it is set at a distance and in contexts which seem inaccessible. As the Kaya has been physically more removed from most people's experiences, for few are allowed into it and even fewer ever stay there overnight or live there, it satisfies these conditions of the sacred as remote and unchallenged.

Of all the Giriama institutions, then, and despite the actions of those very few regarded as having misused it, the Kaya is the most likely to secure agreement as to its definition, history, value and purpose. It is in this sense that it is now epistemologically and ontologically central to much Giriama thinking, and is believed to transcend in time and space all other events. But the Kaya can only keep this self-sealed quality by remaining literally beyond question. It cannot afford to have the information it puts out and the knowledge it verifies subject to debate.

The Kaya *is*, then, both knowledge and effect. By remaining secret the knowledge sustains the Kaya and the people. But when knowledge is divulged to outsiders, the Kaya and people become unprotected. While western thought distinguishes a place of learning from the learning itself, and the learning from its effects, these three are conjoined in Giriama ideas of the Kaya. This composite idea of being and knowledge is indeed reported in numerous other non-western societies, usually under the rubric of secret knowledge, which must not be fragmented from its people, lest the latter cease thereafter to exist (Salmond 1982, 1985; Murphy 1980). The knowledge is their life-force. This was also made very clear to me when, as a young man, I first lived among the Giriama in 1966, and I give a personal anecdote to illustrate how Kaya and other Giriama forms of secrecy are not simply information or knowledge which has been withheld, but are part of those privileged and authorised to have it. I also show how that idea became threatened by commercial considerations over time. The purpose of the anecdote is not to reproach, for we are all involved directly or indirectly,[4] but to pinpoint the effects of what has become worldwide an almost ineluctable process, and the Giriama response to it.

My wife and I arrived in Kaloleni, Giriama, in early August 1966, living for a few weeks in the trading centre and then, from late September until August 1967, three miles from the centre in the homestead of an elder in his late fifties, Johnstone Muramba, who was a member of the Mijikenda Union but not yet considered old enough to enter the Kaya as one of its permanent elders. He was nevertheless referred to as one of the 'Kaya elders' by virtue of his belonging to the Mijikenda Union. He had been deputed by the Mijikenda Union, on instructions from senior Kaya elders, principally the head, Pembe wa Bembere, to 'guide' me in my research among the Giriama, for which I had been given government permission. Despite this government clearance and the fact that I was accepted by the local central government district officer and by the chief, it was very obvious that I was obliged to comply with the offer of guidance by the Kaya elders.

While aware of the fact that I was effectively under surveillance, I was also

---

[4] My point being that, while neither I nor, I imagine, other long-term researchers breached the anthropological rule that one resists paying cash for information (allowing instead reciprocity in kind to become an aspect of the relationship with informants), we are nevertheless visibly taking more from the society than we can possibly give, a point never lost on Giriama who would laughingly, though no doubt seriously, remark on the immense wealth I must have made from my first book on them. No amount of special pleading nor protestation that there has over the years been reciprocity will ever alter this view, for what is at issue is the asymmetry of power, which is undeniable, and which, over the years, is indeed convertible into the relative wealth of a professional career.

glad of the opportunity to live as a full member of a rural homestead where important Giriama elders would often visit. My status was fixed fairly early on. I was allocated the site of a house whose construction had just been started and which belonged to the homestead head's eldest son, who was working in Dar es Salaam and would return only infrequently during my time there. I bought wooden poles, wattle, and palm thatch 'tiles' (*makuti*) and, as part of a team whose members were given customary payment, built the roof of the house while the women of the homestead daubed most of the walls, sufficiently for it to be habitable. The understanding was that, by way of compensation, the eldest son would move into what was by local standards a good house on his return from Dar es Salaam, after my wife and I had had use of it.

Through partial identification, then, I was already provisionally cast in the role of son of the homestead head, my Kaya elder guide. But confirmation was needed, for people in and around the homestead were still uncertain how to address me. I came to know well a man of my own age from another homestead. He prided himself on his fearlessness, being prepared to joke with and even insult chiefs and headmen, yet stopping short of visibly incurring their wrath.

In a typically daring conversation one day, he called my wife *hawe*, meaning grandmother but also used by a man of his brother's wife. People were embarrassed and asked each other questions. Were he and I, then, no more than peers? Was I no higher in status than that? Should he address my wife in that familiar way? I joked back and people concluded, therefore, that his judgement was in fact perfectly sound. My status was settled. We were peers or 'brothers'. I was then called Karisa, son of Muramba, the homestead head, and given his MwaMweni clanship.[5]

This placing of my kinship and generational status had a dramatic effect on my participation in events, whether lavish funerals or more humble afternoon sessions of palm wine drinking. As a young married man and woman still without children, my wife and I had a definite, if rather junior status, which enabled people to know, for instance, what sacrificial meat to give us, which meetings and gatherings I should attend, which dances we should join, and, most importantly, what level of secret customary lore I should be instructed in. I asked about entering the Kaya, but, since my own 'father' himself had only restricted access, I was told to wait until I was more of age. This kind of restriction by age and generation certainly applied also to others at the time. Non-Giriama, and especially Europeans, rarely were allowed in, and, as far as I know, only if they were of at least late middle age and had lived in the area a long time (an example being a British CMS missionary doctor at Kaloleni, Milton Thompson, who was respected by

---

[5] This was in fact the same name, Karisa Mweni wa Muramba, of the absent son I was in effect replacing. Given that he was to take over the house when I left, there is a light-hearted continuity about it. I suspect that there is also another more mischievous irony which I cannot explain here.

Giriama for his many years of hospital service and had been allowed twice into the Kaya).

Over the succeeding years, more outsiders visited the hinterland of southern Kilifi district. These included young American and European social scientists, historians, mineral explorers, ethnobotanists, and even, as package tourism developed on the coast, a few convoys of tourists, sometimes taken by (allegedly) up-country tour guides to visit 'authentic African villages'. Paying for entertainment and information in cash rather than kind became increasingly expected and inflated. By 1981 a team of young researchers calling themselves the Oxford Ethnobotanical Expedition to Kenya were scandalised by the situation, saying, with reference to the Mijikenda Kayas, that ' . . . previous researchers – obviously with fieldwork deadlines – have used money as a convenient means of extracting information quickly. This was particularly the case in Kaya Fungo, where the new "elders" [whose credentials they doubted] have commercialised the parts of the Giriama heritage to which they have access' (Hawthorne *et al.* 1981: 31 n. 2; my brackets). They showed sympathy and respect for Pembe Bembere, ironically the now retired Kaya elder who had first issued instructions for my guidance in 1966, who 'would not divulge the essence of their heritage, the very heart of the Giriama "soul", to the present incumbents [i.e. the Oxford researchers] because he did not consider them worthy of the knowledge' (Hawthorne *et al.* 1981). But there were others who were so willing and whose sale of Giriama secret knowledge was to culminate in the stand taken by elders of the Kaya in 1988 against them and against its further erosion.

This tendency to treat Giriama knowledge as a commodity to be sold at negotiable and therefore ever-increasing monetary value may or may not have been arrested by the purificatory action of the Kaya elders in 1988. While there may well be a pause, it seems likely that this tendency will continue, as has happened elsewhere in countries where innumerable foreign researchers and tourists merge in the eyes of the local population who see all visitors, most of them short-term, as having similar desires, equipment, and lack of commitment to the area. In becoming commoditised, the secrets also become unhinged from the customary view of them as part of the social ranking of Giriama kinship and generational differences. They become separated off from Giriama gradations of personhood. Alongside calls for Giriama to reinstate control over their ebbing cultural knowledge and essence, there is, then, a developing division among the Giriama between those alleged to sell the secrets and those insistent on with-holding and so conserving them.

In this struggle to retain cultural essence, the Kaya and its elders have been regarded as central. As I have indicated, a few have been criticised and even removed from office for allowing Kaya rules to be broken and customary knowledge to be sold. But most are not so regarded and indeed are still seen as custodians. It is the value placed on this custodianship which reinforces the ritual, judiciary and, on occasion, political power which they exercise, and gives them authority and the Kaya the status of sacred centre.

Yet it seems, at first sight, difficult to refer to the Kaya also as a political centre, for this would imply that the Giriama are themselves politically centralised. Or perhaps it is the anthropological notion of political centralisation which is inadequate and which therefore hides the complexity of the Kaya's role in the organisation and definition of the Giriama people.

The myth of political centralisation

I address myself here, then, not to a myth held by the Giriama but rather to that of the anthropologist, who has frequently begun an analysis on the assumption that we can broadly distinguish between politically centralised and uncentralised societies, going back to the pioneering typology of Fortes and Evans-Pritchard (1940). Of course there are gross differences between those kinds of states which are close to tyranny, those which are little more than benign bureaucracies, and those societies which lack formally instituted authority roles. There may even be, as Eli Sagan argues so vividly, some necessary process in the evolution of minor state systems that requires their rulers to engage in violence against fellow citizens in order to emphasise the separateness that has now occurred between sovereign and subjects (Sagan 1985). But the problems of such typologies are now so well known that few would seek to use them. The implications of this distrust of political typologies has pushed anthropologists increasingly towards a view of power itself as generally dispersed and as only occasionally concentrated in the hands of individual persons, statuses, and institutions, as most recently argued by Arens and Karp (1989). Power ebbs and flows, often appearing as separate kinds of power (Augé 1975), or as a combination of capacity, energy and agency (Karp 1989: 105), and literally makes history when it is seen to be the property, though temporarily, of a particular group of people.

This better fits a political description of the Giriama than whether or not they show aspects of political centralisation. Two historians writing of the Giriama talk in terms of an assumed and unproblematic contrast between centralised and uncentralised societies, but nevertheless reveal in their remarks a much more fluid situation.

Spear regards the Giriama as having an uncentralised, segmentary political system, but additionally describes the main Mijikenda Kayas, including that of the Giriama, in the seventeenth and eighteenth centuries as 'central residential towns and politico-religious complexes. They were similar to royal villages elsewhere in Africa, for their physical design was a manifestation of Mijikenda cultural ideals and the Singwaya legend was their master plan' (Spear 1978: 49). Brantley also repeatedly refers to the Giriama as politically uncentralised and gives this as a main reason for their not providing coordinated resistance against the British in 1914 (Brantley 1981), though she also points out that the dispersal of Giriama peoples and ruling elders from their Kaya made them elusive and difficult for the British to administer, both before and after the rebellion.

It seems unlikely, in the light of the fate of major state systems in Africa, that the Giriama would have been any other than defeated even if they had had such a system in confrontation with the British. Or it is possible that they would have been used as delegated administrators in the policy of indirect rule and so become strengthened. In any event, the fact that the Giriama used their knowledge of the hinterland terrain to escape most British efforts at domination and to avoid becoming a source of labour, raises the question of whether the Giriama were in fact conquered. Against British guns they lost men and livestock, and suffered the burning of villages, with 598 men having to enter the Carrier Corps service during the First World War (Mambo 1987: 98–9). But they remained relatively independent of urban wage labour until recently, and even now are much less involved than many other Kenyan peoples.

It would seem that the Giriama played it both ways. Against the British their dispersed social organisation enabled them to move quickly as small, independent units to the west and north and away from the immediate coastal hinterland. Yet, beforehand, under the woman leader, Mikatalili, they had shown some signs of united organisation against the British (Brantley 1981: 85–88). Still earlier, they had lived in the fortified Kaya in an attempt to defend themselves against the raids of the Oromo. Finally, later, from at least the mid nineteen sixties to the late eighties, they once again expressed common political awareness and action through the Kaya elders, as I have described. Moreover, it can be argued that, alongside this capacity to concentrate power through the Kaya elders when needed, the Giriama have begun in the last two decades especially to migrate in search of land and work by using the dispersed network of kinship and clan ties that stretch throughout the province.

Centralisation is, then, a property that can be created or drawn upon, according to situations affecting and even defining Giriama interests. While accepting that the Giriama could not be classified as a kingdom or state in the same way that Buganda, Barotse or Asante have been, the Kaya and its elders have, despite their and their people's dispersal, continued to provide a ready centre on which ideas of power and action can be concentrated and articulated in the name of all Giriama. By contrast, Kajiwe, the witchfinder, claimed to speak for all Mijikenda but wished to push them towards incorporation in Christian and European education and medicine. The Kaya elders spoke only for Giriama (as did those of the other Kayas for their respective groups) and sought authority through customary knowledge supposedly belonging only to the Giriama. In this sense the Kaya and its elders remained the Giriama centre, both politically and metaphysically, while Kajiwe, in his earlier period, sought to undermine that and other ethnically based centres and to bring all Mijikenda within the orbit of the newly emerging, Christianising Kenya state. Yet, despite his stated aims, Kajiwe's actions threw into relief questions of ethnic identity and the pivotal role of the Kaya elders in defining Giriama distinctiveness. In trying to marginalise the Kaya elders, Kajiwe made them more central while he himself eventually became a marginal political figure. The Kaya thus moves to centre stage at the point at which it is challenged by those wishing to usurp its position.

From centre to dispersal
Was this always so? Brantley suggests that a fundamental change occurred when the Giriama people moved out of and away from the Kaya during the latter half of the nineteenth century. Pax Britannica may have reduced Oromo and Maasai raids and made living in the fortified settlement less necessary for the Giriama. Additionally, their population was growing rapidly, making dispersal at some point inevitable.

Brantley suggests that with the dispersal from the Kaya, misfortunes came to be explained more in local terms and in different ways from those used in the Kaya, and that this development therefore weakened the centralising role of the Kaya elders (1979: 116–117). If we regard as unproblematic the dichotomy between centralised and uncentralised politics, this seems a reasonable description of what happened: power simply left the Kaya. But is it as simple as that? I would rather suggest that while power in some senses was seen by Giriama to remain in the Kaya, it also became dispersed outside it, taking such negative forms as increased witchcraft accusations and spirit possession. These in turn reinforced the need for periodic re-concentration of remedial power in the hands of the Kaya elders, when they were called upon to reverse these various evils. They then began to provide ritual power intermittently from the Kaya, as needs were perceived to arise, rather than regularly as part of the organisation of a settled community within the Kaya.

What, then, are the various negative forms of power that flourished with the dispersal from the Kaya?

Witchcraft (*utsai*) and possession by capricious non-human spirits (*nyama* and *pepo*) were much more frequently diagnosed, while ancestral ghosts (*koma*) and breaches of protective oaths (*viraho*, placed in a field or village to deter theft and witchcraft) were blamed much less for personal and homestead calamities. Moreover, Giriama began to regard Islamic medicines and spirits as often more powerful than their own (Parkin 1970: 225).

This happened especially in those well-watered and fertile eastern parts of Giriama country, such as Kaloleni, where from the nineteen twenties onwards migrants came from the western cattle areas and planted coconut palms and other trees instead of keeping cattle. Over the years such Giriama became more involved in the palm wine and copra trade, which was dominated by the neighbouring Rabai, and would sell their produce to Swahili and Arabs in Mombasa and on the coast. Swahili traders and Muslim holy men themselves came to settle in Kaloleni, setting up a Friday mosque there. In this way, Kaloleni, which had itself once been a cattle-raising area, became i. extricably a part of the coastal economy and, to a lesser extent, coastal culture (Parkin 1972: 18–19).

The population density increased enormously, so that by 1966 homesteads would be no more than a couple of hundred metres apart and often much closer. The traditional method of shifting cultivation every five years was abandoned by the nineteen fifties at least, and homesteads remained fixed, with heads jealously guarding their valuable land from encroachment. It was known in the mid nineteen sixties that the government was proposing to register and consolidate land holdings. A scramble for land resulted. Landholders, many of whom had originally come as supplicants for land which did not belong to their own clan, tried to demonstrate their rights to plots on the basis of their extensive tree plantings, a claim which did, in fact, often find favour with the government officers responsible for adjudicating land titles (Parkin 1972: 53–55).

It was against this background of disputation and conflict, occurring not just in Kaloleni but in the locations of Jibana, Chonyi and Rabai, where land registration and consolidation were also about to be carried out, that Kajiwe's witch-hunt of 1966 was seen to be so important. Witchcraft, it was believed, was exceptionally rife.

In fact, as Brantley points out, there had been a succession of witch-hunters from the late nineteenth century after the dispersal of Giriama from their Kaya. It was also with this dispersal that spirit possession may have increased inordinately in these eastern Giriama areas.

The western cattle area was always much less densely populated. It has its problems of cattle disease, water supply and limited transportation, to which I have referred, but homesteads are distant from each other and there has never been much involvement in the farming cash crop economy. Nor is there any other than minimal contact with Muslim Swahili and Arab traders. The latter do come to the area to buy cattle but they have never settled there. In the Gotani area, in which I lived, none of the currently active possessory spirits were Islamic. While life in the cattle area is hard, in many ways harsher than that of the fertile farming zone, its troubles cannot easily be blamed on the jealousy of neighbouring homesteads, which are all at some distance from each other. Individual homesteads are larger, it is true, but this does not by itself give rise to the idea that witchcraft must therefore be extensively practised. It is said, for instance, that in these large homesteads consisting of so many agnates and other relatives living together, the main problem is what we might call adulterous incest giving rise to the afflictions of *vitio* and *mavingane*, which cause the sterility of wives and the death and sickness of their children and so threaten the continuity of family lines.

In other words, it is believed that misfortunes in the cattle area occur more as a result of a disturbed cosmos, arising not from peoples' malice, as in witchcraft, but from thoughtless breaches of customary taboos. It is even said that the secret societies, including the Vaya, are more in evidence in the cattle area, and that the use of oaths is correspondingly more effective in curbing witchcraft.

This alleged difference between 'traditional' west and 'modern' east is not just that of cattle-keepers and farmers. There is for example the hilly, fertile area around Mwangea, which is well inland, and there are other northern inland areas where the terrain is wholly unsuitable for grazing cattle. In fact, cattle are not found further than sixty kilometres north of Gotani. But the division between cattle-keeping west and agricultural east is a significant one in terms of population drift in southern Kilifi district and is spoken of in this way by Giriama themselves, who also refer to problems of witchcraft in the east and those of incestuous homesteads in the west.

The modern characterisation of eastern tree farmers as plagued by witchcraft and spirit possession has, as its counterpart, the view that western cattle-keepers have greater respect for their ancestors and for the work and sanctions of the Vaya and other Kaya elders: this is after all where the Kaya stands. Thus, while witchcraft and spirits were brought in or exacerbated by external coastal contact (some say from 'Arabs' via the Muslim Digo and Swahili), the problem of incest, believed to be more common in the western cattle zone, is at least indigenous to Giriama in the form in which it occurs and, accordingly, can be dealt with by Kaya elders.

This contrast is a variation on that between the west as upholding Giriama tradition and the east as subverting it through its involvement in coastal conflicts and ambitions. It does indeed fit the view that witches and malevolent spirits increased in number after the Giriama moved away from the Kaya; or perhaps we should say that these explanations of misfortune became especially important among those Giriama who migrated to and settled in the farming areas nearest the coast, leaving those in the west with a cosmology closest to that existing in the Kaya when it and its immediate environs accommodated a majority of Giriama.

I am, of course, dealing here not with measurable facts (for who could ever measure the relative incidence of witchcraft as against incest between the two areas?), but with an idealisation of geographical difference, which is partly given substance by a difference of ecology. It is, to refer to an earlier point, the distinction between the remote and ethnically pure on the one hand and, on the other, to the immediate and contingent, and indeed urgent in view of the alacrity with which Kajiwe's promises to eradicate witchcraft were met.

The Kaya elders embody the idea of the continuous, the uncontaminated and the remote, and in this way suggest some of the characteristics of regal authority. But they do not go so far as to constitute royalty. They lack the degree of predictable and institutionalised delegated use of power that is associated with kings or leaders of state, but might, under more favourable circumstances, have acquired it. The Vaya elders, for instance, do not delegate authority to others but, as a secret society, keep it for themselves. They hide the mysteries of their oaths yet reveal publicly, through their presentation of themselves as men to be feared, that their powers are to be respected. Even though, since the dispersal from the Kaya in the late nineteenth century, the Vaya have lived in and operated from their own neighbourhoods more than from the Kaya, they retain their links with the Kaya and are regarded by Giriama as indeed Kaya elders. The Kaya remains central to Giriama cosmology and to the deployment of power. The Giriama are clearly not a politically centralised society if we take a view of power only as to do with the capacity of individuals to influence people and events, a view which unquestioningly assumes that human agents and the institutions they work through are to a large degree self-determining. But we may, instead, regard agency and power as inscribed in activities in an indeterminate and subtle manner. Events then occur as the knock-on effects of different powers identified by people themselves. The Giriama, like most peoples, seek key causes for this apparent randomness in the distribution of power and have seen the Kaya and its elders as being centrally placed to explain it. It is indeed the idea of political centralisation as a repository of explanation, that makes it possible for a people to heed and mobilise around recognised men of power, including such women as Mikatalili, the leader of the 1914 Giriama rebellion against the British.

Just as the this-world marginality of prophets enables them to place themselves at the centre of a new religious world, so witchfinders like Kajiwe draw upon their marginality to similar effect. Yet, in becoming for a short while central, Kajiwe displaced the Kaya elders who, themselves now marginalised, invoked past ideals and so regained the centre. Centre and periphery are thus held by Giriama to sustain each other through their alternating denial of each other.

Powerful manifestations

I have earlier suggested that concentrated power is associated by Giriama with the Kaya and its dispersed usage with the various different areas outside it. It is clear from the above, however, that while the Kaya as a sacred centre is indeed regarded as the ultimate provider of ritual knowledge, this knowledge is also used in various ways and combinations and sometimes for evil as well as for good. Going back to an earlier point, the elders of the Kaya share at least some of the same human frailties as persons not associated with the Kaya. They are not always regarded as doing good, even if the Kaya itself is beyond question. In other words, the uses to which knowledge is put divides the powers in a different way: at one point or place, witchcraft prevails, at another spirit possession dominates, at yet another incest, ancestral vengeance, breech births and bad deaths may take on greater significance, and so on.

Kaya elders and witchfinders touch on all of these, both claiming to confront evil with good, but with the elders outlasting individual witchfinders through their repeated messages of ethnic purity, distinctiveness, and tradition. No Giriama witchfinder has become a prophet and substituted a new tradition for the old, as in the case of the prophets of Zionist churches in South Africa among Zulu (Sundkler 1961) and Tshidi Baralong (Comaroff 1985), though we may specu-late on this as a possible development. The legend of the prophetess called MiPoho, who predicted the threat to Giriama culture and identity through the arrival of white people and their planes, vehicles and what we now call consumer objects, does not refer to her as ever having been a witchfinder though, clearly, her powers of divination were considerable (Thompson 1990: 102–108).

These and other powers described below variously flow through both elders and witchfinder. Each can harm as well as heal. But the spatial association of elders with the Kaya, and of Kajiwe, or another witchfinder, with eastern Giriamaland, broadly divides them, as I shall show.

What, then, are the powers which give the Kaya elders the last word, so to speak, and those which establish such seemingly aberrant persons as Kajiwe? In now introducing these, let me repeat what I described in detail in the previous chapter, that at different times and for differing sections of the population, Kajiwe was regarded as a legitimate authority. As with each new witchfinder, his methods were regarded as unique. He was recognised early on by the Kaya elders and government as well as by ordinary Mijikenda people. He was then denounced by both the elders and government, but not by the people. Still later, when his methods were milder, he was once again recognised as acting legit-imately by both the Kaya elders and people though not by the government, which detained him. The Kaya elders themselves have undergone similar oscillations of legitimacy, under both the colonial and independent regimes of Kenya. But throughout these changes of recognition, the elders and Kajiwe, and people like him, have drawn upon powers which are separately distinguished by the Giriama. In other words, whatever the changing expressions of political legit-imacy, the powers that make up these key figures are always there.

To take an example, *uganga* is the term which we might translate as medicine, and *muganga* as doctor. But, just as a doctor can become a witch (*mutsai*) by turn-ing against society, so *uganga* itself is the power to destroy as well as to cure, if the doctor so intends, and itself becomes witchcraft (*utsai*). Similarly, the Vaya elders, who are themselves sometimes called doctors as well as 'elders of the hyena', may also be referred to as witches, as may other Kaya elders. This might occur if some of their 'protective' oaths, especially those buried in the soil of homesteads and pathways (ambivalently referred to sometimes positively as *fingo* but sometimes negatively as *mbare*) are regarded as having been placed with malicious intent. Again, certain spirits may be divined as having been sent by a witch and therefore as a kind of witchcraft, unlike the more capricious spirits which possess a person independently.

In other words, these are powers where it is recognised that some degree of human intentionality and control may be involved, and that human intentions are both ambivalent and inconsistent, both for and against humanity. We can regard these powers as all coming under the rubric of medicine and witchcraft combined.

By contrast, the powers of the ancestors, of most capricious spirits, and those powers resulting from incest, 'bad births', homicide, and other 'bad deaths', are not easily reducible to human intentionality. The Giriama recognise that an intention can only be for good or for bad. It cannot be neutral. In Western thought homicide (including suicide) and incest are intended acts, which may, even in the case of suicide, be vengeful. The Giriama do not see them as based on malice or revenge, but as arising from thoughtlessness or violent anger. Since they are directed to neither good nor bad, it is irrelevant what the perpetrator thought about before he committed them, and whether he intended them. It is enough that they happened and that their ill-effects be erased. These malign powers do not, then, arise from anyone's intention to spread harm. If anything, they result from negligence, either by the victim or by someone close to the victim.

To distinguish these two sets of powers as intended and unintended does not translate well their sense, especially in view of the ambivalence attaching to medicine and witchcraft and to spirits. Intentionality is not of course a good term to describe those cases of witchcraft reported for other societies where the accused admits in a trial by ordeal that he or she did someone harm but claims to have done so involuntarily through jealousy. The Giriama do not accept this explanation of involuntary harm as sufficient: the accused must have summoned the help of a doctor skilled at avenging clients or willing to provide the knowl- edge to do so.[6] But nor do the Giriama separate the act from the state of mind and circumstances of the perpetrator. Intentions are always part of bodily and emotional dispositions. Feelings of envy and jealousy are even classed by some diviners as illnesses, sometimes caused by rivals, with the result that, on rare occasions, even previously diagnosed malicious intentions can be re-diagnosed as directed by someone else's malice!

However, if we ask how the Giriama treat the negative side of these powers, we can draw a distinction which is less dependent on questions of human inten- tionality. Thus, there are problems which can only be solved by identifying and

[6] I have elsewhere spoken of the Giriama having sorcery rather than witchcraft, along the lines of Middleton and Winter's early distinction. Insofar as sorcery connotes the use and transaction of medical knowledge and, under certain circumstances, medical roots and herbs themselves, the distinction continues to be useful, for the voyages undertaken by Giriama herbalists are indeed in pursuit of one or another medicine (see Parkin 1968). The transactional nature of medical knowl- edge and the extensive journeying can, in this way, be neatly encapsulated in the term sorcery, whereas witchcraft, according to Middleton and Winter, emanates psychically from aggrieved or malicious individuals and is not dependent on physically identifiable medicines. However, on reflection, I now want to include both elements of these definitions in this study, for, while the Giriama do indeed practise sorcery in the above sense, they also see it as motivated by strong and sometimes uncontrollable passions of anger, hatred and jealousy. It is to that extent involuntary, as in the definition of witchcraft, as well as requiring conscious calculation and planning, as in the sense of sorcery. Since both connotations are, in the Giriama view, part and parcel of each other, I here adopt the more conventionally used term, witchcraft (see also Turner 1964).

seeking recompense and restoration from the individual who, whether consciously or not, is causing them. There are also problems which affect a whole community, whose purification and repair is more important than blaming the individual(s) involved. As examples of the first, the ill-effects of witchcraft and of other human-sent powers can be reversed by other humans, either by the evil witch himself or, in the case of a breach of a pledge or prohibition bound by an oath, by the doctor responsible for giving or planting the oath. There is in other words an area of human-made suffering which is caused either deliberately or erroneously by named individuals, who may be identified as malicious perpetrators, or as victims who have brought the trouble on themselves through theft or other wrong-doing, or as doctor-judges simply carrying out protective magic for which they have been paid but which has accidentally harmed an innocent person. Examples of the second kind of problem are incest, the neglect of ancestors or spirits, and involvement in or association with a bad death or birth. These bring misfortunes to a homestead, and not just to an individual, and are eradicated by means of a gift (to spirits) or the sacrifice of a ram in a communal ceremony held in the homestead.

Putting the contrast simply, malice and medicine are directed to the problems of individuals, while the neglect of customary prohibitions, of which the principal one is incest, brings problems to groups which can only be resolved through group activity. The problems suffered by these groups are of a contaminating nature, and able to affect any of its members indiscriminately. The remedial sacrifices are of a purificatory kind.

Spirits which possess people straddle this contrast. The spirits attack individuals. They are ordinarily deemed to intend this, with occasional male sceptics nevertheless claiming that a female victim is feigning the affliction. However, it is sometimes argued that the spirits are really aspects of the victim's own character which surface in crises. More than any other field of Giriama belief and activity, spirit possession defies our conventional distinctions of individual and group, intentionality and accident, centre and periphery, as will be shown in a later chapter.

Both Kajiwe and the Kaya elders claimed to work for the benefit of communities rather than for individuals alone. But Kajiwe's attention was specifically directed to the competitive individual conflicts and interests that are associated with witchcraft, and to cultivating in his fellow Mijikenda an individualistic commitment to modern education and Christianity as routes to so-called progress. He himself turned his practice into a profitable business. The Kaya elders were by no means opposed to making money and included among their members one or two who had accumulated considerable traditional wealth in the form of cattle, trees, wives and children. But upon them alone fell the task of presenting the case for rule by such customary means as retributory oaths and collective purification following incest and homicide.

Conclusion

Let me return now to the distinction between the spacious cattle zone of the west and the crowded agricultural and coastal east, and to that between remote authenticity and contingent immediacy. Incest, it will be remembered, is believed to be found in the western cattle area much more than witchcraft. This area is also that in which notions of Giriama purity, expressed centrally through the Kaya, are thought best preserved. Witchcraft, on the other hand, is said to be found more in the agricultural eastern areas and towards the coast, where economic competition between individuals is held to be most intense, and where ethnic and religious admixture threatens Giriama exclusivity.

The anomaly, spirit possession, is also more associated with the eastern and coastal areas, and though it is normally dealt with communally in large dance seances and so is in this respect like the large purificatory rites held to remove the effects of incest, it is also very much directed at particular persons, usually women, who are seen to be victims in much the same way as are those of witchcraft: indeed, as I have mentioned, certain forms of spirit possession are actually called witchcraft. Given its individualistic thrust, especially through the Islamic spirits which oblige particular persons to become Muslim, it does indeed make sense to think of it, as do the Giriama, as more an eastern and coastal phenomenon than a western one.

In presenting these collective representations opposing the allegedly communal, self-purifying cattle-keeping west with the agricultural and individualistic east contaminated by a range of non-Giriama others, my aim is to show that they are an allegory of a much wider order of power. The coastal peoples as a whole, Giriama, Mijikenda and Swahili, have ceded much of their control of their respective areas to migrants, settlers, ranchers, enterprises and government officers from other parts of Kenya. The rapidly expanding use of fertile coastal land, the ranching and farming innovations, the land settlement schemes, and the growth of tourism, hotels, Mombasa and other towns, have brought about enormous transformations in the political, economic, cultural and religious structure of Coast province as a whole since those days in 1966 when Kajiwe first expressed his own concern. Kajiwe's campaign was not entirely directed at the witches within. It will be remembered that, while emphasising the unity of all Mijikenda, he attacked Mijikenda as well as non-Mijikenda Muslims, a clumsy act for which he paid but which raised the question of the identity of the Mijikenda in a world increasingly governed by interests beyond their control. At the same time, Kajiwe urged people to adopt modern western medicine, education and even Christianity, which, for better and worse, are inextricably involved in the conditions that have given rise to the newly burgeoning material consumerism along the coastal strip of Kenya and which run counter to the values associated with the Kaya.

In this allegory, the cattle-keeping Giriama of the west are represented as independent of the inter-penetration and diversification of the east to which Kajiwe drew oblique attention. The traces of their past political independence, albeit limited, described by Brantley, that at first enabled the Giriama effectively to evade British conscription in the colonial labour market, are seen by many Giriama to rest in the ambivalent powers allegedly located in the west: the Kaya, its elders, their ancestors, their secret societies, and the problem of incest encountered by cattle-keeping people obliged to live in large homesteads. But how do these cattle-keepers of the west live this construction of themselves by fellow Giriama? The next chapter attempts to answer this.

3

View from the west: cattle and co-operation

'A man without cattle is like a man without work'

'If you are lent cattle, it is like work because you can sell the milk'

Hiding the cattle

Wide-flung co-operation is essential in the vastness of the western and northern hinterland of Giriama country. Although clans may claim to be the holders of specific tracts of land on the basis of first and continuous settlement, uncultivated land is nevertheless available to anyone for livestock grazing. It is when people build a homestead and cultivate land that tensions may develop between them and the clan owners. But, given the greater availability of land and the fact that farming is normally secondary to keeping livestock as a livelihood, such tensions are far fewer than in the heavily populated eastern areas. A second area of co-operation, in addition to the common use of grazing land, is the sophisticated system by which cattle owners place their animals in a number of different herds spread out over a large area.

In fact, this placing of animals provides mutual benefits for cattle owners and herders alike. The Giriama actually call the practice that of 'hiding cattle' (*ku-fitsa ngombe*), refusing to reveal to each other how many they have and so guarding their herds against the demands of agnates and tax assessors. As among the Maasai, sons who become herdboys may be encouraged by their fathers to find out the composition and size of other men's herds (Spencer 1988: 51). The information they get is inevitably only ever approximate and, being sought after by all senior men, is therefore both tacit and roughly shared. In describing this system of hiding cattle we obtain some idea of the distinctive independent ethos of Giriama cattle country, and why this area is seen by both its inhabitants and those nearer the coast as the authentic home of custom.

I shall for much of this chapter refer only to cattle, for it is these, rather than goats and sheep, that people point to as shaping the lives and character of home-steaders living in the west. Nevertheless, I should emphasise even at this stage that goats are far more numerous than cattle and overall have greater subsistence value, while sheep, though few, are used in key purificatory sacrifices. Nevertheless, the Giriama regard cattle as the most prestigious animal for funeral sacrifices and for bridewealth and as the most powerful animal, the most demanding evidence of a man's courage and strength. After some six months in the field in 1966, I was sent to pull a bull some miles from the cattle area to the eastern palm belt where it was to be sacrificed at a funeral. Though I received reassuringly excellent assistance, the experience was daunting and not without danger. Organised by a man who was later to become a firm friend, Kahindi Poko of Kaloleni, it was later laughingly explained to me as testing my suitability for incorporation in the society of Giriama men, becoming the theme of a praise song thereafter. The identification of men with bulls is of course common in Africa, as indeed is that of large herds of cattle generally with politically powerful men.

The average size of a herd is fifty head of cattle. This is what Giriama say and is what I counted. For instance, of eleven herds counted in one day in Miyani, the largest was about one hundred head and the smallest fifteen, with a median also of about fifty. Herds of goats, which are very much larger, often running into the hundreds, are normally grazed separately from cattle, unless the latter are few. Numbers of sheep are minimal, being kept solely for the special but less common purificatory sacrifices, as described in chapter six.

We must distinguish between owners and herders of cattle. To put the difference extremely, a man may be owning but not herding his cattle, just as a herder may not own the cattle he herds. In fact, most owners look after some of their own cattle, while most herders own a few of the cattle they herd. Of the 38 heads of homesteads in Miyani, 21 own cattle. Of these, all but six retain at least some of their herd with them in their homestead. At one extreme are those of recognised 'big men', of whom there are two in Miyani. Each owns many hundreds of cattle, with up to 300 of them located in their own homesteads dispersed among different byres, the homesteads themselves consisting of at least thirty separate human dwellings. At the other extreme are some groups of animals numbering no more than ten, in smaller homesteads of only a few houses. In between are those homesteads comprising fifty or so animals and a dozen houses.

Some six other owners place all their cattle in other local or more distant herds. Even the two richest cattle owners in Kayafungo location, mentioned above, place a large and perhaps majority proportion of their cattle with other herds. They themselves will not put a precise number on the size of their herds, but each may well reach six hundred head. Being larger, their herds are the most widely dispersed: some remaining with them, others scattered over a range of different pastures, but in often small groups of one or two score. Each big man is thus linked to a huge number of herders located in all parts of Giriama country where cattle can be raised. Smaller owners are similarly linked, though on a smaller scale.

If we include a few cases of under-reporting, which seems inevitable among those I knew less well, some two thirds of the heads of homesteads may own at least a few beasts, though most of the other more junior men such as younger brothers and sons would have none. On the other hand, they may lay claim to a father's or elder brother's cattle, which is one of the reasons that the head may feel obliged to hide some of his herd elsewhere than in his own homestead.

A herder (*murisa*) may find himself over time acquiring a large number of cattle. First, if his reputation is excellent, the agreement may be that he is allowed to keep the first calf born to a cow which he is herding, and every second calf thereafter, the owner being credited with the others. Alternatively, when the owner retrieves his cattle, perhaps to place them elsewhere, the herder is given a payment of cash or a he-goat (formerly a heifer). In this way the herder can build up his own herd, especially valuable for the sons of poor men who need bride-wealth, but also a means of acquiring extra wives for herders who are already married. However, the main source of revenue for the herder is the right to all milk produced by the animals he herds. He can sell this, sometimes eventually produced as ghee, both locally and to such distant concerns as the Mariakani milk marketing board or the shops and hospitals in Kaloleni town.

Herders may delegate some of the work to boys, and in some cases to girls, of from about twelve years of age upwards, who will be paid 70 shillings cash per month (in 1985). Such an assistant is called *muzingiri* (from the verb *ku-zingira*, to surround something). Some owners employ such young people directly to herd some of their cattle locally, to and from their byres. In herds containing more than fifty head of cattle, at least two boys will be in charge. The employment of young people in this way frees the herder to concentrate on the growth and deployment of his own herd, which is itself partially placed amongst other herds, and gently ushers in the time when, as a young married man, he does less and less actual herding himself.

There is, then, a career process, beginning as herder's assistant at the age of twelve, to herder in the late teens or early twenties, to herder-owner and then owner at any time thereafter. The increased use of girls as assistants has occurred in recent years as a result of a greater number of young boys entering primary school. This has not produced women cattle owners, however, and since few boys continue at secondary school, has merely delayed the point at which the boys develop herding skills. The association of men with cattle is thus unaltered by such developments.

This male association is commonly recognised as in the anecdote given above. People also say that Giriama cattle are more important for bridewealth (*hunda* or the plural form *mahunda*) than for either milk or meat. Of course all three uses are fulfilled. Yet this is no empty claim and is borne out in two ways. First, most transactions of cattle are in the form of marriage payments. Second, a man will often seek to build up a large herd, including cattle received for daughters' marriages, in order to be in a position to make the bridewealth payments of his sons, thereafter allowing the herd to become run down and, effectively, retiring himself.

Cattle enable men to marry, but the cattle used in marriage transactions are in fact mostly heifers. The marriage payment rate in cattle over the last twenty-five years has been between 15 and 17 heifers and one so-called bull (*ndzau*). In the non-cattle farming areas of the east, cash is often substituted either wholly or partially. In the west, as in Miyani, the reverse is the case and most payments will include all or a large proportion of heifers, with no more than a few cows who have already calved. The so-called bull is, however, rarely the animal itself and most commonly consists of palm wine, which is supposed to reach the bride's maternal uncle (*ahu*) and secures for her husband rights over children produced by his wife. In other words, marriage is the means by which men perpetuate themselves through male children, but the marriage is contracted through the exchange of female animals.

Cows are not normally killed for meat unless old, nor indeed sold commercially, but are reserved for bridewealth exchanges. It is mainly male animals, in the form of young bullocks, which are eaten or sold. They are kept for slaughtering at funerals or at other feasts along with some older cows, or they may be sold, often only two at a time, at the stock auctions of Mariakani or Bamba or to fellow Giriama. While young female animals thus continually circulate between different inter-marrying groups, the male animals continually depart, through either sacrifice or sale. The exception is a bull, roughly one in about twenty-five animals, which is allowed to grow to full size and move with one of the predominantly female herds. The parallel with a big man is commonly made by the Giriama.

I have spoken of men reproducing themselves through male children born to them through the exchange of bridewealth. Giriama have a system of patrilineal inheritance of land, moveable property and clanship, and so this statement is consistent, and is moreover shared by Giriama themselves. It must be remembered, however, that the rights over children (male and female) are secured by only a small and relatively non-valuable part of the total marriage payment, the so-called bull. As palm wine, this part of the payment shares the same destiny as a real male animal, which is to be consumed. The remaining heifers are too valuable to be consumed. Their destiny is to reproduce themselves and to continue to circulate, spreading laterally by means of their female offspring in numerous directions throughout Giriama cattle country. The Giriama note the parallel with the movement of women, who move from natal to husband's homes and who, at a husband's death, may move yet again as inherited widows to the home of his agnate (whom the widow may choose but who must be related to the deceased husband within a sub-clan).

This lateral dispersal of cattle and women is therefore as much a feature of marriage exchanges as men's lineal destiny through male heirs. An oft-cited Giriama maxim says it well: the blood of cattle buys brothers/siblings/kin (*mulatso wa ngombe wagula ndugu*). Note that the claim is not that cattle buy children. The saying is in fact sometimes heard when people discuss funerals, and refers to the blood of sacrifice. As well as being occasions when marriages may be arranged, the large and often huge attendances at funerals are made up of what I call serial linking through affinity, and what the Giriama call relationships of *kizhere*. People of the clan or descent group which has suffered the death of one of its members invite their affines to the funeral of the deceased. But these affines are expected to invite their affines, and these latter theirs, and so on, covering a number of links in the manner of a chain. Such invitations are reciprocal and are part of the extensive network of affines that in fact links the different ecological zones of Giriama country.

Given that the Giriama kinship terminology is of the so-called 'Hawaiian' type, and that marriage is permitted within any clan other than the person's own patrilineal one, classificatory kin may become affines and vice versa. Affinity is, however, seen as in some ways prior to kinship as a linking mechanism. Patri-lineal clanship powerfully sharpens foci of identity, but the web of affinity mixes identities, converting non-kin into kin, and kin into different kinds of kin, and transcends boundaries, including that between west and east, and hinterland and coast.

When inviting each other to funerals, parental affines use the reciprocal term of address and reference, *kizhere*, which means that they are linked through the marriages of their offspring. The blood of cattle, in the saying given above, appears to refer to its secondary meaning of reproductive capacity, and draws upon another feature of the 'Hawaiian' terminology: the children of a marriage may refer to each other, and to their cousins and all generation peers on both mother's and father's sides, as *ndugu*, or sibling. The term *ndugu* thus collapses male and female, agnatic and uterine, and close and distant ties but preserves the distinction as a lateral and geographical spreading out of ties existing in the here and now, as distinct from ties which reach back lineally to a past (see Appendix 2).

It is consistent with this thinking that cattle are most commonly placed or 'hidden' not with lineal clansmen or close agnates but laterally with such other relatives as brother-in-law (*mulamu*); father-in-law and daughter's/son's father-in-law (both referred to as *mutsedza* or the latter as *kizhere*); cognates of the same generation, *ndugu*, especially a father's sister's son (also called *tsawe* or grand-father); and less frequently mother's brother (*ahu*). I give more details below on these relationships. For the moment we may note that all arise out of inter-marriage between different patri-clans in the present or previous generation, and that such relatives may look after each other's animals. Moreover, all terms used are reciprocal, so reinforcing further the idiom of relationships based on exchange through marriage.[1]

Why should agnates and patri-clansmen often be ignored among the Giriama as good guardians of a man's cattle? In answer it is said that they may too easily regard the cattle as part of a common patrimony and, by arguing through genealogical entitlement, claim the right to use them for the marriages of their own sons. Nevertheless, in extreme cases, it is among agnates that ultimate trust is located. To take an example to which I shall refer again,when Karisa Kambi of the Ziro clan thought he was dying, fearing that his dispersed herd would be appropriated by certain of his affines and cognates looking after it, he called in thirty of his eighty cattle and allocated them to a younger full brother. The other fifty were, however, left with non-agnates, and the overall distribution may be said to have been a compromise on his part: should he have died, at least some cattle would have been available through his brother for the marriages of his sons, but he would not have lost all his herd if his brother had in fact used them himself; some at least of his non-agnates could be relied on.

Normally, herds are built up with successive bridewealth obligations in mind. It makes sense to place cattle with, say, the father or brother of your wife, or with the father of your daughter's husband, provided you have already finished the marriage payment to them. Unlike in some other societies, Giriama wife-givers do not continuously increase their expectation of bridewealth. A bargain is a bargain, and once the payment has been made, no more will be requested or taken. Such an affine-herder does, after all, benefit materially from the deal through sales of milk and ghee and through the annual payment of goats. He thus becomes a strong ally and will protect a man's cattle, allowing them to multiply so that, in time, the owner can reliably call some in for the marriage payment of another son, whose bride will belong to yet another clan with whom the same process begins.

It is commonly remarked that, by placing the cattle with his daughter's father-in-law (i.e. at the homestead in which his daughter has been virilocally married), a man is able to ensure that his daughter and her children receive a ready supply of cow's milk. The same is also said of a sister and her children, for whom of course the man who places his cattle is a mother's brother. These personal concerns thus fit the more pragmatic considerations of finding the most reliable cattle guardians. They also keep alive links between a woman's natal and

---

[1] At first sight there might seem to be similarities with the ego-centred network of stock-associates described by Gulliver for the Jie of Uganda and the Turkana of Kenya. Among these peoples, a man may go to such friends and ask for contributions to, say, bridewealth. The Turkana particularly value affines among their stock-associates and the Jie maternal kin, with affines being also important (Gulliver 1955: 196–222). As among the Maasai, however (Spencer 1988: 234), such stock-friendships are initiated by gifts, and there is no evident parallel with the open Giriama intention of 'hiding' cattle: the Giriama cattle are given out not as gifts but as subject to rules of contract, with affines and other kin and even friends as the partners to such contract.

in-married homesteads and clans, preparing the ground so to speak for possible marriage between them in a later generation. Cross-cousin marriages, both matrilateral and patrilateral, are spoken of approvingly and, though very few, reinforce in idealistic terms the lateral spread of ties between different clans and the movement of cattle between them.

Let me illustrate these cattle-based links through the example of the man just mentioned, Karisa Kambi. His ownership of eighty cattle is a little larger than average but much smaller than that of the renowned big owners.

Karisa worked for some years in the docks of Mombasa as an overseer, a permanent job. Urban wage employment outside Giriama country is one of the ways in which men can build up their own herds of cattle, and a fifth of those who own cattle have helped themselves in this way. Karisa retired from the work in Mombasa in 1983, in his late forties or early fifties, having at the time acquired the basis of his eighty cattle and one hundred and twenty goats. He also has three wives, two of them recently married and with only small children. Three of the senior wife's children have survived to adulthood, and have all married. Two are daughters and one a son. Karisa has therefore received two lots of bridewealth and given out only one. On the other hand he hopes that his younger sons by his other two wives will themselves eventually marry, for whom he will pay bride-wealth out of his growing herd.

His cattle are placed or 'hidden' at eleven other homesteads. Nine are within a few kilometres of Karisa's own homestead, but two are up to thirty kilometres away. In other words, just as most marriages are between people living locally, so are most cattle kept within easy contact. The larger the herd the greater the proportion of more distant placements, and the greater the likelihood that the herd-owner will arrange marriages for himself or children with more distant families. Even in the case of wealthy herd-owners, however, local ties still account for most cattle placements and marriages.

It is useful here to list the number and type of cattle and the kinship status of those with whom the cattle have been hidden by Karisa Kambi:

1 Full younger brother (*ndugu*): thirty cattle consisting of twelve cows (*goma*), ten heifers (*ndama*), three bulls (*ndzau*), four bullocks (*kitsao*) and one male calf (*katsao*).
2 Wife's (classificatory) brother (*mulamu*): five cattle consisting of three bulls and bullocks and two cows.
3 Male patrilateral cross-cousin (in fact paternal grandfather's sister's son's son, called by the term *tsawe*, with a primary meaning of grandfather and secondary one of brother, following the equivalence of alternate gener-ations): seven cattle comprising four bulls and bullocks, two cows and one heifer.
4 Wife's (classificatory) sister's husband (*mulamu* or *mwanyumba*),

both reciprocal terms: two cattle, comprising one cow and one bullock.

5 Wife's sister's daughter's husband, *mutsedza* (refers also to daughter's husband or wife's father): one bullock and one cow.

6 Father's sister's son (called either, descriptively, son of my father's sister, *mwana wa tsangazimi*, or by the term *tsawe*; see under 3 above): two cows (and very many goats).

7 Father's clan sister's son (called by the same terms as in 6 above): one cow and one heifer.

8 Mother's brother's son (called *tsawe*, see 3 and 6 above): one cow and its recently produced female calf (*kadama*).

9 Mother's classificatory brother (*ahu*): one cow, one heifer and one fully grown ox (that is, castrated male) (*ndewa*).

10 Father's classificatory elder brother's son, whom Karisa Kambi called *mukulu wangu*, which is a non-reciprocal elaboration of the reciprocal term for brother, *ndugu*, which could also be rendered by the reciprocal term for grandfather, *tsawe*: one bullock.

11 The half-brother of no. 10, whom Karisa also calls *mukulu wangu*: two cows, one bull and one bullock.

The other twenty-five or so cattle are managed by Karisa himself in his own homestead and herded by his young sons. These cattle, too, were once placed with other herders, but, when he retired from work, Karisa took control of them himself, so reverting to a common pattern among Giriama cattle owners of splitting their animals among themselves and a range of other herders.

This example is by no means as detailed and complicated as many. From it, however, we can see some recurring features of the practice of hiding cattle. Most placements are of no more than one or a few cattle. With only one exception a female is placed in a herd in order that she reproduce within it: the offspring belong to Karisa, the owner, and not to the herder. Karisa's cattle appear to comprise a large proportion of bulls, some ten out of eighty. Many of these are in fact still young and have not yet begotten calves, but are regarded as more senior than the younger bullocks, hence are called bulls.

What is important here is the set of terms discriminating between the different stages of an animal's growth: for males, there is the progression from *katsao* to *kitsao* and *ndzau*, with *ndewa* a castrated ox, while for females there is that from *kadama* and *ndama* to *goma*. A fully mature woman is also called *goma*, as are a very few men called *ndzau* (with Kitsao a common personal name for men). The use of these terms to describe cattle has to be seen as part of the bargaining process by which the animals are given value. A fully grown ox (*ndewa*) can be worth up to 2000 shillings (1985), a large bull (*ndzau*) somewhat less and a small one (*kitsao*) is worth 800 shillings. A highly fecund cow (*goma*) might sell at

1500 shillings, a heifer (*ndama*) at 800 shillings, with male and female calves (*katsao* and *kadama*) worth up to 500 shillings. In addition, equivalences may be used: for instance, a fecund cow is normally reckoned to be worth two heifers. But even these quoted prices and values are no more than possible starting points for negotiation. The terms for cattle thus set the parameters within which evaluation and bargaining occur.

The value of individual beasts used in bridewealth is more settled, however, rising more in terms of general inflation than as the result of haggling, though the overall amount of bridewealth is subject to bargaining. In 1985, the standard consisted of up to 17 heifers valued at 500 shillings each and the so-called bull at 350 shillings. In pure economic terms it is thus more profitable to insist on receiving a bridewealth of livestock rather than cash, which is what many cattle owners do. On the other hand, those who do not wish to herd more animals than they have, or have an urgent expenditure need, may request cash instead.

Though some relationships between Karisa and his herders arise out of recent marriages, most are rather more distant, with almost half being with classificatory kin. Indeed, what is significant is that the relationships are legitimised as those of kinship, not that they result from an essentialised kinship. Once again, this mirrors marriage ties: since any two Giriama can trace at least a classificatory or clan-based kinship or affinal link, then any marriage can be construed as being between such kin or affines. The extent to which persons engage in such constructions depends on the value they wish to place on the relationship between them. In practice, then, Giriama use the language of kinship to designate the importance of a relationship, as is common in many other societies.

Another feature not yet mentioned is that the herd managed by Karisa himself includes not only some of his own cattle but a small number of those of other owners, including a few of the herders mentioned above who look after Karisa's animals. The hiding of cattle thus involves the dispersal of animals among various herds but includes within it a few reciprocal relations: I herd for you but you also herd for me. Having taken over some of the direct management of his herd only in recent years since his retirement from work in Mombasa, Karisa is involved in relatively few of these reciprocal ties. As his herd and commitments grow, they may be expected to increase and diversify.

Once again, we find a characteristic of marriage reflected in the management of cattle. *Ku-hala* means to take, and is used of a man taking a woman in marriage. The reciprocal verb form, *ku-halana*, means to take each other (of exogamous clans) and has the idea of marriage as a form of exchange or alliance. Similarly, the idea of hiding cattle for each other is the translation of the reciprocal verb form *ku-fitsirana*. In other words, a man does not always just hide his cattle (*ku-fitsa*), he ties himself to another doing the same. The Giriama have a clear notion of the system of cattle hiding as constituting a network of cross-cutting and reciprocal relationships, each dependent on others. They see these cattle-based ties as largely localised, as they do those of marriage, but recognise also that individual strands emanating from personal networks reach out to more distant parts and so link them as people of one area occupied by the Giriama as a whole. The open-ended localisation of activities is thus seen as providing a wider coverage and expression of Giriama collective identity.

It is paradoxical that the concept of hiding something, with its implications of secrecy and privacy, should be regarded as providing the wider-scale contacts by which Giriama can claim publicly to know each other in whatever part of Giriama country. It is however consistent with the continuing history of migration and movement of the Giriama. Since their dispersal from the Kaya in the nineteenth century, they have settled and established communities within which they prefer to marry but between whom a small number of marriages at a distance do occur as a result of the movements of individual families and persons. It is tempting to suggest that the emphasis on local endogamy reproduces the ethos of the original Kaya settlement: the oft-mentioned justification for marry- ing a girl from a nearby homestead is that her and her family's 'character' will be known, which refers not just to her personality but also to whether or not the homestead suffers from diseases, in particular *mavingane* or *vitio*, which cause the death of children and the inability of adults, particularly women, to produce children. Marrying at a distance is therefore risky and rare, but occurs often enough for distant homesteads to be able to trace at least some links with each other if need be, just as having a few cattle placements at a distance brings the possible benefit of richer pastures but runs the risk of owners not knowing of the illicit use or sale of their livestock. In these ways we can see how hiding the cattle and finding a bride, both locally and at a distance, are mutually meaning- ful kinds of exchange. Taking a bride (*ku-hala muche*) means bestowing cattle in the form of bridewealth; hiding cattle means placing them at a homestead from which a bride has been or will perhaps one day be taken.

Moreover, in both cases a balance has to be maintained between acquiring benefits and taking risks. Thus, to take an example, marrying a bride from afar may be a big man's way of forming a long-distance trading alliance, against which must be calculated the undetectable possibility that her homestead is in some way contaminated. Similarly, men hide their cattle for a number of reasons: keeping them away from the persistent demands of agnates and other kin wanting bridewealth or an animal to slaughter at a funeral; distributing them as widely as possible in order to avoid their total loss through any one of the many prevalent cattle diseases; hedging their bets that inadequate rainfall and pasture will not afflict all areas where they have cattle; and helping kin and those desig- nated as kin, who ask to herd cows in order to sell the milk from them, and who may well at a later time be in a position themselves to help the lender. Such advantages as good rain and pasture, and avoiding contagious cattle diseases and covetous kin, are best maximised by hiding the cattle in remote areas. But this also requires considerable trust at a distance, which, unsupervised, may more easily be broken. It is, for instance, a rule that an owner must be informed immediately of the death through illness or accident of one of his animals in a herd managed by another man, in order that he may see for himself that the beast has not been sold or illicitly consumed. But an owner having to travel far to witness the death of an animal may not arrive before the animal has been eaten, as often happens in such cases, and so lacks the complete reassurance that the death is a *bona fide* one.

In short, hiding cattle and arranging marriages reinforce the lateral use of non-agnatic kinship ties: it is not normally with clansmen or agnates that a man places his cattle, and, as I shall explain further in the following chapter on marriage, it is never the case that a man takes a wife from among his own agnates and clan. Both cattle and marriage involve sideways movements, so to speak. On the other hand cattle and other livestock are inherited within agnatic lines and are treated in other ways that constantly remind people of their system of clanship.

Cattle and clans

Most of the land in southern Kilifi District is, or was, Trust Land, that is to say, held in trust for the sole use of its indigenous inhabitants. Other land, especially along the coastal strip, is either State Land or privately owned. It is over the future use of Trust Land that the greatest conflicts between government and ethnic customary views have occurred. At root, these turn on questions concerning the role and destiny of clanship as a form of entitlement.

In the eastern, agricultural area of Giriama country, rights over land and trees became the subject of bitter disputation as the population increased and as it became known, in the nineteen sixties, that the government wished to register and consolidate land. All land in the key, densely populated administrative locations of Kaloleni, Jibana, Chonyi and Rabai has now been registered, with no more than one or two persons within a family recognised as title deed holders. This has certainly altered the view of clanship in these areas, though it has by no means obliterated its significance. For some years yet, clan elders will still be called upon to settle cases of inheritance when no immediate heirs exist. More-over, the recognition of clanship has become more emphasised in those areas containing fewer people and where agriculture is possible, such as Rare. This area, especially along the edges of the river of the same name, has become the home of an increasing number of immigrants who lack adequate land elsewhere. Many of them claim land on the basis of earlier clan settlement occurring two or even three generations back. These claims are for the most part made at the level of local elders and the government chief but not before government officials who have yet to declare their intention of registering the land there too. The scramble and the appeals to clanship (or sub-clanship in many cases) are reminiscent of those which occurred in the early and mid nineteen sixties in Kaloleni and the other areas which have subsequently been registered (Parkin 1972). Since many of the immigrants to Rare are from these populous areas, the result is, as one elder put it to me, that clanship still has plenty of life in it.

In the cattle areas of Giriama country, the importance of clanship is clearly different. We would not expect it to be valued for its access to agricultural land. But, given the right of all herds to graze on unsettled land, we would not expect clan claims to affect pasture land either. After all, as I have explained, herds are made up of the animals of a number of owners who are of different clans. Any one herd is multi-clan in composition, so to speak, and it would seem to be senseless for any one clan which could prove its rights over a section of land to prevent others from grazing their livestock on it. Such a measure would undermine the cross-cutting ties of reciprocity on which the system of hiding cattle is based.

Nevertheless, conflicts between representatives of different clans have occurred. In addition, there has been conflict between many Giriama cattle owners and the government in its attempt to establish group ranching schemes. This, too, has brought to the fore clan claims to pasture. Indeed, the various conflicts are interwoven.

Let me, then, briefly describe the government's long-standing attempt to establish group ranching. This will show the continuing significance of clanship as a concept which both unites and divides Giriama.

A governmental view: 1964–1985 (Case history 2)
It must be emphasised at the outset that government advocates of the ranch scheme, which goes back in its primary form to colonial days, are usually unaware of the way the Giriama hide cattle or how important this is to them as an ecological and social system. A report of 1964 (Kenya Coast Province Annual Report 1964, Ministry of Agriculture and Animal Husbandry) refers to a 100,000 stock owned by a 'small number of people' being let out to the 'mass of the Duruma' (Mijikenda neighbours of the Giriama), who as 'caretakers', are allowed to use the milk from the cattle, the progeny of which however belong to the owners. The report remarks on the tendency of herders to over-milk cows to the detriment of their calves, so causing 'the progressive degradation of the stock'. The report correctly pin-points the strong element of clientage in the system, in which a few large herd-owners flourish through the labour of herders who either lack herds altogether or have only small ones.

What the report does not perceive, however, is the dynamic element of the system by which herders may become large herd owners, whose wealth may nevertheless be lost within a couple of generations through the subdivision of herds to the many sons of many wives on inheritance. The system is not, then, one of self-perpetuating classes of owners and clients. Secondly, no account is taken in the report of the reasons for hiding cattle and the advantage of variable pasture, rainfall and independence from kin that are gained from the practice. None of this is to deny the obvious fact that the system involves at any one time the use of the labour of many for the few, but the redistributional nature of the system also means that the few and the many are constantly changing. Finally, the report gives the impression that herders are prepared to extract milk from cows regardless of the effects on calves and on the size and well-being of the herd. In practice, the reverse is the case, for, from the viewpoint of the herder, the larger the herd the more his supply of milk for sale. On the other hand, it may well be that, in harsh grazing conditions, the quality of herds may suffer while herders are reluctant to reduce their size.

In any event, the government wished to alter this traditional method of cattle dispersal by introducing the idea of forming 'small co-operative ranches, on a clan or co-operative basis. Each ranch must have a registered title and its own permanent water supply'. Information on clan and sublocation areas was then collected with a view to carrying out a pilot scheme in 1965. The idea was that small ranches of this type, set within demarcated areas of land, would make for more individual control within each of the size of herds and of the state of pasture. Inevitably, a necessary implication was that the cattle from other ranches would not be able to graze on pasture that was not their own.

Since the area of each proposed ranch was to be the land 'owned' by a clan, many Giriama believed that the measure would have had the further effect of favouring those clans which had plenty of, or especially good, grazing land. The proposal, when it was made to the Giriama of Kayafungo in a meeting at Gotani in 1968, was therefore opposed, especially by those cattle owners and herders who could not claim much clan land of their own and who depended on the communal right of access to all grazing land. Others opposed the scheme, including those whose clan lands were extensive, out of fear that defaulters on loans given to develop the individual plots would be obliged to sell their land to outsiders, 'Kikuyu or other up-country people', as had happened to registered land plots in the eastern and coastal agricultural area.

A second government proposal was for a much larger co-operative ranch scheme. The two other kinds of ranch established in other parts of Kilifi District, individually owned and private company ranches, were not considered feasible in the Kayafungo area, in view of the difficulties there of re-allocating, and, in some cases of withholding and compensating, clan land owners. But the large co-operative ranches were thought more suitable for existing areas of settlement. The intention in 1974 was, and still is, to establish a large central grazing area, 910,720 hectares in the case of Kayafungo group ranch. Land adjudication was carried out in order to ensure that settlers would receive equivalent holdings outside the ranch and to register the ranch itself, after which it would be eligible for government loans to build cattle dips. People were to live around the grazing area of the ranch, farming as before and grazing their own cattle in the customary manner in the now reduced pastures available. Within the co-operative ranch itself would graze the central herd of cattle specially selected by livestock officers for their grade and species and jointly paid for by members of the co-operative.

Even by 1978 the scheme had not got off the ground. The drought in the Kilifi hinterland which began in about 1968 continued, causing the death both of the few cattle which had been bought for the central herd and of some people's own herds. Nor was the government happy with what it later thought was a membership largely made up of herders who owned few cattle of their own, reflecting the government misconceptions concerning the Giriama system of hiding cattle to which I have referred above. Moreover, even with this larger co-operative ranch, many local people expressed their earlier fear that its failure might mean fragmentation and sale to outsiders. The cattle dips have been constructed through money jointly raised by government and the people and are working satisfactorily, giving benefit at least to individual herds, but there had been no success up to 1985 in collecting funds to buy the central, communally owned herd.

Again, conflicts have prompted protest. Following a land dispute with a neighbour, one large cattle owner opposed the first but supported the second government scheme provided his own cattle were entitled to use the ranch. He did not have much land of his own clan and could only benefit from access to a much enlarged area of pasture. The dispute in Gotani in which he became involved concerned the land accommodating his huge settlement of some fifty dwellings and many cattle byres. He is of the Nzaro clan but the land, like much in the Gotani area, is owned by the Mweni clan. The senior Mweni resident in Gotani demanded that the Nzaro large cattle owner pay a substantial annual rent for the use of the land. The Nzaro cattle man countered by claiming that the land had been settled by his own father and had never been within the Mweni area. The area was outside that which the government had adjudicated for purposes of the ranch and would have had to undergo separate adjudication, a long and costly affair. The case was in the process of being judged by local elders by way of a compromise, when the Mweni claimant died of a heart attack. As far as I know, no open accusation of witchcraft was made, and the matter has been discreetly left by his successor, a younger brother in his sixties. There are other cases of clan leaders seeking to demarcate territory in this way and to secure significant compensation from users.

The ranch scheme has clearly had the effect both of shuffling people into different areas and of highlighting long-standing but unresolved grievances of clan land ownership. Of the 21 cattle owners in Gotani, 14 are settled on their own clan land where they can keep some at least of their herd, if they wish. There have been a couple of attempts by cattle owners to buy the land on which they live. There is in other words a tendency for cattle owners to own also their homestead site, whether through clanship entitlement or through purchase. This would seem to suggest the wish for a balance between clan-based security of land tenure and fluid, territorially dispersed relationships: cattle may be hidden with the latter or kept close by in the homestead, and can be moved from one to the other as needs be.

Case implications

While non-agnatic kinship and affinity is seen by Giriama as an attribute of all relationships among them, though of variable strength, clanship is clearly viewed as immutable essence. Despite some slight but growing differences in, say, the recitation of clan names, the overarching distinction between one clan and another and between sub-clans provides a ready-made framework within which claims for land are made.

Cattle are in a sense themselves divided into clans. Their placement with other herds is marked by the differences of kinship which come from clan distinctions. More than this, owners use cattle brands which usually continue, even today, to denote their clanship. Formerly, cattle carried the brand of a particular clan, consisting of an emblem. That of the Ziro clan for example, was as shown in Diagram 1b. Nowadays this is rarely used. Instead individual owners will use a brand which depicts their own clan name. In other words, they depict in the one brand their clanship and their individuality. Thus, Mulande Wanje is the clan name of an owner of a small herd who is of the Ziro clan. His brand is alphabetic rather than emblematic and presents his clan name initials, M W, as shown in Diagram 1a.

A few owners have broken away from this continued use of clanship and brand their cattle with personal rather than clan names, as in the case of Karisa Kambi, who uses as his brand his 'Mission' name of Jeremiah Kambi in the simple form of J-K.

Such departures underline the tension between the need to retain a system of clan identification in order to claim or retain land, and the wish at times to dilute the claims of clansmen on such moveable property as livestock. As a former urban wage migrant, Karisa Kambi's herd had been largely purchased, rather than built up during a career as herdsman at the centre of collective obligations, and he wished to indicate that he had acquired the animals 'through his own efforts', as he put it. Urban wage labour is often contrasted in this way as being more 'individualistic' than such community-based rural occupations as herdsman, palm-wine tapper, diviner-doctor, and even agricultural farmer.

The tension is evident also in the method by which animals themselves are identified. On the one hand a man's cattle carry on their flanks their owner's initials, usually including his clan membership. On the other hand, a complex use of colour and pattern terms identify each animal precisely, stressing their individuality. (A list of some of them is included in Appendix 3.) No two animals in a herd are referred to by the same name. While fellow clansmen can come to know the identity of a herd through its brand, which they can recognise as one of

Diagram 1. Two cattle brands

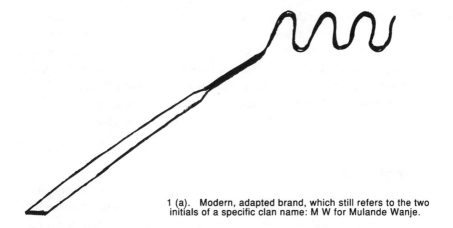

1 (a).   Modern, adapted brand, which still refers to the two
initials of a specific clan name: M W for Mulande Wanje.

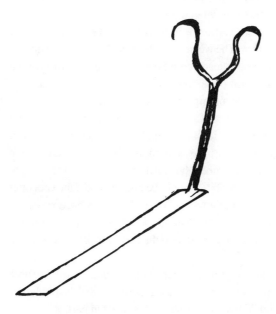

1 (b).   Traditional brand for all Ziro clan, of whom Mulande Wanje is a member.
The Ziro include blacksmiths who make cattle brands for anyone seeking their custom.

their own, it is only the owner, his herdsman, and a small number of other trusted kin, who know the names or precise specifications of each animal in the herd. Such names do not by themselves give anonymity to the animals of a herd, for their distinctive brand can identify them. But they act as a secret code and so enable the owner to communicate swiftly with the herdsman and, should he wish, move particular animals from one herd to another or prepare them for sale or sacrifice. The names do, in short, facilitate the owner's control of his herd more rapidly than would be the case if agnates and fellow clansmen were easily able to intercept information about the whereabouts of the herd and the owner's intentions concerning it.

Controlling the homestead

Hiding the cattle is therefore an attempt to keep the demands of clanship at bay, while their use in marriage payments between clans gives value to clanship, as well as to affinity and marriage itself. Cattle and women link clans in this way, with heifers making up most of the bridewealth and women moving in the opposite direction from a natal to a husband's home. Herding cattle cannot be done from small homesteads: the larger the herd, the larger the homestead. The larger the homestead the greater the number of marriage alliances with different clans centred on it and, in geometric ratio, the more complex the management of homestead relationships becomes. The western cattle area of Giriama country is then noted both for its larger homesteads compared with the eastern farming zone, and for its particular problems of personal conduct within homesteads.

In the eastern area, major disputes among co-resident householders are simply resolved by one party moving off away from the other to found a new though smaller homestead. The precipitating idiom in which this is done is witchcraft accusations. The recent registration of individual plots of land in the east in the name of one or two senior family members has further encouraged the trend to small residential units. Land is not mobile, cannot be hidden, and, since coconut palms and other trees require limited attention once they have become established, can be farmed almost as well by half a dozen people as by three times that number. Alternatively, hired labour can be bought and laid off according to seasonal need.

Cattle by contrast require attention all the year round. Being easily divisible and moveable between different areas they can, as I have described, be hidden by the owner even from members of his own homestead, at least in part.

Surely, the potential tension over access to such elusive property should also give rise to witchcraft accusations. As I have indicated, the Giriama themselves claim that adultery with brothers' wives, a kind of incest, is a more common problem in the large cattle homesteads than witchcraft. My own impression is that witchcraft accusations, being often only resolvable among the Giriama through the separation of the disputants, are indeed relatively inhibited within a cattle homestead by the need on the part of its members to remain together for herding purposes and until the death of the homestead head: thereafter brothers of a homestead may be obliged to live together until outstanding cattle bride-wealth obligations have been settled among them. Even between homesteads witchcraft accusations appear to be less common, on the one hand perhaps because the greater distance between homesteads, averaging a kilometre in Gotani, reduces the intensity of interaction among the same people, and on the other because frequent conflict between homesteads would require the disputants constantly to withdraw their cattle from each other. Hiding one's property with a man of another homestead depends on mutual trust and imposes constraints on their views of each other. Given that cattle are hidden among clans with whom marriages have been contracted, cattle-linked men try to curb the possibility of separation and divorce and to regulate closely the lives of married couples in their homesteads.

Adulterous incest therefore figures more prominently as a concern and an alleged attribute of life in the western cattle area. I repeat that, although I have cases of witchcraft and incest in the eastern and western areas, my interest is in the widespread Giriama characterisation of the two zones, rather than in trying to measure objectively how far it is true. In other words, I share and understand the Giriama impression of a difference along these lines, and seek its implications.

A main implication is the sanctity of the large homestead in the western cattle area. Cattle owners and herders themselves are opposed to sub-dividing homesteads just as they have opposed the government over the division of pasture land into smaller and mutually exclusive plots. They themselves, and people living outside the cattle area, jokingly speak of the very large homesteads as modern equivalents of the traditional Giriama capital or Kaya of Kayafungo. The Giriama are historically aware that Kayafungo once accommodated a large proportion of the Giriama people, in the manner described by Brantley and Spear. They recognise that the Kaya itself has and had powerful political as well as ritual significance, and they point to the large cattle homesteads as nowadays acting as political bases for those who oppose the government ranching schemes. While the comparison is only jokingly made, we can see that the elders of the Kaya itself base their modern political influence on their control of oaths, ritual, and customary knowledge, while the major cattle owners base theirs on their wealth in cattle and on clients with whom they have placed cattle and have inter-married. The Kaya elders, who do not have many cattle, and the big cattle owners thus complement each other as parts of a greater power complex and are together represented in Giriama thought through the idea of huge dwellings, past and present respectively.

The idea of a large central place as at the root of Giriama political affairs has therefore been partially transposed from the formerly large Kaya to the currently few huge cattle homesteads, leaving the Kaya itself as the sacred centre. There is also a sense of continuity. In the past a new Kaya would be built following changes in Giriama migration, settlement and political leadership, producing an image of successive capitals, a couple of which might briefly co-exist. Today, also, there are a limited number of very large homesteads which play key roles in the internal and external representation of Giriama matters, and which rise up anew every generation or so. They are not all in the cattle area, for there is the case of the famous doctor Kabwere Wanje whose village of 166 wives and dependents near Malindi must be the largest under one head throughout the coastal area. But large homesteads tend to be located in the west, and even Kabwere Wanje associated himself with the Kaya there, as has been mentioned in the previous chapter.

In other Bantu languages in Africa the term *kaya* commonly refers to an ordinary village or homestead and not to an especially large one or to a capital as among the Giriama, among whom the term for an ordinary homestead other than the Kaya is *mudzi*. Among the Digo, a Mijikenda grouping which once had a proliferation of competing capitals, no such difference is made and the term *kaya* refers to large and small dwellings alike. The Digo usage appears to be closer to an archetypal Bantu notion of residence which does not distinguish between dwellings on the basis of size or importance (see Beidelman 1986: 53). Etymologically, then, as well as organisationally and conceptually, there is elision between large and small, and customary and modern ideas of central places.

At this point I can describe in more detail the area of Miyani in which I worked and which includes two very large homesteads, which I have already mentioned. The area of thirty-eight homesteads is one roughly demarcated as a neighbourhood by the Giriama with whom I lived, but otherwise it has no clear boundaries. I cannot know how representative of other such neighbourhoods it is. It does, however, share the general Giriama preference for local endogamy, and so is an unbounded unit within which most people marry and hide cattle, while a few do so outside. It has moreover the significance to which I have referred of being close to the Kaya. The aim of my description is to show in what sense large herd ownership and complex homestead management go together.

Surviving and thriving: the people of Miyani
At the southern end of Miyani is Gotani trading centre, so-called, which consists of one poorly stocked shop selling soap, matches, lamp oil and soft drinks, and the office of the chief of Kayafungo location. No one lives at the centre itself. It stands at the junction of roads which are usable throughout most of the year except during the rains and before repair, and which lead north to Bamba, south to Mariakani and east to Kaloleni. Much of the land radiating out from it for a distance of a few kilometres in each direction is claimed by the Mweni clan. To the east of the trading centre there is also a largish area belonging to the Nzaro

clan. Seven other clans also claim to have settled areas of their own. Overall, however, people speaking generally will refer to most of the area nearest to Gotani as Mweni land. The area in which I worked is bounded by valleys on all but its northwestern side (see Map 2), with the seasonal Nderu river running through the eastern one. The 38 neighbouring homesteads which I surveyed are about half of those within this area and stand to the north and west of the trading centre itself.

Of the 38 homesteads, 16 are built on their own clan land (14 of which are headed by cattle owners, as mentioned above). The other 22 (comprising only 7 cattle owners) are on the land of clans other than their own, though in fifteen cases the links are of marriage and close kinship. A couple of homesteads have now purchased their land, in one case in response to an appeal from the owner who needed money for bridewealth. The pattern of land occupancy is rather like that of cattle holdings: more people live on the land of clans other than their own. In the cattle area it is indeed still the tendency for new migrants to seek out non-agnatic kin for permission to settle on their land. There are however signs that the dominant Mweni clan may wish to capitalise on its extensive land holdings, a not surprising development in the light both of the registration of land in eastern Giriama country and of the recent albeit failed government attempts to set up ranching schemes on the basis of clan holdings in the west.

Although 17 of the 38 homesteads stand on Mweni land, only 5 are themselves of this clan, the senior member of which is therefore a kind of landlord of the other twelve homesteads. This senior Mweni member is attempting to charge substantial cash rentals to 5 occupants of Mweni land, instead of the customary much less valuable tribute of minor livestock every year or so. It remains to be seen whether the other non-Mweni occupants of Mweni land will also be expected to pay. The new development flies in the face of the convention that marriage and kinship provide the ties that migrants to a new area use in seeking new settlement.

The remaining 33 non-Mweni homesteads are distributed among 15 clans. In other words the neighbourhood comprises a diverse range of clanship. Among the Giriama as a whole there are some 26 self-named clans, though, as I explain in Appendix 4, this number could be reduced to 21 according to how we define a clan: there are at least 21 exogamous units, a few of which can, however, inherit wives from each other without being allowed to intermarry. For my present purposes, the simple point I wish to make is that, as is the case elsewhere in Giriama country, neighbourhoods are made up of a large proportion of the total number of possible exogamous units.

As I have mentioned before, Giriama clans are divided into six sections which were probably all themselves once exogamous and which Spear calls clans (1978: 6). I include a list in Appendix 4. The Milulu section remains exogamous, its three clans of Mboro, Mbogo and Shungu being allowed to inherit widows but not to intermarry. The same situation applies to two of the three clans of Parwa section (Nguma and Kiwe). In the Milalani section (not often nowadays referred to as such), two of the five clans, Kiringi and Dundu, are similarly treated. The three sections, Milulu, Parwa and Kiza, are often spoken of as if they were corporate units. Having carried the protective *fingo* or *ngiriama* stone from Singwaya, Kiza does in fact have special ritual significance in the Kaya, which, it may be remembered, it itself divided into six areas, one allotted to each section. At least one, and not more than two, extremely aged elders should represent each of the six sections at the Kaya, at least by visiting occasionally if not permanently residing there.

There is some clustering of homesteads from two sections, one of which includes the major landholders, the Mweni clan. Otherwise there is a reasonable distribution of both clans and sections in what is after all a small neighbourhood. Only two or three of the homesteads drawn from a single clan stand alone as a result of fission from a neighbour in the last generation or so. The rest have come as a result of having kinship and clan links in the area beforehand. They have migrated mainly during the early part of this century from even more westerly and northwesterly areas of Giriama country, such as Silaloni.

Although the Mweni are by far the largest landholders, they are not the wealthiest in cattle. Two of the five Mweni homesteads own cattle, one of them having a substantial herd (Salim Katana). The biggest cattle man of the area (Kushonga Zungi of the Nzaro clan) does himself live on Mweni land, and, as I explained earlier, has been involved in disputes with the senior Mweni elder over it. He has also been attempting to buy surrounding land. The other very large cattle owner does live on his own land (Kanyala Mdigo of the Ngari clan). This mixed pattern of land and cattle ownership explains why the Mweni elder should demand compensation for the use of his extensive land by successful cattle owners. But he is also restrained, as are any landowners who might wish to copy him, by the cross-cutting network of cattle hiding and marriage alliances between clans on which so many depend, including the two Mweni cattle owners. In short, the attempt to impose precisely calculated exchange value on land in the cattle area of Gotani would probably promote more conflict between interlinked homesteads than the highly tuned system of cattle distribution could bear. It would be to impose land values emanating from the agricultural east to the dominant cattle ecology of the west.

One result of the tension, however, is for the larger, wealthier cattle homesteads to emphasise their communal strength. Although each such homestead head hides many of his cattle, fellow members of his homestead characteristically approve of this customary tactic. As competing agnates, they see it as safeguarding the herd against what might be their own uncontrolled demands on it.

All homesteads consist of agnates, linked by not more than three generations. Remarkably few non-agnatic kin and affines live in these homesteads, though they may visit for extended periods of many months in some cases. A typical

Map 2. Gotani and Miyani

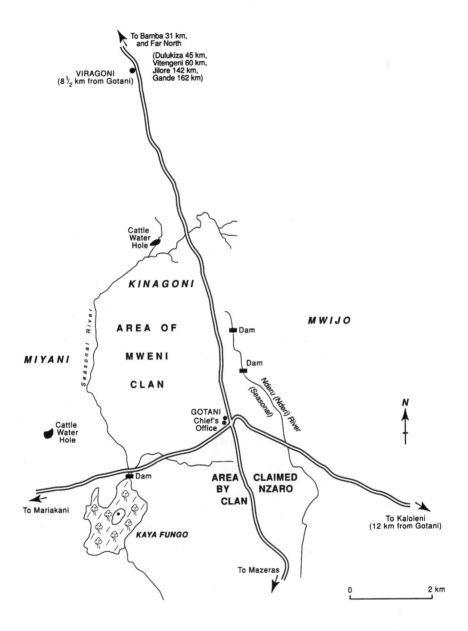

homestead is simply made up of a man, one or two married brothers, and their children, including married sons. The long-term non-agnatic visitors commonly include a widowed sister of the homestead head, together with her son, who reciprocally calls the head mother's brother (*ahu*), and his wife and children. They are not numerous and are regarded as minor clients of the head, who may find them land to settle or may employ them in cattle-herding or farming.

Of 28 homesteads for which I have full data, 15 are based on cattle-keeping and consist of an average of more than 27 persons, including 15 adults and more than 12 children. The 13 non-cattle homesteads average a size of fewer than 13 persons, including 8 adults and 5 children. As well as being more than twice as large, therefore, cattle-based homesteads have a far higher proportion of children to adults than those without cattle. We may recall here the aim of many homestead heads to build up a herd in order to marry off sons who are, as yet, still young. A homestead including many children is also in the best position to provide an apprentice cattle herdsman, who, later, may well be able to turn his skills to building up his own herd in due course. Heads of cattle homesteads have a larger number of wives. In addition, their homesteads have a larger proportion of married women to men, 8.5 to 6.5 on average, compared with a proportion of 4 women to 4.25 men in homesteads lacking cattle. Overall, then, there is a clear syndrome of wealth in cattle, wives and children, and a large number of co-resident, agnatic worker-dependents. By contrast, those lacking cattle live in smaller homesteads, and have fewer wives and children.

To some extent this difference corresponds to contrasting stages of the life-cycle of a homestead, as I have already suggested. That is to say, many heads lacking cattle once had them but used them to marry off younger brothers and sons, while those now wealthy in cattle will in due course discharge similar obligations and intentionally allow their herd to dwindle in size.

This explanation cannot, however, account entirely for the sometimes considerable contrasts in cattle wealth. The cases of the two big cattle men, of the Nzaro and Ngari clans respectively, are of individuals who, as I suggested above, have taken on political roles and have built up homesteads which are central places of regional importance and are regarded as the modern counterpart to the Kaya. This is not to say that within a generation or two following their deaths, their wealth and homesteads may not be dissipated. This, after all, has been the pattern so far among the Giriama, even in this century, for the fragmentation of wealth and political loyalty still precludes the formation of family dynasties. Nevertheless, their significance as markers of present possibilities is considerable. Not only are they seen to be politically effective, even against government in its attempt to establish ranching schemes, but they are regarded as reconfirming core Giriama ideas of Kaya-like largesse. Their personal dramas are publicly discussed, not as examples of what happens to less prominent individuals, but as instances of the furthermost possibilities of Giriama being: they strive within a modern cash economy, yet do so through ecological means and appeals to corporate clanship which pre-date that economy.

It is the dramas of such persons that help create the stereotypes of the cattle-keeping area of Giriama country. Thus, one of the two men, let us call him Nzaro, now has six wives, all of them married from near or within the Gotani area. He is now in his mid sixties. His ambition, people say, was always to have many children. But for much of his life his first two wives produced only two, both sons, who have survived to adulthood. He now has four other children, ranging in age from a few years to the early teens. This is not regarded as a large number for a man of his wealth and seniority, nor, indeed, as satisfying his own ambitions. Particularly galling, it is said, is the fact that his eldest son, a man of less than forty years of age, has himself three fecund wives and six children and so will almost certainly have more children than his own father during the latter's lifetime. Given the normal mixture of concern and rivalry between fathers and adult married sons, this reinforces the ambiguity between the two men: the father wished to have many sons who would continue his name, but did he wish, before his own death, that one of his sons would, so to speak, achieve this ambition on his behalf? People then ask what prevented the old man's wives from producing children in those earlier years? Was it the effects of *mavingane* and *vitio*? The homestead is, after all, immensely large and increases the possibilities of incestuous adultery between men and the wives of their agnates.

Although these questions of causation are raised in this manner at the present time as if the homestead had always been large, there is also a contrary version which points to witchcraft as an earlier cause. The original, much smaller family homestead nearby is known to have split some years back after the death of the original founder, the father of Nzaro. The founder's brother assumed the head-ship but soon came into conflict with his nephew, Nzaro, the son of his brother. Nzaro accused his father's brother of causing his wives' barrenness through witchcraft and set up his own homestead, even forsaking the clan land on which the original homestead stands. Nzaro built up his herds but was still unlucky with children, many of whom died, and despite acquiring more wives.

It is of course common for explanations of misfortune to vary both among people and according to time and place. Here, we see the apparent inconsistency as providing an alternative to the widely held view that incestuous adultery prevails over witchcraft in the western cattle area. It is rather that witchcraft accusations may predominate at a stage in the lifetime of a homestead when it is small and may even precipitate its fragmentation; and that incestuous adultery becomes the main fear should a homestead survive or thrive beyond that stage and become large. Both are used to explain the worst fate befalling a man or woman, namely to lack children or to lose those they have. Questions of fertility are at the root of their explanatory use.

This takes us into Giriama ideas of value: fertility is intrinsically important for the pleasure of having children and the ancestral memory eventually bestowed through them, but fertility also ensures that homesteads are large enough for the labour required in terms of cattle-herders.

Conclusion

'Hiding' cattle, and dispersing them as bridewealth, both create and operate through kin and affines. At any one point in time it is these non-agnatic, non-clan relationships which are here most likely to be manipulated and so sustained. One could be forgiven for wondering whether clanship, which is otherwise regarded so importantly, by men in particular, is struggling for survival in the face of these evidently useful non-lineal relationships. Already, Giriama regard clanship as having been undermined in the agricultural east through, among other things, the registration of land in the name of individuals rather than clans. Even in the west, where wealth in cattle prevails over that in land, strong herd-owners challenge the authority of land-holding clans. Yet clanship survives.

Giriama men and women speak of the value of the clan in separating humans from animals. Humans know how to relate to each other through clanship, while animals, lacking clans, are unaware of the sin of incest and mate indiscriminately. Clans thus confer on humans their personal and collective identity. More pragmatically, it enables one to place a stranger one meets in terms of his or her generational and genealogical relationship to oneself. It helps people create and maintain personal contacts throughout Giriama country, some of which in certain localities may still be used to secure land and settlement.

Giriama use the contrast between the eastern and western areas of their country to give further weight to the value of clanship: the Kaya in the west is organised on the basis of clanship and reflects the corporate ethos of the surrounding homesteads; the east is fragmented, with clan entitlement to land allegedly becoming less relevant, and with people beginning to know less of clan identities.

Stable marriages are, however, said to be the key to firm lines of clanship. There is less divorce in the west than in the east, but the rate is low in both areas. The difference is exaggerated in the reluctance of western men to marry eastern women, whom they regard as incapable of surviving for long in the hard conditions of the cattle area. Indeed, few eastern women who marry into the west do remain there. Their 'escape' from the west back to the east, and the fact that the difference between the two ecological zones enables women to trade between them, raises the question of how much women are or are not controlled by men.

In the other direction, eastern men often value western women for their reputation as customarily hard-working and obedient. In the competition for such women as wives, however, eastern men are disadvantaged compared to western men, for they may need first to convert cash into the cattle required for bridewealth and may lack the local ties that lead to introductions to possible brides.

Yet a few such marriages do occur, which, because they are stable, provide some on-going connections between the two zones. Overall, however, marriage is localised in the west, as it is in the east, so serving to perpetuate the easterners' image of the west as separate and remote from an east which is increasingly involved in non-Giriama relationships and ideas. It is an image to which westerners themselves subscribe, for they do indeed speak of themselves as being closer to the heart of Giriama tradition, as sharing by association as well as in practice in the purity of the Kaya.

4

From west to east: the works of marriage

The blessed and the unblessed

In the old days, women would not leave their husbands because they would have been blessed (*ku-haswa*) at their marriages. This is like being given an oath, for if a wife did leave her husband for another man, she would die or would never be able to have children. But nowadays many marry in a Christian church and so do not get blessed, and that is why more women leave their husbands.

This view of a changing situation was expressed by an old man raised in the cattle area but many years resident in the coastal palm belt, who saw the difference between the two areas as responsible for the change: with traditional marital stability still a characteristic of the pastoralist west, and recent instability that of the farming east.

From the cattle area cases are given which provide another perspective on blessed marriages: a man who follows the customary procedure of approaching a girl's parents for her hand and whose father takes a gift of palm wine for preliminary negotiations concerning bridewealth(*hunda*), has a fruitful marriage which becomes blessed in the course of the customary bridewealth payments; another man who simply chooses a girl from a group of dancers at a funeral but does not consult either his own or her parents, does not have a blessed marriage and so remains childless.

Such examples can always be given to justify the importance of customary procedure. But the distinction between formally arranged marriages and those resulting from elopement is certainly over-drawn, for funeral dances are one of the main ways in which young men and women meet each other. Even if they do insist on their own choice of partner, it is still impossible for them to marry or live together without bridewealth being paid to the girl's family, a ceremonialised transaction which must involve the groom's father or senior agnate in at least the capacity of negotiator or witness, regardless of whether the groom actually raises the money for the bridewealth himself.

The view from the coast reveals an anxiety that wives may run off. That from the cattle area touches on worries that young men and their brides may not respect the wishes of elders in their marriage choices. The first concerns men's control over women, and the latter concerns older men's control over younger men. Both are related, for it is through older men's control over the amount and disposition of bridewealth transactions that women's principal status as providers of children is assured. But while it is important for this status quo that fathers continue to control their sons, the possibility of women's independence from men is the most threatening. Without women's subordination or at least compliance, the system by which women move from their natal home to their husband's and produce children for him and his agnatic line would collapse.

It is small wonder, then, that men and their parents talk so much about the character of a prospective bride. In both the cattle and the coastal areas most marriages are localised, a preference justified by the possibility of having been able to observe a neighbour's daughter at first hand. As well as surveying her personality in this way, and such other attributes as her capacity for hard work, the view from the next village ascertains whether the girl's family suffer from disease, from difficulties in having children, including *vitio*, as well as from other misfortunes.

However, in one of the many comparisons people from both the cattle and coastal areas make between marriage in their respective areas, one view is forcibly made. Separation, which leads automatically to divorce through the return of bridewealth without deduction, is higher the closer one is to the coast, while in the cattle area it is rare.

Facts and fanciful reasoning are undoubtedly mixed here, and yet certain aspects of these claims can be measured. First, as I was able to show in a previous study, the Giriama divorce rate in the palm belt is of a middle range compared with a number of other African societies. But this rate would be much lower if failed marriages occurring during the first year were excluded. Beyond the first year, marriages tend to remain intact for a whole lifetime (1972: 69–71).

The problems afflicting the first year of marriage in the coastal palm belt largely arise from the fact that bridewealth takes the form of cash, the amount of which may have been agreed in the negotiations before the marriage, but which is often spent on such other necessary contingencies as sudden and serious illness, or on funerals which have to be lavishly staged for a deceased family member, or on school fees in an area where education is becoming increasingly valued. Sometimes the cash bridewealth received from a daughter's or sister's marriage is used to purchase land, palms, or other trees which have just come on the market. This money may already have been promised for another marriage, which has already been agreed and for which an initial payment has been made, so allowing the couple to live together as man and wife. Its use, therefore, for other purposes invariably prompts the girl's angry father to demand her return and her marriage to some other suitor. There are even cases of marriages being terminated in their early stages by fathers accepting higher bids of bridewealth for their daughters. Recognising that their natal homes are a lifetime refuge of last resort, most girls are reluctant to go against the wishes of their fathers, and so comply with these manoeuvres, which are clearly made possible by the multi-purpose convertibility of cash.

By contrast, in the cattle area it is heifers that usually make up all or most of the bridewealth. Unlike cash, cattle cannot suddenly be spent on immediate contingencies. They are hidden in different areas and locked into a system of reciprocal herding and caring responsibilities, and can only be released for bridewealth after slow deliberation. The men who herd one's cattle tend to be kin or affines, as explained in chapter three. Withdrawing one's cattle from them is, then, a delicate matter, not to be undertaken hastily and without grace. Indeed, it is only if the owner suspects theft and mismanagement that he will retrieve them swiftly, a rare though obvious act of hostility that will mar or end the relationship.

Schools are fewer in the cattle area and fees therefore less of a drain, though funerals are just as lavish and medical expenses as great. But whereas cash in the palm belt is not specially earmarked for any of these forms of expenditure and so is 'consumed' as each need arises, cattle in the west are kept in reserve, at least for the purpose of bridewealth, and so are in this sense protected. In any event, the dispersal of a man's cattle in different areas, coupled with the reluctance of Giriama to withdraw their cattle rapidly and their skilful curtailment of localised outbreaks of cattle disease, enables him to draw upon them from a number of possible sources should he need to do so. Cattle are not an easily moveable form of capital and, under modern conditions of animal health care, are for this reason more secure than cash.

These factors enable owners to control the disposition of their herds at a pace that can be agreed on between marrying families. Fewer fathers therefore default in their payments during the first and successive years and so few marriages break up for this or other reasons.

The difference in divorce rates between the cattle and palm zones is quite startling. In the Kaloleni palm area fifty-three out of 204 marriages of persons still living had ended in divorce, with thirty-six ending in the death of a spouse (Parkin 1972: 70). This was in the mid 1960s, since when the divorce rate seems to have risen still further. Even allowing for the fact that, after the first year, marriages in the palm area are much more stable than these figures suggest, the contrast with the cattle area is still glaring. There, in the mid 1980s, only thirteen or 7 per cent of 182 marriages had ended in divorce, with nine ending in death.

What about the claim from both sides of the palm curtain that cattle men are reluctant to marry women from the coastal area? Again, there appears to be truth in this. Only twenty-four of the 182 cattle-area marriages, less than one in seven, were with women from the palm zone, while ninety, that is a half, were between spouses drawn from local homesteads within a radius of five kilometres. The remaining forty marriages were with other homesteads also in the cattle area but beyond a distance of five kilometres. Given the distance of on average one kilometre between homesteads, even these non-local marriages include many that are with cattle-keeping families who know each other on a fairly regular basis. Localised endogamy is also a feature of the palm zone (Parkin 1972: 72), and an even smaller proportion of women from the cattle area are married by coastal men, explained by both sides as due to reluctance by fathers in the cattle area to release their daughters, who are needed for relationships of marriage alliance in their natal area.

The picture we have, then, is of two contrasting ecological areas within each of which families practise a high degree of local endogamy but rarely marry across the ecological boundary. The usual reason given, that coastal women cannot stand the harsh conditions of cattle country and have been corrupted by the allegedly easier conditions and possibilities of female independence offered at the coast, is in Giriama eyes borne out by the fact that seven of the thirteen divorces in the Miyani sample involved coastal women. Putting this another way, nearly a third of all marriages with coastal women (seven out of twenty-four or 29 per cent) have ended in divorce, which is much higher than the 7 per cent of all marriages in the Miyani sample. Such divorces stand out as evidence of the frailty of marriage with coastal women. In fact, since only two of the divorces in the sample as a whole concern local marriages, the contrast that Giriama from both areas make between a coast full of independently aspiring women and the cattle zone as made up of stable marriages linking local homesteads is certainly seen by them to be given substance.

Moving east
If so few marriages occur across the ecological boundary and indeed much beyond a few kilometres, how is it that the Giriama can locate kin and affines so easily all over the extensive area that they occupy? Why is it that their relationships are not each more heavily confined to their respective ecological areas?

That Giriama from different ecological areas are in fact in easy communication is the result of migration. In Miyani no homestead has been in its present position for more than three generations, and most have been there for considerably less. The same applies to the coastal palm area. The pattern is for younger and usually disaffected sons and brothers habitually to move away from their natal area to another one at some distance, quite often in a different ecological area. But they will only make such a move after they have married, usually with bridewealth provided by a father or elder brother from the proceeds of a sister's marriage, and have children and therefore recognised status. The usual procedure prior to migrating to another area is to contact a member of their mother's clan, a real or classificatory mother's brother for instance, or of their father's mother's clan, and to ask for land on which to settle in the new area, a practice known as *ku-rombeka*.

During the last three generations, that is to say since the ending of the so-called Chembe war, or Giriama rebellion, of 1914, there have been two main patterns of migration. First, most of the migration across ecological boundaries has been in one direction: from the inland west and north to the more fertile, agricultural coastal areas, such as Kaloleni (see notes 1, 2 and 3 to chapter one). Second, there has been movement within ecological areas. Within the coastal zone people move from one farming area to another, sometimes so close to the coast that they become involved in the third ecology, that of fishing. Away from the coastal districts and within the hinterland, however, there has been extensive migration from the remoter inland northern areas, where neither cattle-keeping nor farming is easily carried out, to those of Gotani and Bamba. In my area of Miyani, near Gotani, none of the thirty or so homesteads originally came from the eastern, coastal areas. They stem instead either from the inland north or from areas to the west of Gotani, in the latter case bringing in their trail a network of marriage ties with the people called the Duruma, a Mijikenda group living in Kwale district.

It is partly the great shift in population from north and west to the coastal east over the last seventy years or so that gives places like Gotani and Bamba (and also northern areas like Mwangea and Jilore) their reputation, according to Giriama, for traditional authenticity. It is the land of grandfathers and great-grandfathers and so deemed to be closer to the historical origins of custom. The proximity of the Kaya gives the Gotani area of the west a special place in this sense of history.

The claim that Gotani men rarely marry wives raised in the eastern palm belt because of their tendency to run back to their natal homes, is certainly consistent with the facts. Yet the claim has further significance. It reinforces and justifies the believed distinctiveness of the western hinterland, regarded as a place where Giriama authenticity can only be perpetuated through marriages arranged exclusively within the area. In other words, the west represents pure custom and this purity can only be preserved through western marriages secured through the traditional exchange of cattle. This, at least, is how the reasoning goes.

Yet, families have for two or three generations been abandoning this alleged haven of uncontaminated Giriama identity in favour of the more fertile land and more reliable rainfall of the eastern zone, where Muslim, Giriama and other Mijikenda identities mix. Such migrants to the east usually lack adequate cattle, leaving behind them those rich in herds and those confident that their present lack or losses will be followed by better fortunes, and that wealth and poverty commonly alternate with the generations.

There is, then, a distinction between poor families who renounce the cattle-keeping west for the fertile east and those families who take a longer-term view of the cyclical nature of wealth and remain in the west, possibly moving around within it. The cyclical, longer-term generational view is thus quite consistent with notions of Giriama customary purity as historically rooted in the west and inland north (from where many present-day Gotani westerners originate).

Objectively, we might say that the cattle-keeping area has a limited man–cattle carrying capacity and that, over the years, some of the surplus population simply had to move elsewhere. This conveniently was the eastern area which had been almost evacuated during the 1914 rebellion against the British. The result is a relatively stable core of families who have intermarried with the cattle-keeping western area but from among whom there is an outflow of members who migrate to the east and with whom contact is retained for a couple of generations or so. The distinction is therefore that between stayers and movers, with the former regarded as more valuable repositories of Giriama traditional knowledge.

Clanship plays a crucial part in this distinction between stayers and movers. In being able to marry a woman from any clan but his own agnatic one, a man may call upon a large number of extended clan ties on both his mother's and his father's mother's sides. Since all clans are dispersed in clusters throughout Giriama country, in all ecological zones, one's own and one's father's matrilateral ties provide the close links both for localised marriage and for the distant links needed prior to migration. In other words the stayers use such ties to remain within the cattle area but are also in a position, should they so wish, to make use of them to move away from the area.

Spreading the links
It is not surprising that marriage with the mother's brother's daughter is spoken of so favourably. There are in fact very few marriages with the daughter of one's real mother's brother, no more than five per cent according to my limited sample in Miyani. There are however an additional ten per cent of men marrying into their own mother's clan. On top of these are another 10 per cent who marry into the clan of a father's other wife or that of a father's brother's wife, both called 'mother'. Though difficult to say how many, there are also a number of marriages with the daughter of a mother's sister, the latter also called 'mother'. To begin with, then, over a quarter of all marriages make direct use of real or classificatory maternal ties. There are also a little fewer than 5 per cent of marriages which are into the clan of a father's mother. Other marriages are made using matrilateral links through grandparents.

Since they are localised, marriages drawing upon ties spanning adjacent or alternate generations clearly reinforce existing ties of territoriality and neighbourhood. Roughly a half of all homesteads are built on the land of others, and so a fair proportion of these marriages with women matrilaterally related in the parental or grandparental generation are effectively between landlords and tenants.

Other such marriages are between cattle herders and cattle owners, who are not, however, necessarily also land tenants and owners respectively. A man poor in land may be a successful cattle owner, while, by contrast, a man who has clan rights to tracts of land will not necessarily own large herds. It may be remembered from chapter three that the great cattle owner of Miyani, Kushonga Zungi of the Nzaro clan, lacks much land of his own and lives and herds some of his cattle on Mweni clan land. His grandfather, Chai, came to Miyani in about the nineteen twenties from Mwangea in the north on the basis of the fact that his father's senior wife was a Mweni. Chai wanted to herd cattle in the open spaces around Miyani, finding the area around Mwangea too thickly wooded for this purpose. Other marriages in Miyani between the Nzaro and Mweni clans followed, with the former as clients and the latter as patrons of land. Kushonga himself arranged a marriage between his son and the current Mweni head's daughter, but is also nowadays sought out as a patron of cattle by other families. In other words this particular Nzaro family has over three generations remained dependent on another clan for some of its land but has emerged as economically powerful through its ownership of cattle, and is currently trying to use some of its wealth to buy land of its own in and around Miyani.

While there are these strategies, so to speak, across the generations, parents seek within the current generation of sons and daughters alliances which reflect the latest changes in personal fortunes among neighbouring families and clans. If a family is newly settled in the area, for instance, which in Miyani means that they have come from another cattle area or from an arid part of the north, an early task is for them to reinforce through marriage the matrilateral tie by which, commonly, they were allowed to settle on the land. This may be done by first having a son marry a woman of the land-owning clan, so providing her father with valuable bridewealth, and later urging him in turn to accept a daughter in marriage, thereby enabling a return of bridewealth.

The extent to which this can be done depends, therefore, on whether the new settlers can raise the bridewealth in the first place. If they cannot, then a second possibility exists. They can approach a wealthy cattle owner and beseech him to take a daughter in marriage, for himself or for a son. They thus receive the bridewealth cattle which enable them then to marry a son to a daughter of the land-owning clan and so on. To return to the example of Kushonga Zungi, most of his six wives (excluding the additional three he has inherited) have been acquired in this way, as have the three wives of his eldest son and most of those of his other sons and grandsons. Since family fortunes fall as well as rise, it is not only new settlers who need such patronage, but also those who happen upon hard times.

The result is that all homesteads are directly or indirectly linked to each other through marriage if they have lived in the area for more than a generation, and that, since the wealth of homesteads may fluctuate over the generations, alternating between comfort and poverty, it is the ties of affinity and kinship which are the most enduring. They are the networks within which over time property moves and ties of patron and client are established, reversed and reversed again.

A look at homestead genealogies shows that a minority of marriages are indeed repeatedly arranged with a limited number of key clans which own land or cattle. But we also see that most marriages are distributed among as many clans as possible. It is in fact only by tracing carefully the matrilateral links of fathers and grandparents that we can see that certain marriages are repeatedly with key clans behind an apparent surface appearance of diversity.

The diversity of clans married into by men and by their sons and daughters is certainly remarkable. Of thirty-one polygynists for whom I have full details, we find two co-wives of the same clan among only two of them. These two men (one of them being Kushonga Zungi referred to above) each has six wives. Most other polygynists have two or three and in no case are co-wives from the same clan. It would seem that taking two wives from the same clan will only occur when a man already has a large number of wives.

There is in fact considerable distaste, even horror, expressed by women at the idea of having a sister as a co-wife, and I have never come across any case of sororal polygyny among the Giriama. Men, for their part, state frankly that co-wives should be of different clans as a means of increasing inter-clan alliances. This, combined with the high rate of local endogamy, further ensures that almost any homestead can point to affinal and kinship links with any other clan in the neighbourhood.

As regards marriages entered into by siblings, we also get a picture of clan-marrying diversity, but it is tempered by a minority of cases in which a brother and sister, or, less often, two siblings of the same sex, have married into the same clan. In nearly all cases these are deliberate attempts to cement a relationship between homesteads of different clans based on differential access to land or cattle, as I have already described.

A slight clustering of affinal relationships with the same clan occurs, then, when a homestead head has already diversified ties with a number of other clans.

Thus, according to my sample, where a man has only two, three or four children, they will each be married into different clans. (In only one case did I find a man doing otherwise: he has a son, and two daughters both of whom are married by men of the Kombe clan.) As a man begets more children, a larger proportion of them are likely to be married into the same clan: in no case however are more than two clans represented twice in the marriages of a man's children. To take the extreme example of one man who has fifteen married children, two sons and one daughter are married into the Mboro clan, and a son and daughter are each married into the Fondo clan. In other words twelve clans figure in the fifteen marriages of his children, so that even in this example diverse affinal links significantly prevail over repeated ones. As might be expected, most marriages into the same clan involve a kind of exchange of brother and sister: one, let us say the girl, marries first into a particular clan, and later her brother takes a girl from the same clan, though not necessarily the same homestead.

As is the case in the choice of co-wives, the first priority is to establish diversity of clan relationships, and only when a man has many children is he prepared to reinforce a marriage tie with the same clan.

Why do homestead heads seek to spread their own and their children's marriage ties among as wide a group of clans within the local community as possible? Why should there be what amounts almost to a prohibition on marrying twice into the same clan except when a man has many wives or many children? The practical and simple answer is that, given the changing fortunes of homesteads of different clans, it is good to be linked to as many of them as possible. The wider the network of affines and kin who are linked to each other through exchanges of bridewealth cattle, or who have access to land, the easier it is to call on any one of them for aid or for hiding one's own cattle. The Giriama are quite aware of these practical advantages, consideration of which governs the talk that precedes marriage choices.

In summary, then, the Giriama prefer to marry within their immediate locality, into as many clans as possible, and are only restricted from marrying into a father's clan.

Centring the mother's brother

One consequence of this preference is that the many clans into which men and their children marry are often connected non-agnatically to their grandparents through the latter's own parents, siblings and affines. Grandparents often provide important advice and suggestions for the marriages of younger people. They know better than others the personal histories of particular homesteads and clan segments and whether or not they are cursed or are suffering from a possibly dormant affliction which may return. Drawing on their own knowledge of clans and homesteads into which their own close kin married in the past, they tend to present these as the safest choices. It is not much of an exaggeration to say that many of the clans into which a man's children marry are in fact those of his grandparents and kin, excepting only that of his paternal grandfather. Such marriage choices complement those undertaken with matrilaterally linked clans.

Thus, just as the mother's brother relationship (*ahu*) is pivotal in the articulation of maternal links which lead to marriage, so those of grandfather (*tsawe*) and grandmother (*hawe*) are key reference points for other marriage possibilities. When used in address, the terms *ahu* and *tsawe/hawe* are reciprocal, as are other key kinship terms.

Broadly speaking one cannot joke (*ku-tseyana*) with one's parents (*baba/ mama*) nor with kin of the parental generation, but must respect them (*ku-ogoha*, also meaning 'to fear'). Conversely, one is expected to joke with grandparents and persons of their generation. One may also joke with persons of one's own generation, though less so than with grandparents, and, in the case of the eldest brother (*mukulu*) of a homestead, no joking is allowed at all by each younger brother (*muvuaha*). The elder brother has a special relationship with his father, who will even tolerate his eldest son's disagreements over the running of the homestead, so suggesting a certain equivalence in their status, for this privilege is not in any way extended to other sons.

Important reciprocal kinship terms used between members of the same generation includes brother/sister/cousin on either side (*ndugu*), brother-/sister-in-law (*mulamu*), and fellow-parents of two persons married to each other (*kizhere*). Grandparents and grandchildren may also call each other 'brother/sister' (*ndugu*), and it is everywhere recognised that alternate generations are equivalent in status and substance to each other. Conversely, certain cousins, for example a person and the son/daughter of his father's sister (*tsangazi*), may call each other grandfather or grandmother (*tsawe* or *hawe*) as well as brother/sister. A man may even inherit the wives of a paternal grandfather, other than his own grandmother, and names of different kinds are transmitted from grandparents to grandchildren, who are also said to inherit grandparents' characteristics.

It is broadly true that members of alternate generations joke, while those of adjacent ones respect each other (with, incidentally, use of singular and plural pronouns and verb forms respectively to denote joking and respect (Parkin 1980b)). Moreover, relationships generally are distinguished by the Giriama as either joking or respect. In actual behaviour there are, in fact, degrees of respect and/or joking within each of these two categories.

Thus, grandparents and grandsons joke most, while fathers and children are the most respectful. Relations with parents-in-law are also respectful (the singular reciprocal term for whom is *mutsedza*), as is, to a lesser extent, that with a father's sister (*tsangazi*). Within the area of professed joking relations (*ku-tseyana*), siblings and siblings-in-law of different sexes joke less than those of the same sex: a man calls his brother's wife *hawe* (grandmother) and she reciprocates with 'grandfather', but obscenities are rarely exchanged. A great-grandfather/great-grandmother (*bamzhere/mamzhere*) stands in the same relation as father/mother (*baba/mama*) and so should be treated respectfully, but in practice may become merged a little with grandparents. Other such details show how in practice there are gradations of respect and familiarity within relations.

The mother's brother relationship, however, stands out as especially ambivalent. You must respect your mother's brother and cannot joke with him, but can take any of his property such as chickens, goats, tools and clothing. The Giriama themselves recognise the ambivalence. During an early period of field work, I was given a neat breakdown of kinship and affinal relationships into those which were based on 'fear' (i.e. *ku-ogoha*, to fear/respect) and those based on 'joking/familiarity' (i.e. *ku-tseyana*). But, with regard to the mother's brother, I was told that he is a kind of father whom one must respect, and not joke with as one might in exchanging obscenities with a grandfather, yet from whom one could take things and with whom one could even 'clown' (*ku-umiria*). This third term was clearly intended to mediate the opposition of 'fear' and 'familiarity' and to denote a kind of respectful playfulness. It was not used to describe any other relationship. This discussion occurred in the eastern agricultural zone. Seven years later, during ordinary conversation in the cattle area, which included two of the very same people (one a visitor, the other a returning migrant), people insisted again that one did 'respect/fear' one's mother's brother, and yet could help oneself to, say, his chickens and even goats. But they would not accept that one could also 'clown' with him, and they could not believe that this had ever been suggested.

Whether or not we regard this as inconsistency, as a difference between the farming and cattle-keeping areas, or as a change towards more formality in the relationship with the mother's brother, the basic ambivalence remains: one does not joke nor is one in any way familiar with him, and one is spoken of as fearing him, but one is at the same time remarkably at ease when visiting him in his homestead, helping oneself to his crops and his utensils, and light-heartedly ordering his wife (*mukazahu*, the wife of my mother's brother) to cook a meal.

In other words, the relationship is ambivalent in terms of the behaviour that accompanies it. But, in classifying it, people do see it as a relationship of fear or respect rather than of familiarity. This means that all relationships of the adjacent generation are seen to be those of respect rather than of familiarity, with not even the mother's brother exempt from this generalisation as sometimes occurs in other societies with patrilineal descent. Such relationships complement those of alternate generations which are exclusively based on familiarity, and which are identified with one's own generation, within which joking also prevails (with the exception of the eldest brother). In this way, the generations are firmly distinguished from each other: adjacent ones are respectful, while alternate ones are playful.

However, the ambivalence in behaviour towards the mother's brother contains the potential for skewing relations between the generations and for blurring the distinctiveness between them. It has, indeed, the potential for changing the whole kinship system from a patrilineal to a matrilineal one, the dynamics of · which can be seen in a contrast between the cattle-keeping and farming areas.

In the cattle zone the transformative power of the mother's brother turns on his right to a bull from the bridewealth received at his sister's daughter's marriage. In 1985, bridewealth in Miyani was seventeen heifers, one (young) bull, and twenty-four gourds or calabashes of palm wine. The cash value of a heifer was 500 shillings, of a young bull 350 shillings, and of the palm wine (*uchi wa munazi*) about 550 shillings.

The initial payment consists of four calabashes of palm wine which is called that of the house (*uchi wa nyumbani*) and is drunk among close relatives and witnesses inside the bride's father's house. The remaining twenty calabashes are drunk over a period of months outside the house by a wider range of relatives.

They are called 'the palm wine which is lined up' (*uchi wa mulolongo*), for the groom's father does in fact place them in a line every time he brings them to the girl's father.

The heifers and any other cash equivalents are also paid in instalments, sometimes over a period of two years. Payment of the bull, either as an animal or more often as palm wine, occurs fairly early on and is in fact the payment for any children that the bride produces thereafter.

The bull is paid directly to the bride's father but, in the cattle area, is normally then passed on to her mother's brother. Sometimes an equivalent of 350 shillings is given to him instead, should he not wish to receive palm wine or an animal. Once he has received the bull, the mother's brother then blesses the girl, an act which should ensure that her first delivery is swift, easy and successful. Should he not receive his bull, then the girl may suffer from an ailment that makes childbirth difficult and is called *mufundo*, which is in fact the term for 'curse' (curiously, the related term, *fundo*, means conception). The mother's brother would then be asked to give his blessing, in exchange for a gift of some kind, perhaps even a goat or a watch, pending something more substantially equivalent to a bull. No mother's brother would refuse to comply, and the act is at least symbolic of his pivotal position.

In the eastern farming zone, this role of the mother's brother is much less emphasised, to the point of sometimes not being mentioned. The payment of the bull occurs after the main cash payments and takes the form of palm wine, which, after being handed over to the bride's father, usually stays with him. The bull still secures for the husband and his family rights to any children produced by his wife, but it is the girl's father rather than her mother's brother who is more likely to be seen to cede these rights. The mother's brother's role is not especially marked symbolically.

This is a difference of degree, highlighted by the differential use of cattle and cash in the two areas. But even as a difference of tendencies, it points up the transformative potential of the mother's brother's role in the cattle area. There he is indeed like a father, as the Giriama say, for it is he who gives away the bride's procreative powers in exchange for the bull, rather than her father. Logically he is in a position to withhold the granting of these powers and to keep them for himself, so becoming the legal 'owner' of any children born to his sister's daughter. This would of course convert the system of affiliation from a patrilineal to a matrilineal mode. Symbolically, this comes out in the power of his blessing: if he withholds it, his sister's daughter may not produce children successfully; but by proffering his blessing in exchange for his rightful bull, he allows her, so to speak, to produce children for another family and clan.

Although there is this difference of view concerning the mother's brother's role in the farming and cattle areas, the main significance is again in the positive image it helps create of the pastoral west. There, as the remarks at the beginning of this chapter suggest, a marriage must be blessed in order that women stay with their husbands and are fertile. A blessed marriage is only possible through respect being paid to the pivotal role of the mother's brother. By contrast, in the eastern coastal area, the allegation is that Church marriages circumvent the need for such traditional blessings, which is another way of saying that the mother's brother's role is ignored. The believed consequence is, as we have learned, that women can escape their husbands more easily and are supposedly closer to the possibilities of leading independent lives. In fact, this characterisation of the eastern Giriama farming zone is a gross exaggeration, and the numbers of women who can secure for themselves an existence independent of their husbands and families is still very few. But their very proximity to the Muslim coast where divorce and separation rates among such Muslim Mijikenda peoples as the Digo are in fact very high, and where at least a minority of women of independent means do exist, casts them sufficiently in this light that the contrast between eastern farming and western cattle areas can be set up and elaborated.

In this world of contrasting images, there are echoes of the dual marriage system found among the Duruma, the Mijikenda group living inland and to the west of Giriama, with whom some Giriama have affinal and matrilateral links.

There, a prestigious marriage is based on a transfer of cattle for bridewealth which secures for the man all rights for his wife's children. A less prestigious marriage, reserved for the poor or for men seeking only women's labour, is based on a bridewealth of cash which does not, however, give the husband rights to his wife's children who remain the property of her brother. The Rabai had a similar dual system, and to this day are also divided into cattle-keeping and agricultural zones, which distinguished the prestigious cattle and less valued cash-based marriages from each other. The Muslim Digo appear to have transformed a similar duality, with its implications also of alternative patrilineal and matrilineal descent systems, into a distinction between lavishly expensive prestigious Muslim weddings and much less elaborate ones in which the rights to a child have to be paid for as each child is born. The prestigious and non-prestigious marriages are in all these cases associated respectively with stable and unstable unions (see Parkin 1980a).

The point of mentioning these neighbouring marriage systems, with their innuendos of double-descent and of women who stay and those who run off, is that they provide ready-made yardsticks by which the Giriama can measure their own tendencies. Women, as well as men, all deplore any development along the lines of the above peoples (and others not mentioned) which could result in destabilising agnatically based families, succession, and inheritance. The exaggerated contrast made by the Giriama, then, between the blessed marriages of the cattle-keeping west and the allegedly unblessed ones of the farming east draws its imagery from more obvious first-hand examples, and is a kind of collective warning of future possibilities.

However, marriage does sometimes occur between the Giriama and other Mijikenda peoples. Moreover, many Giriama clans are of non-Giriama origin. This fact neatly summarises the precariousness of the call for customary purity. The Giriama patri-clans are the means by which consistent agnatic lines maintain the boundaries of the Giriama and their constituent groups. Yet, the very fact that marriages with other peoples occur and that, from out of them, new Giriama clans have become grafted, so to speak, onto previous Giriama ones, negates the idea that only by marrying fellow Giriama in the customarily blessed way can ethnic purity be maintained. It therefore also goes against the idea that such customary purity can only be maintained in the cattle-keeping west, for many of the mixed marriages and grafted clans originate from quite different areas.

Shifting kin and fixed clans
The kinship system, allowing marriage into any clan but one's own agnatic one, is thus one that often identifies kin as affines, potential or real, and affines as actual or likely kin. In other words, kin are always becoming affines and vice versa. It is often claimed by Giriama that they are all related, by which they mean affinally as well as through blood and clanship. In Miyani I was constantly given examples of men and women beginning to address and refer to each other by different terms of kinship and affinity as the result of their own or a relative's marriage.

It is as if the prohibition on marriage within one's own agnatic clan stresses lineal boundedness and so purity, while the absence of other marriage prohibitions threatens to transform it, epitomised by the ambivalent and yet pivotal role of the mother's brother and his right to receive the bull of birthright, and by the capacity of kinship and affinal terms to redefine people in relation to each other.

Thus, marriage to a mother's brother's daughter (real or by clan) means that a man stops calling his mother's brother *ahu* but henceforth calls him *mutsedza* (father-in-law, and also mother-in-law). Similarly marriage to a father's sister's daughter, converts the reciprocal relationship with her mother from one of *tsangazi* (patrilateral aunt) into *mutsedza*. Parallel and cross-cousins call each other *ndugu* (brother/sister) before the marriage of their siblings to each other (excepting patrilateral parallel cousins), but are *mulamu*, brother-/sister-in-law, afterwards. When their respective children marry each other, parents call each other *kizhere*, regardless of what they called each other beforehand. There are other such examples, in all of which it is the latest marriage affecting a relationship which determines which kinship term people use with each other. In other words, a marriage between people related to each other re-orders the pre-existing ties and modes of address and reference between them and their own relatives.

Nevertheless, people who are less closely related to each other are not bound to call or refer to each other according to the latest marriage redefining them.

Such people, including newly met strangers, are constantly excavating their relationships with each other, switching between one relationship and another, in the manner of a game. Sometimes the game results in a more permanent linkage. For instance, two distant relatives, perhaps linked by a vaguely acknowledged non-agnatic common forebear, may have been calling each other 'brother' (*ndugu*), but are discovered through their respective clan names to be of adjacent generations and so are really 'father' and 'son'. One may then marry the daughter of the other, for the girl and her husband are of the same or alternate generation. The two men will henceforth call each other *mutsedza* (father/son-in-law). And so on.

While relations of kinship and affinity are in these ways constantly being redefined through marriage or excavation, those of clanship and of generation provide a contrasting image of continuity and consistency.

Among the Giriama clanship is, however, the lifetime property only of men. Each man has his clan name, though not always much used in everyday activities, in addition to other personal names. Women, however, lack clan names, have only personal ones, and in a sense lose their natal clanship on marriage. It is, for instance, difficult for them ever to return permanently to their natal homes, even in the event of divorce, for their fathers and brothers will marry them off elsewhere as soon as possible. When old they may settle with a son, who is of course of his father's rather than of his mother's clan.

Generational identities also tend to emphasise male rather than female continuity. This is because men's clan names are exactly those of their grandfathers and are given to them at birth in a special ceremony, which itself invokes family ancestors by their clan names. Grandfathers' clan names are limited in number and passed on in a regular order to grandsons, whose own grandsons in turn receive them in due course, ideally ad infinitum (Parkin 1989a).

In other words, men's clan names perform the double task of re-stressing agnatic durability and generational distinctiveness, and are said to impart these same qualities of permanence to the men themselves. Women never become the eponyms of clans or other descent groups. Women as well as men are in fact remembered as ancestors through the placement of short wooden memorial posts. As ancestors, they figure as much as men in dreams demanding some kind of appeasement for negligence. But, in the everyday world of the living, it is men through whom is expressed the idea of the permanency of clanship and, to a lesser extent, that of generations forever alternating with each other.

By contrast, the shifting nature of kinship and affinal identities is a kind of script mainly reserved for women. Men's clan names root them in homesteads and territories, but women are moved from a natal to a husband's home, and from there to another husband's home in the event of divorce or widow inheritance, and finally to that of a son, at each stage shifting further from the possibility of constituting a link in a permanent chain of identities.

It is further consistent with this script that it is women in Miyani who engage in the kind of low-income trade that requires them to walk considerable distances from the cattle zone to the palm belt, bartering milk in exchange for palm wine, for instance, while men either stay put as the producers of such items of trade or engage in buying or selling more valuable products such as ghee, travelling however not on foot but by transport provided by entrepreneurs nearer the coast. Marriage is here literally a working out of the implications of, on the one hand, kinship and affinity prescribing the movement of women, and, on the other, of clanship and generational continuity providing men with roots and a sense of autochthony. Together they make up an allegory of the division of labour: roots presuppose stable production of the goods that must be carried and traded.

Husbanding trade

It is in fact trade more than marriage that takes place between the two ecological zones. Milk, ghee, and charcoal are regularly taken from the road junction of Gotani to the small township of Kaloleni, at the heart of the palm belt, and there exchanged for palm wine, which is tapped by men, and sometimes for the palm thatch used to roof houses, which is made by women. Cattle and goats are also traded in Kaloleni, but usually in response to a specific request: otherwise cattle and other livestock are sold at the western auctions of either Mariakani or Bamba.

The distances walked by women are truly remarkable, and are undertaken for other reasons than just that of trade. Piped fresh water reached Gotani in December 1984, and another cattle area, Ganze, in July 1985, but women of the cattle area still have to cover vast distances to acquire water when local ponds, springs and river beds have dried up during the hot season. Before the Gotani source was installed, they had to seek water near Kaloleni. For Gotani women this source is twelve kilometres distant, while for those in Bamba it is much further: they would leave Bamba at 3 a.m., arriving at their destination at 8 a.m., and then return to Bamba before nightfall the same day. Even nowadays, with water available in Gotani, the journey from Bamba is twenty-seven kilometres. As with their equally extensive trading journeys, women travel in groups of, say, five or six.

For months on end buses in the area commonly do not run at all because of poor roads or unprofitability, though they are used when available by those who trade. Otherwise, as with the collection of water, the women traders walk.

From Gotani the main trade with Kaloleni is milk, which is bought by the mission hospital, and by shops and 'hoteli'. The milk is carried in a large gourd, called *kadzama*, which has a capacity of 20 to 30 litres and which is partially filled with palm wine (*uchi wa munazi*) for the return journey. The milk is sometimes converted into ghee. An increasing number of women are using plastic containers, or, if they go instead to the Mariakani milk scheme to the south of Gotani, carry the milk to supplied aluminium urns, which, during periods when the milk scheme sends out transport to collect them, may hold 42 litres. Otherwise, containing up to 20 litres, all such vessels are carried balanced on the head, the hands kept free to carry other things or used to steady the container occasionally. Younger women may in addition be carrying babies on their backs.

Here, it must be emphasised that Giriama consistently argue that the main economic value in cattle is in their milk and not in their meat or in selling them, just as they equally assert that the main social purpose in keeping cattle is for bridewealth rather than for, say, funerals at which at least one and, in the case of wealthy homesteads, many may be slaughtered. Women's role as purveyors of the milk is, then, central.

Almost all women in the cattle area at some time in their lives will carry milk to Kaloleni and buy palm wine there to bring back, doing so as the member of a team of women from the same or nearby homesteads. There are also some five women in the Gotani area who specialise in the trade and who organise the purchase of milk from local herders and its distribution and sale in Kaloleni and Mariakani. These are entrepreneurs (*muhambi*, sometimes known also by the Swahili term *mchuzi*). They invest their own money in the operation, keep the profits for their own use, and complement in status the male entrepreneurs (also called *muhambi*), among whom there are specialists not only in ghee and milk but also in cattle, goats, hides and skins, numbering some three or four in each case.

Livestock are herded to their destination, and hides and skins transported in hired trucks, but these male and female entrepreneurs use whatever local Gotani women are willing and available for the trek to and from Kaloleni or Mariakani to sell milk and ghee. These will be women whose husbands have no milk of their own to sell or who currently lack the money to buy some for re-sale. The entrepreneurs, whether men or women, thus stand in the metonymic relationship of husband to these local women carriers. They supply them with milk, take profits from its sale, and leave the women to bring back palm wine to sell as their own, as is the pattern in ordinary homesteads around Gotani.

Husbands do not allow their women to stay overnight in Kaloleni or Mariakani, yet, at the same time, claim that women seize the opportunity provided by such a trip, even though carried out only during the day, to arrange to meet lovers. The allusion is more to the fact that women can, as they become settled in a marriage with children of their own, acquire small amounts of money of their own with which to carry out the trade, spending some of their earnings on their children and on clothes for themselves, and so securing a modicum of financial independence. Some husbands even concede that their own propensity for spending money on palm wine legitimates this degree of financial management by women.

Most milk is sold during or shortly after the wet seasons, with charcoal and firewood often taken instead to Kaloleni during parched periods when grass is sparse. At such times, also, women bring back palm wine, which is available all the year round. Thus, while most or all of the profits from the sale of milk in Kaloleni go to a woman's husband or male or female entrepreneur, it is she who deals, on her return to Gotani, in palm wine and retains the profits, usually providing her husband with a little free wine.

Thus, while the sale of milk products is the work of women for husbands, or of a handful of women for entrepreneurs, that of palm wine is by women largely for themselves. Both depend on women's mobility, indeed on their preparedness to walk great distances, and on men's ecological rootedness: raising cattle for milk in the west and growing and tapping palm trees in the east. The shifting nature of kinship and affinal identities, to which I referred above, thus contextualises women's labour, for it is with a changing range of such relatives that women travel and meet in Kaloleni. Conversely, men own, raise, graze, or extract produce from their cattle and palms through permanent clan ties, their own or another's, that give them access to pasture or farmland. Putting this another way, kinship-affinity and women's mobility and labour are expressed in each other, as are clanship and men's productive bases. The fact that some women can become entrepreneurs and act like men is paralleled by obverse instances of men doing what is otherwise regarded as women's work. As with women entrepreneurs, the numbers are few. But they point in the direction of a tendency commented on by Giriama as happening among Mijikenda Muslims along the coast, where it is claimed that men often do women's work and vice versa, and where women can dominate husbands. As with other stereotypes this has no more than a limited foundation: there is probably as much a gender division of labour among Muslims as among Giriama; on the other hand Digo and certain other Muslims commonly claim that it is 'the custom of women to leave men', a practice reported also by some ethnographers among certain Swahili (Le Guennec-Coppens 1983).

In Miyani there is a celebrated case of a man who took the place of his wife in a team of women, after she had fallen sick and was unable to carry out the two-way trade in milk and palm wine. He carried the gourd on his head, as women do, though with initial difficulty, and survived the long journeys. Though the example is sometimes given, as much by men as women, to show how certain gender roles are not naturally fixed, the man was neither ridiculed nor regarded oddly, and anyway ceded his place to his wife when she recovered. There is overlap of a more permanent kind in the production and sale of charcoal and firewood. For men this is regarded as the work of those too poor or untalented to own land and livestock, or have a waged job. Some of those most deeply involved in it spend a number of months in the far west of Giriama country preparing their charcoal and then emerging for a shorter period to sell it in Kaloleni and the east. Their isolation adds to the lowly status of work acknowledged to be difficult for the rewards it brings. But women also produce a little charcoal, doing so locally rather than at a distance, and during lean times when milk is too scarce to be traded in Kaloleni. Finally, while herders are always male, their lowly assistants may be girls as well as boys, although usually the latter, and in either case unlikely to be attending school.

Even when they do the same kind of work, men still tend to earn more than women. But the differences are sometimes reduced and, from the above examples, we have a picture of men as well as of women performing tasks which are the most lowly and harsh, just as, in the case of women and men entrepreneurs, both figure among the most profitable and prestigious. In the middle, so to speak, there is a firm division of labour by gender, a firmness which is underwritten by the control of men over women in marriages occurring between clans. It is, then, at the top and bottom of the trading hierarchy that women and men almost become identified with each other in a play of shifting identities reminiscent of that between kin and affines.

The metaphor describes well the relationship of clanship to kinship and to affinal identities. For clanship is seen by the Giriama as the core identity, which is nevertheless subverted by intrusions from outside, at its edges so to speak. It is through admitting as affines and thence kin those from outside the Giriama, and from outside the wider non-Muslim Mijikenda-speaking group, that the Giriama see their essence as a distinctive people as likely to be eroded. Let us take the example, mentioned during a conversation in the homestead of the great cattle-owner, Kushonga Zungi, of an educated son, a radio broadcaster living in the Kenyan capital of Nairobi, five hundred kilometres away. He married a woman from the Kisii people of western Kenya, even further away. It was remarked that if she was 'like a Kikuyu, she would not stay long but would leave her husband and take the children', with no bridewealth having been paid for her. The comments parallel in an uncanny way those reserved for Giriama men who marry Muslim Digo women. Such men will have met these women while working at the coast or in Mombasa, and have been seduced by them against their better Giriama judgement.

The alleged sexual proclivities of Digo women are talked about by men, who see them as threatening in a wife and as an aspect of her preparedness to abandon the marriage. But Giriama women collude in this negative judgement of Digo women. It is reported, for instance, that Giriama wives fiercely resist any attempt by a husband to have sexual intercourse in any other than the 'orthodox' position (sideways facing, with the husband on his right side and the woman on her left). To adopt any other position is taken by wives as treating them like Digo women.

Parallel and indeed part of men's concern that Giriama women should be prevented from adopting Digo habits, is one which addresses itself to the value of women as sources of labour. Giriama men provide a jocular, rhyming charac-terisation in Swahili of Digo women as being nothing more than a burden, 'Mdigo ni mzigo', the clear implication being that not only will a Digo wife cause a man trouble by using up his property and then leaving him, together with the children, but will not work in the fields or homestead during the time that she is with him. Giriama men depict Muslim women generally in these terms.

Such comments and asides are telling indicators that the cherished fixity and permanence of patri-clanship are not just to do with men's power and lineal immortality, they are also the essence of absolute judgements about men's relationship to their wives, sisters, and daughters: that the labour of women, as mothers, workers and traders, must remain mobile, able to be moved from homestead to homestead linked by kinship, affinity and the exchange of cattle, so serving to perpetuate men's own agnatic boundaries and identities.

Conclusion

While affines are always likely also to be kin, and kin to become affines, in the manner I have described, there is another sense in which affines remain distinct from each other and recognise that they are each a party to an alliance between two clans. This is the aspect of affinity which, then, stresses differences between clans, and marks clans out as marriageable groups. As if fearing the confusion of affinity and therefore clanship that might occur if all affines were regarded as no more than blood relatives, funerals are great occasions at which alliances based on marriage between clans are highlighted. There is nothing unintendedly functionalist about this claim. The Giriama themselves tell us that the attendance at funerals is recruited in this way, by affines inviting their affines, who invite theirs, and so on. 'It is in this way that we know our clans.'

However, as I show in the next chapter, funerals do more than allow for the re-expression and creation of alliances between firmly distinguished clans. They also provide dramatic occasions on which ideas of what constitutes proper Giriama customs become disputed. Funerals are regarded as too important an event not to be carried out according to customary rules, which are held to uphold the distinctiveness of Giriama cultural identity. Yet, perhaps precisely because of this stress on their rule-governed conduct, funerals become arenas of contestation, as competing parties seek to assert and apply their knowledge.

Flowing through such contested certainties, however, a theme seeks its resolution. Death is mocked and banished, and life is celebrated through food and drink, and the end effect is that a clear-cut separation of death and life has occurred. Yet, beforehand, during the period of physical closeness to the corpse prior to its burial, during the burial itself, and in animal sacrifice and appeals to the dead, the sense of one's own mortality and of those dear to one is considerable. Giriama themselves express this and I always experienced it.

Strong figures come to the fore at such times, telling the enfeebled rest what to do, though not always themselves in agreement. As in the relationship of men to women, and of east to west, the boundaries demarcated by rules and stereotypes become fuzzy, allegedly more so in the east than in the west. Funerals begin by breaking people down emotionally, raising the general fear of death, and playing on the horror of the corpse itself. They end with men of authority clearly in control, first by giving guidance and expression to people's emotions of anger, grief and fear, and then by having their interpretations accepted of how to run a funeral.

5

Spanning west and east: dances of death

Scripting funerary rules

As in a number of African societies, Giriama funerals are major occasions. They are attended by hundreds of people and involve lavish sacrifices of cattle and goats, and vast donations and consumption of palm wine. There is the first funeral consisting of a burial and then of feasting and dancing for altogether six days for a woman and seven for a man. Then, some one to four months afterwards, the second funeral is held, extending over three days. Sometimes the second funeral is omitted for someone not regarded as socially important enough, but this is uncommon and may, anyway, be rectified at a much later date following a misfortune in the homestead concerned.

Rather like marriage, funerals among the Giriama are supposed to follow numerous and often complicated rules. But, whereas the rules concerning who may marry whom are generally obeyed, those for holding funerals are invariably contested and are sometimes more evident in abstract argument than in practice. Yet the rules, while probably always in change, provide at least a provisional conceptual framework into which can be fitted activities following a death.

The rules specify when, where and how the corpse should be buried, who should carry it from its resting house to the grave, how young and old, and men and women, should address and behave towards each other and how long the ceremony should last. Making up the underside of this rule consciousness are various practices which are in fact rather more predictable than those supposedly governed by rules yet are not recognised as such. They are part of a series of dramatic responses to the presence and disposal of death and comprise what appears to be socially standardised emotional arousal. There are weeping and wailing, outbursts of anger and of vengeance claims, frenzied jostlings to see the corpse as it is carried to the grave, and, as when young men see a fiancée dancing with another man, there may be jealous attacks, themselves sometimes ending in violence and even death, so perpetuating the cycle.

Such activities do at first seem to follow an informal script. But individual responses and interpretations thereafter may vary and cause surprise. One is indeed expected to feel both grief and anger at the loss of a loved one, and even to seek the help of a doctor-priest specialising in revenge medicine against the witch responsible, but beyond that one's emotions can be expressed and understood in different ways. Will the bereaved withdraw into a personal shell, or publicise their hatred of the alleged witch, or will they quietly resume their life before the bereavement as if, by appearances, nothing had happened to disrupt it? Alongside such variable responses, people question and interpret behaviour. Is the bereaved's tranquillity due to their having secretly and satisfyingly sought out counter-witchcraft against the killing agent? Is their angry rampaging during and after the funeral in fact the effects of yet more witchcraft or perhaps of a burgeoning madness, or even of possession by spirits? Such dramatic turns unsettle the Giriama claim that funerals follow rules. They introduce tension in the conduct and aftermath of the ceremony. Yet, those who through their actions mock the rules, nevertheless speak of their authenticity: funerals must be conducted in the 'proper' Giriama way, for to do anything less is to occasion disrespect for the deceased and to incur his or her wrath.

What, then, are these rules, and since people continually disagree about at least some of them, where is the knowledge allegedly authenticating them?

It is, again, the elders in and around the Kaya who are regarded by Giriama as knowing how funerals should be carried out. Each of the six sectional representatives at the Kaya is supposed to know the different clan variations, and even to some extent those of other Mijikenda groups. During actual funerals there is too little time normally to seek the advice and legitimacy of Kaya elders, and the ceremony gets put together through much contestation in ways that nevertheless reflect the pattern of other recent funerals in the area, without duplicating them precisely. Meanwhile, the alleged superior customary knowledge of the Kaya elders remains untapped and therefore conveniently unquestioned, existing as much in the belief in it as in its recounting.

I have attended some fifty funerals, mainly in the palm belt but also in the cattle area, and while each one has had to be negotiated through its course at different stages, with none of the stages completely the same in any two funerals, there is nonetheless a distinctive shape or family resemblance to them. The contours are broadly discernible, to the extent even of suggesting broad differences between those held in the cattle area and those further east, towards the coast.

Let me, then, outline the common features, pointing up differences between the two ecological areas as they occur.

The homestead as spatial work
To begin with, funerals are organised around the spatial character of a homestead: its inside and outside, its centre and various key points within it, the relationship to each other of the constituent houses, the place chosen for the

grave, the movement taken by people as they enter the homestead and the positions they adopt when they sit, eat, drink, sleep and dance during the days and nights of the funeral, and the sacrificial sites.

A critical distinction between the homesteads of the east and west is that, as well as being larger, the latter include cattle and other livestock byres while those of the east do not. Related to this is the fact that the western cattle-keeping homesteads conform more closely to a general type. This is evident both from observation and from peoples' own descriptions given and in some cases drawn for me. This greater consistency in homestead structure is hardly surprising: the livestock byres are the basis of the homestead, which is therefore organised around them. Given the need to bring livestock in and out every morning and evening, the relationship of byre to the rest of the homestead cannot deviate much from a pattern. The livestock-based homestead is to that extent functionally concerned with internal order.

By contrast, homesteads in the farming areas of the palm belt vary much more. Their internal spatial organisation is concerned solely with human residence, and not with the relationship between people and animals, except for some goats which may be kept at the periphery. Their farms, the family one called *munda* and those worked by each co-wife, *koho*, are external to the homestead, in some cases at some distance from it, given the land fragmentation that has occurred in the more densely populated east. Palms and other trees are often even more widely dispersed: they may have been planted on land now occupied and owned by a family unrelated to the owner of the trees, who retains the right nevertheless to harvest their produce, whether palm wine, coconuts, or, say, cashew nuts. The internal organisation of eastern farming homesteads is therefore unaffected by the distribution of farming land, and so takes various forms.

Interestingly, I found that, even in the farming palm belt, a description or drawing of a homestead would include a cattle byre and spatial structure more like that found in the west. On remarking on the difference between this description and the homestead in which we would be sitting, I would be told that the latter was a deviation from the ideal, which was indeed to be found in the west. By this definition, the east is made up of such alleged departures from custom. In fact, there are certain recurrent spatial features even in the east: the first son's home is normally a long way forward and to the right of the homestead head's; the next son's is sometimes to the left but may at other times also be to the right, on either side of the first son's; other sons may be either to the right or left of the father but always within his view, so that father and sons make up a kind of on-facing, oval-shaped ring dominated by the father's house. There is certainly a tendency for the ring to build up over time in an anti-clockwise direction from the father. But there may also be 'infilling', as when the house of a young son or grandson is built on spare land nearer to the homestead head, but still within the ring. When the father dies, and if the brothers stay together, the senior brother's house then becomes the focus of the ring. Uterine kin and others who have 'begged' for land may have their houses built outside the ring of father and sons, or of brothers, almost making up a separate homestead within a homestead.

Should houses face in particular directions of the compass? While ancestral memorial posts, both those for ordinary men and women and the larger ones for members of the Gohu fraternity (see chapter eight), do face west in explicit acknowledgement that this is the direction of death, with the east associated with new life, this particular orientation is not much talked about in the conduct and affairs of a homestead.[1] The homestead head's house tends to face north, and rarely if ever west, but that of his eldest son (and others) may in fact face in this direction, although there does not appear to be any inauspicious interpretation attaching to this, as is recounted in some other societies. It is tempting to suggest that the western area of Giriamaland has in recent generations taken on such importance as an area of customary authenticity, by contrast with the east and the coast, that the west has lost any sinister associations it might once have had (if indeed it had any): it is the land of the ancestors who are the guardians of custom and cultural identity, but it is not the harbinger of bleak or fearful death. To face it is, perhaps, to be open to the ancestors rather than to incur the misfortunes associated with death.

As with house positions, burial positions, too, are supposed to follow an order. With the exception of those dying from 'bad deaths' and from such contagious diseases as leprosy, which are dealt with later in this chapter, all burials take place within the homestead. A first son is buried to the right of the doorway of his father's house, or where his father's house used to be if both it and the old man have since departed. Second and successive sons and all daughters (that is, those unmarried or divorcees living in their natal home) are buried slightly forward and to the left of the doorway. Widows living in the independent homestead of a son are buried to the left of his doorway. The head of a homestead set up by himself, and with a father buried or living elsewhere, is buried in front of his house and slightly to the right. His wife or wives, and indeed all in-married women, are buried not to the right of their husband's doorway but elsewhere in the internal area of the homestead, the *muhala*, wherever there is room.[2]

---

[1] Champion, a district officer writing in about 1912, notes that the large memorial posts (plural *vigango*) of the Kiza 'clan' or section face east (Champion 1967: 25). It may be remembered from chapter two that Kiza is the 'clan' reputed to have carried the heavy, magically protective stone from Singwaya to the present Kaya, and therefore to enjoy ritual superiority in the Kaya for their efforts. Whether the easterly position once faced by Kiza ancestral memorials is connected with this Kiza role is open to question.

[2] While *muhala* is the central area within the homestead, *pala* is a clearing in the bush or forest outside and at some (walking) distance from the homestead where secret societies meet, male circumcision takes place (there is no female circumcision), and elders from different homesteads may convene for confidential discussions which cannot take place in the homestead. The two terms are presumably related (*h* often taking the place of *p* in other, nearby Bantu languages), and it seems reasonable to suggest that the use of the personifying singular noun class prefix, *mu*, designates the domestic place by contrast with the impersonal noun class (absent prefix) which denotes the 'wild'

While it is normal in due course for new homesteads to be created, either as a result of a sub-division or in the pursuit of new land, men and women are sometimes buried in an area occupied by a now abandoned homestead site, called *gandzo*. This is said frankly to be a way of laying claim to that land, but is also expressed as a preference made on behalf of those who may have spent most of their lives in the former homestead. A number of abandoned sites may be used in this way, especially by residents of a highly populated area, as a way of hedging their bets in future land claims.

Ordinarily a woman is buried in her husband's homestead, except when, as a widow she opts to live with a son in his own homestead, where she will be buried in due course. The co-wives of a man, ranging quite widely in age, will therefore probably be buried in different homesteads. Their dispersal at death inverts their residential concentration in life, for a man's co-wives share his house, though with each normally having her own room nowadays. Most houses in the palm belt are of the so-called 'Swahili' type: rectangular in shape with a pitched roof made up of palm-thatch and walls of mud and wattle. Houses of the traditional beehive shape are made of grass rather than palm-thatch and so are found more in the western bushland than in the east, though even this is changing in view of the regular trade in palm-thatch from the east to the west: the palm-thatches (*makuti*) are made by eastern women and transported to the west in trucks by male entrepreneurs. It was in the large beehive-shaped houses that a man and his co-wives would live, each woman with her own bed and visited in turn by the husband according to what is supposed to be a strict rota. The system of sleeping by rota continues, but, whereas I knew of a few cases in the mid sixties where co-wives slept in the same house without internal partitioning, I encountered none in the mid nineteen eighties. Nevertheless, as in the west especially, the grass houses can still be found, but now have internal divisions approximating to separate rooms.

The larger the homestead the more evident is the processional element in funerals: there is, for instance, ample space to carry the body ceremoniously from its house to the grave. In the eastern palm area, some homesteads are so small and condensed that this element is almost absent: the body is buried only a short distance from its house, visitors to the funeral are dispersed around as well as within the homestead, which thereby loses a clear sense of boundary separating inside and outside, and the burial becomes the main or even sole ceremonial focus rather than the culmination of a number of overlapping stages.

In talking about homestead spatial structure, Giriama distinguish not only the

outside. From my own impression, I doubt that more boys are nowadays circumcised in hospitals than in the *pala*, though Giriama themselves sometimes say this, and specialist circumcisers are still in great demand. Circumcision is carried out not, as formerly, by age-grade or *rika*, but among boys of from about twelve to fourteen from one or two local homesteads, usually without ceremony.

allegedly western ideal from the eastern 'deviation', but refer also to the Kaya. The Kaya is called the 'great homestead' (*mudzi mubomu* or *kaya bomu*) but in fact is quite unlike the western 'ideal' in lacking cattle, which are never kept there. On the other hand, its spatial structure is seen to be distinctive and rule-governed. What the Kaya and the ordinary western cattle-keeping homestead have in common, then, is not spatial structure but an alleged adherence to customary rules.

The Kaya, being largely uninhabited, can continue to be structured according to clear ideas as to its centre, meeting house, different clan areas, and paths and boundaries. But ordinary homesteads, whether in the west or east, have to be adapted to the various changes affecting people who dwell in them. Peoples' descriptions of an ideal homestead are thus each made up of elements variously abstracted from different periods of its existence and so are never seen in practice: people die or move out, their houses are abandoned, or new ones are built on nearby but different sites which alter, even slightly, the spatial relationship to each other of homestead members. My own attempts to draw different examples of homestead spatial organisation reveal an apparently wide diversity, which only becomes more consistent if retraced over time. Nevertheless, crucial distinctions are preserved, more clearly marked in the west than east, such as that between inside and outside, centre and periphery, main and secondary entrances, the back-areas of houses, and the house of the homestead head and those of other people. Men's conversation huts (*kigojo*) are sometimes retained, though, often, the conversations occur in front of houses, within earshot of women and the young, unless matters of secrecy require a more distant venue. There is usually one granary (*lutsaga*), which is an upper part, mounted on poles above the hearth (*mafiga*), of a kitchen-house, but a very large homestead sometimes contains more than one granary.

During funerals, then, organisers have to balance the reality of spatial distribution with their ideas of where a grave should be dug, different commensal groups sited, and the sacrifices carried out. There is probably no one ideal spatial template but instead a number of conceptual starting-points: if the deceased's house is surrounded by ample space, little of it taken up by earlier graves, then emphasis can be placed on the cortège from house to grave, the site for which is therefore chosen accordingly. Alternatively, a sacrificial site may take on more prominence. Overseeing all of this is the position and space occupied by the bereaved, who may be one person or many, and so on. It would be incorrect to say that funeral organisers muddle through as best they can, for they have to think carefully about each stage, yet events do overtake them and they themselves must often adapt to, say, the fact that singers and dancers are more numerous than expected and cause other groups to move.

Despite this need on the part of funeral organisers to work at the possibilities of spatial organisation, I was often presented with firm descriptions of how a homestead should be structured, one of which I now present, if only because it seems to me most to conform to my own image of an ideal type. I am influenced also by the fact that it was drawn by a man in his mid twenties who had been raised until he was twelve in the cattle area, had lived in the intermediary farming area until he was seventeen, and now stays at the coast, earning money through occasional work for tourists (accompanying them to the reef in other men's boats, or 'fixing' services for them) or through buying, frying and selling fish at a market stall, having, with his brothers and widowed mother, built a so-called unauthorised homestead on privately owned land. He seems to comprise the full range of experiences inherent in Giriama ideas of their identity crisis. It is interesting, therefore, that, despite his youth, residence and current activities (or perhaps because of them), his depiction of a homestead should appeal to and evoke an allegedly traditional shape, which, except for its small size, is most likely to be found in the cattle-keeping west, rather than in the east (Diagram 2).

Affines and attendance

In the preceding chapter I mentioned that the close relatives of the deceased who attend funerals will expect their affines to attend. These affines may in turn summon their affines to come, depending on the status of the dead person, and so on. This serial interlinking of affines is summarised in the reciprocal kinship term of reference, *kizhere*, which means a parent of the spouse of my child. It is also summarised nicely in the phrase: 'those who attend funerals follow each other as those who marry each other'.

Most affines are drawn from the local community, as I have explained, with a small proportion coming from further afield. It is these latter who provide the links with other largely endogamous areas, which in turn are linked to yet others. Such affinal chain relationships are thus geographically spread. By coming together at one funeral, different and sometimes distant areas of Giriamaland are represented. Each major funeral, attended by hundreds, thus provides a temporary and partial focus of Giriama unity. A fuller but less frequent expression of unity occurs at and around the Kaya when large congregations attend rain-making ceremonies or gather for political reasons. The Kaya's representation of Giriama unity is often likened to that of the money collected at funerals to help the sponsors. Despite the infrequency and irregularity of its gatherings, the Kaya is regarded as an arch-representation of collective organisation among the Giriama.

While at one level funerals keep distant Giriama in contact with each other and with developments affecting the people as a whole, at another level feasting, drinking, dancing, and discussion groups are differentiated from each other on the basis of age, gender, wealth, and, in the eastern region, the religions of Islam, Christianity and polytheism.

Such different representations of Giriama society are all the more dramatic through the heavy attendance at funerals, when sheer weight of numbers comprising strangers as well as affines, kin, friends and neighbours, forces different and competing groups to come to terms with each other at least for the duration of the mortuary ceremony.

Large attendances, however, are only possible if due notice is given to people, especially those living far off, that someone has died or that, in the case of the second funeral, it is about to be held. For the latter, ample notice can be given. But at the death of someone, the information has to reach outlying areas immediately, for persons are normally buried within twenty-four hours, with the funeral itself (called *hanga*, meaning anguish) starting two days afterwards. Extending over so many days, the burial and first funeral give distant persons an opportunity to attend at least the later stages. The second funeral may be comparatively short, for everyone will have been warned of its occurrence beforehand. Bearing in mind the propensity for variation, which I later discuss, these consecutive ceremonies can first be described in general terms

The burial (*ziko*) and first funeral (*hanga*)
Day One: the burial
Someone dying late afternoon or evening will be buried next morning, while, should the death occur late at night or during the morning, the burial will take place late that afternoon.

As might be expected, the burial day (*siku ya kuzika*, also known as *siku ya mitsanga mitsi*, the day of raw soil, that is, freshly dug earth) is when there is an especially heightened expression of emotion. I present a description taken from my notes of the burial of a fifty year old woman, the mother of a number of surviving children. She was the wife of the brother of a prominent man, known as Ndoro, who owns many cattle in the Gotani area, but also owns many palm trees near Kaloleni. As well as having property interests which straddle both ecological zones, he is well connected throughout Giriamaland. Living together in the same homestead with the deceased woman's husband, it is the senior, wealthy Ndoro who is the homestead head (*mwenye mudzi*), while both men are referred to as the bereaved (*mufererwa*, plural *afererwa*). The two men have been placed on a mat by presiding elders, where they sit silently, the homestead head receiving money called Mijikenda given by newly arriving men.

The number of those designated as bereaved by elders may be as few as one man or as many as, in one instance, fifteen men and women. Elderly or mature relatives of the deceased such as siblings, parents, mother's brothers, and children who are themselves quite senior, are eligible. The dead woman, Kadii, happened to have very few such close relatives. The bereaved must observe four prohibitions throughout the burial and funeral: they must not wash, have sex, shake hands with anyone, nor leave the mat except to relieve themselves. The most serious prohibition is that on sexual relations, the violation of which will

Diagram 2. A Giriama homestead

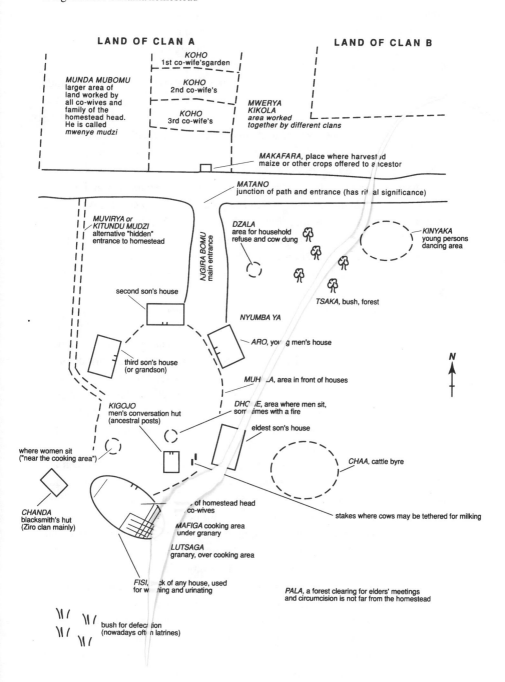

LAND OF CLAN A

LAND OF CLAN B

KOHO
1st co-wife's garden

MUNDA MUBOMU
larger area of
land worked by
all co-wives and
family of the
homestead head.
He is called
mwenye mudzi

KOHO
2nd co-wife's

KOHO
3rd co-wife's

MWERYA
KIKOLA
area worked
together by different clans

MAKAFARA, place where harvested
maize or other crops offered to ancestor

MATANO
junction of path and entrance (has ritual significance)

MUVIRYA or
KITUNDU MUDZI
alternative "hidden"
entrance to homestead

DZALA
area for household
refuse and cow dung

KINYAKA
young persons
dancing area

NGIRA BOMU
main entrance

TSAKA, bush, forest

second son's house

NYUMBA YA

ARO, young men's house

third son's house
(or grandson)

MUHALA, area in front of houses

KIGOJO
men's conversation hut
(ancestral posts)

DHOME, area where men sit,
sometimes with a fire

eldest son's house

where women sit
("near the cooking area")

CHAA, cattle byre

CHANDA
blacksmith's hut
(Ziro clan mainly)

of homestead head
co-wives

stakes where cows may be tethered for milking

MAFIGA cooking area
under granary

LUTSAGA
granary, over cooking area

FISI, back of any house, used
for washing and urinating

PALA, a forest clearing for elders' meetings
and circumcision is not far from the homestead

bush for defecation
(nowadays often latrines)

N

rapidly bring *vitio* and death to children and possibly adults in the homestead. Other obligations become incumbent on the bereaved as the funeral proceeds.

Kadii died in the morning at about six o'clock. It is remarkable that by about noon there are already a few hundred people gathered from near and less near homesteads. It is April and the rains are in the air, though it is dry for the moment. There is an endless succession of groups of women, all with children and grand-children on their backs, and men, in ones and twos, coming separately into the homestead.

Already I have discreetly been told the story of why Kadii died. It appears that Ndoro, the homestead head who is now in charge of the burial proceedings, lost a land dispute to another prominent man of the area. Ndoro is alleged to have gone to a baobab tree where there are nature spirits called *mizimu* and to have wished the death of the victor of the land dispute. But *mizimu* spirits have a sense of justice in these matters and, since there was so much right on the side of the victor, Ndoro's revenge wish recoiled on his own homestead. Within a year he has lost his own mother and now his brother's wife. Ndoro himself does not take this view but instead blames a man, a close relative who has since left the home-stead, of being a witch (*mutsai*).

If even I have heard the story then so must most others have heard it or similar stories. It gives a certain poignancy to the act of giving Ndoro money. One says 'Sorry' (*pore*), though without shaking hands, as is customary, and wonders what is in his and his brother's minds. Do they know that others are blaming Ndoro, while he and his brother apparently blame a witch? Since Ndoro cannot yet have arranged to have a diviner consulted, how do people know that Ndoro already has a witch in mind, and does Ndoro know that people think he has? Already, from the moment of entry into the homestead, there seem to be the beginnings of a labyrinth of guesswork and suspicion.

The grave is already being dug. Its length is from east to west. Women are clustered in and around the house where the body lies. It is they who wash and prepare the body under the direction of senior women, while men carry and bury it, these being neighbours but not relatives of the deceased. Men are in groups of their own outside and at various points in the homestead, with three elders quietly drinking palm wine. There is very little talking at all, a notable silence for such a large gathering. A neighbour, the son-in-law of the dead woman's sister, had earlier provided two mourning mats, and some calico and other white cloth for making the shroud, which he had bought from a distant shop.

The silence is occasionally broken by the weeping and wailing of a few close women relatives who, as they approach to within a few metres of the dead woman's house, clasp the backs of their heads, with elbows spread out, and address the dead woman by one or another kinship term. As I discover later in talking to people, I am not alone in experiencing a kind of fear at this time and until after the burial. It is not exactly fear of the corpse, though everyone finds it difficult to look at it and, for those entrusted with the task, to wash, dress and carry it. It is more a fear of what I can only call deathliness, of death in the air and among us. The Giriama have a name for this, which I shall discuss.

The silence broken by occasional weeping has continued until three o'clock in the afternoon. The grave is still being dug. But at this point an old woman asks a young woman of the homestead to fetch her a winnowing basket. The young woman sends a child into a house for one. The old woman, who is a senior member of the women's society called *Kifudu*, breaks some bottles, puts the pieces in the tray and then, outside the door of the dead woman's house, starts shaking the tray and singing, appealing to other women to join her. Gradually over about an hour she has been joined by a core of forty women, most older or mature, with some younger, but none very young, with a hundred and fifty women silently watching the singers, who also dance to their own music. The dance-song is called Kihoma and is customarily the first to occur. It is similar to and eventually gives way to the dance-songs specifically associated with the women's Kifudu society.

Even while this is going on, and while the grave is still being dug, two or three women, still wailing and with their hands clasped behind their head, walk or stagger round the impenetrable crowd of men gathered round the grave, seeming to be trying to peer into it. At all other burials I have witnessed there is this apparent attempt by women to break through the prohibition imposed on them never to look inside a grave. A woman had once admitted to me that a few close female relatives do try to come near and see the grave, even though they have been told that to do so will cause them and perhaps other occupants of their homestead to become sterile. The attempt does seem to be a mock one, for the wall of men around the grave gives no chance of a view whatsoever. But it is sometimes a close thing, and the men seem genuinely menaced by such women whose own behaviour is that of grief beyond control.

Just as the six or so men are about to go into the house to fetch the body, three things happen more or less simultaneously. The women sing much more loudly, men gather in even greater number around the grave, as if to reinforce it, and the other women's wailing and crying reaches a very high pitch. There is no coffin for the woman. She is to be buried in the customary manner in her shroud enclosed by the two mats. But a wooden plank (though sometimes wooden poles, *tsaga*, are used) has been placed at the base of a narrow recess in the floor of the grave into which the body is to be fitted sideways. A second plank will be placed over the body once it is inserted. The purpose of the recess is to prevent the body falling forward or backward from its sideways position.

The body is carried by the men to the grave. Like the gravediggers and others involved in the preparation of the body, these pallbearers must be of a range of different clans from that of the deceased. The three diggers in the grave receive the body and, standing on the ledge on each side of the recess, lower it into the grave. It is laid on its right side, with its feet pointing west, the top of its head east, and its eyes facing Singwaya or north, from whence the Giriama allegedly came. Men are also laid on the right side in exactly the same position as women and this has been the case at every Giriama burial I have witnessed. Yet a few men, middle aged but not elders, have sometimes insisted that men should be laid on their right side and women on their left. This difference for men and women is in fact recorded earlier this century by Champion, the famous district officer, who is unlikely however to have witnessed any burial positions himself (1967: 24). Nevertheless, that Champion was told so long ago what I have sometimes been told is a puzzle. Perhaps it is a difference that some clans once had, as is the case with certain other Mijikenda groups (cf. Champion 1967: 25). Or perhaps it derives from a confusion with the position adopted for sexual intercourse, during which a man lies on his right or good side, and the woman on her left or bad side. No other sexual position is permitted, least of all by the woman: men who seek to experiment with other positions may be met by the woman's protest that she is 'not a Digo'. In death, however, there is equality of position between the genders, as far as my own observations and those of most Giriama I have spoken to are concerned.[3]

Apart from the general absence of a distinction in this respect between men and women, burial positions and directions and those of memorial posts (see chapter eight) do vary among the different Mijikenda groups, and sometimes within them, as I later note. Where such differences occur, they seem to lend themselves to alternative or modified interpretations of where a people comes from. They enjoy the indexical fluidity of origin myths and indicate not necessarily that peoples may manipulate traditions of origin, but that the idea of origin can be perceived in different ways, just as the Kaya and Singwaya are each often referred to by Giriama as their origin, a claim that need not be seen as inconsistent if the one is regarded as metonymic of the other.

The body is, then, a site of contestation not only in life when medical practitioners interpret its maladies in social terms and so set up as well as reflect and perhaps reconcile human competition. In death, also, its disposition presupposes challenge and counter-challenge. Thus, to return to our description by way of another example, once in the grave, the body is covered with earth as quickly as

---

[3] It is even conceivable that differences concerning the burial position arise from the different regional origins of the different Mijikenda peoples who live near each other along the coastal strip itself. Thus, while Giriama men and women are laid on their right side, with eyes facing Singwaya, as I have described, Duruma men and women are laid on their left side, with their eyes also facing directly north to Singwaya, but with their feet pointing east. The Chonyi, who live in the east and nearer to the coast, are buried on their right side on a south-west and north-east axis, with their feet pointing south-west and their heads north-east, and their eyes looking north-west to Singwaya. In all these different cases, then, the common feature is that the eyes point in some way to Singwaya. The various odd claims that it is Mecca, the sea or the coast that determines the burial position clearly constitute a more recent development, which reflects coastal and Muslim influence and the weakening significance of Singwaya as point of origin and autochthonous reference.

possible, an expectation which clashes, often violently, with that of any Christians in a congregation who wish to say lengthy prayers over the uncovered body. On this occasion, however, 'custom' is allegedly being followed, and there is no delay.

As soon as the first earth is cast into the grave by the man most senior to the deceased (in this case the dead woman's husband, but in the case of a man his father, most senior brother, or son, depending on availability), the core of male relatives begins to weep and wail, also addressing the deceased by a range of kinship and affinal terms. There is immediately a ritualised and rapid passing of the hoe to two or three men at a time who jointly and swiftly fill the grave, passing on the hoe at a touch to others behind them, and building up a mound of earth over the grave.

The work done, the men spring aside. Immediately the closest women of the daughters' generation hurl themselves onto the mound on their knees, four or five on each side, patting the mound and crying in an apparent mixture of fury and grief. After some five minutes they gradually leave the mound, with two or so lingering, and one last woman, a daughter, having to be dragged from it.

This seems to have been an emotional peak. A few close male and female relatives continue wailing for a while but then, with the exception of some women who carry on weeping against the house of the deceased, a relative quiet falls upon the homestead.

There is now what seems to be a wait, while members of the husband's clan are called to one side to discuss how many bulls and goats will be sacrificed at the mourning ceremony to begin the day after tomorrow. I have the feeling that, with the body well and truly buried, we have now left the loosely structured, highly emotional and often competitive initial phase of the funeral. We are now more within the realm of male authority and calculation.

The men of the husband's clan assert that the Mijikenda money which has been collected cannot possibly suffice. It will pay for paraffin for a few lamps and for the palm wine given to those who have worked on the grave and on the body (excepting women who are not normally permitted to drink), but the homestead head and other people must provide the livestock and palm wine for distribution. Members of the deceased wife's clan are also there, and they say what they can offer or bring, together with other close relatives of both the husband and the woman. Offerings by the woman's clan are sometimes expressly made on the understanding that they are to help someone from the husband's clan who cannot afford even a goat.

The group then announces to the large congregation that the mourning ceremony will indeed be held, confirming what always happens, for it is only small children who are given a burial without a subsequent ceremony. Such announcements may also be about an extra day added, as for instance when an important doctor-diviner has died. As evening approaches even more people gather at the homestead, forming small groups each with food and palm wine which they have brought with them. From this night on, women will sleep on mats on the floor in and around the house of the deceased, whether a man or a woman, while men sleep outside on the ground out in the open, also on mats but well apart from the house.

Day Two: resting the hoes (siku ya kusindira madzembe)
The day after the burial is regarded as one of rest after the previous day's labours, also giving the freshly turned soil of the grave mound the chance to dry out. But it is in fact used to prepare for the mourning or *hanga* proper, which begins next morning, the third day. In fact, people say that neither the burial nor the rest day are counted as part of the mourning ceremony at all.

The homestead head, the main bereaved and other close kin set about arranging for livestock and palm wine to be brought to the mourning ceremony. The animals are sacrificed on the fifth day, which gives sponsors some three days or so in which to acquire them. In the cattle area, palm wine has to be brought from the east, mainly Kaloleni and Rabai, but in much greater quantities than is normally the case for daily consumption.

The homestead head and his family meanwhile provide some palm wine and food to special visitors but, otherwise, until the fifth day, those attending the burial and staying on will have brought their own food, mainly maize flour, and will buy their own liquor.

Seeking the livestock for the sacrificial fifth day clearly presents a greater problem for people attending funerals in the agricultural east. Only a few cattle and goats can be kept in the densely settled palm zone, where even maize is grown in patches between the trees, and livestock have to be moved rapidly from one small grazing area to another. Most animals therefore have to be bought and brought in from the cattle area itself. This is of course a reversal of the problem faced by the cattle zone where it is palm wine which has to be imported.

Funerals, in other words, being both prolonged and recurrent, articulate a significant exchange of liquor and livestock between the two ecological areas. The exchange is mapped onto the geographical interlinking of affines who, through their relationships of *kizhere* with each other, attend funerals in both areas regardless of where they live. Funerals, then, facilitate widespread contacts and the exchange of goods.

Day Three: the first water (siku ya kwandza madzi or siku ya madzi ga mosi)
This is the day when the mourning ceremony (*hanga*) begins. It is called the first day of the 'water', to be followed by the second, third, fourth, and in the case of a man, fifth days of 'water'. Why water? Among the neighbouring Chonyi, another Mijikenda group, such days are called those of the 'brush' or 'broom'.

Thus while the Chonyi see their ceremony as sweeping away the taint of death, the Giriama wash it away. The use of water in medicines for purificatory purposes is particularly pronounced among the Giriama, as in the use of the sheep's chyme to cleanse a homestead of *vitio*, described in the next chapter. At the mourning ceremony it is from this, the third day, that people who have been sleeping overnight at the homestead must wash themselves ritually in medically prepared water (*vuo*) placed in a special wooden bowl at four o'clock in the morning (at about the time of the first cock crow). Men wash first, followed by women, who then weep and wail for a short time. The bereaved do not wash.

On this day also, those men and women who are closest to the deceased ask each other, or whoever is willing, to shave their heads for them. Shaving is yet another act of 'clearing away', an aspect of the cleansing and expulsion of death. The circle of kin and affines who have their heads shaved is arbitrarily defined, depending on whoever counts themselves as part of it, though it must include those who have been called the bereaved (*afererwa*). The first to be shaved is he or she regarded as closest to the dead person, starting with a widow or widower, and then the homestead head, and thereafter brothers, sons and parents in no special order. The hair will not be cut again until the second funeral, which may be at any time from one to four months later, when again the heads will be shaved. The prohibition period is also that during which the widow is said to be 'tied' and must not have sexual intercourse with any man until she is inherited. *Kitio cha mufu* will come if either of these rules concerning sex and hair is broken.

The head shaving and early morning washing are regarded by the Giriama themselves as a renunciation and banishment of what I translate as deathliness (*kifo*), a notion which is repeated on the last day of the ceremony and which comes out more strongly in the event of a 'bad death', as I shall show later in this chapter.

Day Three continued and Day Four

Throughout this day and the next, the day of the 'second water' (*madzi ga hiri*), there is dancing and singing of various kinds, some by competing neighbourhood teams of relatively young men and women (not all unmarried), some exclusively of old men and women, and some mixed both as to gender and age. The dancing continues until the final day.

Much could be written on the dances, but here I can only touch on them. I have already mentioned the women's Kihoma and Kifudu dances which introduce the burial and therefore the whole ceremony, and it is appropriate here to return to them for a moment.

The name Kifudu, to describe the dance of the women's society, has remained unchanged for many generations. The society itself has added to its functions, being concerned nowadays with raising money for children's nurseries and schools as well as for instructing women in the knowledge of medical cures for their children, and other medicines.[4] But the Kifudu songs and dances have for as long as can be remembered and recorded (see Champion 1967: 26) accompanied the burial and been prominent in the ceremony.

The words of the Kifudu, and also of the Kihoma, King'ombe and other songs are in verse form (*ma-zumo*). First, women abuse the deceased by name, accusing him or her of having left behind with the living a whole host of problems which he or she is now unable to help with, and of now being sexually useless. Expressions of anger are mixed with those of grief. Clans are also identified as having certain characteristics: their men are jealous of their wives, neglect them, never sleep with them, favour one wife over the rest, are greedy and so on. It is hinted that one or another clan may have caused the death through witchcraft. Later, men respond in like manner, accusing women of drunkenness, laziness, adultery and desiring too much sex (*manahendza uzembe*). The songs thus range in tone and theme from anger and grief, including abuse of the dead body, to a bawdy abuse of clans and of the opposite sex.

Giriama have remarked on the didactic effect of such songs, which both convey some shared opinions about clans and persons and also alert everyone to the realisation that their behaviour is judged and subject to comment. The abuse of the dead and their denunciation as now useless is the most poignantly expressed judgement and is said by Giriama to be a way in which the living tear themselves away in a harsh farewell. At first sight this might seem to amount to a very pragmatic attitude to the dead: especially in the light of a saying that 'the dead can only be buried by the living' (*afwaye ni kuzikwa na ariye moyo*), that is, that the dead are indeed so useless that they are now completely dependent on the living. At the same time, however, there is fear of the dead (women as much as men) avenging themselves on the living. They have to be appeased, in order both to avert misfortune and to remove it. Appeasement thus co-exists with abusive renunciation as an ambivalent attitude to the dead.

One way of dealing with ambivalence and ambiguity is to confront it. Perhaps, therefore, the Kifudu women's abusive dismissal of the recently deceased member of their community (whose death, after all, is still occasioning grief at the very moment that they sing), both belittles death itself and is an initial challenge to the dead in what is expected to be a struggle between them and their descendants for at least a generation: alleged neglect of dead parents, grandparents and other close kin, can literally haunt and harm a man, and sometimes a woman, for the rest of their life unless they accede to a diviner's diagnosis and appease the dead relative. Perhaps the Kifudu woman can issue this challenge because their medicines empower them to take the risk. The result is that their provocative songs and dances blend with the expressions of grief all around them

---

[4] Both Thompson (1990) and Udvardy (1990; and forthcoming) have carried out research on the women's Kifudu society and activities. Thompson has also uncovered information on an interesting predecessor, called the Forudahe society (1990: 91–92).

in the homestead. In the highly charged atmosphere of the occasion, the challenge throws into question the notion of mortal capacity and capability: the dead can harm their living relatives while the latter can be hurtfully negligent towards their dead kin (who may come to a man or woman in a dream and complain sorrowfully of hunger and cold); is it therefore the living or the dead who are more in charge of their destinies and the world? It is a question which recurs throughout the ceremony.

The Kifudu dances and songs apart, there has clearly been much change over time in the repertoire of others, just as there are variations between and even within regions. Dances and their sequence have altered considerably within certain areas even during my twenty years' acquaintanceship with the Giriama. In the cattle area of Miyani in the 1980s, two other sets of dances and songs of abuse were identified as only ever used at a funeral. One is Mwanzele, which is danced at a relatively slow pace with men prominent, and Changilo, said to be the 'younger brother' of Mwanzele, which is danced much more quickly and sometimes has men dressed as women. Changilo means 'speed' and is the name given in the area to the famine of 1979, when people had to dash off to Kaloleni when relief supplies of American maize were provided by the government. The four dance-songs, Kihoma, Kifudu, Mwanzele and Changilo, together talk abusively of death, sex, and 'the secret parts of people's bodies', the men speaking contemptuously for instance of a deceased woman's large vagina (*jini bomu*) and the women of the deceased man's large penis (*mbomo bomu*), both regarded as having become so through too many years of use and so impracticable for sexual and therefore reproductive purposes. Two other dances also only occur at funerals, namely Msego and Uganja, but these include praise rather than abusive songs. It is the dance-songs of abuse which are paramount and excite the most attention. The licence extends more widely on these occasions and 'a man can even abuse his father-in-law', amounting to mild familiarity with him.

Other dance-songs are not confined to funerals and may also be played on such occasions as weddings and local dance competitions held in honour of visitors. None of these dance-songs, however, are the same as those played at spirit possession sessions, which are also, incidentally, subject to changes of fashion in name, content and the sequence in which they are played.

The place of dance and song in the funeral is clearly itself ambivalent. While some, like the Kifudu, are constant markers of the ceremony and highlight its main existential themes, others have the status almost of popular music in the Western world. They are renamed or newly named, incorporate new rhythms and pace, and, like all songs, including Kifudu, experiment with their words all the time, but switch themes much more rapidly than Kifudu. The stated intention is to encourage the bereaved to see beyond their grief: the more witty the verbal repartee the more the bereaved persons 'listen and forget'.

In view of the constant naming, re-naming and thematic variation, it is difficult to know in what sense new songs are created or old ones renovated. Thus it is that the dance-song called Uganja is said also to be known as Mishari, and Kindurumu to be known also as Kilale, while the long-established but still popular Gonda is said to be similar to Sengenya and Mabumbumbu and so on. Dances are distinguished by the use of different instruments and such body movements as shaking the shoulders, stamping the feet, quietly shuffling or leaping athletically, as well as by the content of their singing, and whether or not men, women, the old and the young, or any of these, are entitled to join them.

Dance-songs are much like the conduct of funerals themselves in that they are presented to participants as having broad outlines to be followed but vary in the ways in which they are actually carried out. The on-the-spot working through the dance-songs is both a part of the funerals and an allegory of them. They suggest predictable activities and responses yet are innovative.

The Day of Sacrifice

Day Five: 'the third water' (siku ya madzi ga hahu)

As if to rescue the course of the funeral from taking too wayward a turn, the fifth day, or the 'third water', is firmly marked as the time of sacrifice (*siku ya ku-tsindza*). It is also known as the day of the heads or leaders (*siku ya vitswa*), because this is when sponsors of the funeral feasting, who have donated animals to be sacrificed and eaten, have to decide to whom they will allocate their meat. It is a time of reckoning for men to show their prestige through conspicuous generosity, and to indicate their followers, who, in accepting the meat, accept publicly some notion of the sponsor's seniority or leadership.

Since, over the course of many funerals and even within the same funeral, a man may be given meat by, and may himself provide meat for, a number of the men in the congregation, there is no way nor any expectation that hard and fast ties of binding loyalty should be formed. It is much looser than that, but is nevertheless an effective way of roughly indicating the lines of friendship and, by default, or actual or potential enmity: not to receive meat from a man incurs no debts and may sometimes be taken as a rebuff. Yet no man is wealthy enough to feed everyone and so choices have to be made. The compulsion to be generous conflicts with the inevitable necessity to be ungenerous to some and not others.

Customarily, the sacrifices start with that of a single male goat, whose right ear is taken and spoken into by the main bereaved, who tells it to listen. Through the medium of the goat the deceased is addressed and beseeched to leave members of his or her homestead and family in peace, and that it was God's will that he/she died and not that of anyone in the homestead. This preliminary to the actual sacrifice is called 'laying down the ancestor' (*ku-laza koma*). The ceremony is similar to that by which a boy-child gets his clan name: the goat's ear is taken and, through it, clan ancestors are told to listen as they are told the boy's clan name, an act which is said to reassure the ancestors of their continuity. Thus, at the beginning of life as at death, a spiritual co-existensiveness between forbears and their living descendants is created. For a mature man who dies never having married, a burning wood ember must be placed under his head as he is buried on his side. It is called a *kinga* and regarded as his partner. If this is not done, the ghost of the man will come to the elders in dreams and threaten to 'take' (i.e. kill) a woman of the homestead.

In 'laying down the ancestor' at the funeral, the sacrificial goat's throat is slit and the blood allowed to flow onto the grave. Thereafter, the other animals are sacrificed, sometimes one or more head of cattle next, but sometimes a number of goats, with an alternating mixture depending on numbers of both beasts, and people at the funeral. Though customarily all are expected to be male, an old female animal may be sacrificed if a donor cannot acquire a male. The reason given is simply that of expediency rather than symbolism: females are not killed but are kept for reproduction and, in the case of cows, for milk. Nevertheless, it is tempting to see an inversion of ideas in the exchange of heifers in bridewealth for wives who reproduce humanity, and of bulls for the peace of the dead who are beyond reproduction but can hinder it among the living.

In the eastern palm belt it is almost always Muslims who actually slaughter the animals. This is out of deference to the minority of Muslims likely to be in the community, who cannot otherwise partake of the food. The cattle area contains very few Muslims, and few Muslims visit funerals there, with the result that non-Muslims commonly carry out the killing. This difference, minor in itself, is one of a number, such as the absence of Islamic spirits in the cattle zone compared with that of the east, which reinforce people's image of the eastern area as increasingly under the influence of Islam and therefore less authentically Giriama than the west.

It is considered shameful if the homestead head (who will also normally be one of the bereaved though not necessarily the closest to the deceased) has not provided for the sacrifice of at least two cattle from out of his own homestead's resources. The number of goats is always many more, most being offered by relatives and affines living outside the homestead, some of whom may also provide a bull if the deceased or homestead head is socially prominent and respected.

Another important difference between the eastern palm belt and the cattle-keeping west concerns the way homestead heads actually procure the livestock. In the eastern area heads sometimes have to mortgage palm trees and land in order to raise the money to buy the animals, to the extent sometimes of bankrupting themselves, and in some cases may still not raise enough to buy the minimal two bulls. A homestead head bitterly recounted to me how he saw the pressures to which the head is subject, which I have also observed.

When the elders of the deceased's clan, or that of the husband of a deceased wife, retire to one side to discuss the funeral following a burial, or the prospect of a second funeral, they will say, 'Your father (or whoever) was a big man (or *you* are a big man), and so you must slaughter bulls, goats, and lay on plenty of palm wine'. The head may reply, 'But I have no money to buy many of these things'. 'What do you mean no money – what about these palm trees your father left you?' And at least one of the elders will have many bank notes stuffed in his pocket, and will offer to 'help' to have the trees on mortgage. Since the head may never be able to redeem the mortgage, he will lose not only his father but also his father's inheritance.

In the cattle area, none of this occurs. Livestock cannot be mortgaged like palms and land. Rather, they circulate between families who have intermarried, so that, even if a man is too poor to provide an animal, an affine, most likely a *kizhere*, will provide one for him which was part of the bridewealth originally handed over by the poor man. The cycle of wealth and poverty in cattle is generally accepted in the area as a normal feature of the domestic life cycle, as men use cattle for the marriages of sons and so contentedly relinquish their herds as they get older. In the cattle area, even poor men manage to raise the minimal two bulls which, though they may be donated, are presented as their own. The funerals of which rich cattle owners are sponsors are especially well supplied with livestock, with often treble this number sacrificed and, in some cases, fifty to seventy-five goats.

The main difference between the two areas is that while people in the agricultural east must raise the cash to buy livestock, perhaps by selling their main means of subsistence, people of the west either already possess animals or can more easily draw upon those of affines and kin. Even if their own small herd is depleted, no land is lost and they can if they wish eventually acquire new animals by herding for others as described in chapter three.

The names of the providers of beasts are announced for each animal throughout the day of sacrifice and for the next day or so if many are slaughtered. The meat is cooked and distributed. The male elders who have provided an animal are given the liver (*ini*) which is said to symbolise the male unity required for war, with the so-called finger (*chala*) of the liver going to the homestead head and, usually, the sacrifier (that is, the donor of the animal). They are also given the tongue (*ludhimi* or *ngumba* as it is called in 'the old Giriama language of the Kaya'), and first taste of most other parts of the animal such as the ribs (*mubavu*), lungs (*laga*) and thighs (*viga*). Young men are allowed a second taste of the latter after being given the entrails (*uhambo utsanga*), which they attack with knives and eat raw. Women are also given intestines but clean and cook them before eating them. Persons who have been diagnosed by diviners as suffering from problems of the heart (*moyo*), kidney (*figo*) and spleen (*luwengo*), take care not to eat these parts of the animal, and sometimes eat to one side of the homestead.

Throughout the homestead are separate groups of men drinking palm wine and eating meat and maize-flour 'bread', and of women who cook for them nearby and eat afterwards. Each group, called a *chamiyo*, is associated with a particular animal donor and his followers. People do not move between groups, but may well be invited to another group subsequently. The homestead head and the senior bereaved (who are commonly the same person) try to ensure that no one is left out of the meat-eating groups by discreetly suggesting additions to existing groups or by bringing meat to someone and setting up a new one. This has to be done on the basis of a head's knowledge of local rivalries and possible friendships. This delicate handling of social relations is yet another aspect of the managerial skill and tact that is expected of a homestead head or senior person generally.

By this stage of the funeral, dancing, singing, eating and drinking have transformed the ambivalence of the earlier days into an atmosphere of festivity. Men get drunk, dispute with each other in a raucous manner, which, though jocular at the outset, may touch on sensitive personal matters and so occasionally result in genuine anger and violence. Men claim that this is the time when wives take the chance to commit adultery with a lover, presumably while husbands are drunk or perhaps similarly engaged. Women have, after all, been told by husbands to take food to the funeral and to sleep there out of respect for the deceased and his family, and men tend to accept that this meanwhile lessens their control over their wives. 'We cannot control their adultery at funerals but we will claim compensation (*malu*) from the lover if we catch them in the act.' Given the women's colossal work-load this reasoning sounds fanciful for the most part, though one or two illicit liaisons may occur in the deep of the night as the drums, dancing and singing continue throughout. During the day women talk at their work more freely than at other times, occasionally joining in dances as married or unmarried, old or young, as is appropriate to the particular dance.

This is also the time when games of kinship placing are played, in which men try to assert their seniority either through genealogical reckoning or the generational clan naming system (see Parkin 1989a). There is also more serious discussion of land and property deals, for which funeral congregations provide admirable opportunities. The heightened emotional atmosphere of the recent death does indeed seem to fade, as the dramas associated with grief, fear and the dismissal of the dead give way to those of festive challenge and counter-challenge, often instanced by dances (such as that called *mavunyo*, meaning 'boasting') in which competing teams of young men and women dressed in colourful clothing vaunt themselves.

Days Six and Seven: 'the fifth and sixth waters' (siku ya madzi ga nne/ tsano)

Those who said early on in the funeral that their dances and songs were aimed at cheering up the bereaved can reasonably claim to have succeeded, at least from outward appearances, as the bereaved themselves eat, drink and converse on their mats with people who come and sit with them. The funeral has clearly reached its closing stages. If the deceased is a woman, this is the last day of the funeral and if a man, the penultimate. The last day, for both men and women, is also called the 'day of the mat' (*siku ya kitseka*), for it is when 'people go home, and shake the mats on which they have been lying and sleeping' during the funeral.

A final rite is carried out by the next senior male to the deceased, or, as in the case of a widow, to the deceased's husband. This man leaves the homestead on the last night with a small gourd of medicine (*muhaso*) made up of water and the leaves of a 'cold (and therefore curative) tree' (*muhi wa peho*), such as a baobab (*muyu*) or *mukone* tree. He makes his way to one of these trees, or to a river or road junction, where he is joined by his wife. They do not speak, but have sexual intercourse in the normal side position (he on his right and she on her left), after which they wash their genitals in the medicine and then trample it into the ground, he with his left foot and she with her right. They then return to the homestead without looking back or speaking. To do so would bring further deaths to the homestead. Once back inside the homestead, they can act normally but must refrain from sex until the following evening. They have successfully turned their backs on death.

This is the final act renouncing death in the first funeral. I indicated above that head shaving early on in the funeral, and early morning washing for people other than the bereaved, are seen by the Giriama themselves as contributing towards ridding the homestead of death. In this last rite death or deathliness (*kifo*) is thus finally banished to the outside of the homestead. Moreover it is done at places where deathliness may be made safe, as at a baobab tree whose cooling properties will contain it and where, incidentally, *mizimu* spirits, renowned for their sense of justice, will also guard over it. If the rite occurs at one of the other two permissible sites, the reasoning appears to be that deathliness will be carried away by the flow of the river or, at a road junction, by travellers passing by and taking it with them, away from the homestead. I shall return in due course to discuss this immanent quality of deathliness.

Here I note that, as well as being regarded as part of the cleansing of the homestead, this expulsion of death is sometimes likened to the occasions in the Kaya when the elders get people to 'clear away' the 'dirt' or contamination which derives from foreign influences, evil, accumulated neglect or simply uncontrolled undergrowth.

Minimising grief, causing the bereaved to forget, and banishing death itself through abuse of the deceased and through the ritual action of expulsion, therefore come across as the principal themes in the burial and funeral. The expulsion of death is seen as one of a chain of acts which begins with the symbolic washing with water: 'washing' is the gentle act of the supplicant, while 'clearing away' is a term normally used for cutting undergrowth or ejecting things forcibly, and so borders on violence. The anger that is present at funerals does in fact oscillate between that directed at the witch or whoever is responsible for the death and that felt towards the deceased corpse itself, which is a frightening intrusion and threat. As it was once put to me, 'Those we love are frightening to us when they die.' The horror of the corpse of someone who was and/or should be loved, no doubt produces what we can only translate as guilt, and it is perhaps an unsurprising reaction to confront and reject both corpse and guilt with anger. The washing of the corpse and the expulsion of deathliness are paradigmatically one, yet progress from a gentle to a violent idiom.

Such themes are more in evidence than the idea of regeneration. Regeneration is entailed rather than explicit. It is implied in the last night's ritual copulation between the senior mourner and his wife, after which normal life, sexuality and reproduction may be presumed to continue. It is also entailed in the abuse hurled at the deceased as now sexually useless, the implication here being that the dead person has now yielded the capacity to reproduce to those who are living. But this is the outsider reading into these activities. From the Giriama viewpoint, it is the desperate wish to rid themselves of deathliness as such that is paramount, for unless this is done further life and, indeed, fertility, may be lost.

The theme of banishment is, in fact, especially emphasised on the occasion of a bad death, which I shall describe later. For the moment, let me continue into the second funeral, which is a culmination of the first.

The second funeral
This is called 'the hairs of the month' (*nyere za mwezi*) and refers to the hair that will have grown on the heads of the bereaved since they were shaved at the first funeral. The customary ideal period elapsing between first and second funerals is one month, but is nowadays often longer than this though not normally more than four.

The second funeral can only be started at the sighting of a new moon. A new moon may be hidden by cloud, or, since the moon's cycle varies, may appear a day or so later than the twenty-eight days provisionally expected (the Giriama 'week' consists of four days, with seven weeks roughly making up a lunar month). Livestock to be sacrificed are brought into the homestead a day beforehand, and may therefore be kept waiting if the new moon is 'late' in appearing.

Those coming from afar for the second funeral will have been told of the event and will also arrive on the day before the hoped-for new moon, staying if necessary the extra day or so before it is sighted. Local people are able to attend once the ceremony is under way.

At midnight after the new moon has been seen, drumming, dancing and singing begin, continuing throughout the night as at the first funeral, together with food and palm wine. The dawn is counted as the beginning of the first day, and is when the animals are slaughtered from about seven o'clock in the morning. Among the Giriama, two bulls and a large number of goats are again regarded as a respectful minimum to be offered at a second funeral, though more are sometimes provided and usually more than at the first funeral. Other Mijikenda groups vary considerably in this regard: the Chonyi slaughter no animals at the first funeral, but do so at their lengthy second funeral (called *mab-ulu*) and to a lesser extent at an intermediary ceremony (called *ku-laga mabulu*); the Duruma and Jibana have their own named and different ceremonies (for example *lusinga*) and so on.

The day following the sacrifice of livestock is customarily supposed to be the last of the Giriama second funeral, which should therefore last only two days from the sighting of the new moon. In practice, since more animals may be donated than at a first funeral, the feasting, singing and dancing at the second funeral may continue for three or four days and nights, sometimes called the first, second, third days and so on of the mat (*siku ya kitseka cha kwandza/hiri/ hahu* ...), echoing the theme of the first funeral that people must not only attend the event but also stay there a while. Affines of affines of a socially important homestead head or deceased, who have taken a long time to arrive from distant parts of Giriamaland, are in this way included in the ceremony.

In any event, on the second and nominally final day, or on a subsequent day if it is so agreed, elders of the deceased's clan meet, if he is a man, to discuss the inheritance (*ufwa*) of his property and widow(s). Widows choose their inheritor, who may be a brother or recognised patrilateral parallel cousin (classificatory or otherwise) of the deceased man. It is preferred that the widows be taken by one man rather than being divided between two or more. Even in the event of young widows preferring to be inherited by a grandson of their ex-husband who is nearer their own age, the older widows may also be inherited by him, though only nominally, for they are more likely to live in the homestead of a married son. Grandparents and grandchildren, it may be remembered, commonly call each other 'sibling' and have familiar relations with each other, and this inheritance of widows is then, in effect, that from brother to brother.

The reasoning behind this preference for widows to be inherited by one man is that, otherwise, members of the homestead will not stay together: widows would each go to the different homesteads of their new husbands accompanied possibly by their unmarried sons and daughters. On the other hand, the widows' choice of a junior brother can create a split, for while, ideally, the man chosen as inheritor of the widows becomes the new head of the deceased's existing home-stead, this may prove unacceptable to an existing more senior brother or agnate who may set up his own or force the new heir to do so.

Whoever is chosen by the widows has jurisdiction over the deceased man's livestock, trees, land, other property and unmarried children, though he also assumes the responsibility to enable these to marry through use of the inherited property. Suitors competing for the widows try to persuade the women with tobacco and palm wine, for the advantages in having extra wives for children, labour and prestige, and in controlling additional animals, land and trees, can be considerable.

Once again, there is a difference between the cattle-keeping west and agricultural east. Land and trees are visible and measurable, and their location is generally known, and so they cannot easily be appropriated or sold off by the new heir without others noticing. Some heirs manage to do so, but the main value of such property held in trust is in providing an income from the sale of palm wine and copra and for growing maize for subsistence. The heir to a man's cattle may also benefit from the sale of their milk. But provided he fulfils his obligation to secure marriages for his adopted sons, he can merge the new animals with his existing livestock and reproduce his herd more quickly. The fact that some or all of the animals are hidden and deployed among different herders and locations, as described in chapter three, makes it difficult after some time for the adopted sons and their inherited mother, and for any sons by this latter and her inheritor, to know precisely how many animals make up their heritage. Elders intervene in disputes arising out of this situation, but the advantage is clearly with the cattle-man, who benefits from a greater increase in capital through his herd's expansion than is likely for a man in the agricultural east who acts as trustee for land and trees only.

As well as eventually incurring advantages and responsibilities with regard to property, a man and his inherited widow must, more immediately, cleanse the homestead of the deceased. As in the first funeral, there is ritual banishment of death coupled with an attempt to conserve fertility, by limiting the chances of catching *vitio*, the disease that causes diarrhoea, vomiting, death and barrenness. I give an example of this ritual preceded by an indication of the pressures behind a widow's choice of new husband.

Karisa is the deceased elder full brother of Kenga, who was chosen as her new husband by Karisa's widow. The widow was in fact persuaded in her choice by the mother of both men. The mother had been living in the homestead of her dead son. She reportedly could not tolerate the possibility of the widow and property going to sons who were 'not of her own womb', which might otherwise have been the widow's choice. The mother is herself one of three widows of the one man, the father of both Karisa and Kenga, who therefore have a number of half-brothers.

This decision having been taken, the stage was set for the final ritual of the second funeral. Kenga's newly inherited wife was given medicine made up of water and sheep's chyme, here called *vitio* medicine (*muhaso wa vitio/ mavingane*). She washed her hands in the special wooden bowl containing it and then, shaking the water from her hands at her new husband, said, 'Let not *vitio* seize me'. Kenga did the same. Kenga had then to sleep at his dead brother's homestead with his new wife, spending four days there. He then had to return to his own homestead and sleep with his own wives in order of their seniority, followed by his new wife, so making the inherited one junior to the rest. To do otherwise brings *vitio*.

Until this round of obligations is completed, wives should not commit adultery, which will also cause *vitio*. In fact, they can procure a protective charm to hang round their waist, hidden under their *hando* (Giriama woman's cotton skirt), which lessens the chances of being afflicted with *vitio*. After four days at her new husband's homestead the inherited wife is free to return to her dead husband's home. She remains, however, the wife of her new husband, who may visit her at any time.

Bad deaths

Once again, then, we see that the second funeral, like the first, is concerned to control forces threatening fertility and life. Just as *vitio* has a deathly immanence that must be mastered, so has the more general deathliness known as *kifo*. Averting or being cleansed of the former (*ku-ogeswa vitio*), and averting further deathliness, as in the above example, both involve their banishment to somewhere outside the homestead. The two concepts clearly touch on each other. They bring into question the boundedness of the homestead and its integrity, in the moral as well as organisational sense. But while the disease, *vitio*, arises from recognisable sins of commission and omission and so causes death or *kifo*, the deathliness embraced by the term *kifo* can also arise from unintended, unforeseeable and even incomprehensible accidents. Deaths from accidents, suicide and fights are called by the Giriama 'death from war' (*kifo cha viha* or simply *vihani*), so-called because of their sudden and violent nature. They partly coincide with those labelled in the anthropological literature as 'bad deaths'. The way in which the Giriama deal with such bad or violent deaths draws on the theme expressed in funerals of ordinary deaths, namely how much in control of his or her own destiny can a person be? In normal funerals the theme is subdued and interwoven subtly in songs, dances and addresses to the dead. At the funerals of bad deaths it is the very reason for having a distinctive burial and mortuary ceremony.

The very idea of a bad death among the Giriama is that it has occurred as the result of outside forces over which humans have no control. All they can do is to try and prevent the effects of that bad death striking again. A struggle between human and cosmic forces is at the centre of this concept of bad death.

In fact, bad death is not a good translation of the Giriama concept and we get a better idea by focusing on the last of the Giriama terms in the expression, 'to die in war' (*kufwa kwa viha*). *Viha*, war, is a key concept, best translated as 'violence', for it refers not only to death in battles and fights but also to that arising from domestic disputes, as well as from accidents. Besides having the idea of physical harm being done to a person, *viha* also includes the idea that he or she has been violated or defiled, so that the polluting corpse must be ejected from the homestead.

The central idea is that men and women who kill – in battle as warriors, in homestead or neighbourhood quarrels or by accident – have the blood of their victims on them. They remain in a negative condition called *kilatso*. Unless purified they will be responsible for further deaths by accident or in fights, and including suicide, both within and outside their families. Their motives and reasons for causing such deaths may or may not be clear but are anyway regarded as secondary to the fact that they are possessed by this condition of *kilatso*. It is *kilatso* rather than the person which kills.

While living carriers of *kilatso* must be decontaminated, those who have died *viha* deaths must be ejected from the homestead, ritually dissociated from it, and the homestead itself purified. There are a number of elements here. The victims of bad death are buried outside their homestead, sometimes in the bush and some-times behind the area at the back of their house known as *fisi* (hyena), (but in some Mijikenda groups are actually thrown into the bush); they are not dressed in the calico *sandzu* shroud which is customary for corpses, but are buried in the clothes in which they died; their bodies are not placed on wooden planks in the grave; the funeral is one day less than normal, and the burial position is different (and accords with the nature of the death); and the purification itself is through the slaughter of a ram in the homestead, as with the eradication of *vitio*, after which a customary number of cattle and goats will be slaughtered.

One rite in particular banishes the *kilatso* arising from the bad death and tries to dispose of it elsewhere, far from the homestead. The mother and father of the victim, who may well be a young man, must sleep and have sexual intercourse outside the homestead during the night after the day of the burial. Should the deceased man have no surviving parents, then his widow has to have sexual inter-course outside the homestead ('in the bush' as they say) with a man who is paid for the job but is not of the Mijikenda peoples (that is, who is a complete outsider), and who will unsuspectingly carry the *kilatso* away with him. Sexual intercourse here does not take place until the end of the second funeral. This gives funeral organisers time to find a man willing to take on this task. In fact the unsuspecting man is often characterised as being an up-country Luo, a people who migrate all over Kenya far from their homeland in the western region of the country. He is further characterised as bemused but delighted at the prospect of sexual relations for which he is paid, especially if the widow is attractive. In a parallel manner a Giriama widower whose wife died a bad death must seek a distant prostitute for the same purpose, paying her in the usual way, so that she too is unsuspecting. In this way the *kilatso* is diverted from the homestead, the neighbourhood and Giriama country itself and sent off to another place. Places themselves, such as a bend in a river where animals and people have sometimes been swept away during storms, or a bad stretch of road where fatal car accidents have occurred, or the site of a battle or fight, may also be said to 'have *kilatso*' (*ho hatu hana kilatso*).

Kilatso is the diminutive of the substantive *mulatso*, meaning blood but also personal capacity. A man who is skilled at raising cattle is said to have the blood to do it (*ana mulatso wa kufuga ng' ombe*). But, if his cattle consistently die and he clearly is not proficient, then it is said that he has bad blood (*ana mulatso mui*). Someone for whom things habitually go wrong is identified in the same way, as is a man who may have stolen once but never did so again, yet is suspected whenever a theft occurs. *Mulatso* thus refers to the ability, characteristics, and even luck that someone is fated with. Since *mulatso* is also used to refer to family relationships, there is clearly the hint that, whether good or bad, it runs in a family. In practice the Giriama do not expect a bad cattle herder or person with killing tendencies to produce children who will be like that. They are only too aware of the frequent differences between parent and child. But, as with the inherited tendency to be possessed by spirits, *mulatso* in this metaphorical sense suggests a kind of potential for skill or incompetence which successive generations transmit. It is an idea which gently acknowledges the variable achievements and failings that may run in families but takes the benign view that these are humanly to be expected.

By contrast *kilatso* is only ever negative, is lethal, and is inflicted. If unremoved it will indeed be passed on and run in a family, but otherwise it comes as a result of proximity to death: the carrier is either a *viha* killer or is a relative living in the same homestead of the victim of a *viha* death.

Mulatso has the idea of unalterable personal fate. We might call it innate ability or inability. But it normally holds only with reference to different domains of life: a man may not be good at herding cattle but is renowned for his style of mat- and basket-weaving. *Kilatso* is much more dramatic and is literally a matter of life and death, but can at least be permanently removed through ritual purification.

Kilatso is sometimes spoken of as *kifo*, the more general term for death. As this synonym suggests, *kilatso* is especially associated with the extreme contamination of a bad death, but partakes of the general need to expel deathliness beyond the homestead, in the ways I have described for the funerals of persons who have not died bad deaths.

East – west differences

It is often said among the Giriama that the wide open spaces and ample distances between homesteads in the western cattle area enable the effects of *kilatso* to be more easily dispersed. In the eastern palm belt, however, homesteads more frequently abut each other, causing confusion as to what might be an appropriate distance at which to bury a victim of a bad death. Moreover, since land in the east is registered and owned by title deed nowadays, members of a homestead and the possibly unrelated owners of the immediately surrounding area may not reach agreement on the burial. People from both areas therefore say that there is less problem in the west of carrying out the burial and mortuary rites for bad deaths.

More generally, there is indeed a marked difference, to which people again refer, in the extent to which funerals are marred by disagreements. In the west, there are fewer Muslims and Christians and the area is exclusively Giriamaland, even though a few people of Duruma origin may live in one or two homesteads as client cattle herders. While no funeral, even in the west, is quite like another, there is much more unanimity regarding the rules of procedure. To take an example already touched on, most attending agree that the bodies of both men and women should be buried on the right side with the eyes facing Singwaya, which is recognised as an ancestral point of diffusion. In the east, however, there is increasing differentiation within families between the different religions, as there is of intermarriage between the different Mijikenda groups. As a result there may, after the burial, be a number of simultaneous mortuary rites for the same person, perhaps held in separate homesteads, one Christian, one Muslim and one *koma*, as persons following Giriama animistic beliefs are called. Or, if the different religious groups are present at the same rite, they may disagree vehemently about the relative weight given to their respective religions. Similarly, while the Giriama and Kauma share similar funerary customs, the Giriama and the Chonyi differ markedly, as do various other Mijikenda groups. Yet, from the Kaloleni area towards the coast, the admixture of Mijikenda groups increases, as a result of settlement and intermarriage.

I began this chapter by drawing a distinction between the rules and practice of funerals. It is commonplace in anthropology nowadays to acknowledge that the rules that a people claim for social behaviour are at best provisional guidelines. Nevertheless, the fit between claims and practice may also vary. In the western cattle zone, there is a relatively tight fit which reinforces the view held both there and in the east that this area near the Kaya represents the most authentic source of pure Giriama customary wisdom. As one moves further towards the coast, the fit is less, and disagreements as to meanings increase: in some cases the reason given for the body's position is that its head has to point east because this is towards the coast, with no mention at all of the original homeland of Singwaya; in yet another case the claim is that the eyes have to point *kibla,* that is in the direction of Mecca (which is also north). In other words, even when the body's position is 'correct' (and it is not always so), the reasons given vary.

If this was all there is to the contrast, one would simply note it as a socio-geographical difference and leave it at that. However, the difference also has profound implications for notions of personal fate and external determinacy.

In the west, there is a sense of indigenous control, as in the successful attempt to defeat the government's abortive ranch scheme, described in chapter three, which is reflected in the less complex funerals. People die, are buried, become ancestors (*koma*), and allow *mulatso* (good blood) unhindered by *kilatso* (bad blood) to flow through their descendants. Through hidden and dispersed networks, enough livestock can usually be found for even the poorest bereaved to provide adequate sacrifice and, since the exchange value of land is counterbalanced by the need to keep it open as grazing land for all, no one need bankrupt himself by selling it for a lavish funeral.

In the east, the division by religion and by Mijikenda sub-group provides greater individual choice of faith and spouse but splits families and cuts across wider Giriama clan affiliations. The west is conservative and controls its options, while the east proliferates its options but not in a liberal way, for there is an intense struggle to control land and property in the face both of other coastal people and of people from up-country. Burying those who die good deaths in the west is a relatively secure act of attachment to clan land, while at the same time there is the space to banish unwelcome deathliness or *kilatso*. In the east, burial and mortuary rites are less certain acts, for they highlight growing but unpredictable differences between competing social and religious groups.

Conclusion
The critical feature of Giriama funerals is that they are about the banishment of death, so that life may continue. Banishing death clears and cleanses the homestead and its occupants, and is evident also in the various acts and terms of washing, expelling and shaving. Ritual and, in the case of a bad death, physical banishment outside the homestead presupposes a clear spatial boundary between the homestead as a place where people live and the outside as a place of 'bush' where deathliness can be safely laid. The contrast between the inside and outside is therefore also that between the place that has been cleared and cleansed and that in which the dirt or contamination of death is thrown. Like the Kaya, the homestead must be kept pure.

There are other respects in which funerals make spatial distinctions and orientations between the customarily pure and impure. We see this most obviously in the rules and arguments about the position of a corpse at burial, the positions adopted by men, women, the young and the old in feasting groups and in dances and wailing during the ceremony, and the ritual sexual intercourse occurring outside the homestead at the end of the second funeral. At a metalevel is the spatial contrast between the west as allegedly better able to conform to customary mortuary rules and the east as the least rule-governed and most likely to contaminate the Kaya. Identifying a person's place of origin or residence is commonly used as evidence of his or her personality. It is therefore not surprising to find Giriama from all areas expressing the view that persons living in the cattle-keeping west, being closer to the Kaya and furthest from non-customary influences, define themselves with a clear sense of what kind of Giriama they are, while those towards the coast are more likely to conflate different identities. Politically, what do these two alleged tendencies between purist and mixed identification tell us?

One points in the direction of firm authority, as wielded by the Kaya elders, and the other towards situational authority of the kind exercised by witch-finders such as Kajiwe. At first we might see these as alternatives facing Giriama as a group, that is to say, as a problem of how they should internally govern themselves together with other Mijikenda. Should the Kaya elders rule through a hegemony drawn from the Kaya's unquestioned sacredness? Or should people rule themselves independently of them? For instance, the young Kajiwe ignored the customarily held distinctions between the nine Mijikenda peoples and argued for freedom from the Kaya, from elders, from tradition and from Islam, and for a meritocratic egalitarianism linked to modern medicine, schools and Christianity. By contrast, the Kaya elders, comprising representatives of the nine Mijikenda peoples, reaffirmed the rule of customary law and ensured respect for it through their success in having Kajiwe imprisoned, and discreetly left untouched the question of Islamic ritual power.

Yet, important though they are as political organisers, the Kaya elders have not prevented Giriama in the east from becoming increasingly dependent on agricultural cash-cropping, wage labour and migration, from becoming involved in Christianity, commercialism and consumerism, nor from becoming more numerous and land hungry there. Kajiwe's exhortations anticipated such greater dependency and involvement. His pragmatic opposition to the authority of the Kaya elders was an egalitarian outgrowth of the status normally enjoyed by diviners and herbalists who are individualistic and not directly subservient to the Kaya elders. But, whereas the doctors and diviners fit in as best they can with new developments and with the legal demands of the Kenya state, Kajiwe always spoke and acted to excess, antagonising even those forces of 'modernisation' and civil conformity which he had been recommending.

While Kajiwe was no prophet, he transcended and personified the gap between the customary autocracy of the Kaya elders and the egalitarian professionalism of the doctors and diviners. Funerals are occasions which, through their songs, dances and disputes about traditional procedure, open up such questions of authority, influence and power. Until death is finally and firmly banished, there is always at funerals an ambivalence as to who will die next, who will be accused of sorcery as a result, and who will fail to produce children. Banishing death ensures fertility and life's continuity. But until it happens there is, so to speak, a power vacuum: who will and can control whom? In the context of the funeral, such questions are about who has the power of life, death and fertility over others. Since funerals are large collective occasions, it is not just the fertility and self-perpetuation of a person and family that is at stake, but that of a community, and ultimately that of the Giriama.

6

Alternative authorities: incest and fertility

In chapter three it was shown that cattle-keeping requires that homesteads remain large in western Giriamaland, while high population density and land shortage in the farming east favour smaller homesteads. Eastern homesteads therefore break up at an earlier stage of their development than western ones. The split is triggered by witchcraft accusations between brothers or by sons of fathers. By contrast witchcraft accusations are more contained in the west. People of a homestead need each other. Brothers sleeping with each others' wives, it is claimed, is their main problem, and the dire effects of this also have to be contained.

Speaking in this way gives the impression that adulterous incest and witchcraft are sharply distinguished concepts. In conversation among Giriama this is indeed the case. They will give a clear description of how each differs. In most cases which occur, too, there is no dispute as to what is witchcraft and what incest. But there are the odd cases where the one may be redefined as the other or at least may not be so clearly defined.

What does hold these ideas together, however, is an underlying concern with fertility and the health of parents and children. The concern is obviously fundamental to the continuity of any group. It is an area that is patrolled, so to speak, by figures of authority who try to guard the group from loss and attrition. But should such authorities be tyrants or equals? Should the morality by which they order others be of an absolutist or relativistic kind? Or is this a false choice?

In this chapter I suggest that the two kinds of authority play complementary roles in Giriama society and are often valued as such by Giriama, who also recognise that they represent alternative ways of being governed. Somewhat ambiguously, unquestionable authority is favourably associated with the absolute cultural purity and knowledge that is believed to come from the Kaya and the west, while egalitarian authority is more associated with the east, which has, however, come increasingly under the sway of alien, competing and less easily controllable influences.

I begin by giving examples of how incest and witchcraft can seem at times to be quite distinct yet at others to overlap, for their relationship to each other is paradigmatic of the two types of authority. Unambiguous moral distinctions here go hand in hand with tyranny while relativised ones favour negotiated leadership.

Roaming signifiers and classificatory overlap

On the one hand, the Giriama have an extraordinarily detailed classification of types and sub-types of affliction, and of the means to deal with them. On the other hand, misfortunes which have been diagnosed as not having been caused by witchcraft can later be reclassified as due to it. More than this, a cause which is not normally equated with witchcraft and is seen to be involuntary rather than intentional, may nevertheless become defined as a form of witchcraft while preserving its distinctive identity.

Vitio (plural form) is an example, which was introduced in the previous chapter. The Giriama identify two kinds of affliction. First, there is *kitio* (singular form) *cha lufu/kufu* (the latter meaning 'corpse') which occurs when any one of the following post-mortuary restrictions are broken. A widow must not sleep with another man until after her husband's second funeral (some months after his burial) at which time she is formally inherited by a brother or close agnate of the husband (see the previous chapter). During the same mourning period she must not sleep overnight outside her deceased husband's homestead, though she may leave it during the day to pay visits. Nor must she sleep either on the floor of her husband's house or on his bed. Should she commit any of these acts, she will die. Once inherited, however, she is 'untied' and would not normally need to fear any ill effects of adultery outside her new 'inherited' relationship.

Although the moral onus for avoiding this kind of *kitio* falls mainly on women, men must also observe rules. A man whose wife or close relative has died is free to sleep with other women during the mourning period but if he cuts or shaves his hair during it, he too will be afflicted. A man whose father dies must stay in the father's homestead for an agreed period, say ten or fifteen days, and must not make outside visits.

The second kind of *kitio* refers to breaches of relations within the homestead. The clothes of a younger brother, or of his wife, must never be allowed to enter the house of an elder brother. The younger may be allowed to sleep in the older brother's house, even with his wife present there, but they may not have sexual intercourse. Conversely, while the elder brother's clothes can be left in the younger brother's house during the day, they must not 'sleep' there overnight. More serious breaches are those which appear to flout the seniority of brothers with regard to sexual matters: for instance, an unmarried man without a house of his own should not seduce a girl in his elder married brother's house, nor should a younger brother marry before an elder, unless elaborate precautions and a purifying ceremony are undertaken in the two men's homestead. The most serious cases of all occur if a man sleeps with a brother's wife, father's younger wife, or even son's wife. There are still other reasons for *vitio*, some of which appear to be experimental methods of trying to account for mishaps.

It is the second kind of *kitio*, directly concerned with relationships in the homestead, with which I am here concerned, for it is this kind which people say is most prevalent in the larger homesteads of the western cattle zone. Since it is directly or metaphorically concerned with improper sexual contact and relations among agnates and their wives of a homestead, I call it adulterous incest, or incest for short.[1]

Kitio (or *vitio*) is characterised by vomiting, diarrhoea, the inability to produce children or to give birth successfully, and by eventual death if untreated. It spreads to people living within the same homestead or close neighbourhood, mainly but not exclusively among agnates, and threatens to annihilate a line of descent.

Five brief examples will illustrate its general nature, and the extent to which it may be reclassified as a form of witchcraft. The second and third examples are taken from the agricultural east, and the other three from the western cattle zone. I cannot, in fact, demonstrate numerically whether incest predominates in the west and witchcraft in the east, as many Giriama claim. Both delicts are found in the two areas, of course, and it is likely that a more accurate rendering of the difference is that witchcraft is everywhere the dominant mode of explanation of misfortune, but that accusations of incest are more prevalent *per capita* in the large homesteads of the western cattle zone than in the smaller ones of the eastern agricultural zone. This difference would probably be enough to foster the mutually self-verifying claims of regional distinctiveness made by Giriama. 'Our' reality is to note the signifying power of witchcraft, as in its tendency to absorb other explanations.

Case material

1. Chembe slept with the sister of Kenga Mzee and then afterwards slept with this woman's daughter-in-law, living within the same homestead. Kenga's sister later died while trying to deliver twins, which would not come out. The diviner pointed out that for two women of the same homestead to have adultery with the same man, while one of them is pregnant, always brings *vitio*. In this case, also, an old man had to be appointed to extract the unborn children from the deceased woman in the grave. The baby boy and girl were buried alongside the mother. Failure to do this would have brought further *vitio* upon members of the homestead.

In this case the *vitio* was not regarded as likely to spread once the ceremony in the grave had been carried out, though the fear of further contamination was

[1] More accurately, and following Arens (1989: 3–5), we should perhaps refer to this and its associated domain as that of sexual avoidances, whose transgressions entail different degrees of seriousness.

clearly paramount within the homestead. While problems usually originate in a homestead, the idea of close proximity among agnates, of being from the same place, is also fundamental and gives further scope for the interpretation of otherwise inexplicable infertility, as the following example shows.

2. Having raised his own bridewealth, Karisa fell in love with the second wife of Muzungu, who is a 'brother' (a patrilateral parallel cousin whose 'grandfathers are from the same place'). Karisa eloped with the woman and married her, compensating her husband with bridewealth in the customary manner. The two men continued on good terms with each other. The woman had a good body and health when she was married by Karisa, but thereafter became very thin and aged a great deal. Karisa had in fact been warned by his brother Muzungu that, although Karisa would be entitled to inherit the woman when Muzungu died, she would never bear children if taken by Karisa before then. During her marriage with Muzungu the woman had had a boy, but after six years with Karisa bore no children at all. She became even more sick and wished to join her son at the homestead of Muzungu, her original husband. Muzungu, however, refused to allow this, having been told by a diviner that Karisa and the woman now suffered from *mavingane* [*sic*] and that for the woman to re-enter his homestead would bring the disease there, too.

The use of the term *mavingane* instead of *vitio* in this case may indicate the slightly less serious consequences of the delict: *vitio* seems more used than *mavingane* to refer to cases resulting in death. Otherwise the two terms are used interchangeably, sometimes in the form *vitio-mavingane* or *mavingane-vitio*. What is important is that common to both is the underlying idea of the sickness or infertility as having been caused by two brothers or agnates having sex with the wife of one of them. *Kirwa* refers to yet another affliction which overlaps conceptually with that of *vitio-mavingane*, but focuses more on the obligation of a pregnant woman not to sleep with another man, which is not, it may be noted, consistently regarded also as a form of witchcraft.

3. The wife of Iha produced a son who was born tight-limbed, dry and shrivelled, would constantly contract himself and looked as though he had Kwashikor and would die in a few days. It is the custom when a child is born for its father to be called to hold the child before the wife does. Should the husband himself have slept outside during the known period of pregnancy, he is expected to get a black thread of cloth from the clothing of his mistress and, having called a diviner to supervise the ceremony, tie it round the left wrist of a girl child and the right wrist of a boy. Iha came with his thread but, on seeing the physical state of the new-born child, refused to hold him. He, or rather the diviner, saw the child's symptoms as evidence of *kirwa* and concluded that Iha's wife must have committed adultery whilst pregnant, though neither he nor others suggested that this was with one of Iha's agnates. It is also the custom for the husband to sleep with the wife two weeks after the birth of a child, a custom called *kumzhala muhoho* (to give birth to the child), but this too Iha refused to do, and instead slept with a more junior wife first.

Remarkably the child did survive, though still very weak, until at six months of age he became seriously ill. His survival during those six months was explained as due to the efforts of the midwife (*mukunga*) and others who had originally attended the birth. They did what, according to the diviner, they should have done at the time of the child's birth. They extracted a confession from the woman that she had committed adultery whilst pregnant and then procured a thread of clothing, 'whose colour did not matter', from the adulterer (here referred to as *mwanamume wa tsakani*, a man of the forest, and pointing to the furtive, hidden nature of adulterous liaisons). They tied the thread round the boy's right wrist, pretending to the husband that it served to assuage some other illness. This was done secretly and so ended the *kirwa*, enabling the child at least to survive his early months.

When, at six months of age, the child became seriously ill, the male diviner claimed that, although the *kirwa* had indeed been repulsed, the child was now suffering from *mavingane* as a result of two things: first, the husband had still not slept with his wife in the post-natal ceremony of *kumzhala muhoho* and had meanwhile slept with his other four wives, and perhaps with other outside women; second, the woman had not slept with her husband and, 'because women cannot persevere without sexual intercourse for that many months, must herself have had lovers'.

While Iha's wife had, apparently, been prepared to confess her adultery whilst pregnant to the secret care of the midwife and attendants, so lifting the effects of *kirwa* on her child, she would not confess to this or to later acts of adultery before the diviner in the presence of the whole homestead. She protested her innocence throughout until the diviner privately extracted a name, that of the alleged adulterer, from the midwife and attendant women, passing it on to Iha. A ceremony of purification was performed to eliminate the *mavingane* and it was left to Iha to decide whether he wished to press the adulterer for compensation (*malu*) or to drop the matter.

As different agencies are blamed at successive stages of the investigation, we again have the idea of explanatory concepts overlapping and also of there being a gradation of seriousness: all three are potentially deadly, but *vitio* is the most and *kirwa* the least, with *mavingane* in between or perhaps just a weaker version of *vitio*. Moreover, all three concepts form part of a single conceptual unity which we may call the *vitio* complex. This turns on the need for agnates to preserve their collective fertility by refusing to have sexual relations with each others' wives, by preventing outsiders from doing so, and by respecting domestic rules of agnatic seniority.

The *vitio* complex is both part of and wider than the English translation of incest. Insofar as it provokes horror, it is not so much that of the act itself as that of the consequences for a line of descent. At first, it is the individual man or woman victim who is horrorstricken at the prospect of losing a wife or children or of never again being able to produce them. But later, the homestead as a whole fears the effects of contamination.

Vitio has to be seen alongside the widespread accusations and suspicions of adultery among the Giriama. My impression is that many such accusations are without foundation. Rather like those of witchcraft they reflect ongoing enmities and rivalries. Simple adultery in which the cuckold and adulterer are not agnates is easily settled through the payment of compensation to the aggrieved husband. Just as accused witches may confess to their sin under pressure, and ostensibly for the sake of restoring communal harmony, so accused adulterers may do the same.

But, in large homesteads such as those that characterise the western cattle area, some rivalries will be between agnates, among whom accusations of adultery presuppose matters of much greater seriousness affecting the future progeny of everyone in the homestead.

Touching in this way upon adultery as well as incest gives *vitio* a double aspect. Ordinary adultery is regarded as an inevitable part of the attraction which men and women have for each other. It is laughingly referred to as the perennial problem of old men who have young wives, a not uncommon situation given the high rate of polygyny. Some such men with many wives quietly turn a blind eye until such time as they may wish to claim their compensation. Adultery can at other times lead to jealousy and violence, especially when it involves conflicts between younger men of the same generation. Its conversion into incest, or more properly incestuous adultery, changes its whole complexion dramatically. Seeking compensation is then much less important than removing its heinous effects through purification.

On the one hand, then, *vitio* is recognised as resulting from the 'natural' attractions and lusts which men and women feel for each other. On the other hand, it is seen as the result of such feelings having got out of hand, as beyond mere settlement through compensation. What is significant about both these aspects is that something larger than an individual's intentions are involved: a man or woman cannot help their lusts; nor does their frailty always predispose them to choose the most appropriate liaisons.

Yet, while it is not normally assumed that men and women deliberately seek to bring *vitio* upon their homestead and relatives, there is logically no reason why they should not do so. It remains at least a possibility, albeit an unlikely one, since it would destroy the offender himself as well as those agnates against whom he might wish to exact vengeance. Bordering on this unlikely possibility, however, is the ambiguous idea that *vitio* is wilful negligence: the adulterer cared so little for his brothers that he did not bother to consider the consequences of sleeping with the wife of one of them. Wilful negligence clearly shades into intentionality. It is recognised in the occasional cases in which *vitio* is actually called a form of witchcraft by the diviner who has been summoned to diagnose the cause of communal misfortune, as the following two examples show:

4. Dama was made pregnant by the husband of her elder full sister. She was herself only twelve years or age. Her pregnancy caused her difficulties and, rather late, she was taken to Kaloleni mission hospital for the birth itself. But she suffered incessant haemorrhage and died. The problem was diagnosed by a diviner as *vitio*. But the diviner also referred to it as caused by *utsai wa mbare na nyongoo*, one of many kinds of witchcraft. The diviner said that the man was a *muzinzi wa mudzi*, a homestead adulterer (with the suggestion that the above was not the only time he had been responsible), and that his sin was witchcraft.

5. Chengo Mutunga used to live in Kushonga's huge homestead, one of the largest in Miyani, where many of his herd are kept. However, one after the other a number of the children of Chengo's only wife died. Fearing that his wife had been 'used' by one or more of the younger men in the homestead, Chengo consulted a diviner who indeed confirmed

that, in his words, the cause was the 'witchcraft of incest' (*utsai wa vitio*). Other observers wished to emphasise that though it was quite possible in such a large homestead for this to have happened, it did not rule out the possibility also that Chengo had himself 'used' one of the many wives of the other men there. 'This easily happens between brothers – within the same *lukolo* or *nyumba* when they are living together in such great number.'

While *vitio* retains its distinctiveness as a form of incest, the addition of the term for witchcraft, *utsai*, connotes something akin to malicious intent or at least to the immorality of the act. In example No. 4 the diviner, a woman, linked her use of the term witchcraft to that of the 'homestead adulterer'. In No. 5 the diviner's use of the term accorded nicely with Chengo's great bitterness at having lost his children and having had to set up a new homestead. By comparison in No. 2 Muzungu was not bitter towards his cousin, having after all amicably received the bridewealth for his second wife, while in the first example the view taken was that the two women's adultery with the same man might have had less dire effect had it not been for the unfortunate accident of one of them being pregnant.

Summary of the case material
The five examples together show something of the detailed variations on the theme of *vitio*: *vitio* can be called *mavingane*, with *kirwa* possibly leading to either, and can also be redefined as a form of witchcraft (*utsai*). It seems reasonable to translate *vitio* as a form of incest, for it is placed in the same general category of offences as sex between men and their mothers, daughters and sisters, the only cases of which I have, being between unrelated men and women of the same clan (that is, classificatory kin), all resulting in barrenness. For example, a couple of the Hindzano clan living in Mombasa fell in love and stayed together as man and wife, but their parents refused to hand over and accept the bridewealth for marriage on the grounds that the union would be barren, which indeed it proved to be.

In this and other cases of intra-clan incest, barrenness and other misfortunes are normally explained as the result of improper mixing of the 'same' clan blood, or, as in another case of distant intra-clan marriage, as due to the fact that 'her blood is not strong enough for marriage between a brother and sister'. Since, from time to time, fruitful intra-clan sexual unions may and perhaps increasingly will occur, at least in the towns, this flexible interpretation centred on the incompatibility and weakness of blood allows for such changes. Such barrenness is not normally blamed on *vitio*, which is left specifically to refer to relationships between brothers, fathers and their wives. It is however linked to the effects of *vitio*. The crucial idea underlying the *vitio* complex, then, is that the joining of similar 'bloods' in sexual intercourse will impede the partners' reproductive capacities and will destroy that of the groups to which they belong. The blood of a man and of a woman must be of different origins in order for them to produce children.

While the Giriama do sometimes move through the use of such terms as *vitio*, *mavingane*, *kirwa* and *utsai* to refer to the same underlying idea, we should not see this simply as a case of their classifying phenomena imprecisely and even inconsistently. Their use of different terms in an overlapping way to denote illness or barrenness has the important effect of de-centring, so to speak, any relationship between cause and symptom. Unlike Western biomedical practice which seeks to fix the relationship unambiguously, the Giriama regard any statement by a diviner or herbalist concerning sickness or misfortune as necessarily provisional, and as an ongoing experimentation in diagnosis and cure. When asked to give the meaning of particular medical terms, the Giriama may well provide definitions which strike one as admirably succinct and as distinctive one from the other. But, as pragmatic empiricists well aware of the situational nature of truths, they allow afflictions to be identified and treated from a number of different terminological perspectives, so allowing for the possibility of different kinds of medical expertise to be brought in by different doctors one after the other.

There is however something more to this situational use of diagnostic terms than experimentation. At root is a question of how much humans can determine events and how much they are subject to forces greater than themselves. This comes out in the curious way in which *vitio*, a communal affliction resulting from a man and woman's overpowering, involuntary sexual passions, comes to be spoken of as witchcraft, a coldly calculating act of malice.

The conjoined use of both *utsai* and *vitio* refers in fact to the ambivalence which a victim suffering from the delict may express. On the one hand, the 'sin' could have been avoided if the adulterous or incestuous couple had not disregarded the effects on those living around them: this borders on intentional negligence, a kind of wilful evil or witchcraft according to some diviners and so is called *utsai*. On the other hand, when the suffering is seen as resulting not from such malevolence but out of ignorance and innocent thoughtlessness, not occasioning bitterness, it remains no more than *vitio*.

The heart among the Giriama is as much the seat of intentions as of emotions, as is the head. Reason and passion are inseparably part of each other. The very method by which the diviner works, by entering people's minds by means of capricious spirits which possess him or her, point to this inseparability. Witchcraft shares this inseparability. Unlike the situation recorded in some other African societies, it is not entirely involuntary and is certainly regarded as intended through the use of harmful medicines.[2] Yet, at the same time, it is

---

[2] Following the conventional anthropological distinction between witchcraft as the innate and sometimes involuntary capacity to cause harm, and sorcery as the intentional use of harmful medicines, I have in earlier publications referred to the Giriama concept as sorcery (e.g. Parkin 1968). On the other hand, useful though this distinction is, I am impressed by Giriama statements that any person can be driven to practising witchcraft, and so to purchase the requisite knowledge or expertise, should he feel justifiable vengeance against someone who has, for instance, allegedly killed his

recognised that the reasoning behind witchcraft may occur against a background of jealous frustration, envy, spite and justified vengeance which from time to time may possess any otherwise normal, law-abiding person. Small wonder that phenomena such as *vitio* may become redefined as witchcraft, for it is a force that is both in peoples' hearts and minds and yet is at times greater than them.

As a concept, witchcraft is the most pervasive and threatens to spill over into more and more explanations of misfortune. While people will normally say that *vitio*, *kirwa* and other causes of death and illness are quite distinct from witchcraft, these same people may at other times claim that witchcraft is at the root of all problems. This ambivalence in what is or is not witchcraft and its potential pervasiveness as an explanatory concept also threatens the tidy Giriama characterisation of the eastern and near-coastal part of their country as riddled with witches and the allegedly more traditional west as beset more by problems of large homesteads and incest. When people make this contrast between the two areas in terms of ecology, vulnerability and the authorities dealing with it, they are also talking implicitly about the tensions that surround them all between life-giving and life-taking forces. The Kaya and the west give life, while the east, with its spreading witchcraft and alien invasions of culture, takes it (an extraordinary reversal of a more abstract but rarely made cosmological claim that the rising sun of the east is associated with life, while the setting sun connotes death). That humanity has to contend with forces of death as well as life is of course a universal theme. But the theme can be presented in different ways. The contrast between east and west is one that is relevant to modern political, economic and socio-cultural problems. But it draws on much older presentations of the dilemma which are common to all areas of the country.

Setting up the tensions

According to a Giriama origin myth, humans and animals once talked with each other. But there came a famine and mankind killed and ate hare. Thereafter lion and other beasts started hunting humans and eating them. Mankind in turn hunted animals for food. Animals and humans ceased talking to each other. So, from a state when they exchanged words and lived in peace, they moved to one in which they exchanged death, through hunting and violence.

This is one perspective on the shift from peaceful co-existence to violent differences between animals and mankind.

A second perspective is that which revels in the differentiation of man from animals and wishes to underline it. Thus, I was given this view, quite independently, of the justification for having exogamous clans. 'We have clanship (*mbari*), because otherwise we would be like goats and chickens and not know

wife or child. There is here a broader sentiment that partakes of involuntariness and intention as well as of innate human capacity, and so I have reverted to the more widely known term of witchcraft (see also Turner 1964).

who are our mothers and sisters.' 'You must not marry within your clan, because you are of one blood. This is very important. For if you do your wife may not produce', as in the cases mentioned above. Building on this celebration of incest-avoidance and individual distinctiveness, I was also told, 'You must know your clan so that you yourself may be known', a reference to the often fierce pride that goes with clan membership.

Relations between clans thus involve the defence of personal dignity, through violence if necessary, as well as through marriage. There is in fact a mythical paradigm: peaceful communication between animals and people turned into violent struggle between them; the wish on the part of humans to dissociate themselves from the incestuous practices of animals caused them to adopt clanship; clan boundaries and identity could only be perpetuated through violence or marriage between them; to lose sight of clanship is to revert to animalistic incest; incest, in the form which brings *vitio* as well as that between men and their sisters, destroys human fertility.

It is of course common in many societies for people to engage in the paradox of fighting in the name of clanship yet also reproducing themselves through inter-clan marriage and alliance. Inter-clanship is, then, a means to violence and death as well as to reproduction and life. Negotiation through talk precedes marriages between clans, while violent relations between them occur when negotiations break down or never take place, that is, when clans do not talk to each other. Ideas about clanship thus replicate the theme of the origin myth concerning animals and mankind: that there is a delicate balance between mutual respect, communication and peaceful co-existence on the one hand, and, on the other, disregard for the rights of others in adversity, renunciation of the normal channels of communication, and mutual death and destruction.

Such ideas are so central that they abound in other areas of Giriama life, and clearly are not confined to this people alone. But they are, I suggest, always paradigmatic of some unnamed and unnameable tension between life-giving and life-taking forces. As such they can be referred to in other ways. A contrast which the Giriama make between the dangerously hot leaves of certain plants, which can kill, and the cool leaves or roots of therapy is one of a number of examples. Closer to the expression of relations between mankind and animals, and one which gets to the heart of the idea of incest as the enemy of fertility, is the contrast between dirt (*ukolo*) and cleanliness or purity (*ueri*). We have encountered the latter expression before, in one of the characterisations of the Kaya as the 'pure/sacred village' (*mudzi mueri*).

Incest, in the form believed to be common of adultery between a man and his brother's wife (or sometimes his son's or father's younger wife), brings the *vitio* which can only be reversed through a ceremony of purification at which a ram (*turume*) is slaughtered. The cleansing power of the sheep thus makes it possible for a homestead contaminated by the effects of incest to continue to reproduce itself. Not only is it in the western cattle area that are found the large, heavily agnatic, polygynous homesteads which are regarded as particularly prone to this kind of incestuous adultery, it is from this area, also, that sheep figure among the livestock that are kept in addition to cattle.

Sheep are herded along with goats but are never more than a minority proportion. They are regarded by the Giriama as being more vulnerable than goats to the deadly diseases of foot rot, mouth disease and, occasionally, anthrax (see also Leaky 1977, Vol. a: 231–233), and as preferring a restricted range of pastureland and foods, such as open grass areas. Goats, however, are held to be able to survive anywhere. Sheep, especially black ones, are kept primarily for purificatory sacrifice, whereas goats may be slaughtered on non-sacrificial as well as sacrificial occasions.

The other animal which is also associated with the more remote, western area of Giriama country is the hyena. The two animals, sheep and hyena, complement each other in the contrast between dirt and purity or sacredness. But the contrast is far from unambiguous and leads to other, often at first sight contradictory, associations. Thus, the sheep connotes purity and peace but is mainly used in violent sacrifice. The hyena connotes dirt but is also venerated. These ambiguous contrasts inform ideas of competing types of authority. An absolutist, tyrannical form is allegedly located in the western area where the wild hyena stalks. An egalitarian but also highly individualistic kind is thought to be more prevalent in eastern areas closer to the coast, and is more domestically manageable, like the sheep itself. Let me now outline this contrast in ideas surrounding the two animals, beginning with the sheep.

Sheep

The equation that the Giriama themselves make between cleanliness and peace is evident in the sacrifice of a ram to cleanse a homestead which has been afflicted by the contaminating effects, not just of *vitio*, but also of homicide (Champion 1967: 32–34), a parent's curse, the affliction called *kirwa*, and also when a ram is given in compensation for adultery (*malu*) with a man's wife or daughter. The latter is actually called a peace payment, and requires that the disputants, including the offending man, woman and her husband or father, tie strips of the slaughtered ram's skin around their feet: the right foot in the case of the men and the left in the case of the woman. As mentioned above, the untreated effects of *vitio* are, like the after-effects of a homicide or parent's curse, particularly serious, for they threaten to annihilate the entire descent line of a particular family and may even, it is said, affect those of all other co-resident families, including non-agnatic ones. It is the homestead as a whole and its constituent agnatic lines which are menaced.

Why is the sheep chosen for the special role of purificatory, peacemaking sacrifice? For all other forms of sacrifice, bulls, he-goats and chickens are killed (the latter only for divinations or personal therapy, bulls for funerals, and goats for both funerals and sometimes to spirits). We should first mention that the colour often demanded of the sacrificial ram, black, is that which is used in other contexts to 'capture' or 'expel' witchcraft; the latter is associated with the colour white, which is itself linked to hyena faeces (see below). There are, of course, only a few black sheep in any one flock. Given that the sacrificial animal must be a ram, and that, anyway, the Giriama keep relatively few sheep in relation to goats and cattle, there is already a kind of scarcity value conferred on it. The explanation goes beyond this, however, for it is not always black rams which are sacrificed.

The sheep is accorded special ontological qualities in a number of other societies, apart from Bantu ones. The Semitic religions celebrate the story of Abraham, who was about to accede to God's command that he sacrifice his beloved and only son, when a ram came from heaven as a substitute and as a reward for Abraham's unquestioning obedience. The Lamb of God also connotes love, peace, and the suspension of violence.

The para-Nilotic Maasai, who herd large numbers of sheep and goats together, regard the former as more feminine than the latter. Women's belts are made from sheepskin, but never men's. The Nilotic Luo characterise the sheep as being an animal without sin, and as bringing luck. They make the following contrast. A goat is alert and quick and so is regarded as an appropriate form of livestock to be offered in order to get full bridewealth transactions of cattle under way. But a sheep is seen as a steadier animal and is only slaughtered and eaten when the relationship between the two inter-marrying families and descent groups is viewed by the elders as relatively firm.

There is of course nothing universal about this characterisation of sheep and goats, and among Bantu societies themselves there are wide variations in the degree to which sheep are given special ritual status in relation to goats. The Giriama have a very pragmatic attitude towards the goat, which can be killed and eaten on any occasion. 'You can even slaughter a goat for a girlfriend.' Their view of sheep is quite the opposite. In addition to its purificatory and peace-making uses, the sheep plays a part in ritual adornment: a famous doctor and diviner, Mangi Yaa, used to wear a ram's head as part of his regalia, and at his funeral in late 1969 there was the sacrifice of a solitary white ram before that of cattle and goats, allegedly done only for doctor-diviners of great status. For other people, on no account should a sheep be sacrificed at funerals, for otherwise eaters will get leprosy, or another disease called *mwadzulu* (literally, 'of the above'), which results in body swelling. The sheep is subject to other prohibitions. Sufferers of leprosy (*mahana*, or *ukongo bomu*, literally 'big sickness') and of *safura* (a wasting disease), cannot eat them at any time on pain of immediate death.

An outsider's utilitarian view might see the sheep's greater frailty and often more limited numbers as already giving it greater scarcity value than goats and so immediately qualifying it for ritual focus. But in other parts of Kenya, such as among the Maasai, numbers of sheep approximate and in some cases exceed those of goats, yet the sheep retains something of a special status in relation to the goat. Perhaps all we can say is that it is precisely because sheep and goats (in Africa) are so close in many respects that they have to be differentiated, often by exaggeration, and that their contrast may then be rendered as that between commonplace goats and special-place sheep, as among the Giriama. It cannot be the intrinsic qualities of the sheep which give it special sacrificial status in a number of cultures. Indeed Parkes, writing on a non-Muslim people on the borders of Afghanistan and Pakistan, gives instead an example of the ritual evaluation of goats as sacred animals over and above sheep and cattle (1987). It is perhaps rather that people play on ambiguities, seeking differences arising from similarities, as in the relationship of sheep to goat, and elaborating on them.

Thus, the alleged frailty of the sheep among the Giriama is juxtaposed to its violent sacrifice and becomes part of the tension among humans between life-taking and life-giving forces, and such parallel contrasts as food and poison, and cleanliness and dirt.

Goats, bovines and chickens are slaughtered by throat-slitting. But a sheep (in fact a ram) is stabbed in the stomach and disembowelled, a gruesome and relatively slow death. This is done at the public place called the *muhala* in the middle of a homestead, whereas other animals are slaughtered to the side and apart from it. The first-stomach of the sheep, called *kitavira*, is extracted from the disembowelled insides of the sheep. The first-stomach contains semi-digested grass or chyme which is put into the purificatory medicine called *vuo*, made up of herbs, roots and animals' parts, which has been prepared in a special wooden container called an *mvure*. The still green chyme is called *mavi ga kitavira*, literally 'the excrement of the first-stomach'. It is differentiated from the *mavi ga ifu*, 'the excrement of the stomach leading to the anus', i.e. the colon. The chyme is regarded as a sweet-smelling food (*chakurya*), described as a smooth porridge, and may be eaten as a delicacy (called *ufwifwi* by the Mijikenda group called the Chonyi). It is contrasted with the fully processed, bitter excrement of the colon, which is said to have become such through the 'poison' (*utsungu*) of the bile. Thus, both are called excrement (*mavi*) but one is food while the other is dirt, indeed on the way to becoming faeces.

The herbalist (*muganga*) takes the soluble *vuo* medicine containing the portions of chyme (still a food), and throws it at the members of the homestead who are seated to one side of the central place where the sheep has been killed, on the other side of which the bowl of medicine has been prepared. The medicine is also sprayed over the doors and houses of the people. By contrast, the fully digested grass ('dirty', bodily waste), is taken by the doctor's assistant (*mutegi*) and thrown outside the homestead at the junction of the entrance to the homestead and the path passing by it. Thus, that which is called both 'food' and 'excrement' (*mavi ga kitavira*) is used as a medicine (and here called *muhaso*) to cleanse the homestead and its occupants, while that which is called 'dirt' and 'excrement' (*mavi ga ifu*) and is not made into a medicine, is discarded and not used for cleansing purposes. Neighbours passing by will see this discarded excrement as a sign that the homestead is undergoing a ritual – at a funeral the faeces of a slaughtered bull are also thrown outside – and may take this as an invitation to join the gathering and both eat and contribute towards the expenses.

Giriama are quite aware of the intermediary position occupied by chyme. Terminologically it is 'shit' but also 'food' and 'medicine'. It is located between the intestines (*uhambo*) and the colon/anus (*ifu*). It is green and inoffensive, sweet-smelling and 'smooth like porridge', yet is secured by what is recognised as a violent stabbing (*ku-dunga*) and disembowelment of the animal. It is above all curative yet acquired through such exaggerated violence. Aggressive penetration is an obvious association, and it may be relevant to note the comments of one man who said, 'The ram has not yet been divided into good (*udzo*) and bad (*uii*), into blood (*mulatso*) and dirt (*ukolo*)'. Though the semi-digested grass provides immediate sustenance, its container, the first-stomach, is dried and kept for such future uses as the reversals of misfortune following another affliction, *kirwa*, or for settling disputes.

The soluble, flowing chyme of the first-stomach is thus contrasted with the hard faeces of the colon, yet is also regarded as at an intermediary stage in the process leading from pre-digested food to faeces. Seizing the chyme in this abrupt and violent manner is a way of stopping this ineluctable process. Given the association of fresh food with life and of faeces with death, it is a way of halting the transition to decay and at the same time extracting from the chyme those of its beneficial qualities which remain: returning to the living that which was already semi-digested and had seemed lost to life.

As regards the role of the herbal doctor, he is here attempting to intercede on behalf of the congregation between life-taking forces unleashed by the 'sin' of *vitio*, which has already led to death and disease in the homestead, and the potential offered by the ritual use of the chyme for restoring normality and preserving life. The *vitio* itself will have been identified earlier as the cause of a homestead's problem by a special diviner (*muganga wa ku-voyera*), 'the praying doctor', who uses spirits to guide him. The herbal specialist who actually treats the affliction (*muganga wa kitio*) does not use spirits in these purificatory rites and is always a man.

The herbal specialist utters words known only by himself when he mixes the chyme with the previously prepared herbal medicine, and also when he douses the people and houses with it (an activity referred to as *ku-zizinya*, meaning to cool through the use of medicine, or as *ku-vororya*, with broadly the same sense). His secret words are preceded by a known, formulaic exchange with the congregation, a kind of prayer. The doctor begins: 'Hail!' (*Taireni*), to which the people of the homestead reply, 'Things are of God' (*Za Mulungu*). He continues 'Who is being prayed to?' (*Alombwaye nyani?*) and they answer 'It's God' (*Ni Mulungu*). He asks again, 'Are we praying for good things?' (*Hunavoya vidzo?*), to which they respond, 'Let the good things come' (*Navidze*). The doctor asks again, 'And evil?' (*Vii?*) and they finish by replying 'Let evil be turned aside' (*Navishuke*).

This prayer is that which the specialist male diviner (*muganga wa ku-voyera*) may initiate when called to a homestead or neighbourhood by people who wish him to confirm whether or not they are suffering from witchcraft and who the witch is. Usually he singles out suspects from those attending and eventually narrows them down to a single person. At other times, he ends by identifying someone who is not currently in the homestead or neighbourhood but who lives there or recently lived there. An ordinary diviner no more than hints at the identities of witches usually whilst operating from the safe anonymity of his or her own home, but the specialist goes much further in confronting witches in their homesteads.

However, in the ceremony held to purify a homestead or neighbourhood, the doctor no longer seeks to blame any person for misconduct. The ceremony can only take place once the couple guilty of the sexual liaison bringing *vitio* have admitted their responsibility, with the man agreeing to pay adultery compensation to the woman's husband. In the rare event of their not doing so, there can be no ceremony and the homestead will simply split up and its opposed members move to new and different sites. (See the case reported by Johnston 1976: 318–328.) With the question of culpability out of the way, the doctor seeks a generalised cosmic aid deriving from the medicine in order to restore to members of the homestead their fertility and some measure of control over their destinies.

By contrast, the use of oaths (*viraho*) in trials by ordeal specifically aims to identify and distinguish the guilty and the innocent. Oaths are the blame-pinning devices par excellence. There is among the Giriama a range of oaths which vary in their purpose and degree of efficacy. The most powerful is the 'hyena oath' (*kiraho cha fisi*), whose effect can be so deadly that the colonial government constantly tried to ban it, but failed to curb its clandestine usage. While certain other oracles may be owned and administered by doctors who live outside the Kaya, the powerful hyena oath and its legitimate substitutes, the 'paw-paw oath' and the 'burning axe oath' (*kiraho cha papayu* and *kiraho cha tsoka*), are supposed to be the exclusive preserve of the Kaya elders, particularly the members of the secret society, the Vaya, and are usually administered at the Kaya. It is the role of these elders that Kajiwe, the young witch-finder, temporarily usurped through the use of his own oath.

There are then two sets of associations. The hyena and the secret Vaya elders

constitute supreme arbitrators whose task is to apportion blame and responsibility quite unambiguously. The sheep and doctor, however, connote peace-
making and the cleansing of 'sin', at a point when blaming those responsible has
become irrelevant.

Hyena

The Vaya are often referred to by the Giriama themselves and by non-Giriama
outsiders as the people's 'police', 'government', 'rulers', 'lawmakers', and
occasionally also as priests (Champion 1967: 30; Spear 1981). While it is true
that the Vaya can indeed be regarded as, and may sometimes be called, doctors
by the use of the generic term *muganga*, it is also perfectly clear that they are also
regarded as quite distinct from the range of other specialist doctors who are not
members of the Vaya society, including those mentioned above in connection
with the ceremonial use of the sheep.

They differ not by their sources of power. Indeed, the Vaya are like other
herbal doctors in drawing their power from their use of herbal medicines and
specially placed preparations inscribed with secret incantations. They differ by
virtue of their position as ultimate human judges, bound together by their
exclusivity, their age, their possession of secret knowledge including that of the
hyena oath, and their capacity to create fear among the wider population, at least
during periods of crisis and unrest.

The Vaya are one of the five main societies (*chama*) among the Giriama, the
others being the male ones of Gohu, Habasi and Kinyenzi, and the female one
called Kifudu. Only the Vaya are a secret association. The others are open to
those who can make the payment for entry. All except the Gohu have their own
oath medicines. The most feared, however, is that of the hyena, owned by the
Vaya, who also administer other oaths. Reports as to the composition of this oath
vary. It consists of liquid made from leaves and/or roots and, according to
accounts, kills unrepentant evildoers. For the purpose of the Kajiwe witch-hunt
in 1966, the Kaya and Vaya elders had it mixed with the Habasi and Kinyenzi
oaths, together with a medicine apparently associated with the women's Kifudu
society, *makushekushe*: this, intriguingly, was on this occasion made up of water
in which an old woman past menstruation from each participating Mijikenda
Kaya had bathed her genitals. This specially concocted oath, with its obvious
appeal to Mijikenda unity and the post-sexual cooling effects of old women, yet
with the feared hyena oath at its core, was administered to suspected witches
identified by Kajiwe during his witch-hunt, until he slipped away from the
control of elders and administered his own oath. With regard to both the Vaya's
and Kajiwe's oath, suspects would drink it saying, 'I am a witch. If I bewitch
again, then let me die'. Several cases are given of people who have taken the
Vaya's hyena oath, and who have later lapsed into witchcraft or some other mal-
practice, and who subsequently die.

The secrecy of the Vaya society is evident in a number of ways. Though they are regarded as necessary for ultimate law and order through their administration of oaths in trials of ordeal, the Vaya elders are also regarded as potentially harmful as a result of their own jealousies and misuse of their medicines. Giriama often refer to them as 'bad' people, and point to a number of prohibitions attaching to their activities, including the occasion when they bury one of their deceased members. As one man put it, 'They bury their dead on their own, never allowing people to see. So people wonder where the bodies come from, and believe that the Vaya take the bodies to the Kaya to eat.' During such funerals, especially at night, a special friction drum made with pigskin, called the *mwandza*, is sounded. It gives a far-reaching sound like that of a hyena, which some people fear.

The Vaya commonly administer the hyena and other oaths from the Kaya itself, where they may live for varying periods. But they may also live outside the Kaya, and operate from their own homesteads within a particular, named locality (*lalo*), having been appointed by other Vaya members to do so. There they give oaths other than the hyena to litigants, and also place protective medicines in fields or homes on behalf of owners, in order to ward off thieves and witches.

Although nowadays they live and work as much outside the Kaya as within it, the Vaya retain a tight method of recruitment. First, only mature or old men are eligible (I would say that they must at least have grandchildren), although, as new recruits they do not have to be as old as the ancient, resident Kaya elders (who themselves are not necessarily Vaya members). Second, each of the six Giriama sections of clans should be represented. Third, numbers are limited, though how few is difficult to ascertain. Fourth, potential recruits are approached by existing Vaya elders. They do not themselves apply, as in the other societies. Fifth, there is, as with all the societies, an internal division between novices (*umondo*) and experts (*ubora*), but the experts make up an inner circle who possess the most powerful medicinal and ritual secrets. Sixth, it is this inner circle, sometimes called the 'elders of the hyena' (*azhere a fisi*) who are most likely to live or be based in the Kaya.

Although the Vaya are regarded as themselves capable of evil acts, indeed of being witches when they misuse their power, they are also seen as the ultimate guardians of Giriama integrity and internal peace. They are themselves subject to sanctions. It is said for instance that a witch who enters the Kaya with evil intent will die because the Kaya is a place of peace, while, conversely, a bewitched and suffering person may find sanctuary there.

The ambivalence in which the Vaya are held reflects the attitude towards the animal with which they are associated. While the sheep is characterised as an animal of peace, the hyena is both feared and revered. Giriama who are guilty of killing a hyena are supposed to pay a fine to the Vaya, which is called *kore*, the same term for the fine paid to the family of a person who has been killed. The Vaya imitate the hyena in special dances held in the Kaya before oath-taking on a large scale. An early eyewitness account of 1914 provides a vivid picture both of the Vaya and of the European observers responsible for the description. The occasion is the hyena oath administered by the Vaya on the insistence of the colonial government after the Giriama rebellion, which government forces had just put down. The oath was to commit all other Giriama to live in peace with government officers and to obey them in future. I include most of the report to show that there is considerable continuity in ideas held about the Vaya and their identification with the hyena despite some obvious wider politico-economic changes since then.

The morning came and with it a series of dismal sounds from the bush. Asking what it was we were told they were making the hyena *lia* (Swahili for 'cry' and given also in parenthesis as to speak reluctantly). Enquiries from time to time elicited the fact that the hyena would not do what was expected. It may be mentioned here that, though the Agiryama (i.e. the Giriama) spoke of the hyena as actually there, an active participant in the proceedings that followed, no hyena appeared but only an elder representing him.

Finally we were informed that the elders of the Vyaya [*sic*] (the grade of elders entitled to call upon the hyena and make oath by him) were assembled and ready. Our interpreter (a Giryama but not even an elder of the council as far as I know) was not allowed to be present . . . On the completion of . . . formalities we were led into the bush where the Vyaya was assembled and we found them all stamping (rather than dancing) round in a circle beating their buttocks and repeating a chant to the effect that the hyena was their brother and they were met together. In the centre was the elder on his hands and knees on the ground, covered with a blanket so folded that his head was hidden and the opposite end a corner falling like a tail. From time to time (it was when three circles had been completed) he emitted a peculiar cry, extremely like that of a hyena, accentuated in volume by what he held in his hand, and the others echoed it. He would cry three times, and three echoes would follow, before the stamping dance was repeated. In this connection, I would observe that after each man stamped he slid back his foot with a jerk rather more like that of an animal covering his defecations than the slip of a man treading heavily on clay soil. This performance continued until the actual taking of the oath began.

We then asked to see the paraphernalia and then the man who had been representing the hyena rose to his feet and revealed a tall elder . . . well known to us. He showed us a forest root (perhaps a bone substance) about one foot in diameter which was naturally trenched somewhat like a conch shell. It was by the use of this formation that he was able to accentuate the cry produced. It may be noted that he was sweating violently with the exertion, the sound being made by a retching movement which must have strained the vocal and throat muscles considerably, and all the time the unfortunate man was crouched down and covered with a blanket. He also produced five carrot-coloured roots which had been placed before him.

Before leaving these items I cannot but record the disagreeable impression made upon me by the apparent insistence on the hinder parts. I was on the look-out for a put-up ceremony, a freak performance, and perhaps these details impressed me unduly. But first the sight of a number of old men solemnly marching round with bared buttocks slapping themselves, then the appearance of the big white root (or bone) exactly like the hinder parts of an animal, reminded me so insistently of the unpleasant diet of the hyena that at this point I began to feel that the ceremony was in order. While interested I was repelled, and sceptic, convinced.

After these 'properties' had been inspected he returned to his crouching position and the dance continued. After the third series of cries an elder whose function had obviously been pre-arranged stopped the dance and began an invocation of the hyena . . . The invocation began with a prayer to the hyena 'our friend and brother', going on to discuss the business of the day, and finally introducing us (the European observers) by name. The hyena was informed that our entrance fee had been received and eaten (. . . paid in rupees). The priest or master of ceremonies who introduced us then broke off a green twig with which he tapped the large white root. He then laid curses on all who offered resistance to Government orders, on all who stole and on all who did not obey their elders in Council. After each clause he tapped the grade totem, the 'hyena' howled, and the elders echoed it. The threats were banishment from the Nyika [nowadays a pejorative term for the Mijikenda: DP] to ends of the earth such as Kavirondo (western Kenya) or in some cases death. A rider was added at our suggestion that the Government orders referred to were orders emanating not only from Mr. Montgomery and myself [the author, Assistant District Commissioner, J. M. Pearson], but from all Government Officers, and the oath was amended accordingly. Each curse was repeated and approved by every member present, while the grade totem howled and the rest echoed the cry. The curse ended, the invoker or logos broke the twig and placed the pieces crosswise over the carrot-coloured roots, the dance began again, three series of the cry were repeated, and the impersonator of the hyena, carrying the properties, was led off into the bush.

(An account of the taking of an oath of the hyena by the Giryama elders of Gallana and Godoma in the presence of Mr R. H. Montgomery, Acting District Commissioner, Malindi, and myself, Assistant District Commissioner, J. M. Pearson. 12th March 1914.) See KNA: CP 5/336-II).

Much can be made of this remarkable document. The European author, Pearson, is surprised at the apparently 'genuine' nature of the ritual, though it is also clear that the Vaya are acting under pressure. Nevertheless, the evidently excellent element of theatre, seemingly missed by Pearson, persists among the Vaya until the present time. Part of the persuasiveness of the ritual for Pearson is the way in which it invokes both his fascination and repulsion, again echoed by some comments among modern Giriama. While Pearson may feel safe as a member of the victorious colonial government, he might be expected to feel that other ordinary Giriama would be apprehensive of the Vaya and fear the effects of the collective hyena oath.

Certainly Pearson's observations are interesting for the associations that the Giriama today report on the Vaya: that they 'are' hyenas and act 'behind' things in the 'filthy' manner of the animal. Whilst this is an example of the administration of a Vaya oath to the Giriama as a whole, the nearest to which occurred most recently at the time that Kajiwe's witch-hunt was formally launched, the hyena oath is normally given to individuals in dispute with each other or accused of witchcraft, theft and adultery, including what I am calling incestuous adultery. Peoples' apprehension of the Vaya merges with that of the hyena itself: together the Vaya and the hyena embody and evoke in people a respectful fear.

Local, parable-like examples of the hyena oath at work continue to sustain that emotion, as in the following:

A young man of Chalani was often drunk and beat his wife. His father warned him that he would be bewitched if he carried on like this. The son agreed and said he was himself tired of his excessive drinking. He asked his father to have the elders administer the hyena oath. The son drank it, promising never to take liquor again. He abstained for a year until he was tempted to take some palm wine at a funeral. He became sick and after some time was heard crying like a hyena. Vaya and other traditional doctors said they could do nothing for him at this stage, although they could have reversed the effects of the broken oath had they been summoned beforehand. The hyena-like crying of a sick person is always regarded as a sign of inevitable death. The man died six months after his lapse.

One can see a number of reasons for the Vaya being associated with the hyena. Like the animal they are powerful but operate secretly and hide their activities from public scrutiny. They are often referred to as 'bad' and sometimes as witches, with which the necrophagous hyena is often associated, but as being at the same time the most reliable final arbiters in disputes, clearing away the ill-effects of quarrels, in much the same way that the hyena is regarded as 'good' in his job as scavenger. The Vaya deal in powerful medicines which help humanity but can, should a moody Vaya member so wish, be turned by him against it (in which sense he acts as a witch). The most powerful medicine is of course that of the hyena oath. The senior Vaya are among the nearest in age to death and have the greatest power to decide its occurrence among fellow Giriama, again through their use of the hyena oath. The hyena eats the products of death which are not 'food' to most other animals and humans but are regarded as 'dirt'. Dirt itself, in the form of both human and the distinctively white hyena faeces (the latter ground into a white powder), is associated among the Giriama with the presence of witchcraft, at the borders of which the Vaya operate. The Vaya live on the edge of society as, in a sense, does the hyena, yet are also centrally involved in deciding the balance between life-giving and life-taking forces.

The back of an ordinary house in a homestead is called the hyena. It is some-times where victims of 'bad deaths' are buried, and where people may urinate during the night or wash at dawn or dusk: 'It is behind things, like the hyena'. The same area behind the house may also be called *zingo*, meaning adultery, usually a wife's. A boy born at the back of the house is called *fisi* (hyena) and a girl *zingo* (the verb is *kuzinga*, to commit adultery). It is of course adultery by a woman with her husband's brother, son or father (or, for a man, with his brother's or father's younger wife) that gives rise to the contaminating effects of *vitio*, for which the purificatory sacrifice of a ram is required. That is to say, the dirt and behinded-ness associated with the furtive hyena link symbolically with the incestuous adultery for which the ram, the only animal to be slaughtered in the middle of the homestead, is the remedy. We thus come full circle: the incestuous adultery that is the dirt that stops fertility can only be reversed through purification. But while the Vaya have the greatest power to determine who is responsible for acts causing infertility in a homestead, it is only a specialist doctor who knows how to put things right.

Tyranny and tolerance: ideas of authority
While I did not hear any Giriama relate hyena and sheep and their associations in this way, it is difficult not to see in their relationship some inverse features one of the other (see also Middleton 1960: 109–116). In order to live, the hyena eats or 'incorporates' dead animals or 'dirt', which are its food. In its sacrificial death, the sheep involuntarily 'excorporates' a distinction between the pre-digested food which is called shit and the post-digested shit which is not called food. The hyena is the wild animal medium through which the Vaya resolve disputes between quarrelling humans, while the sheep is the domesticated medium through which the doctor tries to restore the balance between human behaviour and non-human cosmic forces.

The anthropologist is always in a position to create patterns of this kind, which may or may not be acceptable to the people for whom they constitute practical activities. For the Giriama themselves, the hyena and sheep are part of two complementary forms of authority: the Vaya are located in or directly associated with the Kaya, even though a number work outside it in practice, while other kinds of doctors, who also work within their own localities, are only indirectly linked to the traditional capital through the belief that all Giriama medical knowledge ultimately comes from there. The elderly Vaya rule both through a fear of their secret knowledge and of their deliberately cultivated sinister mannerisms and aloofness, and through the use of their hyena and other oaths which are regarded as the most accurate and binding forms of judgement. Doctors such as those responsible for taking away *vitio* may be respected and even feared but, like other kinds of doctors and diviners, are expected to be easily approachable and, at times, docile and even humble in their treatment of cases.

It is no coincidence that a representative number of the Vaya live for at least some of the time in the Kaya and have at various points in Giriama history taken on some of the functions of a weakly evolving centralised political structure. By contrast, the various kinds of doctors, about whom I will speak further in the next chapter, comprising for example young and female diviners as well as older male herbalists, are usually only expected to operate within their neighbourhoods, although their clients are commonly drawn more distantly. It is important, however, to recognise that a few of them, such as Kajiwe, do develop a potential for wider political leadership which is based on peoples' recognition that they have achieved their positions through the individual distinctiveness of their medical and divinatory skills and not through membership of a society.

An older man than Kajiwe but also of modern fame was Kabwere wa Wanje (referred to earlier). In 1966 he was likened to Kajiwe as a doctor of great skills who worked independently of the Kaya. He had earlier been a member of the Vaya society, but had broken away from it, thereafter administering the hyena oath independently away from the Kaya and pocketing the proceeds himself instead of donating them to the society, much to the chagrin of the Vaya elders. He became very wealthy, leaving at his death in 1983 a personally owned town near Malindi made up of allegedly 166 wives and their offspring, complete with its own school, where he also tried to set up a Giriama elders' council in opposition to that of the Kaya, when, as an old man, he was refused entry. In this switch from collaboration with the Vaya to individualistic self-seeking and self-reliance, Kabwere epitomised the two orders of possible authority and achievement.

The contrast is between the Vaya as an institutionalised authority tending towards political centralisation, and the various doctors as egalitarian but sometimes politically mobile and opportunistic figures of influence. The hyena complex adds to the Vaya an element of fear that might, in evolutionary terms, have been necessary to convert their authority into centralised political control. Pressure from the raiding Oroma or Maasai or, later, erosion of their power by the colonising British, may have thwarted that possible development. The sheep, however, gives to the doctor a peacemaking and socially levelling element. Indeed, what is most significant about purificatory rituals is that, although those deemed responsible for a delict such as *vitio* must provide the ram that is to be sacrificed and must ensure that adultery compensation is paid, there is no further question of blame or retribution falling on him or his woman partner. Conflicts between humans are here transposed as being a matter of disturbed cosmos and so are transcended, thereby reducing still further the expression of differences between people.

The secrecy surrounding the Vaya's activities, their oddly central and yet peripheral social position and the constant allusions to their and the hyena's association with dirt, behindedness, death and decay, contrast with the openness of the functions of the doctor and sacrificial sheep. People know where they stand with respect to the sheep; they know that the sheep itself stands for the clarification or straightening out of entangled social relations. Through it fertility is restored to a descent line which had become contaminated. But the hyena and the Vaya, despite the latter's role as supreme and firm arbiters, are regarded as menacingly both about people and yet far from them: for instance, the hyena inhabits the distant wilderness and yet is sometimes frighteningly glimpsed within a homestead during the evening gloom. He is credited with knowing things from afar. Like the hyena, the Vaya can at times be highly visible, as in their dramatic administration of oaths, and yet at other times are hidden from common view, as if between light and dark. They draw their power as much from their capacity to create obsessional fear of the unformed and formless and of matter in the wrong place, as from their capacity to disentangle human relations.

Conclusion

Let me conclude on an apparent puzzle. It will be remembered that the Giriama commonly characterise the Vaya elders as being of the Kaya and its western hinterland, and of *vitio* as being a problem primarily of the large cattle-keeping homesteads of the same area. However, though the Vaya are indeed supreme arbiters who can as a last resort be approached to determine through their use of oaths which couple in a homestead is responsible for bringing *vitio*, it is not them, but in fact a herbalist, preceded by a diviner, who carries out the ceremony of purification involving the sacrifice of a sheep. Yet diviners and herbalists spend most of their time diagnosing, locating, eliminating and reversing the effects of witchcraft, for it is the latter which is held to account for most sickness, death and misfortune. And witchcraft, it is commonly alleged, is more prevalent in the eastern, farming area towards the coast.

Putting this another way, the supreme, somewhat tyrannical powers of the Vaya are not by themselves sufficient to ensure the fertility and therefore repro-duction of the Giriama people; for this they need the specialist doctor, the *muganga wa vitio*, who may himself have other specialisms and be linked in an overlapping division of labour with other specialist diviners and doctors, much of whose work is focused on problems of witchcraft. In this sense the allegedly witch-ridden, heterogeneous east comes to the aid of the west; the fantasy of remote continuity is in fact sustained by the immediate and contingent. Going still further, the Giriama ideal of the west as a pure repository of custom and tradition is an abstraction from the complex conflicts, crises and ambitions of everyday life affecting everyone, cattle and farming folk alike.

What are these common elements? We have seen that the attempt to keep incestuous adultery (*kitio*) out of the homestead links up with the concern to prevent improper sexual relations invading the inner triad of mother, husband and child (*kirwa*). The invasion of the inside by external forces, of the pure by the impure, is a recurrent cosmological theme in both the east and the west. It is behind ideas of witchcraft, the notion of death, especially 'bad death' (see chapter five) and also behind beliefs in spirit possession, where the body may be violated by spirits, but also, ambivalently, sensually pleased by them. The notion of invasion, in other words, like that of incest, here connotes elements of attrac-tion as well as rejection. As a people, Giriama sometimes liken themselves to a body which is under threat, with the heart and mind resting in the Kaya in the west and therefore safer than in the east but as nevertheless potentially vulnerable. But the threat to the integrity of the Giriama social body is, again, not always from outside: there are always some individual Giriama who are regarded as seduced by foreign influences, such as those who allegedly would sell the secrets of the

Kaya to strangers. The risk to the physical body, too, is often due to excesses of behaviour which, in moderation, may be pleasing. Even witchcraft, which causes so much ill-health and death is, in Giriama terms, a kind of excessive passion based on envy and malice. It creates suffering but may also, Giriama admit, originate in the suffering that culminates in sweet revenge. The next chapter considers this ambivalence among Giriama of their experience of illness and of their attempts to contain, prevent, expurgate and cure it, both as individuals and as a cultural group.

The underlying question may be phrased in this way: the Kaya as sacred centre may well provide the ultimate medical legitimacy and customary knowledge that enables elders to rule and doctors and diviners to practice and have influence; but how does the Kaya's sacredness protect people from their desires to be other than they already are? How does its purity prevent them from sometimes wishing to be impure?

7

Alternative selves: invasions and cures

Vulnerability

Greenblatt (1980) may be right that the idea and possibilities of self-fashioning go back in Europe to concerns arising out of the immediate post-Renaissance era. But each age rediscovers the issue with a new urgency, and it may be suggested that the recent and current intellectual preoccupation with person and selfhood in Anglo-American anthropology (preceded by French interest, for example Mauss 1938 (1985) and Dieterlen 1973) is part of the movement of the last fifteen years or so away from the positivistic belief in the objective analysis of measurable structures governed by impersonal rules, systems and forces. Persons and selves have come to prevail over the latter.

However, we may go further than suggest the priority of personal agency and selfhood. We may suggest that selves lack permanent essences or centres, are always redefining and being redefined, and need not be an especially emphasised aspect of human thought and life: people may be culturally and in other ways highly creative without having to contemplate selves, theirs and others, in isolation from other elements of society.[1]

Yet it is also clear that at certain times and places people do develop a marked preoccupation with questions of person and selfhood. Within our own intellec-

---

[1] This amounts to a claim that concepts of the person are so culturally varying that we have in common only theories of human agency, a matter taken up in chapter eight. This appears to be what Marilyn Strathern shows in her comparison of African, Melanesian and, briefly, Western assumptions. She provides a description based on ethnographic accounts of the apparent proclivity in (West) Africa for there to be an already existing pattern of 'roles', 'statuses' and 'offices', into which people are fitted, thereby gaining legitimacy. But the people who are 'entitled' to assume such roles must, in the first place, be judged to have the qualities which will then be legitimately conferred on them. I detect a certain irony in her conversion of this tautology, which surely reflects an earlier anthropological position, into a distinctively African cultural process (1985: 64–65). It is probably true that many or most African societies are concerned with matching people to a structured array of roles and offices. But there is also a strong sense in which, as among the Giriama, one becomes powerful through what one knows, often in defiance of formal ascriptions, especially in the field of divination and cure, and that, in this respect, there are parallels with some of the Melanesian material Strathern analyses. This may become clear as the chapter proceeds.

tual culture, self-consciousness is itself a feature of post-modernism and, in anthropology, of post-structuralism. Reflexivity was until recently a vogue term in anthropology, often substituting for self-consciousness (and therefore completely missing Halliday's original linguistic sense of the term as language referring to itself through itself – 'This sentence is six words long' – and all the analogical richness that this meaning could have provided). But reflexivity has, in the hands of many, become a synonym for a creatively controlling 'I' which is every bit as essentialised as the impersonal structures it replaced.

An essentialised self-consciousness is surely also a feature of the present-day globalisation of the myriad of cultures in the world. Through an unprecedented capitalist consumerism and through rapidly expanding communications systems, we are witnessing the paradoxical process of, on the one hand, a sharing of common elements (for example Coca Cola, American-style soap opera on television, the hit-man as hero, and so on) and, on the other hand, of cultural, ethnic and linguistic separatism throughout much of the world of a kind that in Europe was once called Balkanisation. The self-consciousness of these newly discrete and demarcated cultures, which were previously often no more than clusters of overlapping identities, was often first created by colonial administrators who wanted the convenience of ruling neatly bounded units (Southall 1970), but has been accentuated recently in the face of global cultural generalities which threaten the distinctiveness of these groups. Moreover, under such conditions the process of socio-cultural and political segmentation has accelerated as such distinctiveness becomes a value in its own right. For Europe, this is indeed Balkanisation replayed. But for much of Africa and Asia, it is new: never before has there been the possibility of being able to communicate rapidly and simultaneously to large numbers of different peoples the fact of their co-existence and, in the terms of a global zero-sum game, their mutual competitiveness over resources.

The Giriama, too, listen to their radios (and one day will have access to television) and hear the politicians placing their campaigns and promises in this game-like context. The very fact that the Kenya government discourages people from thinking and competing in regional-ethnic-cultural terms, while at the same time the country's politicians operate from these very bases, literally gives the game away. As a group and as individuals making up that group, the Giriama, like others in the country and elsewhere in much of Africa and Asia, develop a highly demarcated consciousness of self. But to have such marked self-consciousness, whether individual or group, is also to have fears for its preservation and a sense of vulnerability. Raised now to the level of an essence, to that of something essential, the possibility that this self can be appropriated by others, or can simply atrophy, is a final loss that no amount of redefinition could reverse. The very consciousness of selfhood here creates its vulnerability.

Among the Giriama, enmeshment in the eastern cash-crop economy and, for some, in migrant wage labour, creates external dependencies and threatens their notions of their own cultural autonomy and continuity. Meanwhile, sickness, death and infertility in the homestead menace individual lives and ambitions. Personal and cultural vulnerabilities thus easily become part of each other.

There are many examples. A Giriama looking for work in Mombasa competes nowadays with the increasing number of job-seekers from up-country Kenya. Simply being a Giriama rather than, say, an up-country Kikuyu or Luo, becomes more and more a handicap in securing employment in areas dominated by these latter, who have brought with them to the coast ready-made skills and capital from such towns as Nairobi, Kisumu, Nakuru, Thika and Eldoret. It is therefore unsurprising that the 'purely' Giriama western cattle zone is cherished for its alleged independence of such factors and of the vagaries of agricultural cash-cropping to which the eastern farming areas are subject. Yet, while the livelihood in the west, based on cattle, goats and supplementary farming, is indeed more under people's own control than is that of eastern farmers and migrant workers, it is a hard way of life in an often hot and harsh environment. The west has there-fore failed to attract or even hold people, despite its idealisation, yet remains at least a possible area of new settlement.

Similarly, a Giriama who is sick can seek relief and cure from two sources. There are the government hospitals and clinics and some private, Western-trained doctors, all of which vary considerably in the time and care they may give to patients. There is also the still-flourishing alternative system of medicine and health care provided by Giriama and other Mijikenda and Swahili specialists, the so-called traditional doctors. Insofar as we can quantify the difference, tra-ditional medicine and health care is most used. It is neither cheap nor, as far as I can judge from my own observations, especially efficacious. But it is part of a network of social relationships which are culturally familiar to Giriama and per-sonally manageable. They are, in the last instance, relationships and medical knowledge which come from and are explainable through the Kaya and its elders. The Kaya therefore is and represents a personal refuge from sickness and mis-fortune as well as a political rallying point, as described in chapter one.

Giving shape to this vulnerability of Giriama public and private selves is economic uncertainty. Thus, although economic and subsistence hardships take different forms as between the cattle and agricultural areas, they are nevertheless common to both. Wealth differences, whether of cattle or palm trees, may be considerable between homesteads but may be reversed or dissolved by the next generation. The uncertain fortunes of even the wealthy do not always ensure that they and their families constantly have the most nutritious diets and untroubled health. A prolonged spate of sickness, death and childlessness in an otherwise well-off homestead may be part of its decline as well as seeming to trigger it, per-haps at a point, anyway, when maturing brothers begin to quarrel over dividing the patrimony of cattle or of land and trees.

Whatever the cause of such misfortunes, then, another element common to both ecological zones is the heavy dependence on medical and ritual experts, the so-called diviners and herbalists. Yet, even in the organisation of ritual healing, the alleged purity of the western cattle zone and the social mixing of the eastern agricultural area are subtly but sometimes inconsistently represented at various levels. Through this inconsistency, people can redefine a vulnerability as a virtue, or a threat as something to be desired, and vice versa.

Compare the contrasts made by Giriama between herbalists and diviners.

Giriama say that traditional methods of cure used by herbalists come from the remote and autochthonous west and from the Kaya as ultimate source of medical knowledge. They also say that a person becomes a diviner only by being possessed by spirits, the most powerful of which are often not indigenous to the Giriama but are from the outside Muslim world of the ethnically mixed, coastal strip.

On the other hand, diviners charge very little for their services and are depicted as highly moral agents whose work must have the blessing of ancestors, while herbalists charge much more and may become witches through abuse of their medicines. Both categories are thus ambivalently regarded: diviners, who include many women, are moral but are the innocent mediums through whom powerful Islamic and other foreign spirits penetrate Giriama purity; herbalists, who are mostly men, cure bodily and mental ills through knowledge that ultimately comes from the Kaya but may be hired to harm a client's enemies.

Already we see that the personal vulnerabilities that we translate as anxiety or illness, and which need divination and treatment, set in train contrasting ideas of autochthony and foreignness, purity and impurity, morality and evil, and men and women. Medicine is not, then, simply about diagnosis and cure, but concerns all these and other associated notions. It touches on questions of boundaries: of that between the Kaya and the outside, between western and eastern Giriama-land, between the bodies of doctor and patient, as well as those of gender. It sets them up and then plays on them as alternative possible ways of being.

A medical hierarchy?

The career pattern of diviners and herbalists is based on the open demonstration of medical and ritual skills. If he or she gets a reputation for incompetence and poor results, they will lose their clients. They do not enjoy the closed ranks of a powerful secret society such as the Vaya. Their own knowledge of medicines and ritual formulae is secret, and is shared only with those from whom they received or bought it, who cannot help them should he or she fail. By contrast, members of the Vaya society are regarded by Giriama as deriving their power through a collective sharing of responsibility, whether in giving oaths at the Kaya or in holding funerals for deceased members from which non-Vaya are partially excluded. Individual Vaya cannot normally be blamed should things go wrong. But it is as individual practitioners that diviners and herbalists stand or fall.

How accurate is the overall distinction made between diviners as mainly women and earning little, and herbalists as mainly men earning much more? Is there in fact a hierarchy of these practitioners, and how much upward mobility through the hierarchy is there?

It has to be said first that all these specialists, diviners and herbalists alike, are called by the same name, *muganga*, which can be translated as doctor. But each is thereafter identified by his or her field of specialisation, of which there are many. This generic identification underlines the Giriama view of *uganga*, medicine, as making up a spectrum of skills, ranging from divination or diagnosis through to various forms of treatment.

The spectrum is divided into two opposed halves, however, which are presented as such by the Giriama. The use of divinatory spirits is regarded as incompatible with the use of purchased herbal medicines. It is claimed, for instance, that diviners' spirits will refuse to work with the diviner should he or she turn to the use of the medicines used by herbalists. Diviners use 'white' ash in some of their work, but cannot use the so-called 'black medicines' (*muhaso mwiru*) which are the black powder of carbonised leaves, bark and roots prepared by the herbalists. Should diviners do so, their spirits will withdraw their divinatory powers. Conversely, a diviner can only practice herbalism and forsake divination if his or her spirits allow this change of specialisation, which is not very common. Only five specialists, all men, are credited with having become herbalists after first being a diviner in the whole of Kayafungo location, compared with a countless number of 'pure' diviners of various kinds, and twenty straight herbalists, one of them a woman. According to some local people the five are capable of practising spiritual divination as well as healing but as not being interested in it, or doing so only rarely.

Let me begin with one of the opposed halves, divination. In fact, diviners comprise a number of types. A general term for someone who divines through the aid of spirits is *muganga wa kitswa* (doctor of the head), for his or her mind is possessed by 'head spirits' (*pepo za kitswa* or *nyama a kitswa*).

The most prevalent kind of diviner is called the *muganga wa mburuga*, who communicates with spirits usually by shaking a calabash (*kititi*) and then shaking and 'reading' a winnowing tray containing flour or another granular substance (the *mburuga*), or by speaking directly. Such oracular diviners are visited at their homes normally by relatives of a sick or suffering person, rather than by the person him- or herself. The diviners diagnose problems and their causes, and may recommend a consultation with other more specialist diviners or with a herbalist. These first-instance diviners comprise rather more women than men and charge the least for their services. Though always more numerous than men, the proportion of women seems to have increased during the last twenty-five years (Parkin 1972: 44). The men among them tend to be young, or at least not elders. Whether men or women, they tend to be married. At a crude guess, there are at least fifty such first-level diviners in Kayafungo location (population 22,562 in 1979), with some much more prominent and active than others.

Most of the diviners developing extra specialisms are men, and their fees increase with their scarcity value along with their age, but all will have started by having become an oracular diviner of first instance, an involuntary process which I shall describe in due course. Principal among the specialist diviners is the *muganga wa kuvoyera* who is, as I mentioned in the previous chapter, an oracular diviner who has been possessed by extra spirits enabling him (less commonly her) to be called to a homestead or neighbourhood to ascertain by means of 'praying-for' (*ku-voyera*) what is causing a homestead's problems. He can know through his spirits for instance whether a homestead is afflicted by witchcraft or by *vitio* and who the witch or incestuous couple are (see Thompson 1990: 145–154). There are only three such diviners in Kayafungo location, two very old men and one woman in her fifties. Two elderly men are also periodically summoned to the location from their home near Malindi, over a hundred kilometres away. Such diviners prepare the ground for the work of the herbalist, the *muganga wa vitio*, who actually purifies the homestead of the deadly contamination. Of the eleven such herbal, purificatory specialists in the location, only one is a woman. All are elderly except for two middle-aged men. The terms used for such purification are *ku-vororya*, which has a combined sense of cooling and clearing away sickness or affliction, and *ku-zizinya*, which emphasises cooling.

This division of labour typifies the relationship between diviners and herbalists of whatever level of specialisation: the diviner diagnoses and recommends; the herbalist carries out the curative treatment, always at much greater cost than that charged by the diviner.

It is significant also that it is men who make up most of the few specialist diviners there are. The male bias is even more pronounced among herbalists who do not normally use spirits and who must purchase their knowledge, which is, in any event, only ever sold to men and gives them an expertise in the use of leaves, roots, grasses, other natural phenomena and of appropriate verbal formulae and vocabulary.

This takes us to the area of herbalist healing which complements that of divination. The general term for herbal healer is either *muganga wa mkoba* (healer of the basket) or *muganga wa kumbo* (healer of the clearing away), the former term being more common. There are twenty-five such herbalists in Kayafungo location, five of whom also practise divination. These are all men except for one woman who is one of the eleven *vitio* specialists already referred to. A couple of men are in their thirties, and the rest are late middle aged and elderly. The most important kind of herbal specialism, practised by nine of them, is that of the 'doctor who reverses things' (*muganga wa kuhundula*). The latter word means to turn or bend something back such as grass, in order to eliminate a person's tracks, a clear reference to the underlying idea that most ills can only be cured by a reversal of the witchcraft that has caused them. Other specialisms, which in a few cases may be combined with the above or other specialisms, include searching for harmful buried objects which are wreaking havoc in a homestead, or burying an oath on a path which will capture a witch who passes over it (for which the specialist is known as *muganga wa pini*), or searching for articles which have become lost or misplaced, including livestock (known as the work of the *muganga wa kuzuza*). Other important capacities are to be able to mediate with special tree and cave spirits, known as *mizimu*, on behalf of a client who wishes to kill an enemy or to seek the spirit's help in some endeavour, or to locate and recapture for someone their soul or 'shadow' (*kivuri*) which has been stolen by a witch. The doctor is known in these roles as a *muganga wa mizimu* and *muganga wa kivuri* respectively.

Returning now to the most common and general term by which herbalists are known, doctor of the basket (*muganga wa mkoba*), the use of this term, basket, suggests a bridge between the two fields of divination and healing. At the start of his or, more usually, her career, having successfully completed an apprenticeship, a diviner is given a basket in which to carry the medicines and tools of her trade. Making baskets, however, is strictly the work of elderly men. A newly graduated diviner will be given the basket by a senior diviner, which will have been made by the initiate's mother's brother, ideally at least. However, only elderly men actually carry baskets around with them on a daily basis, whether or not they contain medicines.

Thus, while all diviners and herbalists possess baskets in which they keep their divinatory or medical wares, it is only those men senior enough also to be herbalists who are seen bearing them openly. This accords with the fact that almost any very old man will have a curative knowledge, however small, of some minor ailment. Unlike those whose sole occupation is medicine, such old men may only rarely be called upon to treat someone, who would invariably be a homestead member or close neighbour. But the idea of knowledge as a perquisite of age is given substance in this way and is especially marked by their open attachment to a basket.

The idea of *mukoba*, the basket, thus alludes to the oneness or interdependence of divination and herbalism. The items kept in a basket are, for example, a calabash for summoning spirits and perhaps porcupine quills for marking out ritual spaces, or finely selected vegetation and carbonised black powder in small gourds called *vidonga*, and other items. They are some of the visible tools of a complex trade. The basket summarises the curative process from initial divination to varied medical practice supported by secret verbal formulae, all of which is called by the one term, *uganga*.

Yet, while it is a single process, it is also cross-cut by such parallel oppositions as divination versus herbalism, spiritual inspiration versus purchased medicine, moral agency and minimal fees versus monetary self-interest and high charges.

While it is not normally considered possible for a diviner to become a herbalist, though some reported cases do exist ('where the spirits have allowed it'), it is possible within each field for individuals to acquire greater expertise and renown. But these possibilities are really only open to men, for few women ever become the specialist, 'praying-for' diviner called *muganga wa kuvoyera*, let alone herbalist. There are, then, in effect the two medical hierarchies, namely divination and herbalism, within which upward mobility is largely confined to men. An oracular diviner, most of whom are women, receives only 2 shillings for her services, only a *voyera* diviner receiving more, but the fees paid to herbalists run into hundreds and even thousands of shillings, especially if the treatment is prolonged. They often far exceed fees paid to hospitals.

This might seem to negate the view that the authority of the *muganga* is essentially an open, egalitarian one in opposition to the more exclusive authority of the Vaya secret society. After all, if women effectively do not rise much beyond simple and low-paid divination, then in what sense is the profession of the *muganga* egalitarian? In gender terms it clearly is not. Nevertheless, many Giriama women and men will insist that wider success is possible for individual women, and will point to the one or two important women diviners whose status is greater than that of some men and who appear, therefore, to reinforce the idea of equal access. Moreover, the women's own society, the Kifudu, has its own reservoir of medical and ritual expertise, which certainly complements that of male doctors. Compared, then, with the Vaya, the opportunities within divination and within herbalism are greater, while at the same time these opportunities are greatly skewed in favour of men.

The relative openness of the institution of divination and therapy on the one hand, and its career bias in favour of men on the other, is evident right from the beginnings of any one career. Giriama themselves talk of practitioners achieving 'promotion' to a higher grade, and the idea of such upward mobility also exists with regard to the secret societies, which have a distinction between novices and experts.

However, to talk only in terms of a medical hierarchy and career is to ignore the alternative Giriama view of the diagnostic and healing process. It will be remembered that while diviners are low-paid but morally exalted, herbalists do well financially but are believed capable, and are sometimes accused, of practising witchcraft. Witchcraft, being especially associated with the eastern areas of Giriamaland and with the coast, is viewed as having expanded enormously over the years and as being part of the contamination of Giriama propriety and customary behaviour. Diviners, too, are increasingly affected by non-Giriama spirits, especially Islamic ones, but they play on ideas of bodily entry and bodily containment, and their spirit-led diagnoses seem to refer analogically to the problem of the Giriama body of custom being invaded, purged, or protected. Whatever else they may be, diviners are clearly not in the profession for significant financial gain. Made up, so to speak, of both Giriama and more powerful foreign spirits, they do indeed embody the dilemma of the identity and continuity of the Giriama people as a whole.[2]

Thus, while men and, to a much lesser extent, women, do see material advantage to be gained from becoming either a diviner or a herbalist, and while men, at least, may seek to better themselves from such work, much as Kajiwe did, the opposition between morality and money, like that between the Kaya and traditional west and the socially complex and contaminating east, touches on the wider political issues confronting the Giriama.

Let me illustrate this allegorical drama of invasion, expurgation and protection by describing some of the activities surrounding spirits.

Invasions

We may start with divination and with the distinction that is made between spirits which enter the body (*pepo za mwirini* or *nyama a mwirini*) and those which enter the head (*pepo/nyama za kitswa*). Bodily spirits may cause the victim pain or discomfort and mainly afflict women but do not give them privileged information about what people are thinking or doing. Head spirits do provide this capacity to see into other minds and therefore to diagnose who and what is responsible for distress. They afflict some men as well as women.

The Giriama distinguish three main kinds of spirit dance, one of which is specifically concerned to drive out a victim's harmful bodily spirits, and is called *ngoma ya kupunga* (or *kuomboza*) *pepo*. A dance in fact consists of many indi-

---

[2] A whole book could be written on Giriama classification of spirits and their social consequences. Oaths, types of witchcraft and other agencies of misfortune, dance and song types, medicines, and flora and fauna, are all subject to sometimes extensive classification, which varies sometimes considerably over time and place. But the list of spirits is perhaps the most lively. New ones are always being added, most are fashionable only for a limited period, though all, once incorporated, seem at least to be remembered, if less and less invoked as time goes on. There are spirits named after successive waves of people, which I present as they were given to me: Kwavi (Maasai), Mugalla, Somali, Langulo, Muboni, Banyani, Mwarabu, Bulushi, Mbarawa, Mzungu, Digo, Murahai, Musambala, Mukorongo, Mutaita, Mukamba, Kikuyu and others. Some spirits are named after animals which have, or take on, a special metonymical significance: Ndowe or Mudowe (dog), Nyani (ape), Simba (lion), Nuyni and also Nyago (bird) each having particular characteristics. A third group of spirits is of a somewhat indeterminate class: Nyari (bare patch of cliff after a landslide), Dena (a Duruma clan name), Kizuka (something carved like a figurine or mask), Kanyango (a red cloth), Mulungu (God), Milungu (the plural form for god), (Ka)tsumbakazi (female, which laughs, is very friendly, throws off its clothes – *ku-tsumba* means to lean forward and kiss or embrace), Mtumwa (slave), Zimu (ghost) and others such as Muwele and Sandzuwa, which may be ethnic group spirits. A number of the above ethnic group spirits are in fact 'Muslim' or 'Arabic', and are regarded as very powerful and potentially harmful, usually requiring the victim possessed by one of them to 'become' Muslim to the extent of observing the Muslim requirements of fasting, not drinking, not eating pork, and not being buried in the customary, long-drawn-out Giriama manner.

vidual songs which are sung by the diviner in charge, or by another diviner. They are accompanied by drums, occasionally also involving a male diviner, and are danced by those persons, mainly women, who are possessed by the spirit after which each song is named. The songs occur in an order deemed appropriate by the *muganga* in charge. These are general features of all dances.

The dance concerned to drive out spirits can last all day and night and involves some sacrifice of chickens and offerings of, say, fruit to the spirits.

A second kind of dance is concerned with the opposite. It seeks to entertain and pacify rather than drive out spirits, which are regarded as having too strong a hold on a person for this to be possible, and indeed to be constructive of the person, being part of his or her make-up. The spirits are those of the body rather than of the head and so this kind of dance is sometimes called *ngoma ya pepo za mwirini*. It may also be called simply *ngoma ya pepo*, which is additionally the general name for all spirit dances. The pacificatory dance is held regularly, sometimes monthly at the sighting of every full moon, unless rains cause a postponement, and lasts until early morning. The idiom is more than that of pacification, for the spirits are spoken of as needing 'to be loved'. Similarly, in the event, say, of a postponement of a dance, the human victim may cry in desperation that she 'cannot stand the pain of possession any longer and must have the dance tomorrow'. In other words, the idiom is that of passion in the classic sense of both suffering and unfulfillable desire. In the course of conversations with the spirits during the dances, frequent allusions are made to the sexual desires and proclivities of these bodily spirits which have 'entered' the woman, who, for her part, 'needs' to 'satisfy' their needs. An attempt is made to guide these unsettled and unsettling spirits back to their proper 'seats' in the body, for example the heart, or into an amulet specially made and worn for this purpose.

These two kinds of dances are held almost only for women, for it is only they who are deemed to suffer prolonged pain and discomfort as a result of having been entered or unsettled by bodily spirits. Both dances are referred to as small ones in contrast to the large one called either *ngoma ya mburuga*, *ngoma ya mukoba*, or *ngoma ya pepo za uganga*.

As may be clear from my remarks above, each of these terms for this third, major dance refers to the fact that in this case the spirits possessing a person do more than simply occupy his or her body. They are spirits of the mind; and the dance is a response to the demand by the spirits that they sit in the head of the possessed person. Through their capacity to move into and out of the heads of other people, such spirits enable those they have chosen as mediums to know the thoughts of these other persons, and to divine.

Dances of all three types may last all night. Although the so-called major dance is specifically held for an initiate into divination, it may, during the night, develop into a dance in which numerous women become possessed or re-possessed by spirits, which must then be driven out at a subsequent dance. Here, we see taxonomic overlap, for while different dance types are classified by the Giriama, the one may spawn the other and they may merge in some respects.

The initiates at the major dance may, according to report, sometimes include a man as well as women and are, as in all cases, involuntarily possessed. Involuntary possession may occur at any time or place. It may take the form of illness accompanied by a dream in which a grandparent who had him- or herself been a diviner urges the grandchild to take up the craft, perhaps revealing in the dream an understanding of relevant trees, herbs and roots and their whereabouts. Diviners tend to inherit their capacities, in the form of spirits, from grandparents of the same sex as themselves, or from a mother's brother, and less often from a father or mother. (Alternative generations are linked as equals among the Giriama and may refer to each other as siblings.) Or the possessed may simply 'know', sometimes through the revelation of a dream, where such divinatory items can be obtained. In either case, the person is disturbed in some visibly emotional manner, often crying uncontrollably.

As in the case of possession by bodily spirits, relatives of the victim visit one or usually more diviners who reveal that the man or woman is troubled by a spirit wishing to direct the person into divination. The victim has no alternative but to follow this road, lest he or she be forever disturbed by the spirit. Plans are made for the initiate's dance, which will be organised and attended by an established diviner drawn from the surrounding area, who will himself or herself have diagnosed the possessed person's destiny and thereafter serves as the initiate's guide and legitimator (see also Johnston 1976: 52–56).

The three drums needed for a dance are, in any small area, located in a homestead which is known to have been afflicted by spirits and where the drums' owner, who is usually a diviner, lives. The drums are bought for personal use but also for investment. They are let out to other diviners wishing to hold spirit dances for about 15 shillings for the three drums for a day. Diviners who regularly act as mentors for new initiates inevitably buy their own at some stage. As Thompson has described (1990: 68), the sexual and emotional symbolism of the drums is very explicit. The 'male' drum (*mushondo*, from the verb, to pound), is long, narrow and played upright between the drummer's legs. The two 'wives' are smaller, but have within each some incense called a 'heart' or 'seat', unlike the male drum. Through the rhythmically frictional heat of being played, the hearts of the two female drums attract the possessory spirits, which, as they come close to the drums, cause women to 'boil' emotionally and so become possessed. Drummers are always only men, but may be of any age, and are invited to the dance. They number about five, so enabling rests to be taken, and are given at least a large calabash of palm wine for their efforts.

Arranging a day for the dance, ordering and collecting the drums, summoning the drummers, and inviting participants, some of whom will themselves invite others on the day, all require organisational skills and a commanding personality. Women as well as men organise. However, given the tendency of men to dominate the higher orders of the professional hierarchy, they figure among the mentors of new initiates at dances more than their low proportion among diviners might suggest. At the same time, the festive nature of the occasion blends with the professionalism. People are there to enjoy themselves as onlookers, to engage in drama if they become possessed, to take over a drum for a few moments from a flagging drummer welcoming a respite, and to witness the initiation of a new diviner, whose powers of clairvoyance are tested by the mentor before he or she is accepted publicly in their new profession.

The mainly male diviners who develop extra specialisms undergo their promotions in the same way. After a few years as an ordinary diviner they are possessed by a new set of spirits who demand a dance and provide the diviner with extra powers which are publicly tested by an older and more highly ranked diviner-doctor. It is sometimes claimed that specialisms run in clans, with, for instance, the Mkare and Nzaro clans (both allegedly originating from the Shambala people of present-day Tanzania) producing most diviners of *vitio*.

Cures and government control

Although they are not dependent on spirits, herbalists must do more than simply purchase their knowledge. They have to be taken on as an apprentice, *mutegi* ('one who traps', as in catching or countering witchcraft, and also used of some-one who assists in witchcraft divination). They must serve an established herbalist in this capacity sometimes for years. They must, in time, develop the confidence of their tutor and the credibility of the public to practise on their own.

Since the early 1970s, the professionalisation of this process has become even more evident through the creation of a number of medical associations or societies, an important one of which is the Jamii-Tiba Society of East Africa which was established in 1973 and based in Nairobi but with a branch in Mombasa. Another is the Miti ya Shamba Society. In 1975 the government declared that all diviners and herbalists should pay for a licence to practise, only 50 shillings for a diviner using the calabash and operating from his or her home, but 1000 shillings for a herbalist conducting his affairs in a more businesslike manner, often by travelling to patients. Government sanctions against non-payment of this licence include imprisonment and heavy fines.

Although the licences are obtained from government district offices, some people assumed that membership of the medical associations provided the necessary legitimation, and indeed many inland, rural chiefs accepted this as such. For the Jamii-Tiba Society the membership fee is 160 shillings for any member regardless of specialisation (and has remained unchanged). For the Miti ya Shamba it is 300 shillings. To protect themselves, many diviners and herbalists along the coast and in the eastern area of Giriamaland joined the medical associations, which are led and managed by senior, urban-based herbalists, all Muslims, who supply new members with an 'identity card' (*sic*) and a statement of their range of competence, after subjecting them to a test. The typed statement of one herbalist, in whose homestead in the east I once lived, listed sixty cures which he could effect, while that of a woman diviner made no specific reference to her skills. The 'identity card' states the member's name, residential district, location and sub-location, together with the name of his chief, sub-chief and headman.

In the western cattle zone, none of the many diviners, twenty herbalists, and five joint diviner-herbalists in Kayafungo location have to my knowledge joined an association nor secured a government licence. There is almost no central government control exercised in the area, and the relationship between the chief and local people is based on a greater mutual respect for traditional forms of cure and arbitration than in the east and on the coast.

Thus, as with all forms of professionalisation, the recognition of individual skills may be constrained by a centralised and controlling modern bureaucracy. The government has therefore encouraged the expansion of medical societies in an attempt to have a ready-made record of diviner-doctors, but has only been able to reach out to those in accessible and easily patrolled areas.

Another example of increasing government control dating in fact from colonial times is the attempt to curb extensive spirit possession dances. Again, it is only in the east that sorties are made from time to time by government chiefs to exert this control, despite the fact that the edict is meant to apply to all areas.

The regular, all-night dances held to pacify spirits or initiate new or apprentice diviners follow Giriama calendrical notions. A dance therefore starts at the sighting of a full moon, whether or not this occurs in the middle of the seven-day week on which wage employment is based and which government has encouraged. The government view is that workers, whether locally employed or migrant, cannot properly fulfil their duties if the dances occur on a weekday. A common compromise is for a chief to insist that the dances occur on Saturday evenings. If the curb were to extend to a complete ban on spirit possession dances, as has sometimes been attempted, this would hit at the initiation and apprenticeship of diviners. Herbalism would thereafter be legitimised through the medical societies, but divination, as a form of spirit mediumship which necessarily depends on the dances, would lack such legitimation. The hierarchical superiority of herbalism over and above divination would be reinforced even more by these developments.

Giriama inevitably talk about such possibilities and, in so doing, point up the often great differences in income and status between diviners and herbalists, a difference that we can read also as a polarisation of opportunities between women, who figure mainly amongst the lowest paid diviners, and men, some of whom earn large amounts of money as herbalists. The government-inspired attempts to centralise and control the activities of diviners and herbalists has had the paradoxical effect, then, of legitimating and so privileging even more those who already enjoy high position and who can most easily afford to pay licence and society membership fees.

Giriama also point to the ineffectiveness of government bans in the west, including those pertaining to the Kaya. The eastern and coastal areas thus face constraints lacking in the west, a difference which substantiates the overall contrast made between the zones as being spoiled and traditional respectively.

Doctors of seduction

While it is true that the hierarchy of diviners and herbalists in eastern Giriama-land and on the coast threatened to become more pronounced as a result of government-inspired centralised professionalisation, the two kinds of prac-titioners still complement each other. I have already explained how Giriama regard diviners as morally important and herbalists as often motivated by money, and in this way they provide the parameters for a debate about human values facing the Giriama. They complement each other also in their relationship to spirits and medicines. It is true that herbalists are not guided by spirits in their work as are diviners, whose sole or main means of communication is through speech and song. But herbalists do have a direct and often highly personalised relationship with the trees and plants from which they take the roots and leaves which make up their medicines. They talk to their flora and so, in this sense, are in communication with non-human agents as is a diviner with his or her spirits. Spirits move between and in and out of people, are never permanently anchored, and so complement the fixity of plant life.

Under the umbrella of this communicative rapport with non-human agents, however, there are differences in the kind of communication with spirits and herbal medicines. This has relevance, as I shall show, to Giriama ideas about nature and human intentionality. It also reflects how Giriama cope with threats made against them through negotiation and persuasion rather than outright confrontation.

First let me show the difference. While diviners, in their capacity as mediums, enable a two-way conversation to be carried out between a spirit and themselves, herbalists engage in one-way talk with their medicines, promising never to misuse them for evil purposes and encouraging them to work only for human good. Similarly, when about to make an oath in a trial by ordeal, a disputant will talk to the medicine that makes up the oracle, asking it to 'catch' him if he is guilty. Medicines can only be cajoled and persuaded: they cannot themselves communicate with humans, as can spirits. The verb used to describe this speak-ing with either spirits or medicines is *ku-kohotera*.

At dances held to placate or drive out spirits, the conversation that is believed to occur between possessed people and their spirits is also at the level of persuasion and negotiation. The diviner manages the conversation. He is the mouthpiece for the possessed and for the spirits which speak through the possessed. The spirits (or the possessed woman) do make demands which are clearly audible to the congregation of people at the dance, but they also express themselves through cries, whoops, and garbled so-called spirit language, all of which are publicly translated by the diviner in charge of the dance (as if by his own spirit). The diviner's control over the exchange is therefore considerable.

Typically, the diviner in charge of the conversation implores the spirit to leave or release the woman (or in rare cases man), and promises to offer what the spirit requires in return. The spirit (through the possessed woman) states its grievance, for example that it feels neglected, and may demand the sacrifice of an animal of a particular colour (black, white, or red) and that it (that is the woman) be given a cloth and sometimes beads of a colour and kind appropriate to the particular spirit. The diviner may argue with the spirit in an attempt to lower the value of what is demanded. But, as the one who also interprets the sounds emitted by the possessed woman, the diviner also states what it is that the spirits finally insist on. That is to say, although the woman is the medium through which the spirits make their demands, the diviner through his spirit translates and so is able to create an open expression of grievances on behalf of the possessed woman and her spirit, doing so before a gathering of up to fifty witnesses of the dance. A diviner of this level is typically a man.

In contrast to this public conversation between diviner and spirits, which is highly performative and full of word play, there are the words spoken to medicines by a herbalist using a secret vocabulary for plant life and in isolation. The herbalist seeking a particular medicine goes to a tree, bush or other plant, usually in a secluded forest or wooded area, and speaks to it soothingly, often stroking it before plucking its leaves or digging at its roots. He beseeches the herb to serve him in the interests of all humanity and to effect the cure for which it is known to be effective. He vows that the plant will not be used for malign purposes and can have trust in the herbalist.

We can see that this kind of conversation is quite the obverse of that with spirits. Spirit communication is presented as reciprocal, even though in fact controlled by the diviner, and is public and performative with an emphasis on style. The conversation with each spirit is preceded and accompanied by drumming and singing appropriate to each particular spirit. The onlookers are there to witness and evaluate the implicit judgements made on a possessed woman and, usually, her relationship with her husband, to which constant allusions are made by the spirit. By contrast, the herbalist's lonely talk with his plants is a curious blend of the personally performative and the unwitnessed, carried out in a secret plant lexicon which is known only by the herbalist, his former tutor and their tutors, and by his own apprentices. It is also in every way more subdued.

Yet both have in common the idea of persuasion, even of seduction. The diviner in the public dance reveals through the word play and allusions the desire on the part of the spirits to sleep with the woman, who, for her part, is depicted as complaining ambivalently of the discomfort the spirits cause to her body. The allegorical play on man–woman and husband–wife relationships and inadequacies is lost on none of the spectators, who will include the woman's husband (who attends, if only to try and check excessive sacrificial demands, for which he will be financially responsible).

The seduction of plants by the herbalist is of a much more indirect kind, consisting of gentle coaxing by word and touch, accompanied by promises of virtuous usage and results, carried out with only the two of them, man and plant, present.

A variation of the idea that medicines must be talked to in order to do their work is the address made by a disputant to an oracle in a trial by ordeal, such as that presided over by members of the Vaya society or by any owners of oracles. This address is both public and formulaic. It lacks the poetry of the diviner's appeal to the spirits but also has none of the secrecy and gently persuasive tone of the herbalist talking to a plant or tree. Although it draws on the oracular power of medicines, it is nevertheless a form of litigation which may, in a few cases, even reach the district magistrate's court. As such, it is not surprising that it preserves its rather austere formulaic element.

Let me now illustrate, with three examples, the differences in communication with spirits and medicines. I begin with the last-mentioned, the formulaic address to oracles. All cases are drawn from eastern Giriamaland for, while similar in outline to those of the west, they show the conditions under which Islamic influences and those of a cash crop economy and migrant and wage labour are brought to bear.

Public formulae

Kazungu used to tap palms for his neighbour Ngwangu. Kazungu saved enough money from his earnings as a tapper to provide the bridewealth for his son's marriage to a local girl. At about this time he also went to work as a tapper at another place. Shortly afterwards, the girl was bitten by a snake and became very ill. Kazungu and his son went to a diviner who intimated through describing the man and his circumstances that it was Ngwangu who out of jealousy had sent the witchcraft resulting in the woman being bitten by a snake. Ngwangu had allegedly wanted the woman for his own son, having recognised her exceptional personal qualities. Kazungu and his son confronted Ngwangu with the diviner's accusation, demanding that the woman be cured. Ngwangu refused, claiming that he did not bewitch the woman and that for him to attempt to cure the woman would be to admit that he had bewitched her.

Ngwangu himself then suggested that he and Kazungu be judged by an oracle. Permission was sought from the chief to do this and was granted. Kazungu as plaintiff and Ngwangu as defendant each recited the following before taking the oath:

Plaintiff: 'I, Kazungu Kahindi, have agreed to eat the oath because my wife is ill [*sic*, though in fact she is a son's wife, the expression referring to the fact that it is the father who actually paid the bridewealth for her]. If I am wrong, and this defendant, Ngwangu, is not a witch, then let the oracle catch me; but if he is a witch, then let it catch Ngwangu.'

Defendant: 'I, Ngwangu Kalama, have agreed to eat the oath because I have been accused of witchcraft. If I am indeed the witch and have really bewitched the wife of Kazungu, then let the oath catch me, but if I am wrongly accused, then let it catch Kazungu instead.'

It was in fact Ngwangu who was caught by the oath: he and Kazungu each swallowed a piece of paw-paw fruit doused in medicine prepared by the Vaya elders; the fruit stuck in the throat of Ngwangu but not in that of Kazungu who was therefore judged innocent. (It appears possible that persons differ in their responses to the medicine or that, as in this case, the person to whom the fruit is first given is more likely to suffer from the stronger effects of the medicine, or even that the Vaya or other doctor administering the oath gives the offending portion to whoever he believes to be guilty, having heard the two versions of the dispute (see also Johnston 1976: 270–271).)

Ngwangu at first accepted the verdict of the oracle. He got someone to write to the chief on his behalf accepting the verdict, again in formulaic terms: 'I, Ngwangu, was caught by the oracle and I accept that I bewitched the wife of Kazungu with the witchcraft of the snake. I accept that I must have her treated medically so that she is cured, and that I must pay all the expenses incurred by Kazungu.'

However, when Kazungu submitted his expenses (not compensation) of 321 shillings, Ngwangu decided on the advice of an educated relative, but much against the wishes of local elders, to take the case to a district magistrate's court. He then became the plaintiff and Kazungu the defendant:

The defendant, Kazungu's wife was bitten by a snake in the bush and the defendant alleged that I was a witch and that I bewitched his wife. The allegation is false and has caused much disturbance in my home. I now claim 600 shillings compensation and the costs of this civil suit (142 shillings).

The magistrate's court found in favour of the plaintiff, Ngwangu, so obliging Kazungu himself to pay compensation and costs (District Magistrate's Court at Kiifi. Civil Suit 82 of 1978).

Johnston makes the point that the oracle medicines are regarded as inert until they are orally instructed to have their effect (1976: 265). In other words, it is the human appeal that activates them. This is perhaps why a common verb, *ku-kohotera*, should be used to refer to forms of communication as seemingly divergent as those between humans and non-verbal medicines and between humans and highly verbal spirits. Common to all is the idea of interaction between humans and non-humans as being based on persuasion, ranging from the rather more personalised formulae addressed by doctors to plants, and to the highly creative exchanges evident at spirit possession dances and seances. Before moving on to examples of the latter, let me give an example of a herbalist at work, where we see his distinctive kind of secrecy combined with a kind of poetic style in his relationship to plants.

Private poetry

Charo is a married man in his early forties with five children. He was sacked from his clerical job in Mombasa after many years service. He blamed his dismissal on the sudden hostility of his fellow employees and new boss. He consulted a diviner who diagnosed his problem as resulting from his having been bewitched by a jealous rival who prevented him from being liked by anyone at the workplace. This was why he lost his job and could not get another. The diviner referred him to a herbalist, a fellow Giriama, known for his ability to reverse this kind of witchcraft and who was also a member of the Jamii-Tiba Society of doctors.

The herbalist began by addressing two medicines, the first called *Kache na Ganje* and the second *Kundano*. The language used is Giriama, a little of it mixed with Swahili, which I have translated:

It is you Kache and Ganje [female and male names respectively]. Arouse my medical skill so that it works [repeated three times].
   It is you, the reducer of things, the dwarf, who folds and compresses.
   I can compress and shorten everything, yes, I can make everything smaller through you Kache and Ganje.
   Phew! [a blowing sound]. It is you who conquer, you who have conquered the Galla, then the Maasai, and then the Arab.
   There is a war by one person over another, and I don't want to see such war continue or be talked about.
   I have thrown off this strife, I have blown it away and it is no longer here.
   Phew! I have not stolen you. I have bought you with my own property [i.e. money] from the old man [gives the name of his own tutor].

The herbalist then addresses the second medicine.

Phew! I believe it is you who are the stultifier of things [repeated seven times].
   You are the spice in the wilderness, you are the correct one, you are the guide.
   You are the one who quashes every tribe under your two buttocks.
   I have sat upon quarrels or any problem and there is nothing now to be quashed which can disturb me.
   I [gives own name], in going my way, my way is swept clean by the [tail of] a cat and my friend is the dove [of peace] and the partridge.
   I do not meet with any vicissitudes at all. The way I left home is the way I return.
   Everywhere I pass are my former homes [i.e. where I may stay].
   The one who has the reducer [medicine] is the one who is the loved one. The possessor of the reducer medicine does not have to aim for things forcefully. He or she does not have

to reach out for things. Its work is to be loved by women and men. Its work is to be given things from nothing.

Phew! I did not steal you, but I bought you with my own property from the old man [name of tutor].

After these recitations, which were made while shaking the small gourd containing the black powdered medicine, the herbalist treated Charo with the medicine. With a razor blade he cut Charo's right hand index finger twice, so that the blood seeped out, and then twice under both eyes, and twice on the forehead just below the hairline and centrally. All were small downward cuts, into which the powder was rubbed. Charo was then told not to speak to anyone about the details of the treatment, which had to remain secret to be effective.

Charo was also told of the treatment that he had thereafter to administer to himself. He was given two separate bottles in which each powdered medicine was contained. The treatment was to begin back in Mombasa and last for a period of seven days. Charo was required first to recite the appeal to Kache and Ganje. Then, each time in the recitation that he reached the point when he had to make a blowing sound (Phew!), he had to take a pinch of Kache and Ganje powder between the thumb and little finger of his right hand, close his eyes, hold the powder to his mouth, and blow it away. This was repeated three times. With the tip of his right little finger he had then to dab some of the same powder on the underside of the tip of his tongue, under the right eye, and inside the right ear, each three times. Then, after reciting the address to the second medicine, Kundano, Charo was to use his longest or middle right finger to dab the slightly thicker, almost granular Kundano powder under the roof of his mouth and then blow at the appropriate two sounds in the recitation. During the treatment, which had to be carried out morning and evening over the seven-day period, finishing on a morning, the bottles had to be left open overnight.

Although it was well over a year before Charo got another job, he attributed his eventual success to the treatment. The herbalist had been paid a few hundred shillings at the end of the demonstration and instruction. Had Charo been somewhat younger, he might well have asked to be apprenticed to the older herbalist, for it is through such expensive curative sessions that such agreements are reached.

In this example the herbalist talks to the medicines as finished products, so to speak, for they have been converted from leaves into powdered carbon. He flatters them on their powers and achievements, speaking softly in a manner that in the original Giriama has something of the poetic. Although it is a recitation of words and of a performance that have been handed down over the years, there is also an emphasis on the uniqueness of that particular moment of utterance. The formulaic is made emotive.

Beforehand, during the actual collection of plants in a forest area, the herbalist also addresses them. As the same herbalist put it, 'Medical skill [*uganga*] depends on knowing the secret medical names which are different from ordinary names. This knowledge has to be bought and the buyer must also be taught how to use them.' The leaves are taken and gently held while still on the bush or tree and, typically, the following is said: 'Listen, you are so-and-so [i.e. he addresses the plant by its secret name], and I have come here to take you to help people. Some people are vomiting, they are deeply troubled, and are ill. This is therefore my reason for taking you. That is my only work in taking you' (that is, he does not intend to use the plants to kill or harm someone through witchcraft-poisoning). The leaves are then broken off, burnt to carbon and ground to a powder, and are addressed in the same way, 'for plant life [*mihi*, a term which includes large trees as well as small bushes] can hear even if it does not speak'.

One part of the address, then, takes the form of pleas, promises and exhortations. This is the doctor as seducer. The other part is where the address reminds him firmly of his own duties towards humanity. This is the doctor exerting self-discipline over his power to seduce and to cure, a power that can so easily be turned against humanity rather than for it, for all doctors or herbalists are regarded as potential witches. The more austere formulaic address occurs when a person, perhaps already a doctor or someone wishing to become one, buys medical knowledge (*uganga*) from another doctor. The buyer must take an oath (*kurya kiraho*, literally to eat an oath) that the knowledge will be used only for curing and not for witchcraft, in default of which the user will himself suffer from the witchcraft he has set for someone else.

Some herbalists I have spoken to claim that they may buy medical knowledge from up to seven other doctors, both to increase a repertoire and to have different types of treatment for the same ailment or misfortune. On each occasion the oath of good practice must be taken. The seven doctors would be selected as follows. A herbalist's own first teacher, called his *baba muganga* (medical father), tells his pupil who his own teacher was and the latter names his and so on up to seven lineal 'ascendants'. Should one in the chain of seven have died, then his successor is approached instead. I assume that in this transmission of knowledge, not all a man's expertise is passed on and that, also, during the course of their careers each is adding to his knowledge. This would ensure that there is always something extra to be learned from members of the seven-man chain. Since successors to deceased members are also always being substituted, this, too, would increase the network of contacts for buying and selling knowledge. I do not know how closely the practice by which medical skills are transacted conforms to this description, which nevertheless reveals doctors' expectations that there is both continuity and control in the transmission of expertise.

The critical element is the insistence that the purchaser takes the oath of good practice before he is actually given the knowledge, and that this oath is then binding both between the buyer and his medicine and between him and his teacher, with a special link existing with his very first tutor. The parallel is often made between this act of binding obligation and that of blood-brotherhood between friends or agnatically distant clansmen of the same or alternate generation. Blood-brotherhood is called 'eating the scar' (*kurya tsoga*). Each man drinks the other's blood from a lightly made cut on the right arm. It involves a number of possible obligations, such that, should one of them die, he will inherit the other's property and wives, subject to the latter's consent, or that neither will commit adultery with the other's wives. The obligation continues after one of them has died. As an ancestral ghost (*koma*), the latter punishes any negligence or transgression by his blood-brother.

The sense of kinship, continuity and on-going sanctions that characterise the relationships of doctors to each other is therefore part of a more general nexus in Giriama life. Remembering how Vaya members are recruited through a similarly tight network of known and tested associates of a single aged generation, we can see this nexus as a kind of prototype of secret societies. It is based on a mixture of local secrecy and trust that stands in contrast to the modern, bureaucratically centralised, Kenya-wide medical associations located in the major cities of Nairobi and Mombasa, such as the Jamii-Tiba society. It also reveals, through variable use of verbal formulae and addresses to plants and medicines, a poetic side to the practice of medicine in addition to the obligatory and contractual.

Why is there this part-emphasis on style and performance? I suggest that such creativity, both verbal and gestural, stands in counterpoint to the severity of therapy and affliction, and makes the experience of illness an ambivalent one of dread and possible pleasure. It is, of course, no laughing matter when people suffer from disease, die suddenly and in numbers, and lose their fertility, jobs and confidence. For this reason the contractual obligations of diviners, doctors and patients can only be talked about in a language that takes such matters seriously. At the same time, therapy and the understanding of afflictions has to be experimental, for otherwise new cures would not be found. Part of the exploration is into the nature of social relationships which are often held responsible for personal ills and sufferings. The arena in which this creativity comes to the fore is that of spirit possession, when diviners interpret and translate spirit-talk. For here, it is not a question of talking at medicines which cannot reply. Rather, it is basic to the idea of spirit mediumship that the spirits not only respond to questions posed by a diviner, but also pose them, often critically: the diviner as well as a client or central character in a performance may be criticised.

However, the exchange is also a performance in which participants appear to take great pleasure. It is a chance to act centre-stage, to display the power of rhetoric and linguistic manipulation, of other alleged tongues and of poetic argument, together with dramatic physical gestures. None of this is to say that those who are possessed are not in some way ill. The one pleasure that may perhaps be derived from such illness is precisely in being able to transcend it through performative play. For some, of course, it is the theatre that appears to effect the cure, while for others the illness sadly returns.

We may, as outsiders, claim that the verbal and gestural repartee is in reality controlled by the presiding diviner. But it comes across to the assembled group (and probably to the diviner himself) as unpredictable and experimental, as well as theatrical. It thus seeks public solutions to personal crises in an aesthetically pleasing way. The solutions become public even when the consultation with the diviner is private, for they inevitably get talked about after a divinatory session among relatives, friends and neighbours.

Divinatory inventiveness

We can make a simple distinction between private and public divination. A private consultation with a diviner at his or her home will be attended by no more than two or three people representing a victim of sickness or misfortune, and occasionally by the latter themself. They may consult a number of such diviners before resorting to a full public divination or therapy. By public divination I refer to any one of the three spirit possession dances which have been mentioned, or to that which precedes homestead cleansing or witchcraft eradication, as described in chapter six.

A private consultation

Somewhat unusually, Kahindi Poko decided to visit a diviner on his own behalf, accompanied only by myself. He wants to hear for himself what the diviner says, rather than rely on reports. He is a relatively young enterprising farmer who suffers from pains in his back and neck. He has been to the local hospital but to no avail.

The diviner shakes the calabash, calling 'Taireni' (the usual spirit summons), to which Kahindi and I answer the usual 'Za mulungu' ('Of God'). She shakes the calabash again and one of her spirits enters her, expressed by a shout coming from the diviner. She again greets, 'Taireni', and the spirit's voice comes from the woman remarking that the client has something very strange that has to be explained, and that it (that is the spirit) is able to see people who went to look at these inexplicable things. Kahindi assents to this.

The spirit says that these things came from the east to the south and thence to the north. Kahindi urges the spirit to tell him what these strange things are. The spirit replies that they did not arise in a person's homestead but outside it and that they certainly came from where the sun rises (i.e. the east). Kahindi answers that we did indeed visit a place outside the victim's (i.e. Kahindi's) homestead and asks whether these things are really something of this tangible world.

The diviner again shakes the calabash and once more becomes the mouthpiece for the spirit, who claims that Kahindi is really contesting that it went to that place in the east, and asks him why he is resistant to this and why he does not believe what the spirit is saying. The spirit knows it is true because it has just gone, in the form of the woman diviner, to that time and place in the past when Kahindi met a man (later identified by name by Kahindi) and has witnessed the meeting throughout.

Kahindi urges the spirit to continue. It repeats that it has now been twice to that place, and Kahindi concedes that the spirit does know the truth about these things, to which the spirit indignantly asks why, then, did Kahindi contest the spirit? More humbly now, Kahindi states that he accepts that the spirit does inform the diviner correctly, and that he, Kahindi, did go with three men to warn another man not to continue with his abuse against Kahindi. The spirit then tells of a meeting held at that place by the elders (whom the spirit calls 'my sons' because the diviner stands as classificatory mother to them).

The spirit, now speaking in the first person plural ('we'), then claims that it (and other spirits) have brought the diviner close to the body of the sick person having gone back even further, to the week when the strange event occurred, to see what it was. The spirits say that a person was envious because of the victim's land. The envious person could not come to the landowner's home and so he put witchcraft-of-the-snake (*utsai wa nyoka*) in his path instead, so that it would bite him and cause the witchcraft to enter his body. But the landowner (i.e. Kahindi) jumped quickly on seeing the snake and so was not bitten, but received instead a pain from having jumped which has lasted to the present day, much more so than would normally have been expected. If the victim had been a woman, she would have died immediately, said the spirit. But it was intended for Kahindi who is known to be strong.

The spirits state that the pains are in the head, shoulders, back, and the small of the back, to all of which Kahindi agrees. The spirits then say that Kahindi's blood is so strong that the witchcraft did not touch him very much, but that had it been weaker he would have slept on his bed for a whole week.

Kahindi then asks to know what it is he has done to the witch to deserve such treatment. The spirits answer that the witch is motivated only by envy of the fact that Kahindi succeeds in his agricultural work without difficulty. The spirits also claim that another result of the witchcraft is that Kahindi gets irritable and loses his temper with his family (comprising three wives and children and two co-resident brothers and their wives and children), which Kahindi confirms.

Kahindi wants to know more specifically why the witch should feel such envy as to wish to harm Kahindi so much. The spirits answer again that it was envy and the wish to prevent him from becoming prosperous, and that the witch would have got his victim by putting something in his food, except that he never eats at that place (in the east).

Seeming to anticipate now Kahindi's wish to narrow down the possible identity of the witch, the spirits then ask him not to blame the homestead head of the place where the witch is, but that the feelings of envy belong to others there.

Two of them in particular have asked themselves why Kahindi should achieve progress when they, much older than he and with grown sons, should have fallen behind.

Kahindi asks, as if by way of seeking confirmation of the original claim by the spirits, whether the witchcraft medicine had been placed in a field or by some other method. The spirits say that the witch did try to place it in a field, but could not and so placed it on his path in the form of a snake. They had also tried to place it in his house, and if he were a drinker of palm wine he would have died from poison put in it. (Kahindi in fact abstains as a result of having been told to do so after being possessed by a 'Muslim' spirit some months earlier.)

The spirits say that three men wish to 'trap' him (an advance now from the two mentioned earlier). In response to Kahindi, the spirits tell him that one comes from the east, another from the west, and the third from the north, and that all wish to impede his progress, and moreover that they are farmers, like him, whose land borders on his own. Kahindi then identifies them, giving the names of two men whose land does border on his own and a third who has a house on Kahindi's land. The spirits then cut in and tell Kahindi (now evidently known by the spirits to be the victim and not the victim's representative), 'The one whose land borders you and who is your friend and at whose place you sometimes eat, he is the one who has done most of this against you'. The spirits then state that two of the three men are Giriama, and the third a Chonyi (a Mijikenda group).

Finally, the spirits list the kinds of witchcraft that made up the composite witchcraft medicine that has been lain across Kahindi's path. These are eight in number (*utsai wa shula moyo, wa tengo, wa nyoka, wa gundiza, wa kitu, wa jibale, wa manane,* and *wa fumula*). The spirits advise that certain chickens will need to be sacrificed for a cure, to be carried out by a doctor skilled in reversing the effects of witchcraft. These are two black hens, one hen the colour of beach sand, one brown or red cock, and one hen of the kind whose feathers have grown in wayward directions (called by the special name of *kuku wa kidemu*).

Explanations of colour and pattern symbolism given by Giriama vary, though here it was suggested that the black hens are the witches who will be caught by the white (in this case a hen of the colour of beach sand). The red cock is to make the black act upon the white, while the raggedy-feathered hen, which is commonly used in both bewitching and cure, both poses the problem and seeks its resolution, for its feathers indicate that elements are not in harmony. It is distinctive in other ways. For instance it cannot be given as food to a guest unless it is first slaughtered at the threshold of the entrance to the homestead: it is, in other words, a thing from outside.

Analysis
We can here distinguish between theme and performance. The theme is that of 'strange events' (*kimako*) that have occurred in a place to the east. By the end of

the session, these are spoken of as witchcraft that has been practised by a member of a particular homestead. There is, overall, movement from the general to the particular (that is, from events to specific kinds of witchcraft, from the east, west and north to a known homestead and its head, and from envy to a precise statement about the resentment felt by older men that a young man should succeed and they not).

Drawing on the idiom of a bodily and spatial journey, as do all Giriama diviners (Parkin 1979a), and in working from broad to more detailed statements, the diviner progressively elicits more and more of the client's agreement with her remarks. Early on, the diviner cleverly questions the client's allegedly bad faith in the power of the spirits. If the client is to justify his consultation, for which he has already paid 2 shillings he has no alternative but to concede that he believes in the ability of the spirits to travel in time and space. Towards the end the client goes to the extent of actually identifying the miscreants obliquely referred to by the diviner beforehand. The client, in other words, reaches the point when he actually supplies information, leaving the diviner with little more to do than look on. Finally, however, the diviner reasserts the authority of the spirits, who list the different types of afflicting witchcraft and the curative items needed by the client.

Although this is a diagnostic theme broadly similar to that of many diviners, the diviner must nevertheless adjust inventively to the different personalities and doubts of clients coming to her. Kahindi is more sceptical than most and, though he is not personally much known to the diviner, is recognised by her as having an independent and strong character, to which allusions are made in the session by reference to Kahindi's strong blood. The language is suggestive through its use of metaphors which allow inconsistencies to be reconciled, and it takes the form of a rhythmic exchange of statements, questions, and answers between the diviner's spirits and the client, Kahindi. It is in that sense both poetic and a performance (see also Parkin 1979a and 1985).

Public divination

The verbal artistry of the presiding diviner is an especially pronounced feature of the publicly held spirit possession dances. It plays upon ambiguities and even exploits the semantic possibilities resting in Bantu grammar and syntax. For instance, the eight or so Giriama noun classes are each characterised by a particular prefix, each of which has a broad sense. By switching these prefixes around and placing them in front of nouns with which they are not normally used, the sense of the noun is altered, sometimes ambiguously, humorously or worryingly. Thus, to place the diminutive prefix, ka-, which is often used endearingly of people or things, in front of a word for monster or threatening giant is both to negate the monstrosity and to offer a new way of thinking and speaking about it.

More than the speech used in private divination, or of addresses to oracles and medicines, the dialogue at spirit dances often mixes Giriama and Swahili. In addition, both the possessed woman and the diviner will carry out conversations in languages which are identified as those of a particular people or ethnic group, for instance, 'Arabic' or 'Kamba' but which no one but the diviner and spirit (speaking through the possessed woman) can understand. Nevertheless, the spirit (i.e. the possessed woman) does periodically break out in clearly under-stood Giriama or Swahili, so that the diviner is obliged to attend to what she says. She is by no means passive and all along tempers the otherwise almost absolute interpretative authority of the presiding diviner. Indeed, it is a test of the diviner's role to retain control over the discourse.

Punctuating these exchanges between spirit and diviner are the songs sung in turn for each spirit that is greeted. The songs tend to retain their content and remain relatively unaltered from one dance to another, often preserving archaic vocabulary, some of which is unknown to younger people. In ushering in one spirit after another, however, they require the diviner to treat separately those women possessed by each. Does a particular spirit require gentle persuasion and a soothing tone, or should it be spoken to firmly and harshly as having over-stepped the bounds of a reasonable request? The number of spirits recognised by the Giriama is enormous and there is often only loose agreement as to their habits and characteristics. Nor is there always agreement as to what beads, clothes and sacrifices particular spirits desire to be given or have made on behalf of the women they possess.

Once again, the inventiveness required of the diviner can be considerable. On one occasion, a spirit (i.e. a possessed woman) demanded that a white horse be sacrificed. No one at the spirit dance was ever likely to have seen a horse, which cannot thrive in the area, and apart from the inordinate expense which would have been involved in buying one from elsewhere, the request clearly could not have been met. Spirits can be deceived, however, if the diviner's powers of per-suasion and pretence are good enough. The diviner therefore described for the spirit a white horse which swiftly took on the characteristics of a white goat. He then urged the husband of the possessed woman for whom the sacrifice was demanded to supply the animal which, as a white goat, the man was able to do. Naturally, having had the horse described to it in this way, the spirit was happy with its gift.

Underlying the often clever verbal repartee between diviner and spirit are allusions to personal care and sexuality on the part of the possessed woman.

Case

A dance was being held to appease the spirits of the fourth wife of a man called Masha Ngole who had inherited her from his deceased brother some few years previously. She had three children and had been married altogether for ten years. Her problems had begun with a sickness which kept her in bed for a week. Her husband consulted a diviner (*muganga wa mburuga*), a woman in her early thirties, who told him that his wife was possessed by five spirits which needed satisfaction, these being named as Mwalimu, Katsumbakazi, Maiti, Mbingu and Msomali, which constitute a mixture of internal Giriama and outside non-Giriama spirits, including two Islamic ones, the heterogeneity being characteristic of the eastern agricultural zone of Giriamaland.

The woman did not go off into the forest before the dance and collect herbal medicines. Had she done so she would have been regarded by presiding diviners as a possible candidate for inauguration as a diviner. Instead, on the day of the dance she was seated on a mat placed in the middle of the compound of her and her husband's homestead. Her head and most of her body were covered by a black cloth. The individual songs were sung and played on the drums in the customary order, or at least in that deemed appropriate by the presiding diviner. At the beginning of each song played to the spirits possessing the woman, the male diviner took incense, lit it, and when it was smoking, placed it under the cloth over the woman's head, and addressed the Giriama Katsumbakazi spirit in that language and the rest in Swahili, 'Now, you have wanted your [using the plural respect form] *mushindo*, and this is it. Come and dance with joy. Don't stop, get your strength and enjoy.' The spirit shouted back, saying that it had been 'deceived' for too long and had been denied the dance which it needed. It shouted very loudly, apparently trying to overwhelm the diviner with its anger. But the diviner shouted even harder, persisting in his insistence that the spirit had what it wanted. More moderately, the diviner then called the spirit by name. In response, the voice of the spirit coming from the woman spoke 'Arabic words' very loudly under the black cloth which only the diviner among those present understood, and to which he replied, again in 'Arabic', conversing at great length in admirable mastery of a range of guttural and other convincing sounds.

At each song other women danced, as each of their spirits required it of them. At about halfway through the dance, one of the wives of a respected neighbourhood elder who was about twice her age fell and started making a great noise. The presiding diviner took the woman, spoke to her spirits, which were called Kuruani and Maiti. But the spirits shouted him down, saying 'I have been deceived too long. I am not getting my [own] dance, therefore I will not be quiet.' The diviner, firmly but without shouting, then said, 'You must agree to quieten, because there is no opportunity now to get a *mushindo*, not until the woman's husband can afford it.' The woman then fell down again, repeating the same demand, but in Swahili this time rather than in Giriama. She was carried to her house a kilometre away and slept until morning. The spirit affected her ('stayed with her') for two days. She was given herbal medicine to wash herself in and was soon again able to understand what people around her were saying, at which point the spirit left her. The diviner remarked, however, that she will be stricken by the spirits the next time she goes to a spirit dance, until they have had their own dance.

The *mushindo* which spirits seek is a curious term. It is Swahili and its basic meaning is 'shock, blow, explosion', coming from the word *ku-shinda*, to conquer. But it has a derived meaning of 'violent emotion or sensation . . . also used of an orgasm in coition' (Johnson 1939: 423). While it is seemingly used synonymously at times with the word for dance (*ngoma*), its other more emotionally embedded senses are also quite explicit, given the general context of providing 'satisfaction' to the 'needs' and 'desires' of spirits.

The emphasis on spirits' desires thus touches on three aspects: spirits always want material goods, usually dresses, personal ornamentation (both worn, of course, by the afflicted woman after they have been granted) and the sacrifice of an animal; spirits which invade or cause a 'sensation' within a woman's body clearly also seek to satisfy sexual desires; more generally, in their wish for appeasement, spirits seek emotional satisfaction. We shall see in the next chapter how this joint emphasis on material, sexual and emotional desire is re-presented in the new and rapidly emerging coastal culture centred on, among other forces, tourism.

While tourism is a new influence, Islam is an old one, with Christianity also old but having had much less impact until recently.

As regards the older influence, Islam, it was remarked to me at some point by one of the spectators at the session described above that all diviners must be Muslim, since they would not otherwise be able to speak 'Arabic' nor converse with Islamic spirits. Another remarked that this particular diviner did in fact have his special Islamic books written in Arabic which he could understand. Such claims are not uncommon, and certainly the view is often expressed by people in the east that all diviners and healers of any persuasion are necessarily Muslim, either through having been involuntarily possessed by a Muslim spirit or through voluntary conversion.

The eastern fingers of Islam

Typical of a Giriama who fears the poison of enemies and wishes to be exempt from neighbourhood drinking and eating, Kahindi, described in a case above, is a 'spirit Muslim', or what I have elsewhere called a 'therapeutic Muslim' (1970, 1972). That is to say, he is one of those people who have been possessed involuntarily by a so-called Islamic, Koranic, or Arabic spirit (*pepo ya Kiislamu, pepo ya Kurani,* or *pepo ya Kiarabu*). Unlike other so-called Giriama spirits, these require the afflicted person nominally to adopt Islam as his or her religion, at least to the extent of observing dietary and other restrictions on the use of food, abstaining from alcohol, and fasting during Ramadan and sometimes adopting a Muslim name. Complete conversion to Islam is not necessarily required by the spirits, though this does often happen. Partial conversion is at least demanded by the spirits, who will otherwise continue to bring pain and suffering to their victims.

Spirit possession is an area of activity in which Islam is most able to penetrate Giriama social life. It begins through this kind of personal divinatory consultation, but once the victim has adopted Islamic behaviour, becomes a matter of public knowledge. Indeed, it is precisely in this way that someone like Kahindi becomes publicly exempt from the normal round of Giriama eating and drinking obligations. Palm wine is drunk in large quantities, in the way meat is eaten at funerals, and to consume both is ceremonially binding. Meat for consumption by Muslims has to be slaughtered in the traditional Islamic way by another Muslim. Muslims thus eat apart or at least can identify what it is that they are eating and who has prepared it. In reality such separate treatment cannot fully guard against the possibilities of food being poisoned, but it helps. Moreover, there is an associated belief in the power of Islam to overcome many forms of witchcraft. The notions of witchcraft and of poison are often merged, so that Islamic ritual protection and practical precautions concerning the consumption of food are seen as together making an enterprising individual like Kahindi less prone to malicious attacks by jealous neighbours.

While economically enterprising men figure among those who, conveniently perhaps, suffer possession by Muslim spirits, a second, perhaps larger group includes women. From the cases I have there is no evidence to suggest that women of any particular status undergo possession more than others. All such women are married, most have children and a high proportion are second and subsequent rather than senior wives. But beyond these features, no sociological pattern is apparent.

From the Giriama viewpoint, men and women possessed by Islamic spirits are of a publicly forceful character. They are the men who refuse to observe traditional methods of adjudication in such cases as adultery and insist, instead, on overturning elders' judgements by taking cases to the magistrate's court. They are the women who dispute with other women as well as men in a homestead, over such domestic matters as carrying water, cooking and farming. Reports of such behaviour reach the ears of diviners as well as neighbours and so it is not surprising that a diviner pronounces such a person as being possessed by the strong and especially troublesome Islamic spirits. The powerful are matched by the powerful.

Such people are examples to other Giriama of the possibilities of an altered personal existence. Some of the most famous male business entrepreneurs were at some earlier stage of their lives obliged to observe Islamic prohibitions. No women possessed by Islamic spirits have achieved comparable personal and economic independence but, in relation to other women of a homestead, they are necessarily given selective attention. In some cases their sense of Islamic distinctiveness appears to become a pretext for a quarrel with a husband, and then a father anxious not to have to return bridewealth. Neither husband nor father may be able to prevent the woman from migrating to work in Mombasa, and from repaying her own bridewealth and so securing her personal autonomy. Such battles of will thus begin at spirit possession dances where demands are made of a husband by a wife. They continue more insistently if the woman is possessed by Islamic spirits and uses them to distance herself more and more from her husband and even from her children and natal family. In most cases, the ties of children and family limit protest to periodic assertions at the spirit dances. But that a few women do transcend even these ties is regarded by both Giriama men and women as a feature of life in the coastal zone, where Islam and high rates of divorce and separation are seen as going together.

Conclusion

Just as witchcraft is regarded by Giriama as more pronounced in the eastern coastal zone than in the western cattle one, so Islamic spirits are believed to be more prevalent there and to threaten traditional Giriama expectations concerning the status of women and that of entrepreneurial young men in relation to elders. While the hierarchy of doctors undoubtedly favours men's career opportunities in traditional medicine more than those of women, it is precisely at the bottom of the hierarchy, at the level of spirit possession leading to divination, that Islamic spirits sneak in, so to speak, and offer a few women, as well as men, the possibility of breaking away from tradition itself.

By contrast, in the cattle area of Miyani, Islamic spirits are hardly ever listed by diviners as of importance and I met no woman who had been afflicted by them. Instead, so-called Giriama spirits are much more in evidence. Spirit possession is certainly common to both areas, but what it says about the possibilities of being female differ radically in the two cases. In the cattle area women's possession by indigenous Giriama spirits does no more than return them to the fold of Giriama family life. In the coastal area, Islamic spirits may turn women into diviners or offer them at least the thinkable possibility of themselves becoming Muslim women of independent means living in Mombasa. In this respect their independence parallels that of entrepreneurial men who have become Muslims and who then escape certain customary constraints and obligations.

In fact, the Giriama were, until Kenya's independence in 1963, commonly characterised by travellers, missionaries and government officers as a people who resisted change, including conversion to Islam and Christianity. It is certainly true that the numbers of those converted have always been remarkably few, especially to Christianity. The process of involuntary conversion to Islam through possession by Muslim spirits goes back at least to the nineteenth century among Giriama and, especially, other Mijikenda dwelling at or very near the coast, perhaps working for or enslaved by Swahili and Arab plantation owners. As regards Christianity, a CMS (Church Missionary Society) hospital, primary school and church have existed at Kaloleni since the first decade of the twentieth century, with a Catholic secondary school built nearby at a later date, and with Krapf's church established much earlier at Ribe, some ten miles away from Kaloleni. Yet here too there has been very little conversion to such orthodox forms of Christianity among the Giriama. Nor are there Christian spirits comparable to the long-standing Islamic ones.

Since Kenya's independence, however, a much more open and vigorous competition between Islam and Pentecostal Christianity on the coast has developed. The success of Pentecostal Christianity (mainly among the Chonyi rather than the Giriama) may be due to the fact that church members are 'filled with Holy Spirit' at congregations, speak in tongues, and conduct themselves in a manner strongly reminiscent of traditional spirit possession dances. In recent years, also, some limited but organised Islamic proselytisation, confronting Christianity, has extended inland as far as Kaloleni, to the very edge of the palm and agricultural zone before it becomes savannah. Traditional Giriama polytheism has never been more under attack from these two sources than at present.

Yet another factor dominating the coast is package tourism. During the same post-independence period of twenty-five years, it has increased at an accelerated rate (Peake 1984: 11–13). Immigration from up-country Kenya has also become very much greater and coastal trading centres and small towns have sprung up in large numbers (Parkin 1979b).

The phenomenal growth and impact of these changes in independent Africa over the last quarter of a century is well known and hardly needs to be elaborated. Of especial significance, however, and yet to be described, are the new language and objects of western capitalist consumerism.

Possession by Islamic spirits and subsequent conversion to Islam were, and for most Giriama still are, regarded as an unfortunate route into the social, ethnic and religious mixture of the coastal east. However unintended, it represents a turning away from the sacred Kaya, its forest and its knowledge. Entrepreneurs and deviant women who become Muslims in this way are portrayed as helpless victims more than willing deviants, and to that extent are excused. The consolation is that at least they are a very small minority of all Giriama.

However, the ideas and activities associated with Christianity and western consumerism are nowadays often welcomed, especially by the young. They reach a larger number of Mijikenda, including Giriama, through the proliferation of government and Harambee schools, the extension of medical clinics using western medicine, agricultural specialists, and the wider use of the English language and of limited German and Italian in the coastal resorts.

The new consumerism, most evident in the articles possessed by tourists and through stories and objects relayed inland from them, has not encountered the early resistance offered to both Islam and Christianity.

The situation now is that consumerism has joined the recent, more militant and fundamentalist Islam and the new Pentecostal Christianity in seeking to create people's desires for a new moral and social order. It is still only at the coast itself, along the line of the tourist road from Mombasa to Malindi, that it has had success. But Giriama further inland, particularly the middle aged and elderly, express fears that traditional Giriama values are under threat there as well.

There is indeed a kind of politics of desire that typifies modern life at the coast. Despite the claims of Giriama elders that this is new, it reproduces the centrality of desire as a motivating theme in spirit possession. There, it will be remembered, spirits threateningly demand goods and appeasement. Sometimes these are spirits which invade persons', mainly women's, bodies and seek to satisfy their desires there. At other times, the desirous spirits are from within the afflicted person's body, and are depicted as elements making up the person's character, temperament or personality. However it has come about, this is a remarkable analogy with the body of Giriama society: most Giriama see the changes emanating from the coast as external forces invading the inner sanctuary of their way of life, represented ultimately by the Kaya; yet there are those from within Giriama society itself who work or live at the coast and who, together with other Mijikenda, seek to satisfy their new consumer wants and bring them inland.

8

Coastal desires and the person as centre

Coastal complexity

Let me now come full circle. In the first chapter of this book I described how Kajiwe, the witch-finder, argued strongly, in 1966, for the adoption of western education and medicine, as well as Christianity, and was opposed to those of Islam and of the Mijikenda themselves, including Giriama. Not only did he seem to anticipate the increasing acceptance of western goods, ideas and practices, he was part of its realisation. In casting out and burning gourds, effigies, boxes, rods, hides and skins, powders and other alleged instruments of witchcraft (that is, of divination and medicine, depending on one's viewpoint), and in urging women to abandon their traditional *hando* dress and families to send their children to schools and their sick to hospitals and clinics, he helped usher in the medicines, artefacts, clothes, fashions, cigarettes, soft drinks and bottled beer, transistors, cameras, watches and other objects of western affluence.

At that time, these articles were heard about and occasionally seen in the possession of better-off non-Giriama, rather than possessed by Giriama themselves. Of course, Kajiwe's role in encouraging their acceptance was a minor one, but is highlighted in view of his own prominence as a cult-like figure. His intervention marks a turning-point: it occurred three years after Kenya's independence, in 1963, and at a time when western development aid and investment was pouring into Kenya and other parts of Africa. This was still portrayed by both westerners and African politicians as a period of 'hope' for Africa's economic progress, whether from a radical or a capitalist viewpoint.

It was also the time when, as part of the new investment of outside money, package tourism began to become highly developed. Previously, coastal tourists had been either up-country Kenya whites or a small number from Europe and North America. As Peake has described (1984: 18), this soon changed with the organisation of cheap short-term trips from Europe, mainly West Germany, Sweden and Italy. In and around Malindi, near the northern part of Giriamaland, both Giriama and Swahili became highly involved in the tourist industry, together with up-country Africans, either as hotel employees, as fishermen supplying food for the hotels and trips out to the coral reef, or as 'beach-boys' and young women providing a range of services from sightseeing to sex.

Malindi is at the northern boundary of northern Kilifi district, outside the southern part on which this study is concentrated. It is some 90 kilometres north-east of Kaloleni in the southern agricultural palm belt and about 100 kilometres from Miyani in the cattle zone. Malindi town has grown considerably since the beginning of the tourist boom. Although the impact of tourism in southern Kilifi district is much less, especially in the hinterland, there is widespread knowledge throughout Giriama country of the impact of the new industry on Malindi and its environs.

One of Peake's observations is the way in which traditional Giriama dances have been selected and adapted specifically for performance before tourists at Malindi's hotels, usually by having the dancers emphasise, exaggerate and even invent sensual bodily movements without reference to a customary context. Peake then goes on to describe how, on the one hand, elders and other Giriama bemoan this falsification and exploitation of tradition and how, on the other hand, some younger Giriama living nearby have come to accept these new dances and other contrived cultural elements as of genuine Giriama origin. The 'front' put on for tourists has, for a few, become the reality (Peake 1982 and 1984: 22).

The further into the cattle-keeping west (south-west of Malindi), the less the effect of such touristic imaging, and the more assertive people are in their pronouncements concerning the authenticity of Giriama dances. The cultural pastiche of coastal tourism is carried to such other areas by report, with few ever seeing it for themselves. But it reinforces the views of those Giriama, the vast majority, who are not directly involved in the tourist industry, that the coastal strip has assumed a social, cultural and economic form of its own which bears no resemblance to that of the Giriama, and is swiftly compromising even that of the Muslim Swahili and Arabs.

Their view of it is mixed. The effects of tourism and its new sexual morality (for this is what it amounts to) are not normally acceptable to Giriama. But it is seen as part of the other trappings of the western cultural invasion which are increasingly sought after. These include more than medicine, education, learning English and Christianity, but also cassette recorders, video cameras, multi-functional watch-calculators, fashionable European dress (and no longer those worked up by a local tailor), household items and food and drink types. Clearly, such objects and tastes are available to only a very few who can afford them and who live along the coastal strip already. But they are recurrent talking points in conversations among the young who are the most likely to migrate from one area of Giriama country to another.

In talking about them, young and old alike ask whether such objects are desirable or not, or how they may be acquired, and what is being lost tradition-ally through their acquisition. I want to emphasise here that these are sophisti-cated debates which I have myself witnessed even in the remote western cattle zone, for it takes very little time for even the oldest residents to sense the cultural implications of expanding consumerism of this kind.

There are, and for a long time have been, comparable debates concerning the virtues and disadvantages of Christianity and Islam, and the future of animism. The link with consumerism is that the three religions are discussed not only as belief systems but, more significantly, as each prescribing distinctive life-styles, taste, dress, food preferences and avoidances, education, forms of therapy, and as each associated with particular material objects and medicines.

In his speeches to the Giriama during the nineteen sixties, their most famous politician, Ronald Ngala, would always refer to the Giriama people as divided into three categories: Christians, Muslims and *koma* (ancestor) or *hando*. *Hando*, referring to the women's traditional short cotton skirt, and *koma*, were a way of speaking of the vast majority of Giriama, men as well as women, who proudly observed the traditional Giriama pantheistic religion, which comprises ances-tral, possessory and nature spirits, a distant high god, and a belief in a transfor-mational life force straddling humans and non-humans. At that time his remarks, like those of other African politicians, were aimed at persuading his fellow Giriama to abandon or at least modify their animistic beliefs in favour of 'modern progress' (*maendeleo*) associated with European capitalist and con-sumer values and with Christianity. Ngala himself was a Christian, trained in mission schools. For such politicians, traditional Giriama polytheism was seen as aiding and abetting beliefs in witchcraft which had been blamed for the alleged economic backwardness of the Giriama. It was for this reason that Kajiwe was given formal government permission to carry out his witch-hunt. It was hoped by government that he really could eliminate witch beliefs and practices.

As in the colonial era, polytheism has only ever been seen by government negatively. The veneration of ancestors (*koma*) and their link with Giriama ideas of sociability, death and the moral accountability of diviners and doctors, has rarely been given credit nor favourably compared with Christianity or Islam. Colonial officers might occasionally encourage Kaya elders to carry out tra-ditional ceremonies, such as rain-making or greeting the Giriama new year, but only ever for the benefits they might bring in pacifying unrest in the country, and not for their value as part of a wider animistic philosophy.

There are other respects in which Giriama traditional religion or polytheism has been squeezed between Christianity, Islam, western educational and medical values and practices, and central government's condemnation of it as witchcraft and mere superstition (echoing, of course, the views of earlier colonial govern-ment).

Not only, therefore, has traditional Giriama religion been surrounded and menaced by western, Christian and Islamic medical and epistemological values, the Kenya central government has repeatedly, since colonial times through to independence, attempted periodically to ban spirit possession dances and the giving of certain oaths by doctors, and has tried to control the length, timing and amount of money and animals dispensed at funerals, as well as the ritually and socially important drinking of palm wine. The reason given is that these rituals, practices and beliefs waste energy, time and resources that could be better spent on farming, herding or other employment. Government control of such traditional activities has certainly been effective along the coastal strip, with the result that sponsors of spirit dances, and of funerary and oathing ceremonies, have at least to seek a chief's permission, which is not always given. But their effect is less within the agricultural palm belt of the immediate hinterland and entirely absent in the cattle-keeping western area.

One result is that chiefs and sub-chiefs along the coast, most of whom are Muslim and who may have only a loose affiliation through a parent or grandparent with any of the Mijikenda peoples, operate and are seen to operate much more closely with the Kenya central government police and the Kilifi district officers. Both chiefs and government are said to seek to enforce the letter of the law, drawing, it is alleged, on any financial benefits that may accrue from their power to decide favourably or otherwise in particular cases.

Chiefs and sub-chiefs further inland are often depicted as closer to the needs of the people rather than those of the government, and as prepared to interpret the law more liberally and more in accordance with custom. For a start, such chiefs are all Giriama and so have jurisdiction over areas which are exclusively of their own ethnic group, and in which, given the practice of marrying locally, they will have close kin and affines. I have come across a number of cases of homicide, for instance, which have occurred at dances or as witchcraft vengeance killings, and which have been allowed to go unreported to the central government police, something which does not normally happen on the coastal strip. Once again, this identification of chiefs and sub-chiefs with the local people is said to be an especially strong feature of western Giriama country. In the agricultural east, the chiefs are also Giriama and therefore regarded as more attuned to the local people's needs than at the coast, but even here people have begun to criticise their modern chiefs as less understanding of Giriama customary expectations than earlier chiefs remembered in the 1940s and 1950s (Parkin 1974).

From gift to gain

This gradation of characteristics from east to west is certainly also my own impression and not just that of the Giriama who speak about it. No chiefs and sub-chiefs go uncriticised, but there is one respect in which the coastal chiefs, none of them Giriama and few of them 'pure' Mijikenda, are criticised and the inland Giriama ones are not. While the coastal ones are accused of settling many disputes and arrests by taking bribes, I have rarely heard this accusation being levelled at inland chiefs and sub-chiefs. The latter are certainly provided with gifts of maize, milk and other produce, usually as part of on-going relationships of respect. But such gifts are in no way considered comparable to the *ad hoc* payments, invariably of money, allegedly made to coastal chiefs in order to secure specific results, such as release from arrest or light treatment at the chief's own tribunal, or in being issued with a letter for a trading licence.

I am here reporting claims and stereotypes and cannot substantiate or dispute them. They are interesting for their contrasting images of coast and inland, and of east and west. Nevertheless, the Giriama I have spoken to say that the difference between the two types of transaction is not merely semantic, that is to say of calling the same thing by different names, but of substance. The difference is given as follows. Giriama chiefs governing Giriama people may be imperfect but do observe a common morality concerning the need to settle delicts and disorders according to a view of custom, which may need to be negotiated, but which is nevertheless recognisably Giriama. Coastal chiefs exercise authority over a culturally mixed community and so lack a common customary method of assessment and adjudication other than that laid down by central government law and order. They resort more to the morality of the market ('according to their personal needs and greed'), in which each settlement has its price to be bargained for separately.

Here, it should be emphasised that it is Giriama themselves, and other Mijikenda, who distinguish in this way between a system of local authority which is sustained through gift-giving and one which depends on bribes. There is a further significant distinction between them. A gift-giving relationship is said to be only potentially corruptible, in that the chief might receive too many gifts without some kind of return, or might favour certain parties too often, and would suffer severe public disapproval were he to do so. However, a relationship based on bribes is said unambiguously to be based already on avarice. In Kenya bribes, generally referred to nowadays as *chai* (tea) rather than *chakula* (food) as previously, have certainly long since ceased to be regarded as reasonable supplements to a government officer's meagre salary. People now see them as frankly, if unavoidably, arising from greed (*choyo*).

The coastal strip is viewed by both those who live there and those who live outside it as having become premised on material desire. The up-country peoples, such as Kikuyu and Luo, are sometimes blamed by coastal peoples, Muslim and non-Muslim alike, for having brought this materialistic avarice with them on their migrations to the coast. Like the up-country city of Nairobi, like Malindi, the coastal tourist centre, and, recently, like Mombasa, the coast's capital, even the coastal small towns and rural villages are characterised in this way.

Coastal people provide what they regard as evidence to support this view. Land settlement schemes have been increased in number since independence to alleviate the problems of the Mijikenda so-called land-squatters, who have been living, sometimes for generations, on coastal land owned by descendants of Swahili and Arab plantation owners of the nineteenth century (Cooper 1980). This laudable government attempt to give people their own land has, however, been foiled in many cases by the increasing tendency of financially embarrassed individual plot-holders to sell off their holdings to persons, usually from up-country, able to buy them. Such purchasers have been acquiring a number of these plots. Despite holders' entitlement to no more than one plot each, they register them in the name of non-resident but trusted relatives, and farm them together as a commercial concern. Land settlement officers are aware of the practice but simply lack the manpower to track down individual cases and act upon them. Inevitably, accusations of bribery operate here too, though I have no evidence of this.

Similarly, shoreland plots, which have been in the possession of Muslim families for generations and provide the basis for Swahili fishing communities to carry out their craft, have increasingly been sold to up-country buyers who either build holiday homes on them for letting to tourists or re-sell them to tourist enterprises or hotels (Parkin 1989b: 167–169).

Even from these few examples, it is clear that coastal people as a whole, Muslim and non-Muslim, have been losing out economically along the coast since independence to up-country land purchasers and entrepreneurs. As yet another example of this tendency, we can instance the development of small towns along the coastal line of road from Mombasa to Kilifi.

The ninety mile road from Mombasa north to Malindi was paved in 1969 and its alignment slightly altered in parts. Occurring a few years after Kenya's independence and while foreign aid was still relatively plentiful for capital-intensive development schemes, the road immediately attracted new trading centres, some of which swiftly became small towns. For example, three such centres increased in size enormously between 1969 and 1978: Shimo-la-Tewa from 5 to 109 business and residential dwellings, the latter often also built for commercial sub-letting; Majengo from 15 to 103; and Kikambala from 5 to 42 (see Parkin 1979b: 274).

Much of the land on both sides of the line of road on which such trading centres stand belongs to coastal Muslims, mainly Swahili and Arab. These have set up small shops and let out plots for other shops and businesses, some of which are run by non-Muslims. A mix has now emerged. In some centres, Muslim businesses are in the majority and in others non-Muslim businesses predominate. Most operators of businesses, whether Muslim or non-Muslim, are themselves coastal people with, for instance, the Muslims dealing in fish and owning butcheries, and the non-Muslims concentrating on the sale of liquor and fresh local produce. However, the most profitable shops are general stores selling household items, clothes, commercially produced foodstuffs and lengths of specially designed cloth required by spirits, and these are owned either by coastal Arabs or by up-country Kikuyu and Kamba. These up-country people also run the highly successful bottle-beer bars and nightclubs which, while providing exclusively for local African custom, replicate in a shadowy way the drinking and leisure pursuits of the European tourists in the nearby hotels, often by appealing to the same emblems, murals, slogans and modern music, and similarly attracting women prostitutes.

Thus, although in a minority, the up-country non-Muslim businesses are among the largest and reap the greatest financial rewards. There are even cases of some successful businessmen from up-country going into partnership with coastal Arabs. The mix is therefore of Muslim and non-Muslim interests as sometimes competing but sometimes co-operative, but with coastal people generally, both Muslim and non-Muslim, losing land and important business opportunities to up-country entrepreneurs and settlers.

It is hardly surprising that this coastal complexity comes across to Giriama as not only a cultural mish-mash but as one that is founded on personal strivings and desire. Economists and political scientists may be able to discern in this burgeoning petty capitalism some pattern, but to those obliged to live with it, and to observe and fear it at a distance, it is a source of random forces, whose uncontrollable greed is the reason for the continual witchcraft practices and widespread spirit possession found there. It is, as the Giriama say, a place without ancestors, and it is true that ancestral veneration, marked by the traditional *koma* posts, is much less common than inland. It may be remembered that inland Giriama refer to Mijikenda Muslims who live there permanently, and who renounce their Mijikenda origins and speak and call themselves 'Swahili', as having lost their clans and therefore their identity.

The very term 'Giriama' takes on a different meaning for many living or staying on the coast. For up-country people and tourists alike, it refers indiscriminately to all the nine Mijikenda peoples. Given the closeness of their respective dialects and customs, this is not an unreasonable abridgement. It partly mirrors the now disreputable appellation, 'Nyika', which the Swahili and Arabs once used to refer to the Mijikenda, but which, having the meaning of 'bush' or 'wilderness', implies that such people are without cultural grace and understanding and is no longer openly spoken.

Inland and among themselves, the term 'Giriama' and the other Mijikenda ethnic labels are used for making what they hold to be important internal distinctions among them. As I have explained the Mijikenda Union is or was based on this segmentary starting-point, as is the relationship to each other of the various Kayas of the different Mijikenda groups, including that of the Giriama.

Lacking precise ethnic tags and often lacking ancestral land, it is perhaps not surprising that some Mijikenda at the coast, principally the Chonyi (whose homeland is nearest to the coastal strip of southern Kilifi district), fill the identity gap, so to speak, by converting to Pentecostal Christianity. The dancing, singing, entry of God's spirit into the body and mind, and the capacity thereby acquired to speak in other languages and so achieve insights and greater understanding of personal and world problems, sufficiently echo traditional spirit possession that it is unsurprising that this is the first form of Christianity to have mass appeal for any Mijikenda grouping.

The rise of Pentecostal Christianity in the area was, however, no mere accident. The power of Islam worldwide had been given a special boost after the war in 1973 between Israel and Arab countries, when the latter for a while countered the might of the Western world by multiplying the price of the oil they produced. Much of this Middle Eastern money was invested in propagating Islam around the world. A number of new mosques were built or renovated along the Kenya coast from the mid to late seventies, all dedicated to Sunni Islam and explicitly on the basis of competition with Christianity. Sponsored by North American money and personnel, a number of Pentecostal and other churches sprung up or were significantly refurbished during the same period. It was clearly stated by their sponsors that they were set up to counter the influence of Islam on the coast. The sites chosen for such churches and mosques were the new small towns and centres referred to above, with the result that mosque and church physically appear to look out on and vie with each other.

The struggle between church and mosque, and evidence of greater commercialisation, have even come to Kaloleni, the small township that in the nineteen sixties was still regarded as indisputably a traditional Giriama centre, set firmly within the agricultural and coconut palm growing area. In 1966, Kaloleni trading centre, as it was then, had only a couple of African-owned shops and a few kiosks selling fruit, vegetables, matches and paraffin. A dozen well-stocked shops were owned by Asians who had been there for up to a couple of generations. In 1969 these Asians were not reissued with rural trading licences and had to leave Kaloleni to trade in urban areas. African shopkeepers and traders took their place, both Muslim and non-Muslim, and mainly Giriama and other Mijikenda, but including also some Swahili. The road from Mombasa to Kaloleni was paved in 1975. Previously the road had been hazardous, accounting for death by drowning on a couple of occasions in the late fifties and early sixties during heavy rains, when drivers had desperately attempted to reach Mombasa after several weeks of being stranded in Kaloleni. The paving and raising of the road above the periodically swollen Kombeni river immediately eliminated the risk and made it possible to reach Mombasa within the hour. The transformation was dramatic. Water and electricity soon followed, and Kaloleni was designated a township. The number of business dwellings in Kaloleni rose from 40 in 1969 to 109 in 1978, and the expansion has continued since then.

In 1966, there was a very small, ramshackle mud-and-wattle mosque in Kaloleni that catered for the handful of Giriama Muslims wishing to attend it on

Fridays. In 1978 an elegant mosque was built in its place, constructed of permanent materials through Arab sponsorship. In the mid eighties, just outside Kaloleni and in the direction of the cattle area, an even larger and more expensive mosque was built, including within it a well-stocked and serviced health clinic, which was intended to compete with the nearby Catholic church and with the CMS hospital in Kaloleni which had been set up in 1904.

The number of Muslims coming to Kaloleni township from the coast has increased greatly as a result. The distinctive black *buibui* dress of their women, the frequent attendance at the new mosques, the use by Muslims and non-Muslims alike of the clinic has certainly given Islam great prominence. People say that, in cases of spirit possession, the numbers and influence of Islamic and Arabic spirits are much greater than before. Typical of such changes are the names given to children. In 1966 it was rare for Giriama children to be given Swahili names. Traditional Giriama and, in a very few cases, Christian names would be given. By the mid eighties it was common practice for Swahili names to be used by non-Muslim Giriama for their children because Islamic or Arab spirits had demanded them. It was explained that, despite the fact that they were unwelcome intrusions from the coastal strip, the desires of such ferocious spirits could not be refused.

It follows from all this that the coastal strip, for most Giriama, represents two main things. There is, firstly, the socio-cultural, ethnic, religious and politico-economic complexity which, if it continues to absorb their young people and to advance ever more inland, will reduce Giriama identity to one of the already numerous, situationally used ethnic tags of half-recognition, as has already occurred at the coast and in cities like Mombasa and Nairobi. In such places, the inability of outsiders to acknowledge the distinctions between the different Mijikenda groups, and between them and other coastal peoples, causes obvious resentment. The second image of the coastal strip is that it is nowadays organised on the basis of objects, spirits, and persons having and creating desires and being impelled to satisfy them. The agents may be European tourists, African entrepreneurs, their possessions, or the numerous and new spirits which make demands on people.

This duality of proliferating complexity and desire is evident in new beliefs which spring up in the coastal strip and which thereby assert its newly emerging cultural distinctiveness. Before Kenya's independence, the coast was under the suzerainty of the Sultan of Zanzibar and was politically and economically dominated by Muslims and their Swahili language and culture, with Arabic as an important background influence and point of reference. In the twenty-five or so years since, neither Muslims, Christians, coastal nor up-country peoples can be said to be truly dominant overall. Fortunes and trends now change swiftly. Under President Kenyatta, from 1963 onwards, Kikuyu political commissioners and officers governed the coast. Since President Moi's accession in 1978, these have declined in numbers and status considerably and, in accord with his policy of giving less powerful provinces more autonomy and so-called minority peoples a greater say in government, a larger proportion of coastal people, including Muslims, have been given important positions. On the other hand, in commerce, up-country, European, Asian and Arab interests remain strong. Culturally, the greatest single influence are the commodities of the European tourists, the imported western-style consumer articles, and western pop songs, dress and fashion.

I now give an example of what is claimed to be a new kind of 'Arab' spirit which has developed among local people living on the coast, including migrant Giriama and other Mijikenda, and which appears to draw on this complexity premised on individual achievements and wants.

Spirit of desire

Katunusi means fieldmouse, according to the early twentieth century missionary, Florence Deed (1964), though it may have since lost this meaning.[1] Recently, Thompson has met it in northern Kilifi district as referring to a strong and dangerous current in a body of water and thence to a spirit which carries a person away from the mainstream of social life (1990: 199), thus sharing such symptoms with some Islamic spirits, though not in fact one itself.

On the coastal strip of southern Kilifi district, *katunusi* has come to refer to a spirit (*nyama*) which desires a man or woman and, in loving and possessing them, may kill them. 'It eats their blood.' Alternatively, it may so want a woman for itself, that it causes her to hate her own child and to refuse to breast-feed it. Being an 'Arab' spirit it can never want or love those who eat pork, who therefore remain safe from it. But pork is rarely eaten on the coast, even by non-Muslims, and so few benefit from this exemption. The term for this spirit is said to come from the verb *ku-tunuka*, which in Swahili means to desire and in Giriama to be desirable, so straddling the two languages' active and passive modes. But it is also linked to the related term commonly used among Giriama, namely *vitunusi*, which may be translated as resentment or ill-temper, with the sense of having had one's desires frustrated. It is said to be close to the notion of anger, *koro*. A person who is exceptionally withdrawn, sulky and ill-tempered is feeling *vitunusi*, and may be divined as being possessed by a *katunusi* spirit. A number of *katunusi* spirits are known by the same term, *vitunusi*. In this way, an emotional state of

---

[1] Alice Werner writes of a *kitunusi* spirit among the Pokomo, which lives in the forests of the Tana Valley (north of Giriama country). It is of the shape and size of a human being and has various characteristics. One, which may be prototypical of its association with destructive desire, derives from the fact that it wears a dark blue cloth (called *kaniki* and much worn to appease certain spirits). A human who manages to wrestle with the spirit and tear off a piece of this cloth and who then stores it in a covered basket, will become rich. But the spirit is nevertheless malignant, and will cause paralysis of the limbs or some other illness to anyone who does not stand up boldly at its approach (Werner 1933: 203–4).

harboured resentment is linked conceptually to the plural name for a spirit whose feelings are perversely destructive of those it desires. The spirit is a manifestation, then, of loving and desiring to excess. *Hendzo* is the normal term for what we can translate as love, in the sense of both compassion and passion, but is only regarded as a destructive emotion under conditions of stress and rivalry.

Given the depiction by non-Muslim Giriama and other Mijikenda of the coastal strip as an area of invasive and unmanageable outside influences, it is not surprising to learn of the proliferation of visitations by the *katunusi/vitunusi* spirits. In 1980, fifty people tragically died when a bus's brakes failed as it was being driven onto the ferry to cross the Kilifi creek. The bus sank immediately, drowning its occupants. In the following year another vehicle, a taxi (*matatu*), went down at exactly the same spot, with all eight passengers being drowned. Other accidents of a similar nature have occurred at the same place, with the result that this place is now believed to harbour many *vitunusi* spirits, which have sought to destroy those they desired and loved.

The place, the Kilifi creek, is, as a result, said to be imbued with *kilatso*, meaning deathly contamination, which afflicts persons in contact with the victims or perpetrators of 'bad deaths'. As well as accidents, these include suicide and homicide, many of which are crimes of passion arising out of rejection by, or rivalry over, a lover or spouse, and which were described in chapter five. There is, then, a semantic domain which links frustrated love and desire, excessive love and desire, anger and resentment, sulkiness, destructiveness and death. In short, the *katunusi* belief expresses the idea of the coast as a place where too much desire prevails and where even love leads to death. This is precisely how, in ordinary conversation, Giriama sometimes describe the new social and cultural complexity that now characterises the coast, doing so before the subsequent linking of tourism to prostitution and the alleged spread of AIDS.

However, there is something more to the domain of *katunusi* beliefs than this. On the one hand, there is the sense that Giriama and other Mijikenda are innocent victims of a perverse spirit. But, as it was pointed out to me, people may themselves be the victims of their own desires, or, in desiring things, may put at peril, through negligence, their own loved ones, and that this, too, is implied in the emotional state of *vitunusi*. This refers to the alleged widespread greed, *choyo*, that is associated with coastal life and the pursuit of possessions and life-styles there. Frustrated greed, like frustrated love, may lead to *vitunusi*.

The perils of excessive love and desire, said to be characteristic of the coast, contrast with the claims made for further inland. Giriama acknowledge that inland spirits threaten to harm women they possess unless their requests are granted. But they argue that it is rare for death to result from spirit possession, and that most demands made by a spirit can be met. To that extent, and unlike the *katunusi* Arab spirit which comes from the sea, the spirits which possess women inland can be appeased and even beneficially controlled for the purposes of shamanistic divination. Similarly, the kind of popularity medicine, or love potion, discussed in chapter six, by which a person secures the love or attention of, say, a man or woman or an employer, is said never to cause harm, and both inland and at the coast, where it is in fact also used by Swahili practitioners, is subject to strict human control.

In fact, the kinds of heinous results attributed to coastal *vitunusi* spirits are, in Giriama country itself, more likely to be blamed on witches. Again, the difference is one of human control. Coastal *vitunusi* are particularly vicious and fall outside the normal sphere of Giriama spirit management. Inland witches (*atsai*) can be dealt with by the appropriate diviner and doctor or, on a larger scale, by witch-hunters like Kajiwe.

The complaint raised by Giriama concerning the coastal strip, then, is not just that human desires, and their spirit manifestation, are excessive and deathly, but that they are far from their, Giriama and other peoples', control. For human desires to be out of human control is unacceptable. It parallels the conventional Giriama view of themselves and of their cultural identity as being menaced by coastal influences: how may these be held in check and in some areas reversed?

We can begin to understand this question by noting how spirits, anywhere in Giriama country, are commonly referred to as having human characteristics. As also reported by Gaye Thompson working near Malindi in northern Giriama country, they are often regarded as elements making up a person's temperament. That is to say, they do not merely resemble but constitute human character. Spirits speak and are addressed and answered, and, in their bargaining, show a range of human-like capriciousness, as the cases in chapter seven showed. The pronominal affixes by which they are addressed and spoken about are the same as those for humans and animals. They are sometimes referred to as 'people'.

The proliferation of spirits which occurs all the time is, therefore, a gauge of the changing human nature of the Giriama and their neighbours. Every people or ethnic group with whom the Giriama have come into contact are remembered through the creation of a new spirit. Some ethnic spirits may go out of fashion, as new peoples come onto the scene, but they are always part of an expanding repertoire. Each spirit has its own attributes, some of which supposedly reflect those of the people after which it is named, or perhaps which it 'embodies'. In looking at the pantheon of possessory spirits, a Giriama presents him- or herself with a history of ethnic contact. More than this, since the attributes of each foreigner-derived spirit become attributes of individual Giriama, there is here a kind of tacit admission that the Giriama as a people are made up over time through incorporation of other peoples' characteristics. In practice, since it is only women who are possessed in great numbers, this is an observation which applies mainly to them.

As regards spirit possession, then, it is mainly through women that any alleged purity of Giriama identity is likely to be altered or, in the words of some, contaminated. And it is women who are depicted as being at the centre of problems of want and sexual desire, either as objects or as subjects, as is evident from the cases of spirit possession, from the portrayal of tourism as corrupting Giriama and other women and turning them to prostitution, or from the more general fear of such coastal influence on marriageable Giriama women further inland, as discussed in chapter four.

Women seem to express this view as much as men, despite the fact that there are male prostitutes and gigolos serving coastal tourists (Peake 1984: 45–118). But, while female prostitution is openly discussed and condemned, the new, and admittedly rare, forms of male sexuality are not. I can only speculate as to why there is silence on such reversals of the Giriama view of male sexuality. Perhaps to admit publicly that even a very few Giriama men offer themselves to other men, or to older (white) women, poses an even greater threat to the Giriama sense of cultural continuity. When an ethnic group's women become prostitutes, this is explained as a problem of inadequate ethnic and male control. But when one's own men reverse the possibilities of normal reproduction, this is beyond both comprehension and control.

There is, here, a special sense in which the coast represents for the Giriama an area in which their ethnic distinctiveness cannot survive. It is not simply that they are, as a people, submerged by others' cultures and languages. Rather it is that the behaviour that is possible there constitutes an irretrievable break with customary Giriama ideas of what it is to be a person.

After all, Giriama men who migrate to a town for work, sometimes staying there for many years, are not by this fact alone, 'lost' to their home communities. In chapter three, there is a description of a man who in fact built up his herd of cattle in Gotani from money saved from nearly a lifetime's work in Mombasa, during which he had nurtured his family and rural homestead, returning as regularly as he could and always in contact with fellow Giriama both at home and in Mombasa. This straddling of town and country is common in much of Africa and is by no means incompatible with increasing urbanisation and industrialisation, provided rural land remains available.

However, when there is the possibility that men and women may through their behaviour cease to produce children for the homestead and the clan, then the cherished cultural identity is truly in jeopardy. It is not that a new concept of personhood is thereby created, which might after all be part of the reshaping of a people. It is rather that childlessness precludes any such concept. This is, of course, an exaggerated view which becomes part of apocalyptic tales told about the coast, and, in fact, the young Giriama men who work as 'beachboys' for tourists do normally marry and have children, though how many return to or take up rural residence has yet to be discovered. A similar observation can be made for Giriama women. In any event, the number of both men and women who work in such capacities on the coast is still very few.

However, insofar as such issues and questions are raised in conversation among Giriama, sometimes openly as in discussions of marriageable women and the harmful influences of the coast, or privately and quietly about the young men there, they have as a background reference a generalised view of Giriama personhood. As shown in chapter seven, the alternative possibilities for selfhood derive from different 'medical' states. But Giriama still claim that it is in and around the Kaya and the western cattle-keeping area that the most 'authentic' versions are found. This legitimate, generalised notion of the person seems, in fact, to be constructed from perspectives found to varying degrees everywhere among the Giriama and constitutes, as far as I can judge, a frequently reshuffled set of templates according to which ideal figures are cut. Real ones never match up, of course, but may at best approximate and at worst, as at the coast, deviate beyond repair.

I suggest that the Giriama construct their notions of personhood, not by first referring to the intrinsic self-determining features of a human agent, but the other way round, by outlining what they see as the parameters and possibilities of human movement and expression. That is to say, they refer not to a particular 'I', but to the spirits, ancestors, relatives and clan which situate an individual. They define the moving centre, so to speak, by describing its constantly shifting environment. Human desire is thus a product of this environment rather than, as allegedly at the coast, deriving directly from the person him- or herself. It is like the difference between the 'understandable' witch and the truly evil one (see Middleton's distinction between the Lugbara witch and the sorcerer, 1960: 238–250). The first refers to a person who becomes a witch only when others have neglected or harmed him and whose resentment leading to witchcraft is partly excusable. He is a witch created as much by his interpersonal environment as by his own volition. This is indigenous Giriama witchcraft which can be controlled by traditional means. The second is the person whose avarice is constant regardless of circumstances and so who is always a witch. This is the image of autonomous coastal witches, who are said to have increased in recent years as a result of the new climate of material desire at the coast under modern influences.

Ancestral personhood
In order to understand how Giriama construct each other as persons, we can begin with the ancestors (*koma*). The description of funerals in chapter five referred to the practice of ritually laying the deceased person to rest, *ku-laza koma*, when he or she is urged not to disturb the living and to leave them now in peace. In fact, ancestors do sometimes come to disturb the living, signalling their displeasure either through dreams or by causing goats, sheep or cattle to die suddenly. A diviner tells which ancestor is responsible for misfortunes and what is required while, in a dream, the ancestor him- or herself will complain of feeling cold and hungry and demand a goat, rice, or palm wine, or perhaps a second funeral which

had never been held for him or her when it should have been. The person to whom an ancestor appears in a dream has a duty, as with all bad dreams, to tell homestead relatives and friends, for any of them may be adversely affected by the aggrieved ancestor who, as well as causing homestead animals to die, may cause women and livestock difficulty in giving birth and even their infertility. The ancestors remembered in this way are only those personally known to the living and so do not often extend beyond a grandparent. Some Giriama insist that, apart from one's own parents, other ancestors who actually cause homestead disturbances are always on one's father's side. Genealogies, generally, are not recounted beyond three or four generations.

Ancestors who come to the living in dreams or who bring trouble to a homestead are literally marked out, for it is then that special ancestral wooden posts are placed to them with full and due ceremony (Parkin 1982a: 9–10). This 'objectification' of ancestors is, then, highly selective. Those who die and remain docile remain unmarked and are more easily forgotten. Those who make trouble re-enter the homestead as venerated objects and become visible again.

This traditional, selective Giriama treatment of ancestors both contrasts with and yet is a prototype of the kinds of personal achievement possible at the coast. At the coast, individuals are portrayed as pursuing material wants in accordance with the new consumerist ethos which is prevalent there, but, neglecting the memory of their own ancestors, may not themselves become one and so may be forgotten after death. Elsewhere among the Giriama, however, prominent men and women not only carve out reputations within their own lifetimes, but may also re-emerge after death as strong characters making demands on their kin. This strength in life and death is regarded as characterising the renowned traders who have always existed among Giriama and who therefore anticipate many of the current coastal entrepreneurial developments. However, such traders were commemorated and, by coming back as threatening ancestors, commemorated themselves, a reciprocal relationship between the living and dead which hardly ever occurs among people who have stayed long in the coastal strip and who lack ancestral lands and memorials.

Not all ancestors in Giriama country who have marked posts placed for them were traders or especially prominent Giriama. Most, indeed, were known only within their local communities, though always as important or prolific elders, and it is made explicit that totally insignificant persons, for instance the childless or those who have never married, are unlikely to be commemorated even if they are dreamt about. Whatever their level of importance, all commemorated ancestors provide an understanding of personhood through the various personalities they displayed when alive, in addition to the reasons for which they present themselves to the living after death. They thus bear upon the living as examples of what fellow Giriama have been, and can be.

There are, in fact, two kinds of commemorative ancestral post, which together make up a visible statement of gradations or prominence (see Parkin 1982b and Wolfe *et al.* 1981). One is elaborate, tall and nowadays quite rare, and is placed only for members of a society, called the Gohu, who exist in areas well away from the influences of the coast. This post measures from three to nine feet, is carved out of hard wood and sometimes painted, and is called a *kigango* (pl. *vigango*). The other post is found everywhere in Giriama country, right up to the coastal strip itself, and is no more than a foot high, of soft wood, and is not elaborately carved. It is called by the same name as that for ancestor, *koma*.

It has been noted, since the early years of this century, that the large memorial posts are found among most but not all of the half million Mijikenda-speaking peoples: the Giriama, Kambe, Ribe, Kauma, Chonyi, Jibana and Rabai, but not among two of them, the Digo and Duruma (Prins 1952: 90, citing Werner 1915: 343; Hollis 1909: 145; and Johnstone 1902: 33, 41). There has been speculation as to possible links with the Oromo gravestones of northern Kenya and Ethiopia or with those of Madagascar, with which there are some resemblances. My remarks, however, are confined to the Giriama.

Giriama sometimes keep the large ornamental posts with the smaller ones in the men's conversation hut, *kigojo*, which is at one end of the homestead compound, but they may be placed elsewhere in the homestead, and always near where men meet to talk and drink palm wine. Neither kind of post is placed at the time of burial nor at the site of the grave itself. There is therefore a temporal as well as spatial separation of memorial site from grave site. Except for those dying of 'bad deaths', graves are dug a few paces in front of the door of the deceased's house and are sometimes marked by a stone or tree, neither of which is likely to be replaced if it disappears or dies.

Although it is sometimes said that memorial posts of both types should be placed within a year of death (always on one of the two 'bad' days of the Giriama four-day week, for death is bad), it is often much later than this, and only after the deceased has visited a close descendant in a dream. Years may elapse and by this time, of course, the body will have decomposed.

People say that having the grave and the memorial in different places, with the latter placed a long time after death, enables the deceased's spirit (*koma*) to be separated from his or her body (called *mwiri* in life and *ufu* in death). The spirit belongs to the memorial post, where it is propitiated when things go wrong in the homestead. Libations of palm wine are regularly and sometimes daily made to the collection of posts by men when they are drinking. The spirit and its wooden memorial have become identified one with the other, as is evident in the use of the term *koma* to refer to both. Indeed, to refer to the post now as a piece of wood or stick (*kibao* or *kigogo*) would be sacrilege and might infuriate the ancestor. The memorial posts are said to take on the animate power once possessed by the ancestors. They are its new body. The spirit may by now, through decomposition, have lost its mortal body of flesh, blood and bones, from which it was separated, but has taken on a new body of wood: tall and elaborately carved in the one case, and small and plain in the other. Reintegration has occurred.

The body and spirit each becomes tied to its respective territory. The bodily remains are never moved and nor is the small memorial post, even when members of a homestead migrate to a new site. The larger post, the *kigango*, placed for members of the Gohu society, may be moved once only, but even this does not often happen. Being made of hardwood it survives very much longer, and so is remembered even after the family who placed it there have moved away and formed another homestead elsewhere. I know of such posts, standing in fields or bush on a former homestead site, that were erected as far back as the 1880s (see frontispiece) and are still identified, whereas ordinary *koma* posts are quickly lost and forgotten once their homestead is abandoned.

The spirit of the hardwood *kigango* may have a long after-life, but what happens to the *koma* spirit once its wooden body is eaten by termites? Giriama insist that no person's spirit ever dies and that, even without its material representation, it continues to exist and simply joins the countless unremembered spirits (still called *koma*). Giriama only rarely claim that these disembodied, wandering human spirits eventually become the capricious non-human possessionary spirits called either *pepo* (or *peho*) or *nyama*, though, since the latter term also means 'meat' or 'flesh' and is at the root of the term for 'animal', such a transformative link between human and non-human is at least suggested. Nor do ancestral spirits ever turn into the nature spirits (pl *mizimu*) which live at the base of large trees such as baobabs, or deep in caves.

The Gohu society, for whom the elegant memorial posts are placed, consists of elders and middle-aged men, though technically there is no age qualification. It meets expressly to engage in feasting, and is a traditional equivalent of a dining club concerned with conspicuous consumption. There are no restrictions on membership save the expectation that, on entry and at feasts, a member will contribute food and drink generously. Feasts occur at the admission of a new member, at his promotion from a novice (*umondo*) to full member (*ubora*), at a member's funeral and when, sometimes years later, a memorial post is placed for him. At a funeral held in Gotani for a Gohu member in 1978, thirty bullocks were sacrificed and eaten, which was far in excess of other funerals at the time.

Conspicuous consumption among the Gohu is expressed in other ways. The memorial post itself, the *kigango*, is carefully and expensively produced by an expert carpenter. It has carved into it a triangular motif, which cleverly intimates either the body's ribs, or perhaps the intertwining of ropes or even of snakes around the body, and is sometimes arranged to look like the snuff container and chain worn around the neck of some elders and itself making up a triangular pattern. Care is also taken to paint the incised triangles in patterns of red, white and black. The memorial post is topped by a flat, disc-shaped, and even three-dimensional head, which, in the past, might have two silver dollar pieces inserted as eyes.

By contrast, the *koma* post, as well as being shorter and made of soft wood, is distinguished in only two ways. Its male version has a slightly inward curving of the neck, rendering it vaguely phallic-shaped, while the female is straight. Secondly, the *koma* post is dressed in cloth: that of the female resembling a Giriama woman's *hando* skirt, and that of the male with a scarf round its neck. The differentiation is simple and the ornamentation minimal, being based on the practical and fundamental distinction between men and women rather than ostentatiously on abstract motifs, as with the larger, long-lasting memorial posts of the Gohu.

The contrast between the *koma* and *kigango* and the relationship of the Gohu, both to ordinary people and to other important Giriama, depends on the Gohu having resources and organisational ability. The Gohu have the wealth to be more polygynous than most men of their age and, as well as holding feasts, they practise and develop magic to make their wives fertile and prevent them from being unfaithful. They greet each other in a distinctive way, wear a buffalo horn bracelet on the upper right arm, are buried in a special cattle hide, and distinguish themselves in other ways.

The Gohu investiture rite for a new candidate, occurring when a *kigango* post is placed for a dead Gohu's spirit, is a good example of their capacity to draw resourcefully, and perhaps ironically, on the elements of different rites of passage. The candidate's hair is shaved, as if at a funeral, as an expression of bereavement for the departed Gohu whose *kigango* is being placed. The candidate pays a fee which is likened by those present to a bridewealth which marries him to the society. Yet, just as the placing of the *kigango* enables the spirit of the deceased Gohu to be bodily reborn, so the candidate undergoes a physical metamorphosis which transforms him from a junior to a senior Gohu: patterns are drawn in millet or maize paste plastered on his shaven head, he wears the armlet of buffalo horn, is given a new cloth to wear, and has ostrich feathers placed in his ears (Champion 1967).

This human bodily decoration uncannily parallels that given to the wooden *kigango*, the spirit's new body. The ceremony transforms one body and consecrates another. Recalling Sperber's interpretation of butter placed on the Ethiopian Dorze dignitary's head as evoking conspicuous consumption (1975: 59–61), the placing of flour paste on the head of the Gohu candidate can be seen in the same light, especially since lavish material display is a hallmark of Gohu status. The use of bone, in the form of the armlet, and of hard wood, in the form of the *kigango*, also echo from other parts of Africa their association with continuity and permanence, and even immortality (Biebuyck 1973), which is another of the Gohu's primary aims.

As an aspect of Gohu openness, their feasts, while lavish, are not exclusive, and non-Gohu may attend them. Indeed, the intention is said to be to advertise the Gohu as wealthy and yet generous individuals. People are invited from one's own clan, from those of one's mother and son-in-law, and from those of other affines of affines, much in the manner of funeral invitations (see also Champion 1967: 23). This conspicuous consumption and redistribution brings out into the open the fact that a few individuals have acquired quantities of cattle, land and wives well above average. Any resentment of their wealth is said to be much countered by this generosity. The Gohu are, at least, regarded ambivalently: some Giriama refer to them as concerned only with their own greed, while others admire their ability to have transcended the normal lot of humanity.

The Gohu embody some of the characteristics of the modern small-scale entrepreneurs as well as the traditionally successful men. Both wish to increase their control over property and to transmit it to successive generations. But among modern entrepreneurs the priority is to expand holdings of land, trees, shops, vehicles or whatever, and to beget children as the means by which such property is retained. To have few children is sometimes claimed by them to be better for this purpose than to have many. Many entrepreneurs therefore state a preference for marrying only one or two wives, even when they can afford more. The Gohu reverse this priority: land, livestock and wives are called 'property', but are the means by which children are secured, for to be reproduced permanently, so to speak, through one's offspring and their descendants, is the object of existence. The more children the better. Property is the means to that end, not an end in itself.

It is, indeed, a standard expression among Giriama men to define property as consisting of wives, children, land and livestock. To consume property, in the form of funeral feasting and drinking, for example, is an activity involving all Giriama. It is a form of consumption that redistributes the fruits of labour in social and personal relationships, out of which some marriage alliances and forms of co-operation will develop. I discussed in an earlier work (1972) how, in 1966, the newly emerging entrepreneurial small farmers, shopkeepers and truck and bus owners constituted a boundary around Giriama involvement in the international cash and capitalist economy. Since that time, this process has advanced further though, ironically, not through a significant increase in the number of Giriama entrepreneurs, nor in the scale of their businesses, but rather in the domination of coastal enterprises by up-country Kenyans and by the European-dominated tourist industry. The resultant form of consumerism, of which Giriama are now aware and to which some of them subscribe, is clearly not of the redistributional kind associated with the Gohu, but is more oriented to securing aims and objects whose value is in more narrowly satisfying only personal wants, with the partial and special exception of politicians who do periodically invest in their election hopes with public displays of generosity.

The spirit of capitalist consumerism, then, has clearly much more in common with, and is indeed part of, the new *katunusi* spirit of coastal desire, than with the spirit of the Gohu who, for all their personal ambitions and conspicuous consumption, were entirely dependent for their reputations on converting the proceeds of their hard work as farmers and herders into generosity towards each other and towards other Giriama.

Redistributional generosity entails a theory of close identification and resemblance, and typically occurs among kin, as Sahlins observed long ago in his characterisation of generalised exchange (1965). Among Giriama, it is in fact commonly the relationship between paternal grandparents and grandchildren that most typifies ideas of personal resemblance. They are regarded as of equivalent generations and may joke with each other, call each other by the same kin term (grandfather/grandmother, or even brother/sister) and bestow and inherit widows and names. From a dream about a grandparent is often derived the right to enter membership of the Gohu, the women's Kifudu society or, through possession by a grandparent's spirit, the right to communication with that spirit. For their part, it is often through their grandchildren that the dead can be reborn, in the form of a memorial post, after such a visitation.

Physical and metaphysical personhood

The 'Hawaiian' kinship terminology of the Giriama is like many among the eastern African Bantu in placing emphasis on the relationships between generations rather than on deep and ramifying lineage genealogies. Descent reckoning does not go beyond four generations and overall patri-clanship is not precisely differentiated into descent lines. Alternate generations go back indefinitely and share the same patri-clan names, so that it is difficult when a genealogy is being recounted to know whether a named person was in fact of the grandfathers' or great-great grandfathers' generation, for the two become merged through use of the same names. Generation thus comprises and prevails over genealogy, with the major opposition being between adjacent and alternate generations.

A man in a sense *is* his paternal grandfather, and not only draws from the same pool of reserved clan names but is often likened to a grandfather in terms of personality and skills. Adjacent generations are, by contrast, sharply separated and it is less common for a man or woman to inherit the characteristics of their father or mother, with the partial exception of the eldest son who is, anyway, regarded as a kind of father of his brothers and accorded some respect by them. None of this is conclusive and other relatives may be regarded as sources of resemblance, but it is generally the case that alternate generations are regarded as like each other, and to some extent are each other, while adjacent generations are not.

Patri-clanship is also important, as has been shown. The foetus of a baby is said by both women and men to come at conception and for the first three months from the man's sperm (*menye*, or, more euphemistically, *makodzo*, urine, and *mulatso*, blood), and to be nurtured by the blood that would normally have made up the woman's menstrual period (*maada*). Thereafter it is fed by food received by the mother, who is nourished after her child. Most men have sexual intercourse with wives until late in the pregnancy, but their sperm, while it is seen to help the baby grow, may also, in excess, damage it, and so is not essential at this stage. Fertility can only result from a mixing of different bloods, and it is for this reason that marriage may be permitted between any clans except that of the father, with whom, unlike the mother and her clan, common blood is assumed. There are no consistent accounts as from which parent or line of relatives a child's bone and flesh derive, and even the notions that the foetus comes from the father's semen and that the blood is that of the father sit uneasily with the idea that the child is, in fact, mainly nourished first by the mother's menstrual blood and then by her food intake.

Thus, while patri-clanship, and generational opposition and resemblance, are both unambiguously held concepts, the physical make-up of a person from conception onwards is not entirely clear, and only inclines to a patrilineal bias. Similarly, while personality and character are said often to resemble that of paternal grandparents, actual cases may refer to other relatives for examples of likeness. Physical resemblance, too, is supposed to be between a child and his or her father and his agnatic relatives, 'for in this way, he knows that the blood of the child is his blood, and that his wife has not had the child by another man'. Yet, the number of possible agnates is sometimes so large that the idea of resemblance often becomes a convenient fiction.

This area of ambiguity as regards physical make-up, contrasting with the firmer ideals of patri-clanship and generation, takes us more clearly into Giriama perspectives on personhood among them. On the one hand, a Giriama individual is circumscribed by clan and generation, backed up by strong beliefs in the sanctioning power of ancestors. This he or she cannot alter. On the other hand, he or she is physically, and in terms of temperament and competence, regarded indeterminately, and so as made made up of possible directions and tendencies as well as being relatively unconstrained. The Gohu member tries to go further and turn this indeterminacy into personal ambition, while at the same time also acknowledging the constraints around him. He both conforms to Giriama customary expectations of egalitarian generosity and at the same time seeks to stand out from other men. I have similarly suggested elsewhere that, counterbalancing the unalterability of patri-clan names, Giriama male nicknames are sometimes coined by their bearers themselves expressly to draw attention to a desired characteristic (i.e. 'the fearless'), an attempt that may fall flat if others judge the self-laudatory name as unearned by the claimant (Parkin 1989a).

The other side of this ambiguity of make-up is its vulnerability and frailty. From the very moment of birth, there is the question of whether a child is born feet first, or, later, whether its first two teeth grow at the top rather than at the bottom. Such children are called 'bad' (*ahoho ai*) and are sometimes also credited with extra miraculous but evil powers, such as being able to talk at birth (and called *kijego*). Such children must normally be killed lest they bring misfortune to a homestead or later prove to be uncontrollably deviant, being considered in much the same way as twins in some other societies.[2] This is done not by the mother but by an old (and probably unrelated) woman. The child is taken to an area shaded by a 'cooling' tree (*muhi wa peho*), of the kind used in therapy, and there drowned by immersion of the head. The body is not buried but is thrown into the surrounding bush, the place being called *katsaka ka ana ai*, literally the copse of bad children. A child is about six months old when it cuts its first teeth, and parents desperately try to prevent the child's slaughter. Elders, notably the Vaya, may insist that it be carried out, and the government chief or sub-chief can do little more than advise the parents to move to another area. The parents would thereafter be obliged to move on to other areas every two years or so as news of the 'bad child' catches up with them. There is no evidence that parents acquiesce in the elimination of breech-birth children or those who cut their top teeth first. Indeed, the Giriama understand the conflict between parental love and the danger to the community that such children bring. Similarly, a person who has met an untimely death from an accident or homicide, a so-called 'death from war' (*kifo cha viha*) or bad death, must be buried outside the homestead for fear of contaminating it but, since he or she was a loved family member, must also be close to it, so that the burial site is in neutral ground between the homestead and the bush. Such compromises of love and duty point up not only how vulnerable humans are to vagaries of misfortune but also how precarious any definition of the 'whole' person, *mtu muzima*, becomes: a woman may manage to have a successful pregnancy and then delivery, but neither may be enough to ensure that her child is acceptable to the community; a man or woman may be respected and admired, but then is stopped short and rendered communally contaminating through a bad rather than a normal death.

As in many societies, maintaining the 'whole person' is a question of striking a balance between hot and cold elements. For example, strong sperms, most likely to make a woman pregnant, are described as hot (*menye ga moho*), and weak ones as cold (*ga peho*). Yet in other circumstances cooling situations, processes and plants can be therapeutic. An apprentice diviner is impelled to seek the leaves, bark and roots of 'cooling' trees, and a diviner, in turn, may urge a client to seek them out for use in therapy. Cooling trees include a large number ranging, for instance, from the baobab (*muyu*) to such others as the *morya, reza,*

---

[2] The famous Giriama politician, Ronald Ngala, wrote a short account in Swahili on Giriama customs, in which he claimed that the Giriama did kill or dispose of their twins. I had read this account before going to Giriama country in 1966, but neither then nor since have I encountered any claims or reported cases of this practice. This is curious and raises the question of whether the custom did once exist, for it is difficult to know why Ngala should otherwise have mentioned it.

katore, *muhowe* and the *mukone*, from which, incidentally, the *koma* ancestral post is made, with the Gohu *kigango* post made from the *mwanga*, a non-cooling tree. The term *peho* itself extends in meaning from cool to shady and windy. Interesting semantic associations are made: spirits, called *pepo*, are sometimes said to be like gusts of wind, *peho*; the *kivuri*, living soul, is sometimes referred to also as *peho* (as when a diviner might say to a victim, 'a witch has taken your soul/life force', using either the phrase *wahalwa peho ni mutsai* or *wahalwa kivuri ni mutsai*).

But the 'whole person' is only a condition of temporary balance and, in the course of life itself, personal vulnerabilities continue. An example already given is the facility with which individuals, particularly women, become invaded and possessed by spirits, or become unsettled by spirits already existing within and constituting them. Another example, introduced in the above paragraph, is the ease with which one's living soul, *kivuri*, may be stolen by a witch. A witch may take this soul at night while its owner is sleeping, for such souls wander about at night having human-like experiences and feelings. The witch fattens it up, cuts it off from its owner, who will therefore become sick and die, and eats its flesh. Sudden death from heart attack is sometimes explained in this way. Some Giriama claim that there is a coastal secret society, organised by the Chonyi living there, called the *chama cha muvula*, which is made up of such witches.

The repetitive form, *kivurivuri*, means 'shadow'. It can only exist as part of a visible object. Similarly, only visible, living persons can have a *kivuri*, soul. While a newly born baby has a *kivuri*, a foetus in the womb does not, for you cannot see it, although it is understood that the foetus is alive and growing. By the same token the *kivuri* does not survive a person after their death. At that point they become, instead, a *koma*, or ancestral spirit. Thus, while *kivuri* can only exist as an aspect of a visible human being and is, for witches, also tangible and material, the ancestral spirit or soul, *koma*, is the opposite. It exists only in the person's death, is ordinarily invisible except in the special sense of manifesting itself as an ancestral post, cannot be killed, eaten or in any other way appropriated by witches or other beings.

The contrast between *kivuri* and *koma* nicely summarises that between the material transitoriness of human life and the immaterial permanency, in principle at least, of ancestral life. *Kivuri* is without authority. It is often called witch's medicine (*kivuri ni muhaso wa kitsai*), meaning that it can be used to take life. As an object it is only ever taken but never itself takes, and expresses the vulnerability of human existence. The *koma*, or ancestral spirit, however, is the supreme Giriama authority and, when it is angry, will take away the fertility of its living descendants or create other problems. It is invulnerable to the predations of all other beings, never losing its immortality even if, after a few generations, it is forgotten by the living.

These two aspects of Giriama personhood amount to a confession that it is only in life that a man or woman is prey to the malice and evil of others. The remarkable thing about the contrast is that while the *koma* or ancestral spirit is intelligent, cunning, sometimes petulant, but ultimately all-powerful and just, the *kivuri* experiences feelings passively and does not contribute intellectually to the make-up of a living person.

For the Giriama, as for many other peoples, reason and emotion are often part of each other and not sharply distinguished as in much Western thinking. Among the Giriama, the heart and the head are the seat both of the emotions and of the intellect. They are also the locus of possessory spirits. As has been explained, such spirits are capricious and make demands of and through the possessed person, who is usually a woman. Men, as well as women, are the victims of witches who, in taking a living person's *kivuri* soul, are also possessory.

In fact, the Giriama have a rich vocabulary to describe what in English would be translated as emotions and reasoning (Parkin 1979a (1991) and 1985), and have many typical African animal allegorical tales on the human play of cunning, conscience, greed and misjudgement. For them, then, human plans, wishes and feelings are hedged about and threatened by their precarious co-existence with ancestral and possessory spirits, with human witches and with the harmful effects of, say, incest, homicide and other bad deaths and births. Much of their intellectual and aesthetic creativity is precisely in elaborating on these constraints. Hence the extraordinary Giriama pantheon of spirits, dances, verse-singing and satire, funeral and ancestral rituals, divinatory procedures and types of therapy, each inscribed within stylistic performances of the kind described in this book.

Conclusion
The Giriama concept of personhood is made up of imaginative attempts to deal with threats converging on an individual from different directions. Under the uncertain conditions in which the Giriama live, it is at times of personal suffering that they, and others on their behalf, raise the question of whether or not they are independent and self-determining. On such occasions a whole panoply of questions have to be asked. Is my sickness, or that of my child, the result of an envious enemy's malicious witchcraft or of a possessory spirit? Should I, then, combat that enemy by seeking vengeance through the nature spirits, called *muzimu*, which live permanently in caves or at the baobab trees and are renowned for their justice, so much so that a dishonest supplicant seeking to harm someone unjustly will himself become the victim? Has someone close to me in my homestead slept with my spouse or with a forbidden category of persons, so bringing the death and infertility of *vitio*, which only ritual purification will end? Is a bad death, bad birth or some child's injurious deformities causing misfortune in the homestead? And so on. In other words, the person and his or her desires seem most likely to be defined in response to events affecting them from outside, so to

speak. One does not start from one's own desires and work outwards, but, rather, one seeks and devises the means to combat the ill-effects of other people's desires.

It is, then, the desires, motives, aims and effects of other human and non-human agents which provoke one's own and so define them. Thus, while so-called Western individualism lays out a pristine career profile that deals with problems as they are encountered en route, I suggest that a common Giriama view is of a route already marked out by obstacles which must be overcome in order that life itself be possible. It is the obstacles that define the route; there is no abstract path which just happens to be strewn with hurdles. Reversing misfortunes, and expanding and defending family, property and fertility against assumed heavy odds, *is* the Giriama career profile. The obstacles marking the path have as much right to be there as one's own wishes, for they are other people's human natures, envies and ambitions.

The Kaya and the *koma* ancestral spirits legitimate what, in Europe, might be regarded as this rather negative sense of motive and desire. On the one hand, from the Kaya emanates Giriama ancestry and distinctiveness and the customary knowledge of patri-clans and generational differences. On the other hand, the Kaya is the common central point to which most Giriama still refer when things go wrong, when rain has not fallen, when witchcraft is rampant, or when medicines and oaths need to be validated. The Kaya is here desired, and in turn motivates people, not because it materially and spiritually causes the Giriama people to advance, as might be the promise of a new religion or of a prophet-like figure like Kajiwe or of the capitalist spirit, but because it protects against dangers to the people's existence. In this way, the Kaya is a collective centre against which individual Giriama measure their own sense of being, suffering, destiny and achievement. They start with the Kaya and its knowledge, rather than with themselves.

The burgeoning new coastal culture of material consumerism threatens to reverse this. In the absence of commemorated ancestry, the individual who is committed to the coast tends to fashion him- or herself, not by reference to an ideal model located in Kaya wisdom, but to a modern entrepreneurial ethic according to which the desire for material property and political power is like a homunculus operating within him or her. This inner desire, and not the Kaya, is the fount and origin of work upon the world.

The opposition between the Kaya and the coast and, by association, between the cattle-keeping west and the changing agricultural east of Giriama country, is thus a contrast also of two centres of influence. But whereas the western centre is not seen as focused on any one individual, not even on the Kaya senior elder, but, rather, on the knowledge, history and institution of the Kaya as a whole, the coastal centre is, so to speak, the self-determining individual him- or herself. Epistemologically, we may agree with the post-structuralists that the idea of any centre is likely to be a fiction since people act and justify their actions by reference to any number of areas and motives, none of which predominates all the time. Yet the possibility for the Giriama of moving from the fiction of a collective ontological centre like the Kaya to the fiction of a centred, self-determining individual at the coast, is no less a reality than that of the Giriama people as a whole eventually moving from cattle-keeping to cash crop farming, and thence to coastal wage labour or working for the tourist industry. The fictions, and the movement between them, are that reality.

Conclusion

Semantic chains and shapes

It was possible for Skorupski in 1976, in a well-argued essay, to castigate what he called the straitjacket of equating 'ritual', 'sacred' and 'symbolic' and seeing them as one half of a dichotomy opposed to 'practical', 'profane' and 'instrumental'. In 1975 (but too late for Skorupski's study) Needham suggested that anthropologists' analytical concepts are in fact 'polythetic', often akin to Wittgenstein's 'odd job' words, which refer to a multiplicity of phenomena between which there are overlapping family resemblances but not fixed criteria. He had touched on the same issue in an earlier publication but had not raised it to a more general problem of epistemology (1971). The impact of the later article was striking, and a number of studies appeared thereafter, at first acknowledging the influence, which then swiftly became an assumed part of the subject's theoretical capital. Few anthropologists would nowadays fail to subject what they regard as a key concept in their analysis to critical scrutiny, nor to 'unpack' it. Nor, if they make use of such analytical dichotomies, do they do so unquestioningly.

We appear to have moved a long way from Leach's own radical departure from Durkheim, when he rejected the latter's absolute distinction between sacred and profane and proposed instead that these two be seen as aspects, rather than separate types, of action. For, despite Leach's amendment, the dichotomy was preserved, even if as two halves of different strengths (Leach 1954: 12–13). Even with Durkheim, there is inconsistency. While insisting that the distinction between sacred and profane was absolute, he also held that one can become the other (1915: 37ff). Durkheim argued that such transformations are still premised on, and so only made possible by, the unambiguous contrast between sacred and profane. He said much the same thing in subdividing the sacred itself into the two poles of, roughly, the pure and impure (1915: 409ff). With hindsight, we can see this as falling into the teleological trap of ascribing attributes which do not fit into one class as necessarily belonging to the other (since there is no third or nth class which can receive them). The act of becoming sacred, profane, pure, impure, or whatever, is then forced into a two-dimensional either/or process rather than one of innumerable, polythetic possibilities.

Of course, it becomes nonsensical and pointless if terms such as these have to be defined anew every time they are used in a study. It hardly helps if we escape the trap of dichotomous absolutes and get stuck in a quagmire of proliferating terms. Here, there are two apparent possibilities open to us. First, we can claim that it is not the actual terms which matter, but rather the fact that there is an endless signification in people's descriptions and references to things. People interpret and name things in different ways according to their view of the world and their power and position in it. Second, we can counter-argue that the proliferating terms do matter, for they make up a kind of open-ended semantic shape, perhaps a 'shadow of meaning' (cf. Ardener's 'language shadow' (1978: 108–121): it is broadly shared by at least some of those making the descriptions but is, at the same time, always being constructed by them, sometimes discrepantly but at other times in convergence. We might be tempted to think that this rough web of meaning is a collective representation. It is, however, the opposite. It does not represent the object referred to but is the overlapping, contestable and partially shared views of the speakers, who thereby impute diverse qualities to the object. The object, as a result of this diversity, is seen to take on the attributes of other objects, and so on.

I would argue that aspects of both views are important. The first is valuable for its recognition that there is never an isomorphic, set relationship between signifier and signified but that the signifiers, the words we use in speaking of phenomena, always presuppose other meanings, or, by their apparent closure, hint at meanings which have been omitted and so must be supplied. It is also valuable in making audible and visible the vantage points of speakers: thus, they may variously say that the 'holy' man is an ascetic recluse who is close to God; but that he is also His messenger, and therefore sometimes an intermediary between God and humans; and that he therefore has prophetic potential, a condition which is at odds with his being an ascetic and so suggesting his possible transformation from one to the other; and so on. Slight though these shifts and extensions of attribute may be, their cumulative effect in even this short example indicates different, and even contradictory, presumptions of 'holiness' which define the speakers' different positions.

The second claim, that a semantic shape is created on such occasions, is not in fact incompatible with the view of it as part of an endless process of signification. It may be argued that all language is metaphorical and not simply a mixture of this and the literal (Parkin 1982a: xxxii; Hesse 1984). Our constant production of new metaphors and other tropes creates the extra or surplus meaning that, over time, forms an endless chain. But an event or crisis, defined as such by speakers, roughly and arbitrarily delimits an area along the chain, so that it becomes both part of the event and that by which the event is defined. Whenever the Giriama Kaya is said and seen to be part of a crisis, it basks in a sudden light of comment, judgement and appreciation, which does not replicate in all respects those of preceding crises.

Missionaries and government administrators have referred to the Giriama Kaya as sacred. Missionary views have, however, qualified this as 'pagan' sacredness, to be distinguished from that of Christianity and, in other references, as therefore not sacred at all. Government administrators have also called the Kaya sacred but also, on occasions, a 'hotbed of sedition', as during the Giriama rising against the British in 1914 or, more recently, when Kaya elders have contravened government rules and expectations. My own use of the term sacred to describe the Kaya has similarly been qualified and turned about. I share the view of other commentators that, up until about 1860, when the Kaya was a fortified settlement containing a large population, it was pragmatically concerned with military defence and attack and trading routes, and that the special magically protective stone, called *ngiriama*, standing at its centre, was possibly all that might be called sacred about the Kaya: an intentionally narrow and instrumental usage of the term.

I have also tried to follow contemporary Giriama ideas of the Kaya, which comprise wider and often more contestable perspectives than the above but which I have summarised in the term sacred, as have other observers. What, then, are these Giriama ideas and how have I translated them? What kind of semantic shape is suggested by them?

The sacred as cleansing, clearing and expulsion

I regard as the most persistent attribute the emphasis on maintaining or restoring the Kaya's 'purity' (*ueri*). The arch-idiom of 'cleansing' (as with water), 'clearing away' (as of overgrown vegetation and rubbish) and expelling (as in the ejection of deathliness, and sometimes a corpse, outside a living space), is pervasive. It inheres in the occasional Kaya rituals aimed at bringing rain and fertility, as well as in the more numerous homestead rituals concerned to banish, for example, the effects of incest and breaches of seniority rules. The co-extensiveness of the Kaya's condition with that of all other Giriama homesteads, and its status as autochthonous centre, are summarised in the notion that it is the Giriama 'earth', 'country' and 'origin' (*tsi*) which must also be cleansed and kept pure: what happens to the Kaya, and what happens to Giriama persons irrespective of their whereabouts, affect each other.

The term *ueri* is the one used by early Christian missionaries and, thereafter, by the few Giriama Christians to translate the English terms 'sacred' or 'holy'. *Mueri* is translated as a holy person. The root verbal stem *ku-era* is found in different forms in many if not most other Bantu languages and also has the sense of to cleanse or, often, to make white or even cool, almost always in ritual contexts. The terms *ku-zizinya* and *ku-vororya* also describe ritual acts of cooling, which shade into the idea of cleansing. For ordinary, everyday purposes, the terms *ku-oga* and *ku-ogesa* are used to signify the acts of washing oneself or things.

How does the translation of *ueri*, purity, as sacred, accord with the definition proposed by Rappaport, who sees sacred or sanctity as resting on postulates regarded as beyond question by a congregation and which are in their nature neither verifiable nor falsifiable (1979: 209)? It does not in fact negate it. The Kaya, after all, is commonly given an unquestionable quality by Giriama. I would argue, however, that it is the Giriama notion of purity, cleansing and clearing away which dominates their metaphysics, and which is itself unquestionable. It is a notion which presupposes also that there are places, things and people which need to be ritually cleansed from time to time. But the things and people must always be purified in special places, which must be cleansed regardless of the presence in them of people and things, as is often the case in the Kaya or in homesteads held to be contaminated. In this sense, place takes priority over people and objects in the purificatory process, and place and purification are necessarily part of each other: there can be no effective ritual cleansing unless the place or space is appropriate. To talk about purification, which we may translate as repairing or sustaining sacredness, is inevitably to talk about the space in which the operation occurs.

Preserving or restoring the inviolability and sanctity of place is also reflected in the idea that the Kaya is complete, whole and self-sufficient (*-zima*) as regards the customary and medical knowledge which it, its forest and its elders hold. Breaking the rules for its use, or selling the knowledge to outsiders, injures this wholeness and is also contaminating. There are other terms used to describe the Kaya (for example 'our big homestead') and its activities, which I would say are less consistently used, but which add to the store of overlapping perspectives.

However, it is not just these terms which make up the discourse on the Kaya. The Kaya also has its histories to which people variously subscribe and which further increase the semantic web which constitutes it. There is the story of its settlement from a distant, northerly point of even more remote origin, called Singwaya. It was from here that the protective *ngiriama* stone was carried by members of a specific clan, whose status is still remembered and marked in the Kaya. There are other such themes affecting the position and settlement in the Kaya of clans, elders and their wives.

Critically important is the recognition by the Giriama that the Kaya is virtually uninhabited most of the time, there being sometimes no more than the senior Kaya elder and his wives, and occasionally one or two others. But this is seen by Giriama as a positive quality, a proof that the Kaya can have an effect on their world without having to contain people. It is to that extent an (almost) empty place: the Kaya elders, including those belonging to the Vaya society, have their powers, but these are derived, ultimately, from the comprehensive power of the Kaya itself. It is the place, and not the people, from which emanates the power.

The concept of God (Mulungu) is also co-extensive with that of the Kaya and the earth, as is evident in, for example, the prayer which is uttered at times of invocation. And yet I have heard no Giriama say that the Kaya is God. They may partake of each other but the Kaya, like God, has its autonomy as a source of power and influence.

I would privilege the idiom of 'cleansing' and 'expelling dirt/death/disease/ evil' over and above that of 'awe' as the dominant attribute of the Kaya's characterisation and appeal. This goes completely counter to Otto's view of the sacred or holy (which are equated). Otto coined the concept, numen, to express this idea of religious awe. It is more than what he calls 'natural fear' and can be the qualitatively different and not always explicable sentiments of horror and dread. It may also be an overwhelming tranquil quiet, a sweeping ecstasy, or an undetachable fascination. It is summarised in what he calls the 'mysterium tremendum' which seizes one without apparent reason. It is what is commonly called a religious as well as a ghostly experience (Otto 1959: 19–55).

Numen is often used by anthropologists to explain the transcendental, timeless quality of religious faith and claims. Rappaport summarises some of these views and, in a sophisticated argument, suggests that numinous experiences (transcendental feelings) and sacred propositions (unfalsifiable statements) are the inverse of each other but, when joined in ritual, create the conditions for religious belief. In other words, the sacred claims of, say, a liturgy, despite being immaterial and hence unfalsifiable, are made undeniable by the 'reality' of peoples' numinous experiences (Rappaport 1979: 215–217). Although 'awe' was an emotion central to Otto's definition of numen, it does not figure in Rappaport's account, nor indeed in that of most other anthropologists, for whom the transcendental and ecstatic aspects are taken as more significant. All are variously part of the definition of numen, however, which, at times, refers to little more than a state of high emotional agitation, a view akin to Malinowski's on religion as answering the need for reassurance.

But why should people need to feel 'awe', 'ecstasy' or the like in order to believe religious claims? Could not other kinds of experience serve as well? Evans-Pritchard's famous instance of secondary elaboration (1976: 154–158) suggests that a strong and no doubt sometimes desperate desire for explanation, as in the belief that divination *is* efficacious even if particular diviners are not, may be adequate. Is not the emphasis on numen as a precondition of religious belief a view of one Self imposed on Others?

Otto, a theologian, vividly reproduces Christian textual accounts of felt divinity, or experience of the sacred, which sometimes become part of ordinary people's experience, as in W. A. Christian's description of provoked religious weeping in Spain (Christian 1982). But while this centrality of awe in the understanding of the sacred or holy may satisfy Christian theologians and sometimes worshippers, it seems inappropriate for the Giriama and, as far as I can judge, most other African societies.

An early study by Tempels (1949) in fact emphasised how Bantu metaphysics, including its pantheistic religions, rested much more on an idea of a dynamic life-force in nature, including humanity, than on special feelings or reverence and awe addressed by the individual or group towards the object of worship. Other studies have since confirmed the general absence in Africa of the heightened numen that Otto saw as characteristic of the sacred.[1] The most recent is Fernandez's study of the Fang, an egalitarian Bantu-speaking people of Gabon, among whom cleansing (*atunba*) is one of the main religious themes, far out-weighing concepts of awe. As among Giriama, it is related to the idea of variously 'clearing' settlements, the body and 'lines to the ancestors' of dirt, rubbish, creeping vegetation and blockages, as the prelude to revitalisation (Fernandez 1982: 100, 120, 253, 305, 634–635).

The allegedly fundamental role of awe or numen in Judeo-Christian-Islamic religion may correspond more to the former wish of religious hierarchies in Europe and the Middle East to instill dread and terror, and also the promise of passion and ecstasy, in its followers, than to any intrinsic centrality in the idea as Otto proposed. Even so, it is questionable as to how much it percolated down from clerics to the masses of worshippers. How many of the churchgoing Victorian middle and working classes in England, we may wonder, found the preachings of hellfire and brimstone to be truly 'awesome'? Hierarchy may have been served to some extent by such preachings but, in stateless or egalitarian African societies, there would have been less need. Some of the major West African states may be partial exceptions, insofar as the awe of gods was partially transferred to that of divine and tyrannical sovereigns, and might commonly take the form of at least symbolic and sometimes actual human sacrifice (Law 1985: 53–88). But even here, plain terror as much as, or more than, Otto's numen may have been what people were subjected to.

The fear that Giriama have, for instance, of the members of the Vaya society, or of witches, is what Otto would qualify as 'natural' fear: it is broadly explicable and controllable, at least in principle. That is to say, usually one has only to

[1] It is curious, indeed, that, while Fortes (1980: vi) speaks of Evans-Pritchard's approval of Otto's concept of numen, we find that in the passage to which Fortes refers, Evans-Pritchard makes no reference to it and gives the contrary impression that, in fact, the Nuer attitude to divinity is not especially awesome, at least not to the degree nor in the sense proposed by Otto (Evans-Pritchard 1956: 8). What is interesting, however, is that Fortes is responding to Evans-Pritchard's apparent claim that atheistic anthropologists could not understand the religions of non-western peoples. Fortes seems, then, implicitly to have assumed that Evans-Pritchard's analysis of Nuer religion would therefore proceed on the basis of a religiously held experience such as that denoted by the concept of numen. I suggest, however, that, whatever his personal religious convictions and despite his approval of some aspects of Otto's analysis, the concept of numen did not significantly shape Evans-Pritchard's analysis.

admit guilt and pay a fine in order to secure relief from the effects of an inter-diction or oath. The matter is then finished. Even Giriama fear of death, as I have described at funerals, is managed throughout the course of the ceremony and so eventually tamed. By Otto's own criteria, none of these fears amount to what he calls numen. Nor, taking into account his other dimensions of numen, have Giriama described to me an experience which I can easily translate as uncon-trolled spiritual transcendence of a uniquely overwhelming kind. The nearest, perhaps, are the vivid descriptions, mainly by women, of spirit possession and trance. But, again, there is always the recognition that these are publicly managed and controlled experiences, with a senior diviner or shaman in charge, or at least available should a person be seized privately and without warning. The experi-ences are explained coherently in terms of the demands of the spirit pantheon and its logic, by both women and men. However apparently ecstatic the possession, the spirit is to be obeyed, appeased or expurgated as part of a standardised response.

Of course, none of this denies the possibility of any one Giriama individual experiencing from time to time that frisson of chilling and sometimes fearful wonderment that we all know and which informs our encounters with a whole range of phenomena, including curious memories and coincidences, a special work of art, story or literary passage, as well as the prospect of our own or some-one else's death. I simply do not see this numen, if I may call it such, as by itself a precondition for established ritual and religious belief and practice, which appear to be construed through the more urgent immediacy of life-saving expurgation and purification.

In suggesting that 'cleansing/expulsion' rather than 'awe' informs what I translate as the Giriama notion of the sacred, I reveal two separate categories of understanding. Otto presented himself as a representative of a now rather out-moded Christian theology that stresses authoritarian power relations. The Giriama emphasis on purifying and ejecting contamination points up instead reconciliation: it will be remembered, for instance, that rites of purification are less concerned with blaming a culprit than with cleansing his or her homestead of the evil effects of the transgression, as is the case with the Kaya.

At the same time, I described two kinds of Giriama authority figure, one tending towards absolutism and tyranny, and the other more egalitarian. The contrast is that between the Kaya elders (including Vaya), who are regarded as occasionally misusing their powers, and the herbalists and diviners who may also do so, but are additionally subject to greater sanctions and who can only survive and expand their clientele through reputations for good medical results. The former are certainly sometimes feared, and the latter much less so, but it is not a fear which is based on their being sacred or divine figures. It is very much a practical fear of them as ordinary mortals who have access to powers which their own human frailties may tempt them to abuse.

In the various cleansing ceremonies, both types of authority have roles to play. These complementary roles hold in check their own competition for power and leave the Kaya, as a place, in possession of the ultimate purificatory and revitalising power which serves them both.

What, then, is the role of sacrifice in all this? It, too, may instill a kind of fear in people. Giriama privately talk of the unpleasantness bordering on horror of killing animals and, especially, of the violent manner in which the purificatory ram is killed. I have heard Giriama say that the ram takes on the ill-effects of human transgression and that killing it in this unambiguous manner (for violence of this kind is unambiguous) sends away the misfortunes from the homestead. It is a notion akin to the idea that *kilatso*, the contaminating after-effects of someone who has killed another person, must be sent far away, preferably by being passed on to someone who is unrelated to the Giriama and kindred peoples.

The Giriama explanation thus comes close, at least in part, to the scapegoat hypothesis advanced by Girard to explain sacrifice (1977), and, while I would not wish to raise this to the level of a universal theory as Girard does, it fits paradigmatically the Giriama emphasis on cleansing and expulsion as the means by which a space, such as the homestead or the Kaya, is kept free of death, disease and infertility.

The sacred as imaginary space
The Kaya is, indeed, the Giriama homestead par excellence and embodies them all. It is not a tyranny, for only people can be that and it lacks people. When people constitute a tyranny, their subjects will fear them and their gods may sometimes be held in awe. But when a near-empty place like the Kaya is regarded as the fount of the customary wisdom that makes authority possible, it literally leaves open such interpretations. Unoccupied by people, its mouthpiece are those who surround it but have no permanent affiliation with it. But since the Vaya and Kaya elders have left the Kaya and live away from it most of the time, their voice is not sufficiently consolidated as to emerge as a tyranny. They may speak for it but not as of one voice in one place. In this way, the Kaya, as a kind of spatial void, is regarded as autonomously dispersing its own power and of preventing its concentration by humans.

The ambiguity of the Kaya is its alternating image as empty place and as cosmological, and occasional, political centre. I would argue that it is precisely because the Kaya is not visited by many Giriama and is known, through popular report, to be barely inhabited, that it can be imagined and re-imagined in different ways. Few dispute its spiritual centrality, yet few know what it looks like, from either the outside or the inside. Stories of it abound, and of what happens to those who harm it or break the rules governing it. The undifferentiated quality it holds for most people allows for many such stories, which, in turn, add to its amorphous image.

However, during the crises described above, the Kaya becomes a more focused object of attention and description. Politicians, witch-finders and others visit it, and it takes on an image of much greater differentiation: internally in the positions adopted by ritual officiants, clan groups and visitors (as classically demonstrated in chapter six in the description by Pearson, the British administrator), and externally in its relations to Giriama country as a whole, a principal one being the distinction made between the uncrowded cattle-keeping west and the populous eastern and coastal areas.

A major theme of this book is the way in which the east and, especially, the coastal area, constitute threats to Giriama personal and political integrity, and how the west provides an ecological safeguard against such loss. Because it stands in this western cattle-keeping region, the Kaya is seen to impart to the people of this area the autonomy, autochthony and cultural knowledge that is imputed to it. This is a constant feature of the everyday contrasts that people make between the west and the east. A person from the cattle area is deemed, by people from both areas, to be more in control of his or her destiny than one from the east and coast. One *is* one's space.

Yet that space is not constant. During crises the Kaya becomes more accessible than at other times, such that even ordinary homesteaders may be required to help cleanse or clear it and its surrounding forests. In times of non-crisis the Kaya is remotely placed for most people, and cannot ordinarily be entered, except for special oath-taking ceremonies or for consultations by appointment with the elder(s) in residence concerning medical, ritual or customary lore.

This ambiguity of accessibility and remoteness with regard to the Kaya is both spatial and cosmological. It is hard to get at and into the Kaya physically, and few Giriama live near it. But it is also hard to engage with the secrets which are harboured by the Kaya and which are reputedly held in trust by the Kaya elders. Who can ever know how much the Kaya elders agree among themselves concerning this secret knowledge? It does not matter, for there is never a public comparison of what they have to say, which may therefore be as remote or accessible as is judged by those who seek and give such knowledge.

Unmanaged by a political tyranny, unattributed with awe or numen, and set in an ecological contrast denoting the alternatives of ethnic independence and subservience, the Kaya embodies the problem expressed by most Giriama: how to remain independent of what is regarded as the contamination of new economic, political, demographic and ecological developments rapidly occurring at the coast. It is unsurprising that the purified body of the Kaya is held to resonate in that of the Giriama people. To be pure is to be sacred, as it is also to be independent and occupy a place of one's choosing. This is not a myth but a potential programme for action, although, as must be conceded, one that is unlikely to be realised. Such realisation would require the Kaya to act as the centre of a successful political attempt by Giriama to regain control over their own economic activities and cultural identity, a form of concerted action which presupposes more agreement among Giriama over specific wants, aims and methods than may be assumed to exist.

The sacred as deferred centrality

The Judeo-Christian-Islamic notion of paradise, or heaven, engages in a paradox. It is other-worldly and outside immediate everyday experience, and yet central to this-worldly religious imagination. The Giriama Kaya is imputed with no such promises of after-life, except in the special sense that its well-being ensures the fertility and continuity of the Giriama people. Even the specific identities of ancestors are forgotten after a couple of generations, and there is no attempt, nor evident need, to offer an explanation of what happens to them thereafter. The Kaya is nevertheless part of a paradox which similarly plays on the spatial idiom of centrality and marginality as well as of remoteness and immediacy. It is both culturally and spiritually central, but demographically and economically peripheral, at least for the many who are often obliged or prefer to work in the east or on the coast.

The expanding senses do not end here. The Kaya is also held up as the repository of accumulated wisdom from the past, as continuing to provide a cultural identity for the future and, at any time in the present, as a political rallying-point or source of knowledge of forest medicines and litigation. Time differences are here subsumed within the overlapping qualities attributed to the Kaya, its position relative to other areas, and to its forest. The Kaya is, then, central in some respects but not in others, transcending time differences and yet sometimes tied to specific occasions.

The shifting characterisation of the Kaya's centrality appears to result from two related perspectives. Firstly, it is subject to a kind of 'originary delay' (Descombes 1980: 145–152, after Derrida 1972: 3–29), such that its history and boundaries are defined not by any intrinsic quality, but by the alleged differences and similarities of peoples and lands around it. For instance, the Kaya is regarded as a place of customary origin only because it has been superseded by people's dispersion from it and by their settlement in the east, as well as in the west, outside the Kaya. The distinctiveness of the Kaya as a point of origin is only possible as a result of the subsequent development of these other distinctive areas. The latter define the priority of the Kaya, which is therefore indebted to them. Without these areas, the Kaya would be a settlement but with no history from within which people could look back and proclaim it as their 'umbilicus'. The ecological contrasts between the cattle-keeping west, the farming east and the mixed coastal zone highlight the growing divisions among Giriama and are the preconditions of the Kaya being the one place standing above such differences of space and ontology.

This position is aided by the fact that Giriama ideas of the Kaya's history do not focus on a single origin. It may be that, when it was occupied by most Giriama before the mid nineteenth century, the Kaya was itself once seen as no more than an offshoot settlement of the alleged more northerly and distant one at Singwaya in Somalia, just as, more recently, there have been other Kayas in addition to Kaya Fungo. Put simply, event A (for example the Singwaya settlement) could not be the point of origin until event B (for example the settlement of Kaya Fungo) had been identified as having followed A: A without B has no distinctive essence and therefore no origin, so that B has explanatory priority over A. Continuing further, the Giriama judgement that the eastern and coastal areas foster economic and material dependency creates the idea of western independence and, therefore, of Kaya autochthony, and so on.

Secondly, however, we can regard this kind of explanatory deferment as counterpoised to the way in which people apply their imaginations multidimensionally or polythetically. For instance, we may say that Giriama sometimes bring into harmony what might otherwise be divergent historical interpretations of their origins. As well as pointing to the Kaya, they may also, though less often nowadays, refer to the alleged northerly and distant settlement of Singwaya as their place of origin, as when explaining the position in which the dead are laid to rest. More has perhaps been written on the Singwaya legend than on any other aspect of Giriama history, both for and against the likelihood of this having been the place from which the Giriama migrated in the seventeenth century or, indeed, at all (for a list of references see Mutoro 1987). For academic historians, Singwaya either is, or is not, a major point of origin of the Giriama people. The debate is thus framed in terms of descent from a single point in time which presupposes, and so subsumes in importance, all subsequent stages.

Taking a Giriama viewpoint, however, the reference to Singwaya as the place from which they migrated need not contradict the assertion that the present Giriama capital, Kaya Fungo, is the seat of their origins. Sometimes Giriama will, indeed, say that they stemmed from Singwaya, and that they came from the Kaya at a later date. But they can also claim, without such qualification, that the Kaya is where they originate and that Singwaya is also their place of origin. By this they appear to mean that Giriama people are the sum of their customary knowledge and that this Giriama knowledge is in the Kaya and was brought from Singwaya. In embodying such knowledge the Kaya *is* Singwaya: that place is this place, just as past Kayas are aspects of the present Kaya, and just as the Kaya and Singwaya are the knowledge that makes up the Giriama people. People constantly work at definitions which become modified by their own closure and so remain incomplete: a definitive statement of what the Kaya is, or does, always leaves something out, which must then be incorporated in the definition ad infinitum. The Kaya, its origin, and the origins of the Giriama people, are thus always in a state of becoming.

The constantly reworked idea of the Kaya as the point of origin is, then, dependent *both* on the subsequent development and identification of the eastern, coastal and western zones as ecologically distinct (an expression of difference) *and* on people's view of centre and origin as metonymically parts of other such centres and origins in both the past and present (a dissolution of difference). In an earlier chapter, I gave an example of such metonymical thinking. The Giriama protective medicine, a magical stone called *ngiriama*, was purportedly carried from Singwaya to the Kaya(s) for burial at its centre and, I suggested, is seen by Giriama to reproduce the essence of Singwaya, which is the essence of Giriama. It is, however, an essence which they would appear to present to each other in any number of ways: through the contrast of the Kaya with both east and west; through metonymic association with the western cattle area in which it stands, and with Singwaya; and through its capacity to influence Giriama despite being virtually uninhabited – a presence incurred through an absence.

It is this latter dimension which touches on what I understand by my phrase, sacred void. The Kaya can be imagined to fit almost any number of socio-cultural and politico-economic circumstances. After periods during which it seems to recede from public memory and recognition, there are Giriama national crises, judged to have been caused through negligence of the Kaya and its accumulated impurity and contamination. These must be reversed in order to restore the fertility, vitality and defence of Giriama land and life. But in so cleansing the Kaya, its imagined void becomes filled again with content, including many old metonyms, contrasts and associations, but also some new ones. In recent years, for instance, we have seen the east–west ecological axis and its implications for migration and capitalist consumerism supplant the north–south one which characterised much pre-colonial and colonial history. We could well imagine also, and at least one attempt testifies to the possibility, that Christian or Muslim religious movements might become associated with the Kaya, which is at present an unacceptable development for most Giriama, though clearly an imaginable one. The void is, then, that point at which memory is revived and recreated, but also allowed to think what was previously unthinkable. Insofar as it is kept alive against all apparent odds, I would see this as sacred space, to which people then periodically give material form, boundaries and a centre, thereafter cleansing and re-imagining it again in due course.

It is this possibility of imagining and re-imagining that releases us from Durkheim's tautology that space can only be thought of in terms of differentiated space, and that this spatial differentiation must be based on social differentiation. That remarkable intellectual genealogy from Durkheim to Saussure, and thence to Lévi-Strauss and Derrida and converging with Foucault, can be continued, but only through translation, however inadequate, of our ideas into other people's metaphysics.

We presumably are, like Derrida himself, trapped within our own Western 'logocentric' categories of analysis and so cannot possibly think beyond them.

By the same token, such categories do not allow us to see beyond endless *différance*, that is, finding an origin behind an origin masking another origin, and so on. For the moment at least, most Giriama do not privilege a Western metaphysics of presence and so do not seek explanations of phenomena in terms of a final or original essence. They certainly appear to speak of the Kaya in such essentialist terms, as being the fount of medical and other knowledge, but they see no inconsistency in also relating it metonymically to the surrounding western cattle-keeping area, to all Giriama country and people, and to Singwaya in the north. Their idea of origin seems to come close to that identified by Foucault as 'disparity', that is to say, a continual coming into being of diverse and re-interpreted elements, apparently drawing on Nietzsche's term *Herkunft*, as distinct from *Ursprung*, a self-determining fixed, causal point in the past (Foucault 1977: 141–142, cited and discussed in Sheridan 1980: 117–119).

This intellectual preference, shared by many peoples, for linking parts of things to their alleged wholes, themselves linked to other wholes or parts, across time and space, has conventionally been regarded in anthropology as the stuff of myth and fantasy. But what does this mean? That it is untrue, a kind of unfulfilled scientific objectivity? It might indeed be argued that, by focusing on the empty Kaya and on their cultural origins, while they and their land are increasingly dominated by other peoples and another economic system, the Giriama are mystifying themselves, and that they would do better to engage in direct confrontational politics. But who would they confront? Those fellow-Giriama who sell 'secrets' to tourists and other foreigners? Christians and Muslims who deny the authenticity of Giriama knowledge? The people from up-country who have settled on the coast? Their own coastal members of parliament? Other representatives of the Kenya state? Confrontation presupposes clear lines of demarcation which have to be agreed upon.

The success of such confrontation would, then, depend on the Giriama presenting themselves as a solid front with common interests and a clear definition of aims and protagonists. Increasingly, as I have shown, there are fewer such interests, as people compete for land and jobs. It is only the timelessness of the Kaya and its spatial co-extensiveness with other areas which currently provide the outline of a possible common Giriama front. The outline is traced back onto the idea of the Kaya, whose essence is in fact its constant deconstruction and recreation. It suggests another metaphysics: that knowledge does not have to be added to, that survival is through the retention of customary knowledge and secrets, but that this knowledge somehow has to be re-ordered in conformity with a changing distribution of power within and outside Giriama country. It does not inherently have weaker explanatory power than the Western metaphysics of presence. But it does not at present compete easily with the derived Western view of knowledge as cumulative (building up from an original point or 'logos' in the past), infinitely expandable and marketable. The latter is inscribed in the ecologies of rural cash-cropping and urban wage labour which more Giriama are obliged to enter in a growing money economy. Can we, for our part, imagine a reversal of this process: no money, no expansionary knowledge and goods, no search for a single autochthony, and Kaya wisdom as even more strengthened through infinite metonymy?

Appendix 1

The three ecological zones and demographic features in Kilifi district, focusing especially on the southern division

1. *Coastal strip.* This is a mainly fishing and agricultural area which is at or slightly above sea level. It consists of wooded grassland up to about 10 kilometres inland, and often much less, before giving way to a mixture of forest and wooded grassland. Its rainfall is relatively high, especially south of Kilifi, and ranges from about 1270 to 1525 millimetres a year, sometimes a little less between Kilifi and Malindi.

The area includes settlement schemes and so-called squatter settlements formerly and in some cases still owned by Swahili and Arabs and occupied by Mijikenda who have migrated there sometimes recently and sometimes generations ago, and who are now being allowed legally to acquire rights of tenure. The coastal strip up to a distance of a few miles inland was under the suzerainty of the Sultan of Zanzibar but became part of Kenya at its independence in 1963.

From this time on, large numbers of up-country people from the Central, Nyanza and Western provinces of Kenya migrated to the coastal strip, principally to the town and surrounding district of Mombasa, but also to small towns along the line of road from Mombasa to Malindi and to settlement schemes newly established along the coast. In 1962 the indigenous Mijikenda accounted for 57% of the population of Coast Province as a whole. By 1979 their proportion had declined slightly to 54%. However, large numbers of Europeans and Asians had left Kenya, including Coast Province, in the meantime. Their proportion was taken up, so to speak, by up-country Bantu speakers such as Kikuyu, Kamba, Meru, Embu and Luhya and by Nilotic Luo, who increased during the same period from just under 10% to well over 17% of the population of Coast Province. Phrased differently, in 1962 there was roughly a ratio of six Mijikenda persons to one up-country immigrant (413,489 to 71,208). By 1979 the ratio had almost halved (732,820 to 231,949): three Mijikenda for every up-country person in the province. However, almost all the up-country migrants were concentrated in the coastal strip, including Mombasa. In much the same way, the proportion of Arabs and Swahili declined enormously (even allowing for some changes of self-designation). Administrative locations which may be included within the coastal strip of southern Kilifi district include Mtwapa, Mavueni-Takaungu and Junju. The eastern halves of Tezo-Roka, Ganda and Magarini, may also be regarded as within the coastal strip and have attracted considerable immigration.

After noting the very high population growth of Kenya as a whole (3.8% annually), the 1979 Kenya government census report states that 'the characteristically belted arrangement of population had become a more marked feature of the coastal region. Lying immediately along the coast, a belt of population concentration showed densities ranging from 200 to just over 400 persons per square kilometre' (Kenya Government 1979 Census Report, Volume 2: page 10). The World Bank had noted, on the basis of the earlier 1962 and 1969 censuses, that Coast Province had a very high in-migration and a very low out-migration rate (1980: 29). That appears to be a continuing feature affecting the coastal strip much more than other parts of the province. The report also referred to the Mijikenda as one of the country's slowest growing populations (1980: 11).

2. *Central agricultural zone.* This is difficult to define and differs as between southern and northern Kilifi district. In the southern division, with which this book is concerned, the area is dominated by the growth of coconut palms and, to a lesser extent, cashew nut trees. Palms grow less abundantly in much of the northern division. The area is between ten and fifteen kilometres wide in a south to north-northeasterly direction. It is of mixed forest and wooded grassland, except where large clearings have been made for coconut palms. In the locations of Kaloleni, Duruma, Chonyi, Jibana, Kambe-Ribe and Rabai, and to a lesser extent Kauma, these trees dominate spectacularly, with maize grown in between the palm groves. The palms are valued for the coconuts, copra, palm wine and fibre which they produce and which are sold or used for domestic purposes (see Herlehy 1985 and Parkin 1972 for detailed studies of the history and social organisation of coconut palm cultivation and trade). The coconut palm (*mnazi*) is the local counterpart crop to cattle (*ngombe*) which is the mainstay of the western area. Rainfall is between 1015 and 1270 millimetres a year and the land rises in ridges to 270 metres. It is along the tops of these ridges where most of the Mijikenda Kayas are built, except for that of the Giriama which is further into the hinterland in the cattle-keeping zone.

The population density of the locations mentioned above averages at 186 persons per square kilometre, well below that of the coastal strip (at between 200 and 400) but much higher than that of the western hinterland, where the density is 29.

Other locations like Tezo-Roka, and the more northerly Ganda and Magarini, approach densities of some 138 persons per square kilometre which represents considerable population growth over the last generation. Their western halves can perhaps be regarded as part of the central agricultural zone, although this is somewhat arbitrary in that there is relatively little difference in rainfall, vegetation pattern and physical features between their eastern and western parts, in neither of which does the palm grow extensively compared with southern Kilifi district. Traditionally, and to some extent still today, the inland, southern area is called Weruni, and is or was distinguished from the two traditional northern areas of Godoma and Gallana, and from the western one called Biryaa (see Taylor 1891).

3. *Western cattle and livestock zone.* This hinterland area begins in southern Kilifi district at about 35 to 50 kilometres inland from the coast, and reaches for another 30 to 40 kilometres to the Taru desert and, north of that, the Gallana game scheme, with Tsavo Park east beyond that. The cattle zone is truly largely confined to southern Kilifi district, for thick bush in the north, mixed with forest, do not permit easy grazing conditions. The cattle zone does not in fact really consist of open savanna grassland so much as bushland with grassy areas, some quite large. Rainfall may reach 1000 millimetres in the extreme east of the zone in good years but is often much less than this and is commonly well below 510 millimetres in the far west. The area easily becomes dry and arid. Only one crop of maize per year can be grown, and that sometimes fails, even in the more watered parts, compared with two in the central agricultural zone and the coastal strip. There are natural waterholes but these are few and subject to overuse during very dry weather. The government has sunk a number of these and is intending to run piped water to places like Gotani and Bamba, which are points (in the case of Bamba a trading centre) along the trail taken by Somali and Oromo cattle dealers, who take their cattle for sale at either Mariakani or Mombasa.

The locations of Kayafungo, Mariakani, Bamba, Ganze and Vitengeni may be said to include within them the main cattle-herding areas, though in each case they include agricultural areas also. Bearing this important qualification in mind, the combined population of these locations according to the 1979 census was 90,467 people, with a density, as mentioned above, of 29 persons per square kilometre.

Summary
Despite the problems incurred by the fact that location boundaries, on which census figures are based, do not conform to ecological ones, there are some broad differences which are expressed by the censuses. Moving from the western cattle zone, through the central agricultural one to the coastal strip, each defined by the locations I have mentioned, we move from a population density in 1979 of 29 to one between about 150 to 400 (average 164), with Mombasa district a colossal 1,624 persons per square kilometre.

According to the 1962 census the corresponding densities were 17.5 for the cattle area, and 85 for the central and coastal areas, excluding Mombasa and also some northern areas for which information was unclear, but including the large locations of Ganda and Magarini. Mombasa's density in 1962 was about half its 1979 one.

Appendix 2

Giriama kinship and affinal terms

As is evident from the two sets of kinship and affinal relationship terms given below, the Giriama system is broadly of the so-called 'Hawaiian' type, and has two main characteristics. First, siblings, parallel cousins and cross cousins may all be referred to by the same term. Second, there is bifurcate merging in the immediately ascending generation, such that a father and father's brother are called by the same name, but not the mother's brother; and that a mother and mother's sister are called by the same name, but not the father's sister. Marriage may occur with all cousins except a patrilateral parallel cousin, and into all clans except the patri-clan (see Appendix 4).

The links between generational differentiation and relationships of respect and joking are dealt with in the main text of chapter four. Broadly speaking, members of alternate generations joke, while those of adjacent ones respect each other. This is reinforced by the reciprocal use of singular and plural pronominal forms of address respectively. But there are a few complicating factors that may intervene, as is the case with the use of kinship terms. Terms of address between alternate generations are reciprocated by members of the same sex or are reciprocally equivalent between members of different sex. Between adjacent generations, certain terms are reciprocal or reciprocally equivalent, e.g. mother's brother/sister's son, parent-in-law/daughter's husband, but are otherwise reciprocated with different terms. The eldest of a group of brothers is commonly addressed with respect forms and behaviour, unlike other brothers who use familiar forms.

Diagram 3. Kinship terms

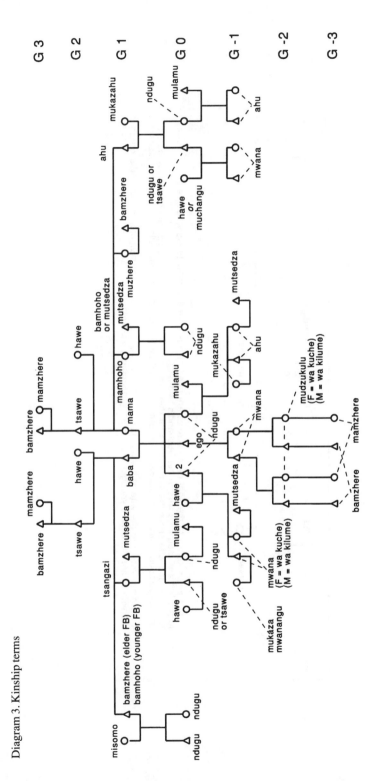

1 What few differences there are between men's and women's use of terms can be seen in the chart on affinal terms
2 The eldest of a group of brothers is called *mukulu* (the big one) and is accorded respect. A younger sibling is *muvuaha*

Diagram 4. Affinal terms

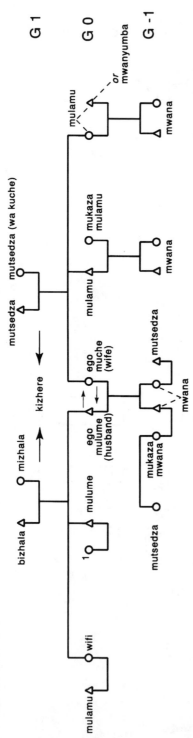

In this chart, terms to the right of the arrows are used by a husband to refer to his wife's relatives. Terms to the left are used by a wife of her husband's relatives. Husband and wife share the same terms for their own children, children's spouses and other members of that generation. Couples of the same generation linked by a marriage of their children, call each *kizhere*.

1 A woman refers to the wife of her husband's elder brother as *mukaza wa (mulume) mukulu*. She refers to the wife of her husband's younger brother as 'grandchild', *mudzukulu*.

Appendix 3

Cattle colour and complexion names among Giriama

As I have explained in chapter three, Giriama cattle owners and herders identify every single member of their herd(s). Nowadays, a list is commonly kept, written by hand in a school exercise book, sometimes with the help of a younger son who is at school but who also helps herd cattle when he is available. A younger son of school age is more likely to be entrusted with this information than an older one wanting to marry, for the latter's 'impatience' to use some of the cattle for bridewealth may conflict with his father's own plans, which may envisage a more gradual deployment of the herd, in order to satisfy the successive bridewealth needs of all unmarried sons. Sons themselves usually agree that it is only their father who is in a position to distribute the cattle fairly for these purposes, although they can also point to what they regard as bad decisions made by fathers. It follows that the father alone, though sometimes aided by a younger son, is supposed to have total knowledge of all the cattle under his charge and held in trust for his family. This means knowing the inventory of terms for distinguishing cattle.

No doubt new terms come into usage, although I have not witnessed such innovation. This should be easily possible, because the cattle names are not dependent on colour terms alone, but draw also on those for different patterns found on the hides of animals.

The three main colour terms are: *thune* (brown/red), *iru* (black) and *ruhe* (white), with other terms drawn from animals and plants. Additionally, cattle are distinguished by gender (male, female and castrated ox) and by stage of growth (female calf, *kadama*; male calf, *katsao*; heifer, *ndama*; bullock, *kitsao*; mature cow, *goma*; bull, *ndzao*; and ox, *ndewa*), by overall size, by body parts, and by particular sores, blemishes and signs of injury or deformity. Taken in combination, these different criteria can produce an almost infinite range of distinct identities.

Evans-Pritchard's early work on cattle names among the Nuer concluded that there are 'several hundred colour permutations' (1940: 44). I do not doubt that, with all the other criteria used by Giriama in addition to colour and colour distribution, their tally could in principle match that number also. Turton has more recently related such practical usage among the cattle-keeping Mursi to more abstract systems of colour classification (Turton 1980). Although it is unlikely that we can regard cattle as occupying such a central ontological role among Giriama as among the Nuer and Mursi, their descriptive range of animal and plant species feeds into, for example, their identification and classification of medical symptoms and curative items.

Here I list, as examples of the more general process, some cattle names which are found most commonly distributed among different herds.

1 *ndzao / thune* bull / brown.
2 *ndzao / ya madamada / mairu / na mathune* bull / with a spread of large patches / of black / and brown [a kind of palamino].
3 *ndzao / ya ngulungulu / ya singoni* bull / with a separate colour [to be specified] from the main body colour / on the face and throat.
4 *ndewa / thune / nyaruhe nyaruhe* ox / mainly brown / but with bits of white.
5 *ndama / thune / ya matumbo maruhe* heifer / brown / with white stomach.
6 *ndama / nyiru / ya waruhe walagani* heifer / black / with white chest.
7 *goma / riru / ra mabata maruhe / ga magongoni* cow / black / with white circles / on the back of the neck.
8 *goma / ra uthune / wiru* cow / of brown / laced with black.
9 *goma / ra maforomaforo / mathune / maruhe* cow / with large stripes/ patches / of brown / laced with white.
10 *kitsao / cha mongo / wa ndire* young bull / along the spine of the back / of sandy colour.
11 *goma / riru / kironda* cow / black / with a sore [if necessary specifying which part of the body].
12 *goma / ra tsengatsenga* cow / with small speckled dots [if necessary specifying which colour].
13 *goma ra mongomongo* cow / having some special colour or mark along the spine [but left unspecified].
14 *ndama / thune / na bandika / kigilu* heifer / brown / with broken leg.
15 *katsao / karuhe / ka mahaka / mairu* male calf / white / with buttocks / black.
16 *kitsao / cha waruhe / uthune* young bull / white / with brown.

Certain of the above terms are regarded as of a single domain: *madamada*, patches; *maforomaforo*, very large patches or stripes (*foro* is a term for zebra, and the term *ndzoro* may refer to stripes such as are found on the zebra);

tsengatsenga, very small dots or patches; *mbato*, medium size dots or circles; *ngulungulu*, a separate whole colour. *Ndire* is a small, light brown, shrew-like rodent, and contrasts with *kunde*, a brighter, even mauve-red, being the colour of water after *kunde* beans have been boiled in it.

Appendix 4

Giriama patri-clan structure

Spear (1978: 52–53) provides a compilation of the six Giriama 'clans' (or what I prefer to call sections since they are not exogamous, though may once have been), and their constituent 'sub-clans' (or what I prefer to call clans, since they are usually the minimal units of exogamy nowadays). Spear's compilation is based on that of earlier writers, including Werner (1915: 326–354) and Champion (1967: 54–55). It differs only slightly from that of Brantley-Smith (1973: 53). In 1966, I found Champion's compilation to be remarkably similar to the list of clans (i.e. Spear's sub-clans) independently cited by people in the area of Kaloleni where I carried out my first fieldwork, although younger people were, not surprisingly, less consistent than elders, especially as regards the relationship to each other both of the six sections and of the constituent clans. In Kayafungo location in 1985, during fieldwork there, I used Spear's list as a basis for reconstructing settlement patterns and movements, and here add comments alongside Spear's compilation. I also have extensive data on inter-clan marriage which, together with local people's own classification, indicate how much more variable are interrelations between clans than our lists have been able to indicate. In collecting such data, I merely asked people what their and their spouses' clans were. I did not indicate that I already had access to a list of clans. The term, *mbari*, means any unit from one of the six major sections, to the exogamous clan, to the smallest unit within which men may inherit widows (with *muryango* and *lukolo* sometimes used, also, for such and even smaller units). In asking someone their *mbari*, one does not therefore prejudge their perception of what to them is the significant unit of interaction. The fluidity of some of the data suggests the possibility of an analysis of the dynamics of clan relations along the lines of Schlee's recent study of Cushitic-speaking peoples (Schlee 1989).

Spear's compilation of Giriama clans

A. KIZA
1 Fondo
2 Iha
3 Wale
4 Hindzano*

B. MILALANI
1 Kombe
2 Ngari*
3 Kiringi
4 Dundu
5 Ndundi*

C. MILULU
1 Mboro
2 Mbogo
3 Shungu

D. PARWA
1 Nguma
2 Gondo (*sic* but must mean Fondo according to my data)
3 Kiwe

E. MAGANJONI
1 Ngowa
2 Ziro
3 Ngore*
4 Kiti

F. KIDZINI
1 Mkweha*
2 Baya Mwaro
3 Baya Gunga
4 Mweni*
5 Toya
6 Nzaro*
7 Mkare*

Parkin's remarks based on fieldwork and a marriage sample of some 200:

The clans
Of the twenty-six clans identified by Spear (his 'sub-clans'), all but two were given independently and without prompting by informants in my sample. The exceptions were Kiwe (D3) and Dundu (B4), who were not mentioned at all. On asking about them both, I was told only that Kiwe could not intermarry with Nguma (D1), and that Dundu were numerous in the location of Mihirini but that they could not intermarry with Kiringi (B3). Kiwe-Nguma can, however, inherit each others' widows, as can Dundu-Kiringi. To be able to inherit a man's widows is to have the status of 'brother' or agnate of the same sub-clan. This would be tantamount to saying that Kiwe-Nguma are one clan, as are Dundu-Kiringi. Unless the original information gathered by Champion and Werner was inaccurate, this contraction of clan status may be demographically explainable.

Thus, although both Kiringi and Nguma were mentioned in my marriage sample, there were, in fact, only two or three examples of marriage cited in each case. It may be, of course, that these four clans are more numerously represented in other parts of Giriama country, as is claimed for Dundu. However, an

* indicates that the clan is allegedly of non-Giriama origin.

alternative possible explanation for their under- and unrepresentation, is that all four clans have so diminished in size over the generations that they are regressing, in effect to the status of related sub-clans which, as such, cannot marry each other but can inherit widows. This regression is made possible by the fact that Kiwe and Nguma are both of the Parwa section, and Dundu and Kiringi are both of the Milalani section. As part of this process, it may be that declining members of the two unrepresented clans, Kiwe and Dundu, are grafting themselves onto the slightly larger clans of Nguma and Kiringi respectively.

The six sections

Kiza (A) is often spoken of as if it were a clan. Parwa (D) and, to a lesser extent, Mililu (C), are referred to in the same way. Remarkably, this accords with Champion's observation in 1914, although I gave no indication of it to my informants (Champion 1967: 11). One may say of an in-marrying wife, for example, that 'she is a Kiza' (*ni mwamukiza*). Further qualification will indicate that 'she is a Kiza of the Hindzano clan (A4) (or Fondo, or whatever)' (*ni mwamukiza wa hindzano*). The same two-part designation may be used for both Parwa and Mililu. In the case of Kiza and Parwa, there is in each a clan called Fondo (A1 and D2), which are not regarded as related. One therefore never hears someone referred to simply as 'a Fondo'. One is always 'a Fondo of the Kiza' *or* 'a Fondo of the Parwa'. The two must be distinguished. But other clans within each of these sections are often preceded by the section designation or simply referred to as either Kiza or Parwa. It is often remarked that both Kiza and Parwa are more close-knit than other sections.

Mililu is also so regarded though to a somewhat lesser extent and, similarly, persons may simply be called 'Mililu', before, and if, the specific clan membership is given. Significantly, it is claimed that the three constituent clans of Mililu, namely Mboro (C1), Mbogo (C2) and Shungu (C3), may not intermarry but may inherit each others' widows. In about twenty-five cases of marriage involving Mililu, there was indeed only one reported case of intermarriage: between a Mboro and a Shungu, and even this was by no means certain.

The two sections, Milalani (B) and Kidzini (F), are never used as personal appellations in the Gotani area, as are Kiza, Parwa and Mililu. You never say of someone, 'he is a Milalani' or 'he is a Kidzini' (a difference also noted independently of Champion's identical observation, 1967). Persons of these two sections are always identified by their specific clans. All seven Kidzini clans are heavily represented in the area, as are the Kombe (B1) and Ngari (B2) clans of Milalani. It follows demographically, therefore, that they would tend to be identified separately. Most often, in the Gotani area, people would speak, not of the Milalani section, but of the Ngari, differentiating it from the other large clan, the

Kombe, which itself appears to be in the process of dividing into two exogamous units: it was claimed by some Kombe (but not by all) that people of the Ruwa sub-clan may intermarry with those from the Kipawa sub-clan, but that this is rare (cf. Champion 1967: 10).

The sixth and final section, Maganjoni (E) is almost unheard of as a term in the Gotani area, though some senior elders know it. Of its four constituent clans, Ziro (E2) and Kiti (E4) are highly represented in the marriage sample, and Ngore (E3) and Ngowa (E1) less so. Interestingly, however, it is claimed that Ngowa and Ziro cannot intermarry but can inherit each other's widows. Since Ziro appears to be large and Ngowa small, is this another case of the small clan grafting itself onto the larger and so 'becoming' sub-clans or 'brothers', or was this, in fact, the case earlier this century, when the basis of Spear's list was compiled?

My own tentative and obviously localised classification of sections and constituent minimal exogamous units is as follows:

A KIZA (often used to refer to any of A 1–4 below)
1 Fondo (but always called Kiza-Fondo)
2 Iha
3 Wale
4 Hindzano

B (MILALANI)
1a Kombe-Ruwa
1b Kombe-Kipawa
2 Ngari
3 Kiringi-Dundu
4 Ndundi

C MILULU
1 Mboro-Mbogo-(Shungu) (no cases of Mboro-Mbogo, nor of Mbogo-Shungu intermarriage, but mutual inheritance of widows allowed)
2 Shungu (one doubtful case only of Shungu-Mboro intermarriage)

D PARWA
1 Nguma-Kiwe (allegedly no intermarriage between Nguma and Kiwe but mutual inheritance of widows allowed)
2 Fondo (but always called Parwa-Fondo)

E (MAGANJONI) (almost unheard of in the Gotani area)
1 Ziro-Ngowa (cannot intermarry but can inherit widows)
2 Ngore
3 Kiti (includes Kibohe: see Spear 1978)

F   KIDZINI
1   Mkweha
2   Baya Mwaro (some claimed that 'part' of Baya Mwaro is of Taita origin)
3   Baya Gunga
4   Mweni (people in Gotani did not accept that Mweni are of non-Giriama origin. However, this clan is a dominant landowner there, a fact which may have altered such judgement over time).
5   Toya
6   Nzaro (both Nzaro and Mkare are claimed by some in Gotani to be of Shambala origin in Tanzania, and also to be most likely to provide doctors specialising in eradicating the effects of *vitio*: see chapter six).
7   Mkare (also reputed to provide *vitio* doctors).

The number of exogamous units is, then, 21 or 23, depending on how we regard the status of Kombe and of Shungu (26 in 1914, according to Champion 1967). This is almost the same as the number of 'sub-clans' given by Spear, with some slight changes. But, to repeat, this is both a localised and a changing picture based on too small a sample to draw conclusions. It does, however, suggest how local circumstances and demographic changes are important long-term factors in delineating exogamous boundaries. It also illustrates why the recruitment of elders to the Kaya does not nowadays simply conform to the six sections, but exceeds this number. Given the propensity of sections, especially the Maganjoni and Milalani, to be known more by some of their constituent clans, the latter have often achieved inordinate significance and take on equal and perhaps in some cases greater representational importance.

Bibliography

Ardener, E. 1978. Some outstanding problems in the analysis of events. In E. Schwimmer (ed.) *Yearbook of Symbolic Anthropology*
  1987. Remote areas. In A. Jackson (ed.) *Anthropology at home* ASA Monograph No. 25, London: Tavistock
  1989. *The voice of prophecy* (ed. M. Chapman). Oxford: Blackwell
Arens, W. 1989. The power of incest. In W. Arens and I. Karp (eds.) *Creativity of power* Washington: Smithsonian Institution Press
Arens, W. and I. Karp. 1989. Introduction to their edited *Creativity of power* Washington: Smithsonian Institution Press
Augé, M. 1975. *Théorie des pouvoirs et idéologie: étude de cas en Côte D'Ivoire* Paris: Collection Savoir
Beidelman, T. O. 1986. *Moral imagination in Kaguru modes of thought* Bloomington: Indiana University Press
Biebuyck, D. 1973. *The Legas: art, initiation and moral philosophy* Berkeley: University of California Press
Bloch, M. 1971. *Placing the dead* London and New York: Seminar Press
  1986. *From blessing to violence* Cambridge: Cambridge University Press
Bourdieu, P. 1973. The Berber house. In M. Douglas (ed.) *Rules and meanings* Harmondsworth: Penguin Books
  1977. *Outline of a theory of practice* Cambridge: Cambridge University Press
  1981. *Le sense pratique* Paris: Editions Minuit
Bourdillon, M. F. C. and M. Fortes (eds.) 1980. *Sacrifice* London: Academic Press
Brandstrom, P. 1990. Boundless universe: the culture of expansion among the Sukuma-Nyamwezi of Tanzania Doctoral thesis presented to Uppsala University
Brantley-Smith, C. 1973. The Giriama rising 1914 PhD thesis presented to the University of California, Los Angeles
Brantley, C. 1978. Gerontocratic government: age-sets in pre-colonial Giriama. *Africa* 48: 248–264
  1979. An historical perspective of the Giriama and witchcraft control. *Africa* 49: 112–133
  1981. *The Giriama and colonial resistance in Kenya 1800–1920* Berkeley: University of California Press
Caplan, L. (ed.) 1987. *Studies in religious fundamentalism* London: Macmillan

Carrithers, M., Collins, S. and Lukes, S. (eds.) 1985. *The category of the person* Cambridge: Cambridge University Press

Cashmore, T. H. R. 1961. Notes on the chronology of the Wanika. *Tanganyika notes and records* 57: 153–172

Champion, A. 1967. *The Agiryama of Kenya* (ed. J. Middleton). London: Royal Anthropological Institute Memorandum No. 25

Christian, W. A. 1982. Provoked religious weeping in early modern Spain. In J. Davis (ed.) *Religious organization and religious experience* ASA Monograph No. 21, London: Academic Press

Church Missionary Society, Log Book 1914–1939. Located at (former CMS) hospital, Kaloleni

Clifford, J. and G. Marcus (eds.) 1986. *Writing culture* Berkeley: University of California

Comaroff, Jean. 1985. *Body of power, spirit of resistance* Chicago: Chicago University Press

Cooper, F. 1980. *From slaves to squatters* New Haven: Yale University Press

Cunningham, C. 1973 (1964). Order in the Atoni house. In R. Needham (ed.) *Right and left: essays on dual symbolic classification* Chicago: Chicago University Press

Davis, J. (ed.) 1982. *Religious organization and religious experience* ASA Monograph No. 21, London: Academic Press

Deed, F. 1964. *Giryama–English dictionary* Nairobi: East African Literature Bureau

Derrida, J. 1972. *Marges de la philosophie* Paris: Editions Minuit

Descombes, V. 1980. *Modern French philosophy* Cambridge: Cambridge University Press

Dieterlen, G. (ed.) 1973. *La notion de personne en Afrique Noire* Paris: Editions du Centre de la Recherche Scientifique

Douglas, M. 1970. *Natural symbols* London: Barrie and Rockliff

Durkheim, E. 1915. *The elementary forms of the religious life* (transl. J. W. Swain) London: George Allen and Unwin

Durkheim, E. and M. Mauss. 1963 (1903). *Primitive classification* (transl. R. Needham) London: Cohen and West

Eickelman, D. 1976. *Moroccan Islam: tradition and society in a pilgrimage center* Austin: University of Texas

Eliade, M. 1954. *The myth of the eternal return* or *Cosmos and history* (transl. W. R. Trask) Bollingen Series XLVI, Princeton: Princeton University Press

  1959. *The sacred and the profane: the nature of religion* New York and London: Harcourt Brace Jovanovich/Harvester

Evans-Pritchard, E. E. 1940. *The Nuer* Oxford: Clarendon Press

  1956. *Nuer religion* Oxford: Clarendon Press

  1976. *Witchcraft, oracles and magic among the Azande* Oxford: Clarendon Press (abridgement, with an introduction, by E. Gillies of the 1937 original version)

Fardon, R. (ed.) 1985. *Power and knowledge.* Edinburgh: Scottish Academic Press

  (ed.) 1990. *Localizing strategies: regional traditions of ethnographic writing* Edinburgh: Scottish Academic Press; and Washington: Smithsonian Institution Press

  1991. *Between God, the dead and the wild* Edinburgh: Edinburgh University Press, and Washington: Smithsonian Institution Press, for the International African Institute

Faruqee, Rashid *et al.* 1980. *Kenya. Population and development* Washington, DC: World Bank

Fernandez, J. W. 1982. *Bwiti: an ethnography of the religious imagination in Africa* Princeton: Princeton University Press

Fortes, M. 1980. Preface to M. F. C. Bourdillon and M. Fortes (eds.) *Sacrifice* London: Academic Press

Fortes, M. and E. E. Evans-Pritchard (eds.) 1940. *African Political Systems* London: Oxford University Press

Foucault, M. 1972a. *The order of things* London: Tavistock

1972b. *The archaeology of knowledge* London: Tavistock

1973. *The birth of the clinic* London: Tavistock

1977. *Language, counter memory, practice* (transl. D. F. Bouchard and S. Simon, and ed. with an introduction by D. F. Bouchard). Oxford: Blackwell

1978. *Discipline and punish* London: Allen Lane

Freedman, M. 1969. *Proceedings of the Royal Anthropological Institute 1968* London

Girard, R. 1977. *Violence and the sacred* (transl. P. Gregory) Baltimore: Johns Hopkins University Press

Gold, A. G. 1988. *Fruitful journey: the ways of Rajastani pilgrims* Berkeley: California University Press

Government of Kenya. Jan. 1964–Oct. 1966. Population Census 1962 (Volumes I–IV), Nairobi: Ministry of Economic Planning

November 1970–April 1971. Population Census 1969 (Volumes I–III), Nairobi: Ministry of Economic Planning

June 1981. Population Census 1979 (Volumes I and II), Nairobi: Central Bureau of Statistics, Ministry of Economic Planning

Annual district reports for Digo, Kilifi, and Malindi sub-districts

Annual Coast Province reports

Greenblatt, S. J. 1980. *Renaissance self-fashioning: from More to Shakespeare* Chicago: Chicago University Press

Gulliver, P. H. 1955. *The family herds* London: Routledge and Kegan Paul

Hawthorne, W. and K. Hunt and A. Russell. 1981. *Kaya: an ethnobotanical perspective* Report of the Oxford ethnobotanical expedition to Kenya, January–June 1981. Department of Botany, University of Oxford

Heald, S. 1989. *Controlling anger: the sociology of Gisu violence* Manchester: Manchester University Press, and New York: Giles Press

Herlehy, T. J. 1985. An economic history of the Kenya coast: the Mijikenda coconut palm economy, c.a. 1800–1980 PhD thesis presented to the University of Boston

Hesse, M. 1984. The cognitive claims of metaphor. In J. P. van Noppen (ed.) *Metaphor and religion, Theolinguistics 2*, Brussels

Heusch, L. de. 1985. *Sacrifice in Africa: a structuralist approach* Manchester: Manchester University Press

Hirst, P. Q. 1985. Constructed space and the subject. In R. Fardon (ed.) *Power and knowledge*. Edinburgh: Scottish Academic Press

Hobart, M. 1978. The path from the soul: the legitimacy of nature in Balinese conceptions of space. In G. Milner (ed.) *Natural symbols in south-east Asia* London: School of Oriental and African Studies

Hodder, I. 1986. *Reading the past* Cambridge: Cambridge University Press

Hollis, A. 1909. A note on the graves of the Wa-Nyika. *Man* No. 85: 145

Hubert, H. and M. Mauss. 1964. *Sacrifice: its nature and function* (transl. W. D. Halls) London: Cohen and West

Hugh-Jones, Christine. 1979. *From the milk river: spatial and temporal processes in northwest Amazonia* Cambridge: Cambridge University Press

Johnson, F. 1939. *A standard Swahili–English dictionary* London: Oxford University Press

Johnston, Marguerite B. 1976. Dispute settlement among the Giriama of Kenya PhD thesis presented to the University of Pennsylvania

Johnstone, H. 1902. Notes on the customs of the tribes occupying Mombasa sub-district. *Journal of the Royal Anthropological Institute* 32: 263–272

Karp, I. 1989. Power and capacity in rituals of possession. In W. Arens and I. Karp (eds.) *Creativity of power* Washington: Smithsonian Institution Press

Kelly, W. F. P. 1960. Kilifi District Gazetteer. Nairobi: Kenya National Archives

Krapf, J. L. 1860. *Travels, researches and missionary labours during an eighteen years residence in eastern Africa* London: Trubner and Company (and 1968, London: Frank Cass)

Kuhn, T. 1956. *The structure of scientific revolutions* Chicago: Chicago University Press

Kuper, A. 1975. The social structure of the Sotho-speaking peoples of southern Africa (Parts I and II). *Africa* 45: 67–81, 139–149

    1980. Symbolic dimensions of the southern Bantu homestead. *Africa* 50: 8–23

Law, R. 1985. Human sacrifice in pre-colonial West Africa. *African Affairs* 84 (334): 53–88

Le Guennec-Coppens, F. 1983. *Les femmes voilées de Lamu* Paris: Editions Recherche sur les Civilisations, Mémoire No. 22

Leach, E. R. 1954. *Political systems of highland Burma* London: Bell

    1958. Magical hair. *Journal of the Royal Anthropological Institute* 88: 147–164

    1961. Two essays concerning the symbolic representation of time. In E. R. Leach (ed.) *Rethinking anthropology* LSE Monograph No. 22, London: Athlone Press

    1983. Why did Moses have a sister? In E. Leach and D. A. Aycock (eds.) *Structural interpretation of Biblical myth* Cambridge: Cambridge University Press

Leakey, L. 1977. *The Kikuyu of Kenya* (Volume *a*). London: Academic Press

Lévi-Strauss, C. 1963. The bear and the barber. *Journal of the Royal Anthropological Institute* 93: 1–11

    1966. *The savage mind* London: Weidenfeld and Nicolson

Lewis, G. 1980. *The day of shining red* Cambridge: Cambridge University Press

Littlejohn, J. 1967. The Temne house. In J. Middleton (ed.) *Myth and cosmos* Austin: University of Texas Press

Mambo, R. M. 1987. Nascent political activities among the Mijikenda of Kenya's coast during the colonial era. *Transafrican Journal of History* 16: 92–120

Mauss, M. 1938. Une catégorie de l'esprit humain: La notion de personne, celle de 'moi'. *Journal of the Royal Anthropological Institute* 68, reprinted and translated in M. Carrithers *et al.* (eds.) 1985. *The category of the person* Cambridge: Cambridge University Press

Metcalf, P. 1989. *Where are you spirits?* University of Arizona Press

Middleton, J. M. 1960. *Lugbara religion* London: Oxford University Press

Moore, H. 1986. *Space, text and gender: an anthropological study of the Marakwet of Kenya* Cambridge: Cambridge University Press

Morris, B. 1987. *Anthropological studies of religion* Cambridge: Cambridge University Press

Morton, R. F. 1977. New evidence regarding the Shungwaya myth of Mijikenda origins. *International Journal of African Historical Studies* 10 (4): 628–643

Murphy, W. P. 1980. Secret knowledge as property and power. *Africa* 50: 193–207

Mutoro, H. W. 1987. An archaeological study of the Mijikenda Kaya settlements on the hinterland Kenya coast PhD thesis presented to the University of California, Los Angeles

Myers, F. 1986. *Pintupi country, Pintupi self: sentiment, place and politics among western desert Aborigines* Washington: Smithsonian Institute Press

Needham, R. 1971. Remarks on the analysis of kinship and marriage. In R. Needham (ed.) *Rethinking kinship and marriage* ASA Monograph No. 11, London: Tavistock

1975. Polythetic classification: convergence and consequences. *Man* (N.S.) 10: 349–369

1987. *Counterpoints* Berkeley and Los Angeles: University of California Press

Ngala, R. 1949. *Nchi na desturi za Wagiriama* Nairobi: Eagle Press

Otto, R. 1959 (1917). *The idea of the holy* (transl. J. W. Harvey) Harmondsworth: Penguin Press

Parkes, P. 1987. Livestock symbolism and pastoral ideology among the Kafirs of the Hindu Kush. *Man* 22: 637–660

Parkin, D. J. 1968. Medicines and men of influence. *Man* 3: 424–439

1970. Politics of ritual syncretism: Islam among the non-Muslim Giriama of Kenya. *Africa* 40: 218–233

1972. *Palms, wine and witnesses* San Francisco: Chandler

1974. National independence and local tradition in a Kenya trading centre. *Bulletin of the School of Oriental and African Studies* 37: 157–174

1979a. Straightening the paths from wilderness: the case of divinatory speech. *Journal of the Anthropological Society of Oxford* 10: 147–160 (reproduced in amended form in P. Peek (ed.) 1991. *African Divination* Bloomington: Indiana University Press)

1979b. Along the line of road: expanding rural centres in Kenya's coast province. *Africa* 49: 272–282

1980a. Kind bridewealth and hard cash: eventing a structure. In J. L. Comaroff (ed.) *The meaning of marriage payments* London and New York: Academic Press

1980b. The creativity of abuse. *Man* 15: 45–64

1982a. Introduction to D. Parkin (ed.) *Semantic anthropology* ASA Monograph No. 22, London: Academic Press

1982b. *Speaking of art: a Giriama impression* Bloomington: African Studies Program, Indiana University

1985. Reason, emotion and the embodiment of power. In J. Overing (ed.) *Reason and morality* ASA Monograph No. 24, London: Tavistock

1989a. The politics of naming among the Giriama. In R. D. Grillo (ed.) *Social anthropology and the politics of language* Sociological Research Monograph 36: 61–89, London and New York: Routledge

1989b. Swahili Mijikenda: facing both ways in Kenya. *Africa* 59: 161–175

Peake, R. E. 1982. 'Transformation of the Giriama dance: the case of Mambumbu' Unpublished paper presented to the Department of Sociology, Nairobi University

Peake, R. 1984. Tourism and alternative worlds: the social construction of reality in Malindi town, Kenya PhD thesis presented to the School of Oriental and African Studies, University of London

Pearson, J. M. 1914. 'An account of the taking of the oath of hyena' Unpublished record. Nairobi: Kenya National Archive: CP 5/336-II

Prins, A. H. J. 1952. *The coastal tribes of the northeastern Bantu (Pokomo, Nyika, Taita)* London: Ethnographic Survey for the International African Institute

Rabinow, P. 1989. *French modern norms and forms of the social environment* Cambridge, Massachusetts: MIT Press

Rappaport, R. A. 1979. *Ecology, meaning and religion* North Atlantic Books

Rasnake, R. N. 1988. *Domination and cultural resistance; authority and power among an Andean people* Durham, North Carolina: Duke University Press

Sagan, E. 1985. *At the dawn of tyranny* London and Boston: Faber and Faber

Sahlins, M. 1965. On the sociology of primitive exchange. In M. Banton (ed.) *The relevance of models for social anthropology* ASA Monograph No. 1, London: Tavistock

Sallnow, M. J. 1987. *Pilgrims of the Andes: regional cults in Cusco* Washington DC: Smithsonian Institution Press

Salmond, A. 1982. Theoretical landscapes. In D. Parkin (ed.) *Semantic Anthropology* ASA Monograph No. 22, London: Academic Press

    1985. Maori epistemologies. In J. Overing (ed.) *Reason and morality* ASA Monograph No. 24, London: Tavistock

Sanday, P. 1986. *Divine hunger* Cambridge: Cambridge University Press

Schlee, G. 1989. *Identities on the move* Manchester: Manchester University Press for the International African Institute

    forthcoming. In E. Croll and D. Parkin (eds.) *Bush and base, forest and farm: perspectives on eco-cosmology* London: Routledge

Sheridan, A. 1980. *Michel Foucault: the will to truth* London and New York: Tavistock

Skorupski, J. 1976. *Symbol and theory* Cambridge: Cambridge University Press

Southall, A. W. 1970. The illusion of tribe. *Journal of Asian and African Studies* 5, 1–2: 28–50

Spear, T. T. 1978. *The Kaya complex: a history of the Mijikenda peoples of the Kenya coast to 1900* Nairobi: Kenya Literature Bureau

    1981. *Traditions of origin and their interpretation: the Mijikenda of Kenya* Center for International Studies, Africa Program, Athens: University of Ohio

Spencer, P. 1988. *The Maasai of Matapato* Manchester: Manchester University Press, and Bloomington: Indiana University Press, for International African Institute

Sperber, D. 1975. *Rethinking symbolism* London: Cambridge University Press

Strathern, M. 1985. Knowing power and being equivocal: three Melanesian contexts. In R. Fardon (ed.) *Power and knowledge* Edinburgh: Scottish Academic Press

Sundkler, B. 1961. *Bantu prophets in South Africa* London: Oxford University Press

Taylor, W. E. 1891. *Giriama vocabulary and collections* London: SPCN

Tempels, R. P. P. 1953 (1949). *Bantu philosophy* Paris: Collection Présence Africaine

Temu, A. J. 1972. The Giriama war 1914–1915. In B. A. Ogot (ed.) *War and society in Africa* London: Frank Cass

Thompson, S. G. 1990. Speaking 'truth' to power: divination as a paradigm for facilitating change among Giriama in the Kenyan hinterland PhD thesis presented to the School of Oriental and African Studies, University of London

Thornton, R. 1980. *Space, time and culture among the Iraqw of Tanzania* London and New York: Academic Press

Turner, V. W. 1964. Witchcraft and sorcery: taxonomy versus dynamics. *Africa* 34: 314–325

    1974a. Pilgrimage as social processes. In his *Dramas, fields and metaphors: symbolic action in human society* Ithaca: Cornell University

    1974b. Pilgrimage and communitas, *Studia Missionalia* 23: 305–327

Turner, V. W. and Edith Turner. 1978. *Images and pilgrimages in Christian culture: anthropological perspectives* Oxford: Blackwell

Turton, A. 1978. Architectural and political space in Thailand. In G. Milner (ed.) *Natural symbols in south east Asia* London: School of Oriental and African Studies

Turton, D. 1980. There's no such beast: cattle and colour naming among the Mursi. *Man* 15: 320–338

Udvardy, M. 1990. Gender and the culture of fertility among the Giriama of Kenya Doctoral thesis presented to Uppsala University

    forthcoming. Kifudu: a female fertility cult among the Giriama of Kenya. In Anita Jacobson-Widding and Walter Beek (eds.) *The creative chaos: African folk models of fertility and the regeneration of life* Uppsala Studies in Cultural Anthropology, Stockholm: Almqvist and Wiksell International

Van Gennep, A. 1960. *The rites of passage* (transl. M. B. Vizedom and G. L. Caffee) Chicago: University of Chicago Press

Walsh, M. 1987. 'Mijikenda origins: a review of the evidence' Unpublished paper

Werbner, R. P. (ed.) 1977. *Regional cults* ASA Monograph No. 16, London and New York: Academic Press

    1989. *Ritual passage, sacred journey: the process and organization of religious movement* Washington DC: Smithsonian Institution Press

Werner, A. 1915. The Bantu tribes of the East African Protectorate. *Journal of the Royal Anthropological Institute* 45: 326–354

    1933. *Myths and legends of the Bantu* London: Harrap, 1968 edition, London: Frank Cass

Willis, R. G. 1968. Kamcape: an anti-sorcery movement. *Africa* 38: 1–15

Wolfe, E., D. Parkin and R. Sieber. 1981. *Vigango: the commemorative sculpture of the Mijikenda of Kenya* Bloomington: Indiana University Press for African Studies Program, Indiana University

World Bank. 1980 (see Faruqee above)

Yamba, B. 1990. Permanent pilgrims: Hausa migrants in the Sudan Doctoral thesis presented to the University of Stockholm

Index

Cambridge Studies in
Social and Cultural Anthropology

Editors: ERNEST GELLNER, JACK GOODY, STEPHEN GUDEMAN,
MICHAEL HERZFELD, JONATHAN PARRY

* available in paperback